PETERSON'S SUCCESS WITH WORDS

Joan Carris

THOMSON

PETERSON'S

Australia • Canada • Mexico • Singapore • Spain • United Kingdom • United States

THOMSON
PETERSON'S

About Thomson Peterson's

Thomson Peterson's (www.petersons.com) is a leading provider of education information and advice, with books and online resources focusing on education search, test preparation, and financial aid. Its Web site offers searchable databases and interactive tools for contacting educational institutions, online practice tests and instruction, and planning tools for securing financial aid. Thomson Peterson's serves 110 million education consumers annually.

Petersons.com/publishing

Check out our Web site at www.petersons.com/publishing to see if there is any new information regarding the test and any revisions or corrections to the content of this book. We've made sure the information in this book is accurate and up-to-date; however, the test format or content may have changed since the time of publication.

Excerpt from *Celtic Mysteries,* copyright 1975, by Crossroad Publishing Company, New York, NY. This was reprinted by permission of Crossroads.

Excerpts from *Black Women Writers at Work,* copyright 1983, edited by Claudia Tate, New York, NY. This was reprinted by permission of Audrey R. Wolf.

Excerpt from *Economics, A Self-Teaching Guide,* copyright 1988, by John Wiley and Sons, New York, NY. This was reprinted by permission of John Wiley and Sons.

Excerpt from *It Began With a Stone,* copyright 1983, by John Wiley and Sons, New York, NY. This was reprinted by permission of John Wiley and Sons.

Excerpt from *The Urban Naturalist,* copyright 1987, by John Wiley and Sons, New York, NY. This was reprinted by permission of John Wiley and Sons.

Excerpts from "Fire and Ice" and "Provide, Provide" from *The Poetry of Robert Frost,* copyright 1969, by Holt, Rinehart and Winston. Additional copyrights 1962, by Robert Frost, and 1975, by Lesley Frost Ballentine. Used with permission of Henry Holt and Company, Inc.

Excerpt from "Mad Dogs and Englishmen" by Noel Coward, copyright 1932, by Chappell Music Ltd. Copyright renewed; international copyright secured; all rights reserved. Used by permission.

For more information, contact Peterson's, 2000 Lenox Drive, Lawrenceville, NJ 08648; 800-338-3282; or find us on the World Wide Web at www.petersons.com/about.

COPYRIGHT © 2004 by Joan Carris

Previous edition © 1987, 1994, 1998

Editor: Wallie Walker-Hammond; Production Editor: Alysha Bullock; Manufacturing Manager: Judy Coleman; Composition Manager: Linda M. Williams.

ISBN: 0-7689-1698-4

Printed in the United States of America

10 9 8 7 6 5 4 3 2 1   06 05 04

Fourth Edition

CONTENTS

INTRODUCTION

Can you answer yes to any of these questions?	1
Why a workbook format?	1
Vocabulary and the PSAT, SAT, and ACT	1
Enhancing vocabulary when school is over	2
How to use this book . . . as a student	3
How to use this book . . . as a teacher	4

UNIT I   WHAT YOU ALREADY KNOW

List 1   The Root of It All   11
Reviewing the origins of our language

List 2   Figure It Out   20
Reviewing number roots

List 3   In the Beginning . . .   25
Reviewing some essential prefixes

UNIT II   VOCABULARY IN AND OUT OF CONTEXT

List 1   You've Got to Know the Territory   33
Studying context as a key to the meaning of words

List 2   Help! Hollered the Puzzled Reader   41
Finding synonyms or antonyms in context as keys to
the meaning of words

UNIT III   THE VOCABULARY LISTS

List 1   Look, Jane, Look!   51
Verbs, the action words

List 2   Excuse My Onomatopoeia   62
Terms from the arts

List 3   Four-Letter Words   73
Short words full of meaning

List 4   O Ye Gods! Part One   84
Words from myth and legend

Lists 1–4   Review   97

List 5   The Incredible Hunk   102
Prefixes that give meaning

List 6   An Eldritch Cry   116
Adjectives, the describing words

CONTENTS

List 7   Parlez-Vous Français? Absolument!   126
French words commonly used in English

List 8   Mrs. Malaprop Is Alive and Well   136
Words about language and speech

Lists 5–8   **Review**   147

List 9   A Hirsute Simian   153
Words from the animal kingdom

List 10   Bigots and Bagatelles   162
Nouns nice to know

List 11   See Spot Run   172
Verbs one more time

List 12   Mind and Matter   183
Psychological and medical terms

Lists 9–12   **Review**   194

List 13   Accentuate the Positive   199
Words with a positive connotation

List 14   Eliminate the Negative   210
Words with a negative connotation

List 15   Test Tubes and Dinosaurs   220
Terms from science

List 16   Presto, a Bonanza!   231
Words from Italy and Spain

Lists 13–16   **Review**   241

List 17   Pardon the Pun   248
More words about language and speech

List 18   Latina Vivit   259
Common Latin words and phrases

List 19   Call My Lawyer!   270
Legal terms

List 20   Jane and Spot Grow Up   282
Verbs yet another time

Lists 17–20   **Review**   293

List 21   Here's to You, Simon and Garfunkel   299
Terms from music and the arts

List 22   O Ye Gods! Part Two   310
More words from myth and legend

List 23   Torrid vs. Hot   322
Adjectives, the describing words

List 24 The Low-Down Noun   333
    Nouns with a negative connotation

Lists 21–24 **Review**   343

UNIT IV **A BOOK LIST YOU CAN LOVE**
        Vocabulary builders that are fun to read   351

UNIT V **YOUR BEST ON THE TEST**
        Answering the verbal questions on
            Standardized Tests   359
        How to get more answers right than wrong   359
        How to answer sentence completion questions   363
        Reasoning your way through to the answers   366
        How to answer questions on reading passages   374
        Why are reading passages such a big part of a
            verbal test?   375
        Do you want to score high?   375
        Time to write right   393

THE ANSWER SECTION
Answers to Unit I   399
Answers to Unit II   402
Answers to Unit III   403
Answers to Unit V   436

INDEX   439

Introduction

CAN YOU ANSWER YES TO ANY OF THESE QUESTIONS?

- Do you need a fat vocabulary to conquer a standardized test like the SAT, PSAT, ACT, or your exit-level exam?

- Do you want a great job?

- Do you need to be more confident in job interviews?

- Do you suspect that your language will shape your life and that you need to improve your vocabulary **now**?

If you said yes to any of the above, this book is for you.

Success with Words is a major step toward all of the goals listed above. After all, a large vocabulary that demonstrates your knowledge doesn't just happen. People work at acquiring words. But that work needn't be an awful process, as this book proves.

First, you need to begin reading. Read the cereal box. Read Stephen King. **Read anything that gives you pleasure** . . . but **read**. Anyone who's a regular reader will tell you that the verbal sections on standardized tests are fairly easy. Vocabulary comes with reading, painlessly.

How do you learn to think? You are not born knowing how to think in a logical way. Most of us have to learn how. Logical, orderly thinking comes to those who first read, then learn how to write. Nothing teaches logic like having to organize a big paper and present it with absolute clarity.

You learn how to write because it teaches you how to think clearly. Thinking and writing clearly and precisely require a large vocabulary. The words you need are in this book.

WHY A WORKBOOK FORMAT?

You've heard this saying: *Use it or lose it.* That's especially true with vocabulary. People have to read or use a word six to eight times in order to make it *their word*. (Honest. I did not make this up.) Each lesson in this book offers you so many chances to read or play with the words that you can't help but learn them.

Frequent review lessons will cement those words into place before you have a chance to forget them or before too many have paraded by. *Do just what this books says*—with a teacher guiding you or without—*and you can't help but learn these words.*

VOCABULARY AND THE PSAT, SAT, AND ACT

Few tests explore the depth and understanding of your vocabulary as well as the College Board's Preliminary Scholastic Assessment Test (PSAT), taken by high school juniors (increasingly, sophomores also), and Scholastic Assessment Test (SAT), taken by college-bound high school juniors and seniors.

The PSAT is composed of former SAT questions and comes to most juniors as a distinct shock. The possible scores on the verbal portion of the PSAT range from 20—given to anyone who can write his or her name correctly on the form—to 80, the highest score. The critical reading portion of the SAT has a range of 200 to 800. In 2003, the average SAT verbal score was 507, with an average score of 519 for the math section.

Since 50 on a PSAT or 500 on an SAT indicates a score of 50 percent, or only half correct, anyone can see that these averages are dismal. Students' attitudes toward these tests are often correspondingly dismal.

Questions on the PSAT and SAT include sentence completions and reading comprehension. *While these appear to be different types of questions, they often are not.* Whenever the vocabulary in a sentence-completion or reading-comprehension question is demanding—and it often is—the entire question depends on vocabulary knowledge. You may understand the question perfectly yet not recognize some of the words or phrases given as answer choices.

The math portions of the PSAT and SAT also call for strong verbal skills, especially reading comprehension.

The ACT Assessment exam, prepared by ACT, Inc., demands a level of achievement similar to that of the SAT. Questions on grammar and usage test English skills. Students need strong reading comprehension skills to answer questions about social studies and natural sciences. Math problems on an ACT resemble those on a PSAT or SAT.

All of these college entrance exams require just what current students appear to lack: good working vocabularies. Any test that lasts for 3 hours, like the current SAT, can do a good job of pinpointing people with weak vocabularies.

Because of the particular demands of these tests, and because students are intimidated by them, I have included a special unit titled "Your Best on the Test." This unit explains how to approach the various PSAT and SAT questions and suggests techniques that lead to correct answers. Many practice questions follow, so that any test taker will know exactly what to expect on the Big Day. Practice in answering the reading comprehension questions should be especially helpful if you're preparing for the ACT.

ENHANCING VOCABULARY WHEN SCHOOL IS OVER

Whether you simply enjoy words or have a need to increase your language skills, I hope that you have fun with the following pages. That's right, *fun*. You will delight in knowing crossword-puzzle words that had formerly eluded you. You'll love the look on your boss's face when you volunteer to give a speech, write a brochure, or make a presentation. As you add new vocabulary, word skills, and language mastery to your life, you will find that this knowledge enriches nearly everything you do. Words are an expression of ideas, after all, and who does not enjoy being rich in ideas?

And now, take a look at Unit I, "What You Already Know." You have a substantial fund of knowledge—more than you may realize. This knowledge is the basis for the next step in learning, and I wish you success.

HOW TO USE THIS BOOK . . . As a Student

You can work well with this book alone, without a teacher or classroom full of other students. The best way to achieve your goal of a bigger, better vocabulary is to set a schedule that suits your life. *Regular study sessions,* planned in advance, always bring you greater rewards than a haphazard approach.

FIRST, check the abbreviations on the last page of this book.

NEXT, look briefly at the table of contents.

THEN, check out the handy index at the back of the book. If you have a question about a word's meaning, the index tells you where to find a definition. The page number in **bold type** indicates which page has the fullest explanation of your word.

What Should You Do First?

Play with Unit I, "What You Already Know," as your first step. It will prove to you that you already know a lot about the most important aspect of our language—its roots. You'll gain terrific confidence from this unit.

Just follow the directions for each section and always check your answers with the key that begins on p. 405. *Always check to see how many you got right. And how many wrong, too. You may learn the most from what you missed.* Taking time to write the correct answers in place of the wrong ones is an excellent idea. Writing fixes words in the mind.

Move on to Unit II, "Vocabulary In and Out of Context"

This is the most critical unit for all readers of all ages. You'll learn how to be a brilliant and accurate guesser for words that are new or strange to you. This is the unit that helps most with standardized tests like SATs and ACTs, your state's exit-level exam, and it goes on helping as you grow older. Absolutely everybody needs to know how to derive the meaning of an unknown word from context (a word's surroundings). Again, *always* check your answers with the answer key, and correct any that you missed.

Time to Tackle Unit III

Unit III is the major portion of your book, with twenty-four teaching lessons and six review lessons. The lessons are all different, to prevent boredom.

For each lesson in Unit III, do the practice work *in the order presented*. Take a stab at figuring out the words' meanings from their use in context *before* you study their definitions. Next, work the exercises in order, as they become progressively more difficult. Make flash cards if learning words is difficult for you. Ask other people to help whenever you're stumped.

But *don't give up*. Anyone holding a job will tell you that a strong vocabulary is a valuable asset in the workplace and a joy to its owner.

"A Book List You Can Love" Is the Fourth Unit in Your Book

The books on this list have been recommended by high school students over a long period of time. Some are easy, some are quite demanding, but all were judged big favorites by readers your age. There are few "classics" on the list because lists of them are everywhere. You'll need to know many classics to be well prepared for college, but you also need to discover that reading is tremendous fun. The highly enjoyable books on this list are here to help you enlarge your vocabulary and to make the point that reading should play a major role in everyone's life.

Kicking Some Serious _ _ _ _ on Your Exit-Level Exam, SATs, PSATs, and ACTs

Yesss! A tidy review for you in this final unit—helping you to do your best on college entrance exams. The verbal questions (and some of the math ones!) depend on your knowledge of words.

The test tips you absolutely *must have* are in this unit.

Now, do the practice exercises and check the answers. This is the place to miss questions, remember? We often learn the most from what we miss.

ACT test-takers, as well as those of you taking high school exit-level exams, PSATs, and SATs, should pay particular attention to the reading comprehension passages.

As much as 90% of your work in college will depend on how well you comprehend what you read.

HOW TO USE THIS BOOK . . . As a Teacher

As a teacher, you may flip through this text and quickly get ideas about its use for your students. My comments are offered strictly as suggestions and as a way of sharing experience with others in my field. Your comments would be welcome; Peterson's will see that I receive all letters.

This text is meant to help you teach vocabulary as easily and effectively as possible. English teachers have so much to teach—writing, understanding of good literature, grammar, speech—that we need our students for a couple of hours a day, not a measly 45 minutes. We know from talking to pupils and seeing their test scores that their vocabularies are often pitifully limited. The problem is how to enlarge their storehouse of words *without* spending hours on lesson plans and too much time in a class that *never* has enough time. (Have you ever been wildly jealous of the chem or bio teacher who gets extra time for labs? I have!)

This Book Is Self-Teaching and Self-Explanatory for Students

Using this text allows you to teach the maximum amount of vocabulary in the least amount of class time, with the least amount of your involvement.

Why is that so great? Because you don't have enough class time to teach all the aspects of high school English and because students learn best that which they teach themselves. All the instructions are in the book. Answers to exercises are there, too.

Making your students independent of you as learners is the finest thing you can teach them. You know that language shapes lives. It shaped yours and it will do the same for all of your students. Putting young people in charge of their own learning makes all kinds of sense, and this book does just that.

Unit I, "What You Already Know," is meant to get the year off to an encouraging start. Students are usually amazed at their own knowledge of roots and prefixes. This unit can be completed as quickly as you want, depending on class ability.

Unit II is called "Vocabulary In and Out of Context." It explains how to derive the meaning of an unknown word from its context and offers many practice exercises. Throughout the book, students will meet new words in context first, so that they will learn to glean meaning from context by year's end. As with Unit I, you can complete the work as rapidly as the class permits.

The major portion of the text is Unit III, which consists of twenty-four vocabulary lessons and six review lessons. A review appears after every four vocabulary lessons, for a total of thirty lessons.

HINT: You may want to cut out those review lessons before passing out books and use them as unit quizzes after every four vocabulary lessons.

ANOTHER HINT: Ask students to write quiz questions. Questions must be of high quality, comparable to your own. Successful quiz/test units earn extra credit or exemption from the test itself. Any student who can understand how PSAT/SAT questions are formulated—and learn to write some for class use—will be miles ahead of the competition on the real tests.

Invite Pros Into the Classroom

The vocabulary lessons focus on different aspects of life (law, medicine, music, science, et al.), so you may enjoy having professionals in those fields make brief visits to your classroom.

Ask questions of the pros. What words do *they* think the public should know in their fields? Live bodies from the "real world" make words come alive for everyone in class. Most businesspeople and professionals are happy to give 20 minutes of their time to promote education.

How About Those Critical Language Roots?

Learning Latin and Greek roots is essential for any study of English, which is 60 to 70 percent derivative from those two languages. But learning long lists of roots is dull. It seems to have little meaning for students. This book presents only a few roots connected to each lesson—little manageable hunks of knowledge that have relevance in the overall language study.

Practice Exercises That Do the Job

Success with Words gives students more chances to use their new words than any other text available. Educational research has shown that people need to use a new word six to eight times before it becomes their own, and this book adheres to that principle. Exercises tend to increase in difficulty within each separate lesson, with the most demanding one at the end.

Student-Designed Flash Cards

A quick way to learn—and pronounce correctly—the words on each week's list is by working with giant flash cards. You can make them yourself or assign the lists to your students. Either way, class can begin with a zippy 3-minute run-through of the week's word list. With only sixteen to seventeen new words, plus a few roots, this practice is quick yet amazingly effective for learning. For the one-third of students who learn best through their ears, this oral review is invaluable.

What to Do with Unit V, "Your Best on the Test"

As each class has different needs, each teacher will make a different decision regarding the last unit in this book. Even so, I urge you to examine recent SATs, PSATs, and ACTs. Is there anything on those tests that you *wouldn't* want graduating students to know? For example, even if your students are not taking a college entrance exam, isn't it valuable for them to understand how an analogy works? Life is full of analogous relationships, after all, and learning how to reason our way intelligently through life is surely a central goal of all education.

Increasing students' comprehension of what they read is the main goal of SAT/PSAT prep as I see it. It was my main goal as a high school English teacher. Perhaps some "play-time" with the reading passages in this test-prep unit could have long-lasting, positive results for all of your students.

Last, you should know that this is not a formal textbook but a rather informal one. I learn and teach better when I can laugh occasionally.

UNIT 1

What You Already Know

LIST 1 The Root of It All
Reviewing the Origins of Our Language

You already know over sixty Latin and Greek roots, plus half as many prefixes. This unit will prove that to you. You have absorbed these language tidbits over time, just as easily as you learned the words and tune to "Happy Birthday."

Roots and prefixes are the guts of language—basic bits of information you use without thinking. That the basics are Latin and Greek should come as no surprise. You learned in history class that the Latin-speaking Romans occupied Britain for a number of years. They left behind not only mosaics, hypocausts, and walls but much of their language as well. (And Latin had already been influenced by Greek.)

Remember 1066, when William the Conqueror won the Battle of Hastings and became ruler of Britain? William spoke French, a Romance language, so-called because it came from the Romans. William's French became the legal language of Britain until the fourteenth century, and French is roughly 85 percent descended from Latin. (See how circular this is? We can't escape Latin.)

So it happens that today's English is a blend of the Anglo-Saxon original with Latin and Greek, plus French overtones—plus tons of words added in the last few centuries. It's a linguistic stew, richer in flavor and variety than the old Britons could ever have dreamed.

Reminding yourself that you know many of these language roots is reassuring proof that your brain hasn't been fried to a potato chip by the summer sun. As you go through this unit, *you should be encouraged by the extent of what you already know.*

LESSON A   Basic Roots

Below are some old friends—basic roots of our language. As a helpful memory aid, write their meanings on the lines provided.

1. An *Aqua-lung*™ is a device that lets a scuba diver breathe under water. An *aquarium* is a water-bearing container for fish or marine life. An *aqueduct* is a conduit for flowing water.

   AQUA/AQU means _____.

2. A *hydrant,* also called a fireplug, is connected to the water mains. A *hydrate* is a compound or complex ion formed by the union of water with another substance. Travelers on the desert, where there is no water, often worry about *dehydration.*

   HYDR means _____.

3. *Biology* is the science of living organisms and life processes. A *biopsy* examines tissues, cells, or fluids from the living body. A *biography* is the story of someone's life.

   BIO means _____.

4. *Kodachrome*™ is a brand name of film used for color photography. Certain small, brightly colored African fish are termed *chromides*. The portion of the cell nucleus that stains well with dyes (assuming various basic colors) is the *chromatin*.

   CHROM means _____.

5. A person with a sizable, bulky body may be described as *corpulent*. A corps such as the Marine *Corps* is an organized body of people. A *corporation* is an association or body of people organized as a legal entity for the purpose of conducting business.

   CORP means _____.

6. An *egoist* (or *egotist*) uses the word "I" frequently. Your *alter ego* is your "other self," one who shares your beliefs and personality to an amazing degree. An *egocentric* person concentrates on himself and his own interests.

   EGO means _____.

7. *Geology* is the science and history of the earth, especially as revealed in rocks. *Geometry* comes from Greek roots meaning to measure the earth. *Geophysics* concentrates on the physics of the earth and includes hydrology, meteorology, and other sciences.

   GE/GEO means _____.

8. One type of *bibliography* is a list of sources (books, articles, tapes, personal interviews) consulted by the author of a book. *Bibliophiles* are crazy about books. The French word for library is *bibliothèque*.

   BIBLI/BIBLIO means _____.

9. If you want to study management of soils, fields, and crop production, enroll in a course in *agronomy*. A broader term, *agriculture,* includes the study of crops, fields, and soils and the raising of livestock. The old Roman *agricola,* bowed over his hoe in the field, farmed the soil.

   AGR means _____.

10. Parents gaze at their newborns with fond *maternal* and *paternal* glances. Mothers are the rulers in *matriarchal* societies, whereas fathers dominate in *patriarchal* ones. Known for his *patriotism*, Abraham Lincoln believed that his fatherland must be a unified country.

    MATER and MATRI mean _____.

    PATER and PATRI mean _____.

LESSON B   No Surprises

You will recognize these roots and their derivative words just as you did those in Lesson A. Write their meaning on the lines provided.

1. An *audible* signal is one you can hear. *Auditorium, auditory, inaudible,* and *audience* also derive from the same root.

    AUD/AUDIT means _____.

2. To be *cognizant* is to know or be aware. Related words include *recognize, cognitive, incognito,* and *cognate.*

    COGN means _____.

3. When I *dictate* words, I'm saying them aloud. Some other members of this giant family are *diction, predict, dictionary, abdicate, benediction,* and *dictator.*

    DICT/DIC means _____.

4. *Dormant* talents are asleep, waiting to be discovered. Relatives include *dormitory, dormer* (originally a bedroom window), and *dormouse,* the one who snoozed at the Mad Hatter's tea party.

    DORM means _____.

5. To *err* is to wander astray or make a mistake, as when answering a Trivial Pursuit question incorrectly. *Erroneous, error, errant, erratic,* and *aberration* belong to this word family.

    ERR means _____.

6. Knees bend or *flex,* a common muscle action, just as *inflection,* literally a bending or curving of the voice, is common in speech. Derived from the same root are *deflect, inflexible, circumflex,* and *reflection.*

    FLECT and FLEX mean _____.

7. A sentence of five years of hard *labor* means that tough work lies ahead. *Laboratory, laborious, belabored,* and *elaborate* come from this root.

    LABOR means _____.

8. A science is a body of knowledge, normally systematized. The same useful root is buried in *omniscient, conscious, prescient,* and *unscientific* and gives the key to their meanings.

    SCI means _____.

9. A *scribbled* signature that resembles chicken tracks is not as easy to read as one in fine *script.* Well-known relatives include *scripture, inscription, description,* and *prescription.*

    SCRIB and SCRIPT mean _____.

10. *Video* is a fairly modern word directly related to *visible*. Also in this family are *vision*, *envision*, *provide*, *revise*, and *visit*.

    VID and VIS mean _____.

11. To *sense* something is to feel it, sometimes without any obvious reason. A *presentiment* is the inexplicable feeling that something will happen. *Sensitive*, *resent*, *sensual*, *consent*, and *dissent* are derived from the same root.

    SENS and SENT mean _____.

LESSON C   More Roots You Know

Yes, you will know this list of roots, too. This time, you isolate the root and write it on the line, followed by its meaning.

1. *synchronize*—to bring or happen together in time, as *to synchronize watches*
   chronological—arranged in order of time
   chronometer—an exceptionally accurate timepiece

   The root _____ means _____.

2. *cosmic*—like the great and comprehensive universe
   microcosm—a tiny world, typical of the larger one
   cosmopolitan—worldwide in scope; sophisticated, worldly

   The root _____ means _____.

3. *civil*—of the state or its citizens; polite, mannerly
   civilization—the state of cultural development
   civic—of citizens or a city, e.g., *civic concerns*

   The root _____ means _____.

4. *pedal*—a foot lever, as on a piano or wheeled cycle
   podiatrist—a professional who cares for feet
   pedometer—a walker's recording instrument to measure distance

   The Latin roots _____ and _____

   mean _____.

5. *psychiatry*—a branch of medicine dealing with the health of the mind
   psyche—the mind or innermost soul or self
   psychosomatic—referring to the interaction between mind and body (usually refers to a mental conflict that results in physical symptoms)

   The root _____ means _____.

6. *pediatrician*—physician who cares for children and teens
   pedagogue—originally a slave who walked children to school; now a teacher or instructor
   pedant—from the word pedagogue; now a nitpicking teacher or educated show-off

   The Greek root _____ means _____ .

7. *via*—by way of or by means of
   viaduct—a road or railway bridge supported by pilings
   trivial—insignificant, unimportant

   The root _____ means _____ .

8. *urban*—referring to a city
   suburbs—outlying yet attached areas of a city
   urbane—sophisticated, suave, as a city dweller may be

   The root _____ means _____ .

9. *tempo*—pace; rate of motion or speed, as in music
   temporary—of limited duration (not permanent)
   contemporary—simultaneous; existing or occurring at the present time; also, n., someone near your age

   The root _____ means _____ .

10. *zoo*—an assortment of animals for display
    zoology—the science of the animal kingdom
    Protozoa—a subkingdom of acellular or single-celled animals; primitive animals

    The root _____ means _____ .

11. *equine*—referring to horses; horselike
    equestrian—one who rides horses; adj., referring to horses, as *her equestrian skills*
    equerry—one who cares for horses

    The root _____ means _____ .

LESSON D   Roots One More Time

Over thirty roots already and you're still going strong, right? This time, complete the matching portion of each question by writing the number of the definition in the blank opposite the appropriate word; then write the root and its meaning on the lines provided.

1. _____ a. tricycle   (1) storm revolving around a center
   _____ b. Cyclops   (2) three-wheeled vehicle with pedals
   _____ c. cyclone   (3) mythical giant with one large, circular eye

   The root _____ means _____ .

2. _____ a. false   (1) erroneous idea

   _____ b. fallacy   (2) untrue; not correct

   _____ c. infallible   (3) without error; certain or sure

   The roots _____ and _____

   mean _____ .

3. _____ a. grave (adj.)   (1) to worsen; to intensify

   _____ b. gravity   (2) serious, weighty, somber, important

   _____ c. aggravate   (3) seriousness; great weight, as "the earth's gravity"

   The root _____ means _____ .

4. _____ a. amity   (1) filled with love

   _____ b. amicable   (2) strong friendship or accord

   _____ c. enamored   (3) friendly, peaceable, congenial

   The roots _____ and _____

   mean _____ and _____ .

5. _____ a. negative   (1) self-denial, renunciation; denial

   _____ b. neglect (v.)   (2) characterized by denial or prohibition

   _____ c. abnegation   (3) to ignore, pay no attention to

   The root _____ means _____ .

6. _____ a. novel (adj.)   (1) beginner, novice

   _____ b. innovate   (2) to attempt something new

   _____ c. neophyte   (3) element in air, used in electric lamps

   _____ d. neon   (4) original, fresh, new

   The roots _____ and _____

   mean _____ .

7. _____ a. vacuum (n.)   (1) space totally empty of matter

   _____ b. evacuate   (2) empty or dully foolish

   _____ c. vacuous   (3) to remove or empty the contents of

   The root _____ means _____ .

8. _____ a. equate   (1) lack of equality

   _____ b. inequality   (2) unclear as to meaning, almost as if voicing several opinions

   _____ c. equivocal   (3) to make equal; to treat as the same

   The root _____ means _____ .

9. _____ a. fragile   (1) portion or piece of the whole

     _____ b. fracture (v.)   (2) delicate, easily broken

     _____ c. refractory   (3) stubborn, difficult to manage

     _____ d. fragment (n.)   (4) to break, destroy, or shatter

     The roots _____ and _____

     mean _____.

10. _____ a. minus   (1) insignificant, of minor import

     _____ b. minuscule   (2) less, without, subtracted from

     _____ c. minimal   (3) tiny, almost immeasurable

     _____ d. minimize   (4) to reduce in importance; to diminish

     The roots _____ and _____

     mean _____.

USING THE WORDS

Yes, you know the roots. But do you remember those words given as examples? You will want to know all of the words in this unit, so here is a quick self-test.

Exercise I. Fill-Ins.

Select the most appropriate word from the choices offered, based on clues in context. The word form or capitalization may need changing. Each word is used only once.

hydroponics	dormant	matron	novice
collaborate	temporal	pedant	biopsy
dissension	amorous	podium	trivial
corpulent	fraction	audience	

1. Once a scrawny kitten, Marigold has become lazy and _____ because she interrupts her naps only to eat.

2. The _____, plaintive howls of neighboring tomcats have often disturbed our sleep since the lovely Marigold joined our family.

3. This cat has been the subject of much _____ in our household—some of us arguing in favor of her charms, the others decrying her faults.

4. When Marigold was under anesthetic, the veterinarian did a routine _____ on the growth he removed from her neck.

5. Contrasting her once youthful figure with her current shape, Mom said, "Darn it. I never planned on looking like a _____."

6. The popular game _____ Pursuit poses many questions about basic, useful knowledge—not solely items of minor importance, as its name suggests.

7. The visible tip of an iceberg is but a(n) _____ of the vaster bulk that lies hidden underwater.

8. The practice of growing plants in liquid nutrient as opposed to cultivation in soil is called _____.

9. The _____ bulbs that rest underground most of the year emerge when the season is right, and we are ready to appreciate them all over again.

10. "Can everyone in the _____ hear me?" asked the speaker.

11. We raised enough money to donate an oak _____ for our orchestra director, who needs the extra height this platform gives her.

12. My friend Brian is a(n) _____ at directing, but with the band director's help he's becoming more professional every day.

13. Brian and the band director have _____ on a new arrangement of the school's fight song to play for the opening game of the season. (Use sentence logic as another key.)

14. Ministers of all faiths often urge their congregations to concentrate on spiritual matters rather than the _____ ones of our current time.

15. A(n) _____ who prided himself on his knowledge of cats would delight in telling you that a group of cats is a "clowder" and a litter of kittens is a "kindle."

Exercise II. Antonyms.
Find an antonym or contrasting expression in the right column for each word in the left column. As a help, remember to identify the root in each word you are considering.

_____	1. **urbane**	(a) patriarchal
_____	2. **negligence**	(b) impolite
_____	3. **civil**	(c) unsophisticated
_____	4. **vacuous**	(d) attentive care
_____	5. **minuscule**	(e) correct
_____	6. **fallacious**	(f) huge or vast
_____	7. **omniscient**	(g) ignorant
_____	8. **cosmic**	(h) regular, dependable
_____	9. **matriarchal**	(i) bright, intelligent
_____	10. **erratic**	(j) narrow in scope

Exercise III. Fill-Ins.

Select the most appropriate word from the choices offered. Each word is used once. And again, pay attention to those roots.

agrarian   dictatorial   equivocal   envision
patrimony   deflect   anachronism   grave
precognition   psychology   geological   cyclic
polychrome   equestrian   inscription   protozoans
egotistical

1. something out of place in time, a(n)_____ like the hourglass or a steam locomotive

2. thorough _____ surveys of the oil fields

3. her hard-won _____ skills at show jumping

4. a(n) _____ tone of voice, not appreciated even in business boardrooms

5. wasted the vast _____ left to him by his father

6. beyond her ability to _____ life in the next century (Also use logic.)

7. lectured on weighty matters in a(n) _____ tone

8. brightly colored pottery known as _____ ware

9. wise _____ policies to preserve farmlands

10. combining studies of physiology with _____ to ensure a total picture

11. psychic whose skill at _____ is controversial

12. a(n) _____ answer that dodged the issue, as if she were refusing to voice her actual opinion

13. the regular, _____ pattern of the seasons

14. a humorous, memorable _____ on the tombstone

15. study of the earth's early life forms, the _____

16. using a garbage can lid to _____ the snowballs

17. the _____ answer: "*I* always know what's right for *me*!"

Figure It Out
Reviewing Number Roots

Life would be infinitely happier if we could only be born at the age of eighty and gradually approach eighteen.—Mark Twain

The significant words in Twain's comment are numbers. With each of those numbered ages come vivid mental pictures. Obviously, numbers are used for more than math problems.

LESSON E   Demi to Dec

1. A *demitasse* cup is half the size of a normal one. A *semicolon* is half a colon, with the bottom half a comma to indicate that the sentence continues. The Northern *Hemisphere* refers to the northern half of the world. Something *medium* is halfway, or in the middle.

   DEMI, SEMI, HEMI, and MED/MEDI mean _____.

2. A one-wheeled cycle is a *unicycle*. Speaking in a *monotone* is talking on one pitch. You play *solitaire* alone—in *solitude,* perhaps.

   UNI, MONO, and SOL mean _____.

3. A *sesquicentennial* is a 150th anniversary, or one centennial plus half of another. Anyone who has a *sesquipedalian* vocabulary uses words a foot-and-a-half long!

   SESQUI means _____.

4. "Two roads *diverged* in a wood," wrote Robert Frost. A *biplane* has two sets of wings. *Duplicity* is false double-dealing. It takes two people for a *duo* or a performing *duet.* A *diploma* was originally folded over double.

   DI, BI, DU/DUO, and DIPLO mean _____.

5. Any school on the *trimester* system has three divisions to its school year. A *tertiary* treatment is the third stage of treatment.

   TRI and TER mean _____.

6. We who walk on two legs are bipeds; *quadrupeds* walk on four. A *tetrarchy* is a government run by four equally powerful heads, each one referred to as a *tetrarch.*

   QUADR and TETR mean _____.

7. The *pentathlete* must compete in five different events. A *quintuplet* is one of five children born in a single birth. A period of five years is a *quinquennium.*

   PENTA, QUINT, and QUINQUE mean _____.

8. A *sextet* has six members, just as a *hexagon* has six sides.

   SEX and HEX mean _____.

9. *September* was originally the seventh month of the year in the Roman calendar. Any line of verse with seven metrical feet is called a *heptameter*.

   SEPT and HEPT mean _____.

10. In the original Roman calendar the eighth month was *October*. An *octave* is one scale of eight notes. Eight muscular arms characterize the *octopus*.

    OCT, OCTA, and OCTO mean _____.

11. A figure with nine sides and nine angles is a *nonagon*. *November*, formerly the ninth month, and *novena*, a nine days' devotion in the Catholic church, share the same root. Any group of nine is an *ennead*.

    NON, NOVEM, and ENNEA mean _____.

12. *December* used to be the tenth month of the year. Ten track and field events make up the *decathlon*.

    DEC means _____.

LESSON F   Duodec to Omni/Pan/Panto

The following list of roots that give number, amount, or quantity is less well known, so it's time to pay attention. You'll be familiar with most of them, and writing your answers on the lines will help to fix even the strangers in your mind.

1. The roots DUODEC and DODEC have added the prefixes _____ and

   _____ to the root DEC, which means _____.

   Since 10 + 2 = 12, DUODEC and DODEC mean _____.

   A *dodecahedron* is a solid with _____ faces.

2. All of the teenage years are expressed as one number plus the suffix-TEEN, e.g., *sixteen, seventeen.*

   Ten and is written _____.

3. *Twenty, thirty, forty*, and so on are numbers that include the suffix-TY, meaning *times ten*.

   Times ten is written _____.

4. A *centennial* is a celebration commemorating 100 years. Someone who is a hundred years old or older is a *centenarian*. One hundred meters is a *hectometer*. Today, *hecatomb* means a great slaughter; in ancient Greece it was the sacrifice of 100 oxen.

    CENT, HECTO, and HECATO mean _____.

5. *Million, millimeter,* and *milligram* share the root that means *thousand*. The Greek form KILO is found in *kilowatt, kilogram*, and *kiloliter*.

    MILLI and KILO mean _____.

6. The root MYRIA means *10,000*—or rather, it used to. Today, a *myriad* of items is a large but not specific number of things.

    MYRIA means _____ or _____.

7. *Megaphone* and *megalomaniac* share the root meaning million. It also means great or large, so that earning *megabucks* doesn't necessarily mean earning a million dollars. A *megacycle* is a million cycles in a measured sequence, not a giant motorbike.

    MEG/MEGA means _____ or _____.

8. *Archaeology* often reveals facts about the lives of *primitive* people, some of whom are said to have dwelt in the forest *primeval*. *Principal*, first-in-line in school administration, and *prototype*, the first of its kind, have the same prefix meaning.

    ARCH, PRIM, PRIN, and PROTO mean _____.

9. An *ambidextrous* person uses both hands with equal skill. A good *amphitheater* offers fine acoustics for both sides of its audience, or all around the circular shape.

    AMBI and AMPHI mean _____.

10. Countries have rarely been ruled by an *oligarchy*—a group of a few people. The Latin form of this root appears in *paucity*, meaning few or scanty in number.

    OLIGO and PAUCI mean _____.

11. We'd all like a *multitude* of friends, a *myriad* of pleasures, and the joy of being a *polymath*, someone with wide and varied knowledge.

    MULTI, MYRIA, and POLY mean _____.

12. *Omnivorous* readers read everything they can find. A *pandemic* illness may occur throughout an entire population, in all areas. A mime show that is all mime, no talking, is called *pantomine*.

    OMNI and PAN/PANTO mean _____.

Figure It Out

Exercise I.
Matching. Select the correct definition for each of the numbered words or phrases. Again, you must use the example words to fix them in mind. As you work the following exercises, be sure to identify each word root.

_____ 1. omnipresent

_____ 2. -ty

_____ 3. digraph

_____ 4. hecatomb

_____ 5. archetype

_____ 6. fourteen

_____ 7. quincentenary

_____ 8. hemiplegia

_____ 9. sesquipedalian orator

_____ 10. monolith

_____ 11. Heptateuch

_____ 12. paucity

(a) speaker using lengthy words

(b) one great stone, or a single impressive structure

(c) 500th anniversary

(d) first seven books of the Bible

(e) times ten

(f) scant quantity

(g) in all places all the time

(h) a great slaughter

(i) model or prototype

(j) four plus ten

(k) two letters pronounced as one sound, e.g., *ch*orus, br*ea*d

(l) paralysis of one side of the body

Exercise II. Fill-ins.
In this admittedly crazy story, please insert the appropriate words based on clues in context. (Hint: *Read the entire story first,* then go back and fill in the missing words.)

ennead	decennial	megalomaniac	dodecahedron
sextet	ambivalent	principal	millipedes
triad	omnivorous	pandemonium	one
octet	solitude	myriad	multitudinous

Once there lived a fellow with a passion for grandiose things—a true _____
1
who collected _____ strange and usually worthless objects. This man's
2
international residences—a _____ of homes in Hawaii, Tibet, and Peoria,
3
Illinois—were stuffed with his possessions. In Hawaii he kept half a dozen peacocks, which

_____ he flamboyantly termed an ostentation of peacocks. There also he
4
drilled his insect army of _____, those said to have a thousand legs. For
5
entertainment he listened to a simian _____ made up of four gorillas on
6
drums and four chimps on clarinet. Of course, the peacocks chased the insect army and the monkeys

bedeviled the peacocks, so that the resulting _____ drove him to his moun-
7
tainous retreat in Tibet.

He felt somewhat _____ about Tibet. At times he adored the peaceful

8

_____ of the area; at other times he loathed being alone. Still, there were his

9

treasures to supervise, and as he was a(n) _____ collector, the Tibetan resi-

10

dence was also crowded. A gaggle of geese honked underneath the feet of his nine llamas, a(n)

_____ that needed daily brushing to be presentable.

11

His _____ *objets d'art* had to be polished, washed, and arranged on their

12

shelves. When he wearied of the labor and the loneliness, he hied himself to Peoria, his birthplace and

_____ home.

13

His dwelling in Peoria was a multisided mansion, a(n) _____ designed

14

to show off his twelve major collections. In the year of his _____, after

15

he had remained in Peoria for ten solid years, his fellow Peorians gave him a

_____-way ticket back to Tibet.

16

Exercise III. Logic.
Answer the questions and complete the statements by decoding the italicized words.

1. How old is an *octogenarian*? _____.

2. Given the nature of human beings, why have there been so few *oligarchies* in the history of
world governments? _____

_____

3. A *pentavalent* element would have a valence of _____.

4. The extensor muscle of the front thigh, called the *quadriceps,* is divided into
_____ parts.

5. What is the problem with an *ambiguous* answer? _____.

6. The root TER or TERR means land. How do you suppose the *Mediterranean* Sea got its name?

_____

7. The slur "They're so _____!" could
be applied to people guilty of *duplicity.*

8. Virgil's *Aeneid* was written in dactylic *hexameter,* so we know that there are
_____ metrical feet to each line.

9. A *millennium* is a period of _____ years.

10. A series of _____ folding panels, often with artistic decoration, is called
a *triptych.* The support for a movie camera is termed a _____.

In the Beginning . . .
Reviewing Some Essential Prefixes

As you know, a prefix is a small group of letters tacked on to the beginning of a word. Prefixes are chock-full of information that can be extremely helpful when you're decoding a mystery word.

For example, the word *prefix* breaks down to PRE + FIX. You know what *fix* means, and the idea in *pre* is *going before* or *ahead*. So, a prefix must be something fixed on or attached before (in front of) something else.

The following two groups of prefixes are ones you will quickly recognize because you use them all the time.

LESSON G   Prefixes

1. RE-, RETRO-, and POST- give us the ideas of *back* (in place or time) or *after*, just as the *postscript* (P.S.) in a letter comes after the body of the letter.

    a. To *review* means _____.

    b. To *replace* means _____.

    c. A *retro-rocket* fires in which direction compared to the aircraft? _____

    d. Considering past events is looking at them _____ *spectively.*

    e. To *postpone* a meeting is to _____.

    f. A *postbellum* Southern mansion was built _____ the Civil War.

2. The prefixes ANTI- and ANT-, MIS- and MAL-, UN- and NON-, and CONTRA- and COUNTER- convey the ideas of *not*, *against*, or *bad(ly)*. Using this information, define the following:

    a. unsocial or antisocial _____

    b. antiaircraft _____

    c. antithesis _____

    d. misfortune _____

    e. nonsense _____

    f. uneasy _____

    g. counteract _____

    h. malfunction _____

    i. nonallergenic _____

    j. contradict _____

3. Well-known opposites are MICRO- meaning *small, miniature,* or *tiny* and MAGNA- meaning *great* or *large.*

    a. Something of considerable *magnitude* is _____.

    b. A *magnifying* glass _____.

    c. A *microscope* allows us to examine objects that are _____.

    d. *Microbes* are _____ organisms or germs.

4. The prefix PRO- means *before, for* (in favor of), or *forward.*

    a. *Progress* is movement in a _____ direction.

    b. If you *promote* an idea, you are _____.

    c. Anyone *pro-liberal* is _____.

5. A familiar Greek prefix is AUTO- meaning self.

    a. An _____ *didact* is someone who has taught himself or herself.

    b. The prefix _____ is a synonym for car, which is self-propelled.

    c. Any business that is independent of outside control is an _____ *nomous* concern.

LESSON H   Yes, More Prefixes

Prefixes aren't exciting, but they ARE useful. Often they'll give you the clue to a strange word's meaning. Write the completing words on the lines provided.

1. The prefix CIRCUM-, meaning *around,* is found in

    a. *circumference* meaning _____.

    b. *circumnavigate* meaning _____.

    c. *circumvent* meaning _____.

2. INTRO- or INTRA- means *inside* or *within.* Using this knowledge, assemble the word parts into known words.

    a. Intro + spective = _____ (looking within oneself).

    b. Intra + mural = _____ (activity within a community, such as between classes in a school).

    c. Intra + molecular = _____ (within the molecule).

    d. Intro + vert = _____ (self-contained, as opposed to being outgoing or *extro*verted).

3. PRE- and FORE- mean *before* or *ahead* (in time or place).

    a. *Forewarned* means _____ .

    b. A scene in the *foreground* is _____ .

    c. *Foregoing* means _____ .

    d. To *predict* an event is to _____ .

    e. An idea that takes *precedence* over another does what? _____
        _____ .

4. The prefixes EXTRA-, EXTRO-, and EXTER- mean *outside* or *beyond*.

    a. Something *extraordinary* is _____ .

    b. An _____ problem is the opposite of an internal problem

    c. An *introvert* is the opposite of an _____ .

    d. *Extrasensory* perception (ESP) refers to _____ .

5. The meaning of INTER- is *among* or *between*.

    a. The *interregnum* period in a monarchy is the period _____ the
        reigns of two monarchs.

    b. *International* dialogue is talk _____ nations.

    c. An interlude may be a lull _____ one activity and the next.

6. The prefixes OVER-, HYPER-, SUPER-, SUPRA-, and SUR- give us the ideas of *over*, *above*, *excessive*, or *extra*.

    a. Over + cooked = _____ (cooked too much).

    b. Over + lord = _____ (a ruler over others).

    c. Hyper + active = _____ (excessively active).

    d. Hyper + bole = _____ (greatly exaggerated speech or writing).

    e. Super + impose = _____ (to place one thing on top of or above another).

    f. Supra + national = _____ (beyond or outside the boundaries of national interest).

    g. Sur + mount = _____ (to overcome).

7. ULTR- and OUTR- mean *beyond*, as an *ultramodern* shopping center is beyond what we expected, appearing to be the most modern center possible.

    a. An *outrage* is _____ .

    b. *Ultrapure* water is _____ .

    c. If her clothing is outré, it is _____ .

USING PREFIXES

Exercise I. Antonyms.

Find an antonym or opposing phrase for each word or phrase in the left column.

_____	1. **toxic**	(a)	prospect
_____	2. **progress**	(b)	normal
_____	3. **contradict**	(c)	preliminary study
_____	4. **retrospect**	(d)	outré
_____	5. **postgraduate work**	(e)	antagonist
_____	6. **protagonist**	(f)	dependent on others
_____	7. **usual, customary**	(g)	agree with
_____	8. **supernatural**	(h)	regress
_____	9. **autonomous**	(i)	antitoxic
_____	10. **ultraism**	(j)	conservatism

Exercise II. Chart Fill-In.

Enter the missing items in the chart. The first one serves as an example.

PREFIX	+	ROOT	=	WORD	DEFINITION
1. pro	+	long	=	prolong	to lengthen in time
2. mis	+	begotten	=	_____	illegitimate; deserving contempt
3. _____	+	vene	=	contravene	_____
4. _____	+	reader	=	_____	one who does not or cannot read
5. intra	+	_____	=	_____	within one galaxy
6. _____	+	_____	=	microcosm	_____
7. magni	+	loquent	=	_____	_____
8. _____	+	adroit	=	_____	awkward, clumsy
9. _____	+	_____	=	circumscribe	_____
10. hyper	+	_____	=	_____	exaggerated speech or writing

Exercise III. Fill-Ins.

Select the most appropriate word from the choices offered based on clues in context.

extrajudicial	misnomer	recurrent	foregone
counteract	unassuming	postmortem	profusely
malevolent	superhuman		

1. Malaria has been called the disease that never gives up; it is a _____ problem for the victim, who must cope with successive bouts of illness.

2. The _____ examination performed on the body of an ancient Chinese woman was surely one of the more unusual scientific inquiries into the past.

3. Carrie's allergy medication made her sleepy, but she drank enough strong coffee while studying for the caffeine to _____ the medicine and she wasn't groggy.

4. The wicked fairy Maleficent in *Sleeping Beauty* cast several _____ glances at the infant Aurora, so that the film audience knew trouble was brewing.

5. When Rory spilled his chocolate milkshake on Jan's new skirt, he apologized _____, but his repeated, elaborate apologies only made Jan lose her temper.

6. Superman is known for his fantastic, _____ efforts to uphold the law and foil dastardly criminals.

7. The judge kept his _____ opinions on legal cases to himself, rarely revealing his thoughts to family or colleagues.

8. Calling that scrawny, hairless dog Fluffy is the funniest _____ I've heard in ages.

9. The seniors' vote in favor of a day off was a _____ conclusion; everyone knew what the outcome would be before the actual voting took place.

10. Brian's talents and intelligence could have been intimidating to others, but his quiet, _____ manner earned him many friends.

UNIT II

Vocabulary In and
Out of Context

You've Got to Know the Territory

Studying Context as a Key to the Meaning of Words

VOCABULARY . . .

Your vocabulary is more than the words you know—it is your storehouse of ideas. Each word represents an idea or concept. Some are straightforward and simple, like *horse*. You know what a horse is. Other words, such as *democracy,* express fairly involved concepts.

Words open the door to the world of ideas. That's why it is worthwhile to have a large vocabulary. People rich in ideas are the ones who get the most out of life—in personal enjoyment as well as material benefits.

. . . AND CONTEXT

Context is environment. The context of a word includes the other words in the same sentence as well as the sentences before and after. When the context changes, so may the word's meaning.

People change just as words do—if only we alter their environment or context. For a minute, think about a close friend. Would he or she behave one way at school and another way at a beach party? One way at home and another way on a camping trip?

Context makes an enormous difference—to words and to people. Consider the verb *to fire* in the following sentences, and note how its meaning changes as the context does. Jot down its different meanings in the blanks.

MEANING

1. Roger was *fired* from his job last Friday. _____.

2. Jan *fired* one shot after another at the basket, scoring 20 points in as many minutes. _____.

3. We were so *fired up* after the victory that we jumped to our feet to sing the school song. _____.

4. One match *fired* the kindling, which, in turn, lit the brush pile. _____.

5. We hope to keep peace without *firing* a single shot. _____.

6. "I promise I'll listen," Dad assured Andy. "*Fire away* and I won't interrupt." _____.

Obviously you can use the context of a word to determine its meaning in the sentence. Often the logic of the sentence will tell you what a strange word means, even if you've never seen the word before.

Example: As they gathered around their fallen leader, the eerie *keening* of the tribe rose above the clearing, penetrating the night with a mournful chorus.

What sort of sound is *keening*? _____.

Given the context of the sentence, it can only be a sound of sorrow and a creepy sound at that. It's described as *eerie* and *a mournful chorus*. Also, it *penetrates* the night, giving us the idea of shrillness and/or loudness. It is definitely not a sad, soft sigh.

Sometimes the context of the sentence actually offers a **definition of the word** you are trying to puzzle out.

Some sentences contain **synonyms or synonymous phrases** that point the way to meaning. Others may offer an **antonym or contrasting idea**, which tells you that your mystery word means just the opposite of those words you recognize.

This text refers to all of these hints or clues to the meaning of words in context as **KEY WORDS**. Practice in locating key words will make you good at it. You will learn to depend on context to reveal the meaning of a mystery word.

KEY WORDS IN CONTEXT

Using Logic or Common Sense

Remember to use the entire meaning of each sentence to point toward the probable meaning of the word in italics. Occasionally you may see a nearly synonymous word that will help. *Read for the overall tone of the sentence.* If stumped, substitute a word you know for the italicized word. Does the sentence make good sense with your word? If so, you're in the right neighborhood.

Now, take a thoughtful look at these sentences before you fill in each of the blanks.

1. The *dank* odor of the swamp filled his nostrils, reminding him how he hated anything damp or moldy.

    Key words _____.

    Dank probably means _____.

2. All around her rose the *puling* sounds of starving infants, children without hope who cried as if they knew.

    Key words _____.

    Puling probably means _____.

3. His appearance told the story: ill-fitting clothes hung on his slender body. *Lank,* dark hair framed a face as devoid of liveliness as the rest of him.

    Key words _____.

    Lank probably means _____.

4. The River Itchen in southwest England is famous for its clear waters *teeming* with trout.

    Key words _____.

    Teeming probably means _____.

5. The *rift* between Jan and Ed is obvious. She will no longer go anywhere where Ed is apt to appear.

    Key words _____.

    Rift probably means _____.

6. "Just pay and be done with it," Mom advised us. "This isn't a marketplace where you can *haggle* over price."

    Key words _____.

    Haggle probably means _____.

7. "He's got a lot of *chutzpah* asking me to work more hours," Carrie exclaimed indignantly, "when I've already worked more than anyone else!"

    Key words _____.

    Chutzpah probably means _____.

8. Sheepishly, Sara put her dime in the collection plate and hoped that no one would notice what she felt was a *paltry* offering.

    Key words _____.

    Paltry probably means _____.

9. Old Merlin was a gray yet impressive figure, his *hoary* beard mingling almost indistinguishably with the silver cloak draped over his stooped shoulders.

    Key words _____.

    Hoary probably means _____.

10. Tim's summer job was so *lucrative* that he saved enough to pay for all books and to provide him with allowance money for his first year in college.

    Key words _____.

    Lucrative probably means _____.

Double Check: How close were you?

1. dank   *wet, damp*
2. puling   *whining, whimpering*
3. lank   *lean, lifeless*
4. teeming   *abounding*
5. rift   *break, breach*
6. haggle   *to wrangle, argue*
7. chutzpah   *gall, nerve*
8. paltry   *trivial*
9. hoary   *gray with age*
10. lucrative   *monetarily rewarding*

Finding a Definition in Context

This time you are looking for a fairly explicit definition of your mystery word within the sentence itself. Enter your answers before checking those that follow this practice.

1. The *sinuous* road curved narrowly up the mountain, winding in and around like a long black serpent.

   Context definition _____.

   Sinuous probably means _____.

2. Matt hoped fervently that Clyde's insensitive remarks and rude gestures would be lost in the party hubbub, because such *crass* behavior would cost them both.

   Context definition _____.

   Crass probably means _____.

3. Aunt Dolly's *effusive* praise washed over me in a flood, making me wonder why she had to rave on and on about my every achievement.

   Context definition _____.

   Effusive probably means _____.

4. The *piquant* sauce is my favorite—a sauce that will tickle the palate and add zesty flavor to food.

   Context definition _____.

   Piquant probably means _____.

5. "He's only a *stripling*," my older cousin said, trying to get a rise out of me by suggesting that I was barely a teenager, years away from college.

   Context definition _____.

   Stripling probably means _____.

6. When he was younger, Andy thought of Santa Claus as someone *ubiquitous*, a presence that was everywhere at all times.

   Context definition _____.

   Ubiquitous probably means _____.

7. She turned a *vapid* face to us and we gave up, knowing we would learn nothing from a countenance lacking life and intelligence.

   Context definition _____.

   Vapid probably means _____.

8. As only a few small items were stolen, the theft was considered a *petty* crime.

   Context definition _____.

   Petty probably means _____.

9. Bess's poem titled *"Reverie"* attempted to describe that dreamlike state of thought and memory into which we all escape at times.

   Context definition _____.

   Reverie probably means _____.

10. A *pestilence* swept through the tiny town, ravaging each household with an infectious disease later named the bubonic plague.

    Context definition _____.

    Pestilence probably means _____.

Double Check: You should be right on target this time.

1. sinuous   *winding, snakelike*
2. crass   *rude, vulgar, boorish*
3. effusive   *gushing*
4. piquant   *zesty, spicy*
5. stripling   *youth, boy*
6. ubiquitous   *ever present*
7. vapid   *empty, flat, dull*
8. petty   *minor* (also means *low* or *mean-spirited*)
9. reverie   *dream*
10. pestilence   *plague, disease*

USING THE WORDS

Use the meanings you have learned for the foregoing twenty words to work the following exercises.

Exercise I. Antonyms.
Find at least one antonym or contrasting definition for each word on the left.

_____ 1. **crass**	(a) major, important
_____ 2. **paltry**	(b) refined, sensitive, polite
_____ 3. **chutzpah**	(c) straight (not winding)
_____ 4. **piquant**	(d) restrained
_____ 5. **hoary**	(e) full of body, springy
_____ 6. **ubiquitous**	(f) timidity, lack of nerve
_____ 7. **lank**	(g) noticeably bright or interesting
_____ 8. **sinuous**	(h) youthful
_____ 9. **effusive**	(i) lacking zest or flavor
_____ 10. **vapid**	(j) absent

Exercise II. Logic.
Here are some of the first twenty study words as they are apt to appear in writing. Write the answers where indicated. If you're still stumped, ask a friend, parent, or teacher.

1. Reword the phrase *a petty act, unworthy of her.*

   _____.

2. Why is the phrase *lank hair* not a compliment?

   _____.

3. A brain *teeming* with ideas is

   _____.

4. Besides *stripling,* what other words can you think of that use the suffix *-ling* to indicate *little*?

   _____.

5. At certain times, could you describe five children—all underfoot and under 5 years of age—as a *pestilence*?

   _____.

Exercise III. Fill-Ins.

From the choices offered, select the most appropriate word for each sentence. The word form may need changing.

dank	haggle	sinuous	ubiquitous
puling	chutzpah	crass	vapid
lank	paltry	effusive	pestilence
teeming	hoary	piquant	reverie
rift	lucrative	stripling	petty

1. Overjoyed at his promotion, Alan informed his parents that his new position was

    _____ enough for him to afford his own apartment now.

2. Long ago, serfs were accustomed to little and could quickly pack up their

    _____ belongings for a move.

3. The director told his actors, "It's no use _____ over minor changes,

    especially when you know that I'm going to win the argument."

4. Hoping to mend the _____ in their relationship, Ed sent Jan a dozen red

    carnations.

5. *Give me your tired, your poor,*

    Your huddled masses yearning to breathe free,

    The wretched refuse of your _____ shore.

    Send these, the homeless, tempest-tost to me,

    I lift my lamp beside the golden door!

    —Emma Lazarus, "The New Colossus," poem on pedestal of the Statue of Liberty

6. The anxious, _____ sounds of hungry animals resounded through the

    kennels each day at feeding times.

7. A remembered phrase from Edgar Allan Poe's creative gloominess describes a "deep,

    _____ tarn," which helps readers to picture a scummy old pond or

    swampy area.

8. *Incens'd with indignation Satan stood*
   Unterrifi'd, and like a comet . . .
   . . . and from his horrid hair

   Shakes _____ *and war*

   —Milton, *Paradise Lost*, Bk. ii

9. Peppermint Patty is often lost in _____, but Marcie sits behind her in school and politely (or otherwise) wakes her up from time to time.

10. Mom reminded my sister Carrie that tattling was a(n) _____, mean-spirited action calculated to make the rest of us despise her.

11. Huck Finn's father loathed "the guvmint," believing it to be _____ — ever present and inescapable.

12. In *A Day No Pigs Would Die*, Rob is only a _____ when his father dies and Rob becomes the man of the family.

13. Marigold rejected the advances of a scruffy tomcat whom she considered a(n)

    _____, loutish fellow and mated instead with a refined Siamese from

    across the street.

14. The _____ movements of the hula dancers kept my dad's attention throughout their performance.

15. The calculus teacher was distressed to see all of us gazing _____ at the blackboard after he'd explained the new problem set.

Help! Hollered the Puzzled Reader

Finding Synonyms or Antonyms in Context As Keys to the Meaning of Words

USING SYNONYMS IN CONTEXT

Look for the synonyms or synonymous phrases within the context of each sentence. The meaning of the italicized word will be close to the key words that you identify.

1. Our family always wonders what *bizarre* apparel Aunt Dolly will appear in next, because the oddities of her clothing cause people to stop and stare.

   Key words _____.

   Bizarre probably means _____.

2. Roger behaved as though he were completely stupid on stage—an utter *dolt* without a memory.

   Key words _____.

   Dolt probably means _____.

3. Parts of London were *razed* by wartime bombing, yet the destruction was overcome by a city eager to rebuild.

   Key words _____.

   To raze probably means _____.

4. Knowing that Marigold had *filched* two of our tropical fish from the aquarium, we were on guard to see that our marauding feline stole no more midnight snacks.

   Key words _____.

   To filch probably means _____.

5. "You've drawn a *dour* face on Macbeth," the art teacher commented. "Was he all that gloomy and harsh, or was he more tortured in his soul?"

   Key words _____.

   Dour probably means _____.

6. Aunt Dolly's new hat is a *pert* navy pillbox that gives her a jaunty, saucy look instead of the outlandish appearance she usually affects.

   Key words _____.

   Pert probably means _____.

7. Marigold's good behavior on Saturday was only a *ruse*. No one was fooled by her deception, especially on Sunday when she resumed aquarium fishing.

   Key words _____.

   Ruse probably means _____.

8. Marigold's kitten, Poucette, is herself a fishing *tyro* who, as a beginner, has yet to make her first catch.

    Key words _____.

    Tyro probably means _____.

9. The *chagrin* on Andy's face was obvious, although he tried to cover his embarrassment by whistling nonchalantly.

    Key words _____.

    Chagrin probably means _____.

10. College students *scrutinize* each semester's list of course offerings, examining each selection carefully before making their new schedules.

    Key words _____.

    Scrutinize probably means _____.

Double Check: Did you find those synonyms?

1. bizarre   *outlandish, odd*
2. dolt   *clod, dumb person*
3. to raze   *to tear down, destroy*
4. to filch   *to steal something minor or small*
5. dour   *gloomy, harsh*
6. pert   *saucy, perky*
7. ruse   *deception, stratagem*
8. tyro   *novice, beginner*
9. chagrin   *embarrassment*
10. scrutinize   *to examine*

USING ANTONYMS OR OPPOSING IDEAS IN CONTEXT

Time to find those antonyms. Remember that an antonym is an opposite. It shows contrast. Watch for the contrast set up in each sentence. (Usually there is only one antonym or opposing phrase. Otherwise, English would be filled with bulky sentences.)

1. "Why do we always haggle over curfews?" Dad asked. "Can't you two just *acquiesce* for once?"

   Opposing word(s) _____.

   Acquiesce probably means _____.

2. Classes on drug abuse emphasize not only the danger from a pure drug but also the deadly potential of an *adulterated* one.

   Opposing word(s) _____.

   Adulterated probably means _____.

3. The trouble with my younger brother Andy in a family picture-taking session is the broad *smirk* he adopts instead of his normal smile.

   Opposing word(s) _____.

   Smirk probably means _____.

   (NOTE: *Instead* indicates an opposing idea.)

4. Because Joe couldn't make a firm decision, he *vacillated* between agreeing with our plan and rejecting it.

   Opposing word(s) _____.

   To vacillate probably means _____.

5. If pessimism and a dour outlook are bad for our health, let's concentrate on the *salutary* benefits of humor and an optimistic attitude.

   Opposing word(s) _____.

   Salutary probably means _____.

6. "Is Dad going to continue being stubborn about our curfew," my sister Jan asked, "or will he *capitulate?*"

   Opposing word(s) _____.

   Capitulate probably means _____.

   (NOTE: *Or* indicates an opposing idea.)

7. Terry's tendency to *dissemble* rather than reveal his true personality confuses nearly everyone he meets.

   Opposing word(s) _____.

   Dissemble probably means _____.

   (NOTE: *Rather than* indicates an opposing idea.)

8. The coach said, "Regular workouts and tough practices will make this team tops. *Indolence* never won a medal."

   Opposing word(s) _____.

   Indolence probably means _____.

9. The legendary Brave Little Tailor knew he should tell the truth about killing "seven at one blow"; nevertheless, he *prevaricated*.

   Opposing word(s) _____.

   Prevaricated probably means _____.

10. "Those vapid, mournful looks won't do," cried our play director. "It's a look of *rapture* we need, not clinical depression!"

    Opposing word(s) _____.

    Rapture probably means _____.

Double Check: How close were you?

1. acquiesce   *to agree, say yes*
2. adulterate   *to add impurities*
3. smirk   *sickeningly sweet grin*
4. vacillate   *to waver*
5. salutary   *promoting health*
6. capitulate   *to yield, give in to*
7. dissemble   *to pretend*
8. indolence   *laziness*
9. prevaricate   *to lie, tell an untruth*
10. rapture   *extreme joy*

USING THE WORDS

Exercise I. Fill-Ins.
Select the best word from the choices given, based on clues in context.

pert	filching	smirk	vacillating
rapture	bizarre	capitulation	tyro
razed	scrutiny		

1. entire crumbling block that needed to be _____

2. the FDA's _____ of each new drug prior to approval

3. easy _____, rather than lengthy debate

4. her _____, sassy retort that irritated Mom

5. obviously a professional, not a _____

6. an unpleasant _____ of smug self-satisfaction

7. a feeling of _____ as he heard his own symphony performed for the first time

8. _____ a couple of quarters and pretending that it wasn't important

9. a _____ account that sounded highly unlikely

10. made a choice and stopped _____ at last

Exercise II. Thinking About the Words.
Use common sense and logical reasoning to help in answering the following questions. If your knowledge is thin in spots, consult a dictionary.

1. Will the second-ranked senior give a *salutary* or *salutatory* address at graduation?

   _____

2. How would you rank the following adjectives in order of degree, beginning with contentment as the lowest degree? contentment, rapture, delight, happiness, exultation

   _____

3. *Dissemble*, *semblance*, and *resemble* make up a word family. In the phrase "only a semblance of her former self," what does *semblance* most probably mean?

   _____

4. One good synonym for *indolence* is *sloth*. Why is that an appropriate name for the animal who bears it?

   _____

5. How many synonyms can you find for *ruse*?

   _____

6. In sentence 4 of "Using Synonyms in Context" (p. 41), what does the word *marauding* have to mean?

   _____

Exercise III. Antonyms.
Suggest an antonym or contrasting phrase for the following words.

1. bizarre _____

2. dolt _____

3. capitulate _____

4. sloth _____

5. salubrious _____

6. vacillate _____

7. raze _____

8. prevaricate _____

9. dissembler _____

10. dour _____

11. adulterant _____

12. pert _____

13. acquiescence _____

14. rapture _____

15. scrutinize _____

REVIEW LIST OF WORDS TAUGHT IN UNIT II

Unit II presented forty words, with only six exercises as practice. Its purpose was to offer practice in deducing meaning from context, *not* mastery of vocabulary. According to learning specialists, you must see a word or work with it six or seven times in order to fix it in your mind for sure. That is why the vocabulary mastery portion of your book will stress repeated usage of the words being taught.

But before we leave this unit, please write a synonym or brief definition beside the words we've covered. If you miss one, flip back to find its meaning and write it on the correct line. *The act of writing is a powerful memory tool.*

1. dank _____

2. puling _____

3. lank _____

4. teeming _____

5. rift _____

6. haggle _____

7. chutzpah _____

8. paltry _____

9. hoary _____

10. lucrative _____

11. sinuous _____

12. crass _____

13. effusive _____

14. piquant _____

15. stripling _____

16. ubiquitous _____

17. vapid _____

18. petty _____

19. reverie _____

20. pestilence _____

21. bizarre _____

22. dolt _____

23. raze _____

24. filch _____

25. dour _____

26. pert _____

27. ruse _____

28. tyro _____

29. chagrin _____

30. scrutinize _____

31. acquiesce _____

32. adulterate _____

33. smirk _____

34. vacillate _____

35. salutary _____

36. capitulate _____

37. dissemble _____

38. indolence _____

39. prevaricate _____

40. rapture _____

UNIT III

The Vocabulary Lists

LIST 1

Look, Jane, Look!
Verbs, The Action Words

In Context. Before studying the definitions, try reasoning out the meaning of each word, using context as your guide.

1. Hoping to *atone* for waking Dad up, Andy promised, "I'll be very quiet the next time you take a nap, okay?"

   Key: Logic   **Atone** means _____.

2. My folks said they planned to spend spring weekends watching their garden seedlings *burgeon* healthily in response to love, weeding, and fertilizer.

   Key: Logic   **Burgeon** means _____.

3. "You can't *coerce* me into going," Jan teased, "but you could persuade me."

   Key: Opposing word   **Coerce** means _____.

4. Aware that the enemy was about to *defile* the sacred Ark of the Covenant, Indiana Jones warned his companion not to look for fear of what would follow the Ark's desecration.

   Key: Logic   **Defile** means _____.

5. After I hooted at Jan's attempts to drive our old stick-shift Ford, she stormed indoors, shouting, "I'm telling Dad! You've *disparaged* my driving for the last time!"

   Key: Synonymous idea   **Disparage** means _____.

6. Trailing a catnip mouse behind him, Andy *enticed* Poucette and Figment into the garage for the night.

   Key: Logic   **Entice** means _____.

7. Marigold *evinced* no interest in the catnip lure and settled herself determinedly on my bed for the night.

   Key: Logic   **Evince** means _____.

8. "Repent and be saved!" was what the street-corner preacher *exhorted* the crowd to do.

   Key: Logic   **Exhort** means _____.

9. When we call Marigold, she *feigns* deafness if she doesn't want to come in, but she never pretends to be hard of hearing when the dinner bell rings.

   Key: Synonym   **Feign** means _____.

10. Jan told Dad, "It would have been okay if Jeff had just *intimated* that I had a little trouble shifting, but he kept announcing it to everyone in the car!"

    Key: Opposing word   **Intimate** means _____.

11. When Andy started raising gerbils, he *nurtured* them with the care of a practiced, tender parent.

    Keys: Logic, partial definition   **Nurture** means _____.

12. The fun of reading an Agatha Christie murder mystery, or any modern whodunit, is deducing who *perpetrated* the crime.

    Key: Logic   **Perpetrate** means _____.

13. My folks observed that it is impossible to *redress* the wrongs of war, because there can't be any compensation to parents for the death of their children.

    Key: Synonymous idea   **Redress** means _____.

14. Poucette and Figment fight over possession of the catnip mouse, each trying to get the other to *relinquish* it.

    Key: Logic   **Relinquish** means _____.

15. In Hale's story, written to inspire patriotism, Philip Nolan was *stigmatized* as "the man without a country"—a man condemned to live aboard a ship that roamed the seas until he died.

    Key: Logic   **Stigmatize** means _____.

16. "No use *truckling* to me, thinking I'm so soft in the head I'll give you more of an allowance," Mom warned Andy. "I can tell when somebody's buttering me up."

    Key: Synonymous phrase   **Truckle** means _____.

WORD STUDY

With any luck at all, you were able to get a fair idea of what each word in this list means. You plucked each meaning from the context because the sense of a sentence depends more on the verb than on any other part of speech. The verb is IT, in other words.

A seventh grader (eager to make points with his teacher as they both surveyed his poorly written essay) said not long ago, "Gee, I wish I had great verbs."

This list contains some "great verbs" to help your writing come alive. Consult the list of abbreviations on the last page of this book for the names of foreign languages from which these verbs are derived.

1. **atone** (ə-'ton) v.   To satisfy or appease by making amends; to make up for a wrong or a deficiency; originally, *at one* in harmony

   No memory of having starred
   Atones *for later disregard,*
   Or keeps the end from being hard.
       —Robert Frost, "Provide, Provide"

   Relative: *atonement*
   Synonym: *expiate*

2. **burgeon** ('bər-jən) v.   To grow, often rapidly (said of people, conditions, plants); to exhibit growth such as buds or sprouts; from L. *burra,* shaggy cloth

   Now fades the last long streak of snow
   Now burgeons *every maze of quick*
   About the flowering squares and thick
   By ashen roots the violets blow.
       —Alfred, Lord Tennyson, "In Memoriam"

   Synonyms: *flourish, bloom, sprout, blossom* (none exact)
   Antonyms: *wither, dwindle, shrink*

3. **coerce** (kō-'ərs) v.   To dominate by force or threats; to bring about by superior strength; from L. *coercere,* to enclose, shut up

   Although they didn't like the idea, we *coerced* our cats into staying in the basement while a crew cleaned our downstairs carpeting.

   Relatives: *coercion, coercive, coercible, coercively*
   Synonym: *force*

4. **defile** (di-fī[ə]l) v.   To make impure or unclean—anything from sanctuaries (with an unholy act or word) to new books (with suggestive notes or drawings); to corrupt, befoul, or debase; from F. *défouler,* to trample

   Nor one feeling of vengeance presume to defile,
   The cause, or the men, of the Emerald Isle.
       —William Drennan, "Erin"

   Relatives: *defiler, defilement*
   Synonyms: *contaminate, sully, dishonor, befoul, debase, besmirch, corrupt, deflower* (denude of chastity), *violate*
   Antonyms: *honor, exalt, respect*

5. **disparage** (dis-'par-ij) v.   To belittle or minimize another's skill or accomplishments; to degrade someone; from F. *despargier,* to marry beneath one's class

"I don't want to *disparage* your achievement, dear," Mom told Carrie, "but I wonder how you can mess up the whole living room just by sewing one costume!"

   Relatives: *disparagement, disparager, disparagingly*
   Synonyms: *belittle, denigrate, downgrade, depreciate, decry*
   Antonyms: *applaud, cheer* (for), *laud*

6. **entice** (in-'tīs) v.   To tempt or lure onward in a clever, artful manner; from L. *in + titio,* firebrand

My son, if sinners entice *thee, consent thou not.*
      —The Bible, Prov. 1:10

   Relatives: *enticement, enticingly*
   Synonyms: *lure, tempt, allure*
   Antonyms: *scare, frighten, alarm*

7. **evince** (i-'vin[t]s) v.   To show or display clearly; from L. *evincere,* to conquer, vanquish

The tour guide warned his group not to *evince* a speck of interest in the beggars who might tag along at major tourist sights in Paris.

   Relative: *evincible*
   Synonyms: *reveal, display, show*
   Antonyms: *conceal, hide*

8. **exhort** (ig-'zȯ[ə]rt) v.   To rouse and urge onward, as *the leader exhorts his troops to step up the pace*; to warn or advise urgently; from L. *exhortari,* to incite

We bent rhythmically forward and back in the racing shell, determined that our crew would be first, while the onlookers *exhorted* us to "Pull, pull!

   Relatives: *exhortation, exhortative, exhortatory*
   Synonyms: *urge, press, spur* (first meaning); *admonish, caution* (second meaning)

9. **feign** ('fān) v.   To pretend or dissemble, as *he feigned illness*; from L. *fingere,* to shape, mold, conceive

Not wanting Dad to know he'd been reading by flashlight under the covers, Andy curled up and *feigned* sleep when Dad peeked into his room.

   Relatives: *feigned* (adj., not genuine), *feigner*
   Synonyms: *pretend, dissemble, assume*

10. **intimate** ('int-ə-māt) v.   To suggest indirectly or hint in a delicate, subtle way; from L. *intimus,* innermost

"Sally makes me so angry," Jan said. "Yesterday she hinted that I dyed my hair, and today she *intimated* that it could use a touch-up, but this is my real hair!"

   Relatives: *intimater, intimate* (adj., private, personal), *intimate* (n., close personal friend)
   Synonyms: *suggest, hint; imply* and *insinuate* (usually negative in connotation)
   Antonyms: *proclaim, announce*

11. **nurture** ('nər-chər) v.   To foster growth and development by giving food, education, emotional support, etc.; from L. *nutrire,* to suckle or nourish

Of the American Revolution, Samuel Morison wrote, "Independence was no conscious goal, secretly *nurtured* in cellar or jungle by bearded conspirators, but a reluctant last resort, to preserve 'life, liberty, and the pursuit of happiness.' " (Note past participial form, used as an adjective.)

   Relatives: *nurturer, nurturance, nurture* (n.)
   Synonyms: *nourish, foster, feed*
   Antonym: *starve* (deprive of nourishment)

12. **perpetrate** ('pər-pə-ˌtrāt) v.   To cause to happen, as *he perpetrated the crime;* to commit; from L. *per + patrare,* to accomplish

Pointing to the empty cookie jar, Mom said, "I'd give a pretty penny to know who *perpetrated* our latest theft."

   Relatives: *perpetrator, perpetration*
   Synonym: *commit*

13. **redress** (ri-'dres) v.   To right a wrong by offering compensation or by removing the cause for complaint; to avenge or exact reparation; from F. *redrecier,* to make straight

There is no grievance that is a fit object of redress *by mob law.*
      —Abraham Lincoln, address delivered in Illinois, 1838

   Relatives: *redress* (n.), *redresser*
   Synonyms: *compensate, rectify, correct* (first meaning); *avenge* (second meaning)

14. **relinquish** (ri-'liŋ-kwish) v.   To give up or renounce, usually with regret; to cease holding on, or to yield control of; from L. *relinquere,* to leave behind

Time does not relinquish *its rights, either over human beings or over monuments.*
      —Goethe, *Elective Affinities*

   Relative: *relinquishment*
   Synonyms: *yield, surrender, abandon, resign, waive*
   Antonyms: *keep, retain, maintain*

15. **stigmatize** ('stig-mə-ˌtīz) v.   To brand or mark, either physically or verbally, in a severely negative way; to disgrace utterly; from Gr. and L. *stigma,* brand or mark of a pointed instrument

Aaron Burr, who undoubtedly had some good qualities, managed to *stigmatize* himself forever as a traitor to his country.

   Relatives: *stigma, stigmatic, stigmatism, stigmatization*
   Synonyms: *brand, mark, denounce*
   Antonyms: *honor, decorate, laud, cite* (for service, bravery, etc.)
   Derivation: Romans and Greeks used to brand a slave on the forehead with red-hot irons. Colored matter was then rubbed into the wound, and from then on the slave was called a *stigmatic.*

The plural term *stigmata* often refers to the marks on Christ's body made by the crown of thorns and the nails driven through his feet and hands. Since that time, similar marks have been thought by devout Christian believers to have appeared on the bodies of certain people, notably St. Francis of Assisi. Religious paintings of the Renaissance era often show holy figures marked by stigmata.

The eye dysfunction called *astigmatism* comes from this same root and refers to a defect of the refractive system of the eye, often an irregularity of the cornea.

16. **truckle** (ˈtrək-əl) v.   To behave as a lowly servant in an obsequious, fawning manner; from L. *trochlea,* block of pulleys

    Disappointed and bitterly frustrated, Jonathan Swift wrote of the Irish people in 1731: "A servile race in folly nursed,/Who *truckle* most when treated worst."

    Relative: *truckler*
    Synonyms: *toady, grovel, fawn*
    Derivation: A *truckle bed* was a child's trundle bed, customarily trundled out of sight during the day and hidden under the higher bed. The idea of truckling comes from the lowly position of the bed itself.

ROOT STUDY

A short list of word roots follows each Word Study section in this unit. It is boring to memorize long lists of roots—and hard to remember them—but tucking four or five into your memory at a time is relatively easy. Also, knowledge of a root meaning often helps you to puzzle out the meaning of a strange word.

Read the example words for each root slowly and carefully. Say them aloud as well. They will appear as quiz items in some of the exercises. You need to include these words in your growing vocabulary.

1. **EV (AEV)** means *age* or *time*.

    longevity—long life
    primeval—of the earliest known ages or times
    medieval (or *mediaeval*)—referring to the Middle Ages, also called the Dark Ages, from the late fifth century to the late fifteenth century, when the Renaissance began in western Europe, printing was invented, and Columbus discovered America

2. **PHIL** means *love* of.

    philosophy—the love of wisdom
    philosopher—lover of wisdom
    philologist—lover of words
    philatelist—collector (and lover) of stamps
    Anglophile—lover of England and things English
    Francophile—lover of France and things French

3. **ANTHROP** means *humankind.*

    anthropology—the study of humankind's cultural development
    anthropomorphism—attributing human characteristics to nonhumans
    philanthropist—one who loves and helps human beings
    misanthrope—one who hates people

4. **VINC** and **VICT** mean to *conquer.*

    invincible—unconquerable
    convince—to persuade strongly; to assure, prove, satisfy
    Vincent, Victor, and *Victoria*—conqueror
    victorious—conquering, triumphant

USING THE WORDS

By this point in each lesson you will have seen the words of the basic list at least three times. Now, operating on the principle of "use it or lose it," you need to use those words.

List 1 Review

atone	disparage	feign	redress
burgeon	entice	intimate	relinquish
coerce	evince	nurture	stigmatize
defile	exhort	perpetrate	truckle

Exercise I. Definitions.

Write the vocabulary words beside their definitions. The first letter of the correct word is given as a hint.

1. to brand or mark in a negative way   s _____

2. to commit   p _____

3. to renounce with regret   r _____

4. to behave in a fawning manner   t _____

5. to nourish, educate, or foster   n _____

6. to show clearly   e _____

7. to suggest or to hint indirectly   i _____

8. to corrupt, befoul, or debase   d _____

9. to pretend or dissemble   f _____

10. to tempt or lure onward   e _____

If you missed one or two, look back at the definitions and enter the missing word(s) in the proper location.

Exercise II. Switcheroo—verbs become nouns.

Although the words in List 1 were explained as verbs, most have noun forms as well. Match the noun forms with their correct meanings.

_____ 1. **coercion**	(a) reparation or satisfaction
_____ 2. **enticement**	(b) downgrading
_____ 3. **exhortation**	(c) one who profanes or desecrates
_____ 4. **intimation**	(d) brand of infamy
_____ 5. **atonement**	(e) lure
_____ 6. **perpetrator**	(f) urgent appeal
_____ 7. **disparagement**	(g) force
_____ 8. **redress**	(h) compensation or correction
_____ 9. **stigma**	(i) one who commits a foul deed
_____ 10. **defiler**	(j) hint, suggestion

Exercise III. Analogies.

Complete the analogies with the best pair possible, using words from List 1 and Roots.

The analogies given in Lists 1–24 are offered for practice in logical reasoning and vocabulary mastery. They are meant to help teach the words. Analogy questions on standardized tests are often more difficult, as they test your knowledge of trickier implied relationships.

_____ 1. wax : wane ::

    (a) moon : crescent
    (b) burgeon : wither
    (c) bud : flower
    (d) redress : wrong

_____ 2. nurture : growth ::

    (a) improvise : rehearsal
    (b) entice : lure
    (c) exhort : action
    (d) defile: reputation

_____ 3. philosopher : wisdom ::

    (a) philologist : logistics
    (b) books : bibliophile
    (c) chlorophyll : plants
    (d) Anglophile : England

_____ 4. disparage : praise ::

    (a) truckle : command
    (b) stigmatize : brand
    (c) denigrate : decry
    (d) intimate : entice

_____ 5. evince : interest ::

    (a) truckle : toady
    (b) redress : wrong
    (c) perpetrate : benefit
    (d) nurture : parent

Exercise IV. Fill-Ins.

Find the most appropriate word for each phrase from the words in List 1 and Roots. The word form may need changing.

1. seeking _____ for grievous wrong

2. a _____ attitude totally inappropriate to modern life

3. obsequious employees who _____ to the manager

4. Aaron Burr, _____ forever with the name traitor

5. resigned gracefully, thereby _____ his control of the company

6. noted _____, whose love of words showed in his vocabulary

7. an offer so tempting we were _____ into going after all

8. a warship we christened *The* _____ because we hoped it would be unconquerable

9. hate being _____ into doing something I dislike

10. wondering who _____ the theft of his tapes

Exercise V. Antonyms.

Select the correct opposites, one for each word on the left. (Note: Not many words have exact antonyms. Choose the best one of the choices offered.)

_____	1. **stigma**	(a) accusation	(b) citation	(c) cicatrix	(d) fixation
_____	2. **misanthrope**	(a) arthropod	(b) philosopher	(c) philanthropist	(d) anthropologist
_____	3. **primeval**	(a) futuristic	(b) ancient	(c) archaeological	(d) postwar
_____	4. **evince**	(a) reveal	(b) display	(c) devolve	(d) conceal
_____	5. **coerce**	(a) urge	(b) please	(c) better	(d) cajole
_____	6. **nurture**	(a) stunt	(b) nourish	(c) mother	(d) delay
_____	7. **feign**	(a) seem wary	(b) appear willing	(c) be truthful	(d) feel depressed
_____	8. **defile**	(a) benefit	(b) encourage	(c) respect	(d) arrange
_____	9. **longevity**	(a) declivity	(b) brevity	(c) activity	(d) nativity
_____	10. **intimate**	(a) proclaim	(b) personal	(c) apparel	(d) preclude

Exercise VI. Word Analysis.

This set of exercises is the place to exercise your brain cells. Let logic and reason do some mental calisthenics for you. If you're temporarily stumped, holler for help. Also, you can always check a good dictionary.

But don't give up. "Word Analysis" is meant to expand your consciousness about words.

1. Many acclaimed books and movies feature *anthropomorphic* characters. They have been given the characteristics of humankind. (Remember the scary trees in the forest of the *Snow White* movie?) You know Peter Rabbit, Wilbur the pig, and Ferdinand the bull, who loved to sit under his cork tree smelling the flowers. How many characters, book titles, or movie titles can you list in which *anthropomorphism* is evident?

   _____

   _____

   _____

2. Context profoundly affects word meaning. In the following pairs of sentences, note the different meanings on the appropriate lines.

   _____ a. (1) *"The* hardly *fought election had put him in the limelight."*—Agatha Christie, *Sparkling Cyanide*

   _____ (2) In the last round he *hardly* fought at all.

   _____ b. (1) Don't *depress* me with any more bad news.

   _____ (2) Remember to *depress* the clutch first.

   _____ c. (1) The trail *inclined* steeply and left us breathless.

   _____ (2) Is he *inclined* to go hiking each summer?

   _____ d. (1) After marriage, the couple will *cleave* together as one.

   _____ (2) Don't attempt to *cleave* the diamond until you have examined it thoroughly.

   _____ e. (1) You're just *plumb* crazy if you think I will go!

   _____ (2) We'll *plumb* the complexities of that book in class discussion.

   _____ f. (1) Did he *intimate* that I was acting fooling?

   _____ (2) *"'Twas one of my most* intimate *enemies."*
   —D. G. Rossetti, "Fragment"

3. How is the derivation for *atone*, "at one in harmony," consistent with our modern usage of the word?

    _____

    _____

4. Synonyms for *relinquish* include *yield, surrender, abandon, resign,* and *waive,* yet the **connotation** (the feeling) of each is slightly different. Try to explain the connotative meanings of the different synonyms. For instance, if you *abandon* a ship, how is that different from *relinquishing* it?

    _____

    _____

    _____

    _____

5. Explain this sentence: "He *insinuated* himself into our group and made himself at home."

    _____

    _____

Excuse My Onomatopoeia
Terms from the Arts

In Context. Before studying the definitions, try reasoning out the meaning of each word, using context as your guide.

1. After reading *Animal Farm,* everyone in our class wrote a paper about that *allegory,* discussing the human personality type and philosophy that each animal represented.

    Keys: Near definition, logic   **Allegory** means _____.

2. "I'm not fond of the *baroque* in either art or music," Mom announced. "The art and architecture are overdecorated—entirely too elaborate for my taste—and the music is cluttered with improvisations so that I lose track of the theme."

    Keys: Synonymous phrases,
         examples   **Baroque** means _____.

3. *Burlesque,* a form of comedy that often mocks by caricature, is a favorite technique of gifted actor Robin Williams.

    Key: Definition   **Burlesque** means _____.

4. "You like only *classical* styles, Mom," Jan said. "You drool over the clean lines of Greek architecture and listen to Haydn and Mozart. You're such a classicist I can't believe it!"

    Keys: Explanatory phrases,
         examples   **Classical** means _____.

5. I enjoy the slapstick buffoonery of Eddie Murphy as well as subtler *comedy* that isn't trying for a laugh every other line.

    Key: Logic   **Comedy** means _____.

6. "I never know 'whodunit' until the *denouement,*" Carrie complained as she closed her mystery novel. "The author always has to explain everything, telling me what wonderful clues were planted if only I'd been bright enough to spot them."

    Key: Definition   **Denouement** means _____.

7. Because our family loves a good *farce,* we enjoy the old slapstick movies of Mel Brooks, such as *Blazing Saddles* and *High Anxiety.*

    Keys: A synonymous phrase,
         example   **Farce** means _____.

8. My English class thought that writing a poem in *free verse* would be simple, but we discovered that free verse, even though it hasn't a fixed meter or rhyme, takes planning and hard work to sound right.

    Key: Definition   **Free verse** means _____.

9. My favorite literary *genre* this year is fantasy, but last year I read only westerns, and when I was a kid I liked detective stories.

    Keys: Logic, examples   **Genre** means _____.

10. Jan and Carrie like *Gothic* novels that are set in castles or other romantic spots and have plots stuffed with mysterious characters, haunted rooms, and village folk hinting that the dark past is about to overtake the present.

    Key: Definition   **Gothic** means _____.
                                           (here applied to literature only)

11. In *My Family and Other Animals,* Gerald Durrell ridicules his sister Margo and brothers Larry and Leslie in a series of hilarious, memorable *lampoons.*

    Key: Synonymous phrase   **Lampoon** means _____.

12. Each year hundreds of *parodies* for the International Imitation Hemingway Competition are submitted to judges who must decide which author has imitated Hemingway's style most faithfully and achieved the most ridiculous result.

    Keys: Definition, logic   **Parody** means _____.

13. As the *protagonist* in many films, Clint Eastwood portrays a classic hero, surmounting all odds to triumph in the end.

    Keys: Synonym, example   **Protagonist** means _____.

14. Decorated in the eighteenth century, many rooms of the Viennese royal summer palace are *rococo* in design, featuring pierced wood or metal sculpture, highly elaborate ceilings, and ornamental wall coverings and carpets.

    Key: Definitive phrases   **Rococo** means _____.

15. Justly famous for his gentle *satire,* Stephen Leacock wrote one essay, "Boarding-House Geometry," that uses his own original axioms and postulates. In it, Leacock satirizes life in an early-twentieth-century boarding house. (E.g., "Any two meals at a boarding house are together less than two square meals.")

    Keys: Synonymous word,
    example   **Satire** means _____.

16. Renowned Welsh *thespian* Richard Burton acted in Shakespearean productions as well as Hollywood movies.

    Key: Synonymous word   **Thespian** means _____.

17. "This is a *travesty* of justice!" my dad exclaimed over the paper this morning. "Sentencing a criminal to jail and releasing him only months later is a mockery of the entire penal system."

    Key: Synonym   **Travesty** means _____.

WORD STUDY

Literary, dramatic, and architectural terms number in the thousands, and many of the words you already know, such as *prose* and *poetry*. You've probably studied the Greek word *onomatopoeia*, for words that sound like what they mean: *meow, dingdong,* and Poe's famous "bells, bells, bells." You remember that a *tragedy* is a work in which the main character's downfall results from a fatal character flaw. The soap opera features characters who are either mainly good or really rotten—and usually get what they deserve—in this *melodramatic* form.

These terms are easy because they are clear-cut and known to us all. Other general terms, more difficult to grasp, form this lesson.

1. **allegory** ('al-ə-ˌgōr-ē) n.   A story that uses figurative characters and language to make an idea more interesting or persuasive; from Gr. *allegoria,* to speak figuratively

    Bunyan's *Pilgrim's Progress* is an early religious *allegory* relating the wearisome progress of the hero, Christian, from the City of Destruction to the Celestial City.

    Relatives: *allegorical, allegorist, allegorization, allegorize*

2. **baroque** (bə-'rōk) adj.   Referring to the elaborate artistic style of expression most popular in the seventeenth century: in art and architecture, by curved and highly ornamental, extravagant design; in music, by improvisation, the use of contrast, and "powerful tensions" (Webster); in literature, by the use of complex and inventive yet often unclear imagery and form; from Pg. *barocco,* irregularly shaped pearl, through F.

    Visitors to Hampton Court, the "country palace" where King Henry VIII courted Anne Boleyn, are fascinated by the *baroque* gilt and plaster ornamentation embellishing many rooms.

    Relative: *baroquely*

3. **burlesque** ([ˌ]bər-'lesk) n.   A comedic form that makes people, actions, or literary works seem ridiculous through incongruous imitation; mockery through caricature; from Sp. *burla,* joke, through It. and F.

    Carol Burnett's exaggerated portrayal of Scarlett O'Hara in a *burlesque* of *Gone with the Wind* is memorable for anyone who loves comedy.

    Relatives: *burlesque* (adj.), *burlesquely*
    Synonym: *caricature* (not exact)

4. **classical** ('klas-i-kəl) adj.   Referring to ancient Greek and Roman cultures, especially their art, music, literature, and architecture; from L. *classicus,* highest class of Roman citizen

    Colleges are naturally interested in what *classical* works of literature incoming freshmen have studied.

    Relatives: *classic* (n. and adj.), *classicist, classicism, classically*
    Synonyms: *Attic* (referring to Athens and the Greek civilization)
    Antonyms: *modern, up-to-date, contemporary*

5. **comedy** ('kȯm-əd-ē) n.   A literary work/production designed to amuse and to end well for the main characters; from Gr. *komos,* revel, + *aeidein,* to sing

    Situation *comedies* like *Frasier* and *Friends* are especially beloved by viewers like me, who think that laughter is necessary for relaxation and health.

    > Relatives: *comedian* (male), *comedienne* (female), *comedic*
    > Synonym: *humor*
    > Antonym: *tragedy*

6. **denouement** (ˌdā-ˌnü-'mäⁿ) n.   The "unknotting" or unraveling of the plot of a literary or dramatic work; the outcome or result of a chain of events; from L. *nodus,* knot, through F. *desnouer,* to untie

    A reader would feel cheated of both answers and literary satisfaction without a *denouement* to resolve any questions raised by the narrative.

7. **farce** ('färs) n.   Comedy featuring rowdy, sometimes violent, action, with audience laughter as the main goal; slapstick comedy, often not logical or realistic; from L. *farsus,* savory stuffing, forcemeat

    Following in the footsteps of *farcical* comedians Charlie Chaplin, Jerry Lewis, and Fanny Brice, Billy Crystal portrayed a typical modern businessman in *City Slickers.*

    > Relatives: *farcical, farceur* (a writer or actor of farce)
    > Synonym: *mockery* (close but not exact)

8. **free verse** ('frē 'vərs) n.   Verse more rhythmic than prose yet written without a regular metric pattern, usually lacking rhyme; from L. *versus,* turn, line, line of writing, verse

    The poems of Walt Whitman, Carl Sandburg, and E. E. Cummings are typical examples of *free verse* that read almost like prose.

9. **genre** ('zhän-rə) n.   Kind, sort, or type; a category in art, music, or literature recognizable by its particular form, content, or style (e.g., science fiction is one literary *genre*); from F. *genre,* kind, gender

    Favorite authors in the satiric *genre* include Mark Twain, Sinclair Lewis, Dorothy Parker, James Thurber, and the more contemporary Nora Ephron and Peter deVries.

10. **Gothic** ('gäth-ik) adj.   A medieval architectural style popular in western Europe till the late 1500s, characterized by slim, upright supports (plus extra buttresses) to bear carefully calculated weight and stress; pointed arches, rather narrow windows; and vaulted ceilings. In literature, Gothic style features desolate, typically romantic settings (castles, dungeons) and macabre or sensational plots with ghosts or seemingly supernatural occurrences.

    Familiar classic *Gothic* tales include Mary Shelley's *Frankenstein,* Poe's short stories, and Emily Brontë's *Wuthering Heights,* all models for today's authors creating material in this genre.

11. **lampoon** (lam-'pün) n.   A (usually lengthy) verbal picture thoroughly ridiculing an individual; may be lighter, mocking satire; from F. *lampons,* let us drink

   Lampoons vary from the rather fond, teasing appraisal of family members by Gerald Durrell in *My Family and Other Animals* to the biting approach of less-restrained authors.

   > Relative: *lampoon* (v.)
   > Synonym: *ridicule*

12. **parody** ('par-əd-ē) n.   A form of high burlesque that ridicules a particular literary work or style by copying its major features and applying them to trivial or unrelated matters; from Gr. *para + aeidein,* to sing

   If you were to imitate *Macbeth* and depict the characters as ants instead of people yet maintain a grave seriousness throughout, you would be creating a *parody* of the famous Shakespearean tragedy.

   > Relative: *parody* (v.)
   > Synonym: *caricature* (see *burlesque*)

13. **protagonist** (prō-'tag-ə-nəst) n.   The leading part (in drama) or main character; from Gr. *prot + agonistes,* competitor at games, actor

   The uninhibited audiences in Shakespeare's time cheered for the *protagonist,* who aroused their sympathies, and pelted the antagonist with rotten fruits and vegetables.

14. **rococo** (rə-'kō-[,]kō) adj.   Extremely ornate or fancifully intricate, as more elaborately baroque; referring to an eighteenth-century architectural style featuring fancy carved designs and pierced ornamental work; in music (also eighteenth century), a light, happy ornamentation different from typical baroque music; from F. *rocaille,* rockwork

   The term *rococo* has acquired the connotation of "too elaborate to be tasteful," yet in its day that style was probably a logical development of the preceding baroque period.

   > Relative: *rococo* (n.)
   > Antonyms: *classic, simple, unadorned*

15. **satire** ('sa-tī[ə]r) n.   Comedy using laughter as a weapon to evoke attitudes of contempt and scorn along with amusement; biting humor or sarcasm to expose human failings; from L. *satur,* sated, enough

   Swift's *Gulliver's Travels* derides all mankind, just as Twain's *Huckleberry Finn* exposes the narrow-mindedness of middle America in the late 1800s. Both are famous, frequently studied examples of *satire.*

   > Relatives: *satiric, satirical, satirize, satirically, satirist*

16. **thespian** ('thes-pē-ən) n.   An actress or actor
   Most *thespians* would leap at the chance to perform on the world's major stages, such as those in London or New York.

   > Relative: *thespian* (adj., dramatic)
   > Synonyms: *actor, actress, performer*

   Derivation: Supposedly, the first actor to speak lines separate from the Greek chorus was *Thespis,* who was awarded a prize for tragedy around 534 B.C. Since then, *thespian* has been synonymous with actor or actress.

17. **travesty** ('trav-ə-stē) n.   Humor that mocks its serious or lofty subject by treating it in lowly or grotesque terms; a low, inferior, warped imitation, as *a travesty of justice;* from L. *trans + vestis,* dress or garment

If you were to rewrite *Hamlet,* putting crude or silly expressions in the mouths of those noble characters, your result would be a *travesty* of Shakespeare's original drama.

   Relative: *travesty* (v., often synonymous with the verb *parody*)

ROOT STUDY

You will recognize the first three roots as the bases for words in List 2. The fourth may be an old friend; after all, who does not like a *bonus*?

1. **GEN** means *kind* (or *type*), *birth, race, cause.*

   ingenue—innocent, unsophisticated young woman
   ingenuous—innocent, open, candid, natural
   ingenuity—inventiveness, cleverness, or skill
   genesis—birth, origin; coming into being
   engender—to cause or produce; to beget; to cause to develop

2. **AGON** means *struggle.*

   agony—anguish, torture, intense pain or distress
   antagonist—adversary, opponent (of the *protagonist* perhaps)

3. **VERS** and **VERT** mean *turn, line, line of writing,* or *verse.*

   verse—one line of metrical writing; language having meter, poetry
   divert—to deflect or turn from one course to another; also, to amuse or distract from something
       unpleasant
   versatile—turning easily from one thing to another; all-around
   reverse—v., to change in a contrary manner, literally, *to turn back;* adj., the opposite of normal,
       as *reverse order*
   diverse—unlike or different; also, possessed of various shapes or characteristics; v., *diversify*

4. **BON** and **BENE** mean *good* or *well.*

   bonus—an extra payment or reward (above what was promised or expected)
   bonny—appealingly attractive; excellent
   bonhomie—comfortable geniality, warmth, friendliness (the hail-fellow-well-met attitude)
   beneficent—producing good, as an act of charity; *beneficial*
   benevolent—kindly, marked by goodwill and high intentions

USING THE WORDS

List 2 Review

allegory	parody	classical	Gothic	burlesque
satire	denouement	protagonist	comedy	travesty
free verse	rococo	farce	baroque	genre
thespian	lampoon			

Exercise I. Fill-Ins.

Select the most appropriate word from List 2, based on clues in context. Word form may need changing.

1. a delightfully scary _____ tale, replete with supernatural events

2. preferring _____, that poetry unfettered by meter

3. admired the _____ lines of Greek and Roman architecture

4. foolish production of *Othello*, a _____ of that impressive tragedy

5. Poe's "The Murders in the Rue Morgue," a first in the detective _____ of mystery fiction

6. expected an interesting _____ that would unravel the plot's complexities

7. the _____, who was actually an antihero for the first half of the book

8. her skills as a _____ desperately needed in a demanding role

9. _____ design even more elaborate than baroque ornamentation

10. a vicious _____ of the mayor that stopped just short of libel

Exercise II. Matching.

Match the List 2 words with their definitions or synonyms. Remember that several study words have multiple meanings.

_____	1. **baroque**	(a) the opposite of tragedy
_____	2. **Gothic**	(b) illogical, often unrealistic slapstick comedy
_____	3. **allegory**	(c) a medieval architectural style
_____	4. **comedy**	(d) wit used as a weapon to evoke scorn or contempt
_____	5. **burlesque**	(e) low or distorted imitation of the real thing
_____	6. **farce**	(f) ridiculing verbal portrait of a person
_____	7. **satire**	(g) high burlesque ridiculing a literary work or well-known literary style

_____ 8. **travesty**   (h) elaborate seventeenth-century artistic style

_____ 9. **lampoon**   (i) mockery through caricature

_____ 10. **parody**   (j) a tale using figurative characters and language

Exercise III. Analogies.

Complete each analogy with the best possible pair.

_____ 1. thespian : comedian ::

    (a) teacher : instructor
    (b) apple : fruit
    (c) doctor : pediatrician
    (d) obstetrician : mortician

_____ 2. Notre Dame Cathedral : Gothic ::

    (a) rococo : Pentagon
    (b) Parthenon : classic
    (c) Paris : capitol
    (d) Smithsonian : museum

_____ 3. classical : Attic ::

    (a) cluttered : basement
    (b) baroque : current
    (c) lampoon : tragedy
    (d) genre : category

_____ 4. prologue : denouement ::

    (a) beginning : culmination
    (b) thespian : tragedian
    (c) free verse : poetry
    (d) comedy : satire

_____ 5. comedy : amusement ::

    (a) tragedy : drama
    (b) satire : contempt
    (c) smile : humor
    (d) farce : frown

Exercise IV. Identification

Match "the famous" with the appropriate vocabulary word from Lesson 2. (Hint: Ask a friend or teacher if you're stumped.)

_____ 1. *Huckleberry Finn*

_____ 2. Dustin Hoffman

_____ 3. *Animal Farm*

_____ 4. Winchester Cathedral

_____ 5. *Revenge of the Pink Panther*

_____ 6. *The Hobbit*

_____ 7. *Watership Down*

_____ 8. Juliet or Romeo

_____ 9. a Greek or Roman temple

_____ 10. *Leaves of Grass,* by Walt Whitman

_____ 11. Beethoven's Fifth Symphony

_____ 12. *The Once and Future King*

_____ 13. "Chicago," by Carl Sandburg

_____ 14. a navy business suit

_____ 15. Kenneth Branagh

_____ 16. *Wuthering Heights*

_____ 17. Hester Prynne (of *The Scarlet Letter*)

_____ 18. "The Nutcracker" ballet

_____ 19. *Candide,* by Voltaire

_____ 20. flying buttresses

Exercise V. Word Analysis.
Remember that this section is meant to stretch your ability to work with words. If at sea, don't hesitate to ask someone else's opinion.

1. One useful synonym for a literary classic is the French term *belles lettres*. Look up the dictionary translation and definition for this term. Can popular, current fiction appropriately be classed as *belles lettres?*

   _____

2. The Latin root **gen**, meaning *kind, race, birth,* or *cause,* has at least fifty derived English words. From the clues below, try to build a few of those words. Each dash indicates a missing letter.

   a. shown to good advantage in a photograph   p __ __ __ __ GEN __ c

   b. a major class or kind   GENu__

   c. a refined, "well-born" man   GEN __ __ __ m __ __

   d. someone born brilliant   GEN __ __ __

   e. birth or beginning   GEN__ __ i __

   f. that which passes on hereditary traits   GEN__

   g. relating to heredity   GEN __ __ __ c

   h. to beget, foster   __ __ GENd __ __

   i. native, not imported   __ __ d __ GEN __ __ __

   j. open, simple, naive girl   i__GEN__ __

3. Antonyms abound in the arts world. See how many sets of opposites you can match.

_____	1. **protagonist**	(a) romanticism
_____	2. **tragedy**	(b) honest representation
_____	3. **assonance**	(c) finale
_____	4. **realism**	(d) antagonist
_____	5. **hyperbole**	(e) dissonance
_____	6. **travesty**	(f) sophisticate
_____	7. **overture**	(g) comedy
_____	8. **ancient**	(h) classical
_____	9. **ingenue**	(i) modern
_____	10. **rococo**	(j) understatement

4. *Divers* and *diverse* are a plagued pair of words that people frequently confuse. With the help of a dictionary, define them and use each in a sentence of your own.

   _____

   _____

   _____

   _____

   _____

   _____

5. Keeping *good* or *well* in mind as the meanings of **bon/bene,** put the following derivatives into their proper phrases.

bona fide	bonhomie	bon voyage	benefactor
beneficiary	bons mots	benediction	benefit

   a. the genuine article, a _____ Ming dynasty vase

   b. my _____, a generous aunt who sends me a regular allowance

   c. hilarious comments, or _____, that keep us chuckling

   d. waving good-bye, hollering _____ in cheerful voices

   e. his kindly blessing, a _____ we all waited to hear

   f. radiating _____ and friendly warmth in an irresistible way

   g. been the _____ of so much kindness from others

   h. a long lecture, supposedly for my _____

6. How does the meaning of "struggle" for **agon** fit in the modern words *protagonist* and *antagonist?*

   _____

   _____

Exercise VI.

Think of some current movies, TV programs, or literary examples of the following terms: *farce, burlesque, parody, satire, travesty,* and *Gothic,* and compare your list with one your parent or teacher can give you.

_____

_____

_____

_____

_____

_____

Four-Letter Words
Short Words Full of Meaning

In Context. Before studying the definitions below, try reasoning out the meaning of each word, using context as your guide.

1. Rory's desk *abuts* mine when we work on our biology lab project, and that way we don't disturb the rest of the class.

   Key: Logic   **Abut** means _____.

2. When asked how she felt about having four children, Mom *averred* sincerely that she wouldn't take a million dollars for any one of us.

   Key: Logic   **Aver** means _____.

3. Listening to the *cant* of some politicians is discouraging. Their mindless repetition of trite phrases is so obviously hypocritical.

   Key: Definition   **Cant** means _____.

4. With a violent or unexpected *coup,* a well-organized army of rebels can overthrow a shaky government.

   Keys: Synonymous idea, logic   **Coup** means _____.

5. "I don't care who the tomcat was," Mom said with exasperation. "The *crux* of the matter is whether or not Marigold is going to have more kittens!"

   Key: Logic   **Crux** means _____.

6. Our family loves the minty chocolate Girl Scout cookies, so we *dole* them out one by one, wishing they'd last longer.

   Keys: Example, logic   **Dole** means _____.

7. It's not so easy to *dupe* Andy now that he's 8, but when he was younger he was such a perfect pigeon that we fooled him constantly.

   Key: Synonymous ideas   **Dupe** means _____.

8. The Lord might have said, *"Fiat lux"* (Let there be light), but today's *fiat* could never be such a sweeping decree.

   Key: Synonym   **Fiat** means _____.

9. One of the more grisly torture methods was *flaying* the victim alive, a process whereby the skin was pulled off in strips.

   Key: Definition   **Flay** means _____.

10. Jan responded to my *gibes* about her inept gear shifting by becoming an expert driver, thus forcing me to praise her after all.

    Keys: Logic, opposing phrase   **Gibe** means _____.

11. "Don't get *mired* down in details on your report," the history teacher warned us. "If you get sucked into that bog, you might fail to present the overall historical significance of your topic."

    Keys: Synonymous idea, logic   **Mire** means _____.

12. Andy's a *rank* beginner at fishing, but he shows real aptitude for the sport.

    Keys: Opposing idea, logic   **Rank** means _____.

13. A basic tenet of the religious *sect* termed Shakers is celibacy. Once that *sect* numbered 16,000 followers; fewer than 10 survive today.

    Key: Logic   **Sect** means _____.

14. Jan's pearl necklace is a *sham,* of course, because a necklace that long composed of genuine pearls would cost lots of money.

    Keys: Antonym, logic   **Sham** means _____.

15. The last chem exam was a killer, so for this one I'm *wary* enough to spend extra time studying.

    Key: Logic   **Wary** means _____.

16. "It doesn't make a *whit* of difference," Jan moaned, "whether you study for the chem test or not. You'll beat me anyway."

    Key: Logic   **Whit** means _____.

17. One celebrated World War I spy, known for her feminine *wiles* and deceptions, was the dancer Mata Hari, who was executed by the French in 1917.

    Key: Synonym   **Wile** means _____.

WORD STUDY

Short words, often Anglo-Saxon in origin, are good words to know. They have a vigor and punch that the longer, Latinate words lack. Writers Ernest Hemingway and E. B. White openly preferred the small word that does a big job.

> *"Do not be tempted by a twenty-dollar word when there is a ten-center handy, ready and able."*
> —Strunk and White, *The Elements of Style*

1. **abut** (ə-'bət) v.   To border or have a common, touching boundary, as *their property abuts on ours;* to end at a contact point; terminate on or against; from L. *ad + bout,* blow, end, and F. *abuter,* to come to an end

   Where the yard next door *abuts* on my folks' vegetable garden, it forms a meeting point for my parents to discuss local news with the neighbors.

   > Relative: *abutter*
   > Synonyms: *touch, border*

2. **aver** (ə-'vər) v.   To state, assert, affirm in a positive way; to declare as true; from L. *ad + versus,* true

   Asked why he had stayed after school, Andy *averred* that he'd been helping his teacher voluntarily, not as punishment for misbehavior.

   > Relative: *averment*
   > Synonyms: *declare, attest, assert, affirm, state, avow*
   > Antonyms: *disavow, disclaim* (neither exact)

3. **cant** ('kant) n.   Hypocritical talk, especially trite religious sayings; dialect of a particular group or jargon; trite talk; from L. *cantare,* to chant or sing

   A lawyer friend, frequently on business in prisons, says that he cannot comprehend the *cant* of prisoners.

   > Relatives: *cant* (v., to lean or slope at an angle or to pitch to one side, as *that table cants off oddly); cant* (n., a slanting surface)
   > Synonyms: *argot* (jargon of the underworld), *dialect, jargon*

4. **coup** ('kü) n.   A successful, sudden act or stroke; an upset or overturning; from F. *couper,* to cut

   Carrie felt that she had scored a *coup* by winning the gymnastics competition when she was a freshman.

   > Synonyms: *upset, overthrow*

5. **crux** ('krəks) n.   The major, vital point, as *the crux of the situation;* an unresolved problem or question; plural: *cruxes, cruces;* from L. *cruc-, crux,* cross, torture

   "I don't mind getting a puppy," Mom said, "but who will care for it? That's the *crux* of the problem."

   (Note: The *crux* family includes *crucifix, crucible, crusade, crucifier,* and *excruciating.*)

6. **dole** ('dōl) n.   A ration or allotment portioned out in regular amounts; a grant of money (or something distributed) to the poor or unemployed;   v.   (with *out*) To apportion or distribute; from OE *dāl*, portion

   We have warned all the family to *dole* out Marigold's food sparingly, as that cat will eat whatever she's allotted.

   Synonyms: *ration* (n., v.), *parcel (out), distribute*

7. **dupe** ('d[y]üp) n.   Someone easily fooled, deceived, cheated;   v.   To fool, deceive, cheat (see "Derivation")

   Every night, without realizing they're being *duped,* Poucette and Figment chase into the garage after Andy, who trails a catnip mouse behind him as the lure.

   Synonyms: *gull* (v., remember *gullible?), trick* (v.), *fool* (v.), *hoax* (v.), *pigeon* (n.)
   Derivation: Of French origin, *dupe* has meant someone easily fooled since the 1300s.

   Although there's doubt, etymologists think that *dupe* comes from the hoopoe bird and his stupid appearance. It is *cant*—a slang form of *hoopoe*.

8. **fiat** ('fē-ət) n.   A decree or similar arbitrary command; an authoritative sanction; from L. *fieri. Fiat* is a complete Latin sentence meaning "Let it be done."

   Americans have never been fond of government by *fiat,* preferring instead that duly elected representatives debate and vote on issues.

   Relative: *fiat money* (paper currency decreed legal by government, not backed by gold or silver)
   Synonyms: *decree, edict*

9. **flay** ('flā) v.   To pull off the skin in strips; to strip of possessions or to fleece; to criticize verbally in a severe, harsh manner; from OE *flā,* to flay

   When Jan and I arrived home late, the folks nearly *flayed* us alive with their blistering lecture.

   Synonyms: *fleece; excoriate* (last meaning)
   Antonyms: *praise, commend, compliment* (all for last meaning)

10. **gibe** ('jīb) n.   taunt or scornful comment;   v.   To taunt, deride, or tease in a scornful manner; from F. *giber,* to shake or handle roughly

    After my team lost the basketball game, Andy *gibed* at me until I locked him out of my room to shut him up.

    Relative: *giber*
    Synonyms: *scoff* (n., v.), *taunt* (n., v.), *sneer* (n., v.)

11. **mire** ('mī[ə]r) n.   Marsh or bog; wet, soggy slush or mud;   v.   To drag down or entangle as in deep mud or marshy terrain; to be bogged down, as if by mire; from OE *mōs,* marsh or moss

    We had to walk home from our last hayride because the wagon became *mired* in the deep mud of the country road.

    Relative: *miry*
    Synonyms: *marsh* (n.), *bog* (n.), *entangle* (v.)

12. **rank** ('raŋk) adj.   (1) Healthy, even excessive, growth, as *the rank outcropping of weeds took over the park;* (2) disgustingly crude, gross, foul; (3) highly noticeable in a negative sense, flagrant, as *rank disobedience;* (4) complete (an intensive), as a *rank amateur;* (5) disgusting in taste or odor, rancid; from OE *ranc,* overbearing, strong

    On our return to the lake this spring, we were appalled at the *rank* growth of lawn threatening to engulf our little cabin.

    Relatives: *rankly, rankness*
    Synonyms: (1) *excessive;* (2) *foul, gross;* (3) *flagrant;* (4) *complete, total;* (5) *rancid, malodorous, putrid*
    Antonyms: (1) *minimal, slight;* (2 and 5) *appealing, luscious, praiseworthy;* (3) *hidden, unnoticeable*

    [Note: Remember the other *ranks,* as *to rank in order of preference,* to rate (v.), and *a member in the ranks of common soldiers* (n.).]

13. **sect** ('sekt) n.   A group unified by beliefs; a religious denomination; from L. *sequi,* to follow

    The religious *sect* called the Puritans settled America; today, a *sectarian* is someone thought to have a narrow viewpoint.

    Relatives: *sectarian, sectarianize, sectary, nonsectarian*
    Synonyms: *party, faction*

14. **sham** ('sham) n.   Fake, imposture; hypocrisy; an imitation or simulation of the real thing;   v. To deliberately mislead, delude, or feign; perhaps from E. *shame*

    Their pretense of being interested was such an obvious *sham* that we weren't surprised when they left the exhibit early.

    Relatives: *sham* (adj.), *shammer*
    Synonyms: (n.) *imposture, hoax, pretense, hypocrisy;* (v.) *feign, assume, pretend*
    Antonyms: *truth, veracity*

15. **wary** ('wa[ə]r-ē) adj.   Characterized by wisdom and awareness of possible danger; prudently keen, alert; from OE *waer,* careful, aware, wary

    Marigold and her kittens are exceedingly *wary* of the big black Newfoundland across the street.

    Relatives: *warily, wariness*
    Synonyms: *cautious, circumspect*
    Antonyms: *foolhardy, rash, bold, brash*

16. **whit** ('hwit) n.   The tiniest particle or bit imaginable; from E. *wiht, wight,* creature, thing, bit

    Jan said she didn't care a *whit* about her former boyfriend; but she is shamming, and we know she still cares.

    Synonyms: *bit, particle*

17. **wile** ('wī[ə]l) n.   Trick or clever stratagem for deceitful purposes, or a charmingly playful trick;   v. To entice or lure; to pass time pleasurably, as *to wile away the hours* (in this sense, *while* is a synonym); from OE *wigle,* divination, witch

    Marigold instinctively uses her feline *wiles* to sneak up on an unwary bird.

    Relative: *wily* (Remember Wile E. Coyote of "The Roadrunner"?)
    Synonyms: (n.) *trick, guile* (v.) *entice, lure*

ROOT STUDY

This group of roots is basic to your understanding of the English language and nearly 100 words, although only *ver* is related to List 3. Four-letter words are often the roots themselves, surviving with minor spelling changes.

1. **ANIMA** means *spirit, soul, mind,* or *nature.*

   animus—disposition, nature; sometimes ill will, malevolence
   animal—living being that is not a human being or plant; mammal
   animated—lively, vivacious; endowed with life, as *animated cartoons*
   equanimity—evenness of disposition; a calm temperament, composure, self-possession

2. **CRED** means *believe* or *trust.*

   credible—believable, trustworthy
   credit—bank balance; time allotted for payment; reliance on the truth of something; esteem
   credential—testimonial, certificate, diploma
   credo—set of beliefs
   credence—acceptance as true or real

3. **SEQU** and **SECUT** mean *follow.*

   sequence—a series, its order in space and time
   consecutive—succeeding in regular order
   persecute—to pursue persistently, often with bad intent
   execute—to carry out (a plan); to inflict capital punishment
   sequel—one development that follows another; an installment

4. **VER** means *truth.*

   verify—to confirm or establish accuracy, truth, or reality
   verdict—judgment after a trial, opinion
   veracity—truthfulness
   veracious—truthful, honest
   verisimilitude—the appearance of truth or genuineness; literally, *similar to the truth*

USING THE WORDS

List 3 Review

abut	dole	gibe	sham
aver	dupe	mire	wary
cant	fiat	rank	whit
coup	flay	sect	wile
crux			

Exercise I. Fill-Ins.

Select the most appropriate word from List 3, based on clues in context. The form of the word may change.

1. When Oliver first joined Fagin's gang of pickpockets, he was the perfect _____, innocent and easily fooled.

2. A _____ calling themselves Scientologists has been the subject of considerable investigation and media probing.

3. "Three at a crack!" Carrie informed us. "A brilliant _____ with my invincible flyswatter."

4. The nearest large dock _____ the shore at Devils Point, right by our lake cabin.

5. We felt stripped and raw, _____ as we were by the coach's stinging halftime rebuke.

6. The hyena circled his newly discovered meal _____, alert for any sound or scent of the predator returning to the kill.

7. The _____ of any murder case is typically motive plus opportunity.

8. We ignored Lee's taunts, figuring that his repeated _____ only revealed how envious he was of our school's success.

9. Convicted of _____ insubordination, the sergeant was reduced to a private.

10. "It matters not a _____ that you mean well," Mom lectured Carrie, "unless you do something to prove it."

Exercise II. Synonyms.

Choose two for each vocabulary word. Write their letters on the lines provided.

_____ 1. **aver**   (a) avoid   (b) attest   (c) avow   (d) deny

_____ 2. **cant**   (a) jargon   (b) contradiction   (c) argot   (d) talk

_____ 3. **dole**   (a) senator   (b) put   (c) distribute   (d) parcel (out)

_____ 4. **mire**   (a) bog   (b) mush   (c) briar   (d) entangle

_____ 5. **rank**   (a) gross   (b) excessive   (c) score   (d) lack

_____ 6. **sham**   (a) feign   (b) spread   (c) mellow   (d) hypocrisy

_____ 7. **wile**   (a) during   (b) guile   (c) entice   (d) guilt

_____ 8. **fiat**   (a) decree   (b) edict   (c) auto   (d) design

_____ 9. **sect**   (a) crowd   (b) belief   (c) faction   (d) party

_____ 10. **rank**   (a) bottom   (b) complete   (c) lever   (d) flagrant

Exercise III. Analogies.

Complete each analogy with the best pair possible, using words from List 3 and Roots.

_____ 1.   truth : sham ::

    (a) abut : border
    (b) honesty : guile
    (c) cant : jargon
    (d) wariness : caution

_____ 2.   gull : dupe ::

    (a) coup : state
    (b) pigeon : robin
    (c) touch : abut
    (d) parcel : gift

_____ 3.   sect : political ::

    (a) execution : end
    (b) averment : declaration
    (c) fiat : command
    (d) verdict : guilty

_____ 4.   coup : downfall ::

    (a) veracity : falsehood
    (b) stillness : animation
    (c) sequel : chapter
    (d) credentials : employment

_____ 5.   noticeable : rank ::

    (a) wily : ingenious
    (b) enticing : appealing
    (c) whit : particle
    (d) bold : wary

Exercise IV. Famous Fill-Ins.

From the choices offered, select the correct word to insert in each of the following quotations.

shamming	wiles	flayed	verisimilitude
gibes	cant	mire	rank
coup			

1. *Oh! Death will find me long before I tire*
   Of watching you; and swing me suddenly
   Into the shade and loneliness and _____
   Of the last land!
       —Rupert Brooke, "Oh! Death will find me" (sonnet)

2. Asking about the fiendishly clever Odysseus (Ulysses):
   "Tell me, Muse, of the man of many _____.
       —Alexander Pope (trans.), Homer's *Odyssey*

3. *"I see it says that Dennis Radclyffe is seriously ill also."*
   "Probably _____, *the dirty blackguard."*
       —Agatha Christie, *Partners in Crime*

4. *"Wife, spouse, my dear, joy, jewel, love, sweet-heart and the rest of that nauseous*
   _____, *in which men and their wives are so fulsomely familiar."*
       —William Congreve, *The Way of the World*

5. *"O! my offence is* _____, *it smells to heaven."*
       —Shakespeare, *Hamlet*

6. *"Though I've belted you an'* _____ *you,*
   By the livin' Gawd that made you,
   You're a better man than I am, Gunga Din!"
       —Rudyard Kipling, "Gunga Din"

7. *"Merely corroborative detail, intended to give artistic* _____ *to an*
   otherwise bald and unconvincing narrative."
       —W. S. Gilbert, *The Mikado*

8. Hamlet, to the skull of Yorick, in Act V:
   "Where be your _____ *now? your gambols? your songs? your flashes*
   of merriment that were wont to set the table on a roar?"
       —Shakespeare, *Hamlet*

9. *"You've got it, sir....we haven't been able to get a clue to it. This is a fine*
   _____ *of yours, sir."*
       —Agatha Christie, *Partners in Crime*

Exercise V. Antonyms.

Find an antonym or opposing phrase for each word on the left.

_____	1. **excoriate**	(a) circumspect
_____	2. **equanimity**	(b) praise
_____	3. **wary**	(c) large amount
_____	4. **aver**	(d) reality
_____	5. **crux**	(e) disclaim
_____	6. **rash**	(f) commend
_____	7. **deride, taunt**	(g) unbelievable
_____	8. **sham**	(h) nervousness
_____	9. **whit**	(i) extraneous detail
_____	10. **credible**	(j) foolhardy

Exercise VI. Word Analysis.

1. What happens to words derived from **cred** (belief, trust) when the prefixes *in-* and *dis-* are attached (e.g., *incredible, discredit)?*

   _____

2. We have several musical terms from the Latin *cantare,* to sing. With a dictionary's help, match the derived words with their meanings.

_____	a. cantata	(1) one segment of a long poem
_____	b. cantabile	(2) a singer or chanter in a synagogue
_____	c. canticle	(3) musical direction: in a singing manner
_____	d. canto	(4) sacred choral music, usually with accompaniment
_____	e. cantor	(5) a religious song from the Bible

3. What link does **crux** have with the meaning of the word *excruciating?* (Hint: Webster knows.)

   _____

   _____

4. The word *crusade,* from **crux,** can be used in different contexts. Write two sentences that illustrate the modern use of *crusade.* What does *Crusade* mean when capitalized?

   _____

   _____

   _____

   _____

   _____

5. The French word *couper* (cut) has given us some of our most colorful and useful modern expressions. How many can you match with their corresponding meanings?

    _____ a. coup d'état   (1) two-door automobile

    _____ b. coup de grace   (2) to deal with successfully

    _____ c. coupe   (3) detachable ticket, certificate

    _____ d. coup de theatre   (4) a fatal blow or finishing event

    _____ e. coupon   (5) sudden, violent overthrow of government

    _____ f. cope   (6) theatrical success

6. What does the word *nonsectarian* mean?

    _____

    _____

LIST 4   O Ye Gods! Part One
Words from Myth and Legend

In Context. Before studying the definitions, try reasoning out the meaning of each word, using context as your guide.

1. Jan and I want to have a graduation party, but our folks are afraid it will be a wild *bacchanal* that will disturb the neighbors.

   Keys: Logic, synonym   **Bacchanal** means _____.

2. Carrie's absorption in her growing bank account has caused Dad to tease her, accusing her of *cupidity*.

   Keys: Partial definition, logic   **Cupidity** means _____.

3. "You'll be the *cynosure* of all eyes in that dress," Dad assured Jan as he admired her modeling of the latest style.

   Key: Logic   **Cynosure** means _____.

4. Our new principal's relaxed style of governing is in marked contrast to the *draconian* methods of our former principal.

   Key: Contrasting phrase   **Draconian** means _____.

5. Mom coached Carrie for her part in the play. "Remember to be delicate, a sort of spiritual and *ethereal* girl—someone just on loan to the earth."

   Key: Synonymous phrases   **Ethereal** means _____.

6. My camp counselor Rob was the best *mentor* I could have had, and I've patterned myself after him in many ways.

   Keys: Synonym, logic   **Mentor** means _____.

7. Changeable Charlie is a private name for my cousin Chuck, whose *mercurial* temperament makes us wonder what he'll do or say next.

   Keys: Synonym, logic   **Mercurial** means _____.

8. The first *mnemonic* device I learned was "*Mary's violet eyes make John sit up nights, period.*" Is that how everyone remembers the names and order of the planets?

   Keys: Logic, example   **Mnemonic** means _____.

9. Our guidance counselor suggested that a "touch of *narcissism*" was probably normal for seniors, who had to focus intensely on themselves and their immediate future throughout the year.

   Key: Partial definition   **Narcissism** means _____.

10. The *nemesis* of our school is East High, as we rarely beat them in athletics and usually tie in scholastic awards.

    Key: Logic   **Nemesis** means _____.

11. Our new basketball coach, unafraid of *Promethean* tasks, devised a brilliant offense that we think will outwit East High.

    Keys: Logic, example   **Promethean** means _____.

12. The *saga* of our first game against East High is a long and complex tale, ending in a narrow defeat for us.

    Key: Definition   **Saga** means _____.

13. After reading the mythology about Saturn, an often gloomy, authoritative figure, I began describing our grumpy neighbor as *saturnine*.

    Key: Synonyms   **Saturnine** means _____.

14. Dad would like to think he's a *solon*, a wise lawgiver, but he admits that guiding four kids is trickier that he had imagined.

    Key: Definition   **Solon** means _____.

15. When our cat Marigold is sleeping and we vacuum nearby, she opens one *somnolent* eye to glare at the noisy, hateful machine.

    Keys: Near synonym, logic   **Somnolent** means _____.

16. Last Halloween was a night of *stygian* darkness, murky and forbidding enough to send the younger trick-or-treaters home earlier than usual.

    Key: Synonyms   **Stygian** means _____.

17. At eight, Andy is small, but he's a *titan* when we go camping. He sets up our camp almost single-handedly.

    Key: Antonym   **Titan** means _____.

WORD STUDY

Greek and Roman mythology seem far away and not very important anymore, until we realize how many of those ancient gods, goddesses—and some real-life figures—have survived and come into our language as everyday words. Most of their names are now common nouns, uncapitalized, and no longer of epic proportions, but once they were important elements of a set of beliefs held by early people with limited scientific knowledge.

1. **bacchanal** ('bak-ən-əl,ˌbak-ə-'nal) n.   A wild party, drunken carousal; a reveler or carouser (person)

    Plato once remarked that he had seen the entire population of Athens drunk at a *bacchanal* in honor of Bacchus.

    Relatives: *bacchant* (n.), *bacchanalia* (wild orgy)
    Synonym: *orgy*
    Derivation: Bacchus (Dionysus to the Greeks) was god of grapes and wine. Worshiping Bacchus involved gallons of wine, grapes on every table—and you can imagine the rest.

2. **cupidity** (kyü-'pid-ət-ē) n.   Excessive greed and desire, often for wealth

    When he refused to donate any of his vast fortune to the library's building fund, the businessman was accused of *cupidity*.

    Synonyms: *avarice, greed, lust*
    Derivation: Eros to the Greeks, the Roman Cupid originally symbolized only physical desire. Gradually he came to embody strong desire of all sorts, especially greed for money. Until his conversion, Scrooge was guilty of *cupidity*.

3. **cynosure** ('sī-nə-ˌshù[ə]r) n.   A center of attention or attraction, as the North Star in the constellation Cynosure. Ursa Minor (Little Bear) is Cynosure's other name.

    Meadows trim, with daisies pied,
    Shallow brooks, and rivers wide,
    Towers and battlements it sees
    Bosomed high in tufted trees,
    Where perhaps some beauty lies,
    The cynosure *of neighboring eyes.*
        —John Milton, "L'Allegro"

    Derivation: Cynosura, a nymph of Mount Ida, was one of the nurses to Zeus, king of the Greek gods. When she died, Zeus transformed her into the constellation Cynosure, "Dogs's Tail" (Gr., *kynos oura*), which we call the Little Dipper.

4. **draconian** (drā-'kō-nē-ən) adj.   Extremely severe or harsh (usually applied to laws, rules, methods)

Most of today's prison administrators realize that the *draconian* regulations of the past did not help to rehabilitate their inmates.

   Relatives: *draconic, Draconism*
   Synonyms: *rigorous, harsh, cruel, severe* (none exact)
   Antonyms: *lax, weak, loose, slack*

Derivation: The Greek statesman who first codified Athenian laws was Draco, a farsighted fellow who nonetheless imposed barbarously harsh laws and punishments. An orator of the time said that "Draco's code was written in human blood."

5. **ethereal** (i-'thir-ē-əl) adj.   Exceedingly delicate and lovely; heavenly, intangible as air itself

And all my days are trances,
      And all my nightly dreams
Are where thy grey eye glances,
      And where thy footstep gleams—
In what ethereal *dances,*
      By what eternal streams.
         —Edgar Allan Poe, "To One in Paradise"

   Relatives: *ether* (the heavens); *ether* ($C_4H_{10}O$), the light flammable liquid *anesthetic/solvent*), *ethereally, etherealize, etherealness*
   Synonyms: *celestial, unworldly, heavenly, spiritual*
   Derivation: Daughter of the Greek Nox (Night) was Ether, who symbolized the soul of the universe.

6. **mentor** ('men-ˌtȯ[ə]r) n.   A respected guide and counselor, more than just a tutor or teacher

Each person struggling to make a career in the arts hopes to find a *mentor* who will be both friend and advice-giver along the way.

   Synonyms: *counselor, coach, tutor* (none exact)
   Derivation: When the Greek Odysseus (Ulysses) left home to fight in the Trojan War, he appointed his most trusted friend, Mentor, as counselor to his son Telemachus.

7. **mercurial** (ˌmər-'kyu̇r-ē-əl) adj.   Greatly variable or changeable, as mercury is in a thermometer (often used to describe personality)

Old belief said that the little finger was the *mercurial* finger; if square, it denoted sound judgment, and if pointed, it indicated eloquence.

   Relatives: *mercurially, mercury* (the element)
   Synonyms: *inconstant, variable*
   Antonyms: *impassive, phlegmatic, saturnine, constant*
   Derivation: Mercury (Hermes to the Greeks) was the original hyperactive kid, zipping blithely through the world. He was god of communication, conductor of souls to Hades, and god of business. His name remains in *commerce, merchant, mercer, merchandise,* and the planet *Mercury.*

8. **mnemonic** (ni-'män-ik) adj.   Assisting memory; **mnenonics** is a technique to improve memory

"I'll never survive this art history class," Jan said, "if I don't create some *mnemonic* aids to remember the major works of art in their proper time periods."

Derivation: Mnemosyne was only one of Zeus's many wives. She was goddess of memory and parent with Zeus of the nine Muses: *Calliope* (eloquence), *Clio* (history), *Erato* (love poetry), *Euterpe* (music), *Melpomene* (tragedy), *Polyhymnia* (sacred lyrics), *Terpsichore* (dance), *Thalia* (comic and pastoral poetry), and *Urania* (astronomy). The noun *muse* can mean *the poet* or *the poet's inspiration*. As a verb, *muse* means *to ponder* or *think over slowly*.

9. **narcissism** ('när-sə-,siz-əm) n.   Extreme fondness of or absorption with oneself; self-centeredness

Sometimes an artist is unfairly accused of *narcissism* because he or she is so totally absorbed and solitary, but usually this absorption is with the work, not the self.

Relatives: *narcissist, narcissistic*
Synonyms: *egoism, egocentrism*
Antonyms: *selflessness, altruism*
Derivation: After the lovely nymph Echo faded into a faint sound because Narcissus failed to return her love, Nemesis punished him by causing him to fall in love with his own reflection in a fountain. Narcissus yearned for himself until he, too, died and was metamorphosed into the trumpet-shaped white and yellow flower we call by his name.

10. **nemesis** ('nem-ə-səs) n.   A relentless pursuer of evildoers; an opponent who usually wins

I did well in math until I reached advanced calculus, which may prove to be my *nemesis* this year.

Synonyms: *bane, jinx, hex* (none exact)
Derivation: Nemesis was the sister of Ether—both daughters of Nox (Night). As the goddess of fate, Nemesis made sure that criminals or those guilty of excess pride were found and punished.

11. **Promethean** (prə-'mē-thē-ən) adj.   Unusually creative and original; life-giving (note that the capital letter remains)

From women's eyes this doctrine I derive;
They are the ground, the books, the academes,
From whence doth spring the true Promethean *fire.*
   —Shakespeare, *Love's Labour's Lost*

Derivation: Prometheus was the Titan who formed man from clay and stole fire from Mount Olympus for humankind's use, giving them the potential to rival the gods. As punishment, Zeus chained Prometheus to a rock and each day sent an eagle to eat his liver, which grew again at night while the eagle slept. (It was not smart to cross Zeus.)

12. **saga** ('säg-ə,'sag-) n.   A lengthy prose story or account including all the details; from OE, *saga*, saw

Jan spent hours preparing an oral book report on *Kristin Lavransdatter,* which is the best *saga* ever written, as far as Jan's concerned.

Derivation: Saga was a Scandinavian goddess who was a friend of Odin, king of the Norse deities. Her name, now in lowercase, refers to any long tale reminiscent of the old Icelandic sagas.

13. **saturnine** ('sat-ər-,nīn) adj.   Gloomy and heavy of temperament; steady in nature, slow to change

Is there in the world a climate more uncertain than our own? And, which is a natural consequence, is there anywhere a people more unsteady, more apt to discontent, more saturnine, *dark, and melancholic than ourselves?*
    —William Congreve, *Amendments of Mr. Collier's False and Imperfect Citations*

Relative: *saturnalia* (orgy, bacchanal, bacchanalia)
Synonyms: *dour, dull, heavy, surly, gloomy*
Derivation: Saturn, Roman god of sowing, was generally regarded as a grim disciplinarian, yet festivals in his honor were wild and unrestrained bacchanals. A *saturnalia* began on December 17, close to the winter solstice on the twenty-second, and lasted for days and days.

14. **solon** ('sō-lən) n.   An extremely intelligent lawgiver; a member of a legislative body

Many have suggested that the *solons* in our Congress would have more time to enact sensible legislation if they weren't always running for reelection.

Derivation: The original poet and statesman Solon lived in Athens in the sixth century B.C. and brought about wise legal reforms that allowed citizens to share in government.

15. **somnolent** ('säm-nə-lənt) adj.   Drowsy, sleepy; apt to bring on sleep, as a *lengthy, somnolent lecture*

When I asked Jan if she would watch a midnight TV movie with me, she gave only a *somnolent* "Mmmhm," and I knew she'd be asleep before the end of the opening credits.

Relative: *somnolence*
Synonyms: *sleepy, drowsily, lethargic*
Antonyms: *alert, wakeful* (and sometimes *wary*)
Derivation: Somnus was the Greek god of sleep, also called **Hypnos**, from which we get *hypnotism* and *hypnosis.* **Morpheus**, son of Somnus, gave his name to the addictive narcotic *morphine.*

16. **stygian** ('stij-[ē-]ən) adj.   Forbiddingly dark and gloomy, as was the river Styx

What *stygian* corners in an author's mind can give rise to tales so ghoulish that we remember them years later?

Derivation: The route to Hades (the Greeks' underworld) was across the daunting river Styx. Charon ferried dead souls across for the price of a coin placed in each corpse's mouth prior to burial.

17. **titan** ('tīt-ən) n.   Anyone huge in size, great in power, or both; an extraordinarily high achiever, as a *titan of industry*

    Joseph Kennedy, a *titan* in the American business world, passed on his ambitious drive to a family of sons and grandchildren.

    Relatives: *titanic* (colossal), *The Titanic* (ship), *titanism* (rebellion against conventions)
    Derivation: Titans were the twelve giants (six male, six female) who ruled when the Earth was new, until the gods of Olympus took over. Famous Titans include Prometheus, Mnemosyne, and Oceanus, who was in charge of the seas. Atlas was the son of the Titan Iapetus.

ROOT STUDY

Roots *arch*, *dei*, *div*, and *the* plus *somn* have an obvious connection to List 4. *Brev* is what these ancients proved not to be in history.

1. **ARCH** means *rule, law, order*, or *ancient*.

   monarch—one who is a sole ruler
   hierarchy—structure of elements ranked in order of importance
   anarchy—lack of law and order
   matriarch—female ruler; *patriarch*—male ruler
   archaeology—study of artifacts of ancient civilizations
   (Note: Remember that the prefix *arch-* means first, main, or chief.)

2. **BREV** means *short* or *brief*.

   brevity—briefness, shortness of duration or extent
   abbreviate—to make shorter or to curtail
   breviary—a small book of hymns, prayers, songs

3. **DEI, DIV,** and **THE** mean *god*.

   deity—a god or godlike figure
   deism—a religion based on reason, emphasizing morality
   divine—supremely good, perfect; of God or a god
   theology—a distinct system of religious beliefs
   pantheon—temple for all gods; the gods of a people; any group of illustrious persons
   atheist—one who denies the existence of God

4. **SOMN** means *sleep*.

   somnambulist—a sleepwalker
   somnambulism—sleepwalking
   insomnia—the inability to sleep

USING THE WORDS

List 4 Review

bacchanal	mentor	nemesis	solon	cupidity
mercurial	Promethean	somnolent	cynosure	mnemonic
saga	stygian	draconian	narcissism	saturine
titan	ethereal			

Exercise I. Fill-Ins.

Select the most appropriate word from List 4 and Roots, based on clues in context. The word form may change.

1. Dad said, "If I were a _____ of industry such as Mr. Iacocca, when would I ever have time to play golf?"

2. Marigold's lazy, _____ movements as she stretches after a nap mirror the motions of African lions, her far-off cousins.

3. "Has Rembrandt run to Venice?" was Jan's _____ device for remembering the seventeenth-century Dutch painters.

4. When I began running track, the fourth mile was my _____. I could never get past it without a short walking spell.

5. Mom says that E.B. White has been her literary _____, even though she's only studied his work and was never able to meet the author in person.

6. "Imagine," Mom says, "the humorous yet _____ beauty of Charlotte's web glistening with dew in the sunlight and containing the words 'SOME PIG' above Wilbur's pen."

7. In the _____ of angels, Satan was once the archangel until he fell from grace. (Hint: Check out those roots.)

8. "Bob's _____ absorption with himself makes me burn," Jan fumed. "He never thinks of anybody else!"

9. Our neighbors had a party last weekend that was a real _____, and the whole street is still talking about it.

10. Almost any movie star appearing at her premiere hopes to be the _____ of the evening.

11. Marigold and her kittens, Poucette and Figment, dance about on their hind paws and swat delicately at the fireflies winking above the grass. "A feline _____ performance," Dad says laughingly. (Hint: Turn a Muse's name into an adjective.)

12. When our guide turned off the lights down in Kentucky's Mammoth Cave, Jan grabbed my arm and complained of the _____ darkness.

13. James Bond, the legendary 007, has need of _____ skills and a constantly ingenious mind to match as he reels from one adventure to the next.

14. Someone with a _____ temperament might find a desk job too confining and routine to suit his quicksilver nature.

15. Many stimulating late-night discussions in a college dorm revolve around _____, especially when classmates of several different religions expound their views. (Hint: Search among the roots.)

16. After he realized that he'd been guilty of _____, Scrooge's stingy and _____ personality altered radically, so that he became both generous and lighthearted.

17. One of the most beloved _____ of all time was the lawyer Abraham Lincoln, who became our sixteenth president.

18. China's desperate attempt to control population by limiting each couple to one child seemed _____ on first hearing, yet most Chinese understood the reasoning behind this severe policy.

Exercise II. Analogies.

Complete each analogy with the best pair possible, using words from List 4 and Roots. Now that analogies are more familiar to you, they will be offered with five answer choices, as on many standarized tests.

_____ 1. titan : weakling ::

    (a) infant : fledgling
    (b) mother : father
    (c) giant : midget
    (d) gnome : troll
    (e) dancer : artist

_____ 2. saturnine : dour ::

    (a) nightly : daily
    (b) harsh : strong
    (c) atheistic : devout
    (d) mercurial : inconstant
    (e) matriarchal : feminine

_____ 3. deity : Zeus ::

    (a) leader : assistant
    (b) dancer : Winston Churchill
    (c) nymph : Echo
    (d) goddess : Somnus
    (e) artist : Mother Teresa

_____ 4. miser : cupidity ::

    (a) mentor : leadership
    (b) enemy : fear
    (c) judge : bias
    (d) postman : letters
    (e) grocer : philanthropy

_____ 5. alert : somnolent ::

    (a) groggy : exhausted
    (b) stygian : dead
    (c) Promethean : inventive
    (d) divine : exalted
    (e) selfless : narcissistic

_____ 6. Cynosure : sky ::

    (a) pine : forest
    (b) house : property
    (c) Mount Olympus : myth
    (d) Styx : underworld
    (e) Oceanus : heaven

_____ 7. physician : medicine ::

    (a) waitress : tips
    (b) landlord : welfare
    (c) solon : law
    (d) patriarch : philosophy
    (e) archaeologist : construction

_____ 8. religion : Deism ::

    (a) college : university
    (b) Muse : Terpsichore
    (c) titan : giant
    (d) god : pantheon
    (e) science : Einstein

_____ 9. daringly inventive : Promethean ::

    (a) amazingly strong : saturnine
    (b) extremely cute : mercurial
    (c) unfailingly generous : ethereal
    (d) unusually complex : mnemonic
    (e) brutally harsh : draconian

_____ 10. *The Mikado* : opera ::

    (a) "The Three Little Pigs" : saga
    (b) cartoon : "Peanuts"
    (c) *Gone with the Wind* : short story
    (d) "The Raven" : poem
    (e) *Julius Caesar* : lampoon

Exercise III. Antonyms.

Find an antonym (or opposing phrase) for each word on the left. One lettered choice is used twice.

_____ 1. **draconian**

_____ 2. **mercurial**

_____ 3. **anarchy**

_____ 4. **abbreviate**

_____ 5. **saturnalia**

_____ 6. **stygian**

_____ 7. **Promethean**

_____ 8. **saturnine**

_____ 9. **divine**

_____ 10. **cupidity**

(a) funeral

(b) cheerful, pleasant, bright

(c) soft, lax, weak

(d) deadening

(e) hellish

(f) responsible government

(g) generosity

(h) steady, constant

(i) extend, lengthen

Exercise IV. Word Analysis.

1. *Somnambulist* literally means sleepwalker because *ambul,* or *amb* means *walk* in Latin. With this knowledge, match the English derivatives with their meanings.

_____ a. ambulatory

_____ b. amble

_____ c. ambulance

_____ d. perambulate

_____ e. preamble

_____ f. perambulator, a "pram"

(1) vehicle for moving those who cannot walk

(2) baby carriage

(3) introductory remarks

(4) stroll idly, in a relaxed manner

(5) capable of walking, not bedridden

(6) walk on an inspection

2. Knowing just one fact about a mythological being can enable you to create the modern-day word in our dictionary. Have a go at the following:

   a. The old sea god Proteus could change form at will.
      Adjective meaning *imaginatively adaptable, diverse* = __ __ __ __ ean.

   b. Juno, queen of the gods, was a handsome, statuesque woman.
      Adjective referring to a *tall, attractive, impressive female* = __ __ __ __ esque.

   c. Urania, daughter of Mnemosyne, was the Muse of astronomy.
      Noun that is the *name of a planet* = __ __ __ __ us.

   d. Aeolus was god of the winds.
      Adjective *referring to the winds* = __ __ __ __ ian.

   e. Eros (Cupid) was god of passionate love.
      Adjective referring to *passionate or sexual love* = __ __ __ tic.

   f. Mars was god of war.
      Adjective meaning *warlike*; *suited for army or military life* = __ __ __ tial.

   g. Mount Olympus was the home of Zeus and his royal court.
      Adjective meaning *majestic, regal, or commanding* = __ __ __ __ __ ian.

3. The prefix **pan-** used with *pantheon* and *pandemic* means all or entire. The following words, also prefixed by *pan-*, are useful to know. Can you make the intelligent guess at their meanings?

WORD	**OPPOSING IDEA**
a. panorama	_____
b. Pan-American	_____
c. pandemonium (literally, *all demons*)	_____
d. Panhellenic	_____
e. panhuman	_____
f. pantomine	_____
g. panacea	_____

   (Hint: Panacea was daughter of the god of healing.)

4. From memory, jot down an *antonym* or *opposing phrase* for the following words from List 4 and Roots:

   WORD   **OPPOSING IDEA**

   a. saga   _____

   b. somnolent   _____

   c. saturnine   _____

   d. narcissism   _____

   e. mercurial   _____

   f. draconian   _____

   g. cupidity   _____

5. The names of planets and the heavenly constellations derive mainly from classical mythology. With the exception of Earth, which is the oddball (forgive the pun), list the other classically named planets. How about the constellations? The signs of the zodiac?

   _____

   _____

   _____

   _____

   _____

This lesson reviews the words and roots in Lists 1–4, giving you opportunities to use these words ONE MORE TIME. You should say each word aloud as you read through the following lists. You may be one of those people who learn best by *hearing*, not seeing.

LIST 1	LIST 2	LIST 3	LIST 4
atone	allegory	abut	bacchanal
burgeon	baroque	aver	cupidity
coerce	burlesque	cant	cynosure
defile	classical	coup	draconian
disparage	comedy	crux	ethereal
entice	denouement	dole	mentor
evince	farce	dupe	mercurial
exhort	free verse	fiat	mnemonic
feign	genre	flay	narcissism
intimate	Gothic	gibe	nemesis
nurture	lampoon	mire	Promethean
perpetrate	parody	rank	saga
redress	protagonist	sect	saturnine
relinquish	rococo	sham	solon
stigmatize	satire	wary	somnolent
truckle	thespian	whit	stygian
	travesty	wile	titan

ROOTS

AGON	BON/BENE	EV/AEV	SOMN
ANIMA	BREV	GEN	VER (truth)
ANTHROP	CRED	PHIL	VERS and VERT
ARCH	DEI, DIV, and THE	SEQU/SECUT	VINC and VICT

USING THE WORDS

Exercise I. Fill-Ins.
Select the most appropriate word from the choices offered, based on clues in context.

atoned	defile	relinquished	titan
classic	dole	satire	whit
coup	feign	sect	wiles
cynosure	mnemonic	thespian	

1. a masterful _____ that seized control of the region

2. remembering long lists through use of _____ aids

3. _____ his claim to the property with regret

4. once a tiny _____, now a religion numbering millions

5. only necessary to _____ eagerness and we'll fool them

6. not even a _____ of interest in the subject

7. a veritable _____ where work is concerned

8. amused by the _____ of Thurber's perceptive story

9. having _____ for his error with repeated signs of goodwill

10. the simple, _____ lines of the fashion collection

11. awesome creation, the _____ of all eyes at its unveiling

12. the practiced _____ of the detective as he elicits information

13. no longer on the _____ and proudly independent

14. a dramatic role that calls for an experienced _____

15. impossible to _____ so fine a reputation overnight

Exercise II. Analogies.

Complete each analogy with the best pair possible. Remember to clarify the given relationship first, *before* you begin hunting the answer.

_____ 1. genre : Gothic ::

    (a) bacchanal : saturnalia

    (b) theosophy : religion

    (c) disposition : mercurial

    (d) somnolence : drowsiness

    (e) sequence : order

_____ 2. nemesis : jinx ::

    (a) bane : travesty

    (b) animation : quiet

    (c) coercion : force

    (d) verity : falsehood

    (e) solon : ruler

_____ 3. dim : stygian ::

    (a) smelly : rank

    (b) rococo : elaborate

    (c) wary : cautious

    (d) primeval : primitive

    (e) weak : invincible

_____ 4. books : bibliophile ::

    (a) stamps : stampophile

    (b) Germany : Anglophile

    (c) cuisine : musician

    (d) philanthropist : business

    (e) French : Francophile

_____ 5. classic : rococo ::

    (a) comedic : farcical

    (b) complimentary : disparaging

    (c) divine : nice

    (d) nervous : tense

    (e) saturnine : dour

_____ 6. dupe : credulous ::

    (a) satirist : tragic

    (b) Prometheus : inventive

    (c) anthropologist : dull

    (d) Zeus : truckling

    (e) protagonist : pitiful

_____ 7. episode : saga ::

    (a) comedy : lampoon

    (b) cathedral : St. Patrick's

    (c) Gothic : novel

    (d) Norman Conquest : Dark Ages

    (e) World War I : Boer War

_____ 8. somnolence : yawn ::

    (a) burlesque : laughter

    (b) archetype : prototype

    (c) deception : wile

    (d) stigma : brand

    (e) exhortation : misery

_____ 9. satirist : words ::

    (a) leadership : mentor

    (b) diplomat : coercion

    (c) victor : credibility

    (d) professor : position

    (e) philosopher : wisdom

_____ 10. mire : entanglement ::

    (a) sham : verity

    (b) animus : motion

    (c) allegory : animal

    (d) lampoon : ridicule

    (e) redress : refinement

Exercise III. Find the Oddball.

Select the one word in each group that does not fit with the others in meaning. (Note: Words in a group may not be synonyms but members of a larger category, e.g., architectural terms.)

_____	1.	(a) dour	(b) gloomy	(c) omnipresent	(d) saturnine	(e) heavy
_____	2.	(a) archenemy	(b) archrival	(c) archetype	(d) duplicity	(e) archangel
_____	3.	(a) deity	(b) divine	(c) theology	(d) pantheon	(e) heavenly
_____	4.	(a) dishonor	(b) laud	(c) brand	(d) stigmatize	(e) mark
_____	5.	(a) disclaim	(b) intimate	(c) hint	(d) suggest	(e) imply
_____	6.	(a) allegory	(b) parody	(c) travesty	(d) lampoon	(e) farce
_____	7.	(a) comedy	(b) protagonist	(c) tragedy	(d) baroque	(e) antagonist
_____	8.	(a) engender	(b) ingenuous	(c) genius	(d) gene	(e) germane
_____	9.	(a) flourish	(b) burgeon	(c) nursery	(d) sprout	(e) grow
_____	10.	(a) bacchanal	(b) solon	(c) mercurial	(d) cupidity	(e) Junoesque
_____	11.	(a) nemesis	(b) pretense	(c) sham	(d) deception	(e) feigning
_____	12.	(a) bonus	(b) beneficial	(c) benevolent	(d) bond	(e) bonhomie
_____	13.	(a) entice	(b) lure	(c) whim	(d) beguile	(e) tempt
_____	14.	(a) assert	(b) affirm	(c) assist	(d) declare	(e) aver
_____	15.	(a) verse	(b) vestments	(c) divert	(d) versatile	(e) diversify

Exercise IV. Antonyms.

From the choices offered, select an antonym for each word or phrase.

coerce	denouement	wary	abutted
evince	verify	nurture	free verse
invincible	animated	narcissism	somnolence
gibe	brevity	cupidity	

_____ 1. to discourage or inhibit growth or progress

_____ 2. to hide or disguise

_____ 3. separated

_____ 4. compliment, praise

_____ 5. foolhardy, rash

_____ 6. generosity

_____ 7. to deny or refute

_____ 8. sluggish, dull

_____ 9. prologue

_____ 10. easily conquered

_____ 11. length

_____ 12. to encourage or request politely

_____ 13. insomnia

_____ 14. concern for others

_____ 15. metered rhyme

Exercise V. Fill-Ins.
Select the most appropriate word from the choices offered, based on clues in context. The word form may need changing.

exhort	redress	truckle	crux
perpetrate	baroque	cant	flay
fiat	ethereal	mentor	anthropomorphic

1. Some rooms are interestingly furnished with a few _____ pieces among furniture of simpler, plainer design.

2. Refusing to comply with an authoritarian decree, the rebellious mob ignored their dictator's _____.

3. The Siamese cat from across the street _____ to Marigold in the most subservient way, meowing pathetically as he approaches.

4. Hidden in the dark hold of the steamship, the stowaway listened to the _____ of the sailors but learned little from their jargon.

5. _____ by her harsh criticism, I went to the woods to think over her words.

6. When we counted the fish in our aquarium, we found that Marigold had most likely _____ another wily theft.

7. Some readers prefer that books be faithful records of real life, but Jan and I enjoy _____ characters like Hazel, Fiver, and Kehaar in *Watership Down*.

8. A respected _____ as well as a friend, my uncle Alan is a frequent, welcome visitor in our house.

9. Where I work this summer is not as important as my boss and my fellow employees are. They are the _____ of the situation for me.

10. A magnetic and dynamic speaker, Abraham Lincoln _____ his country-

    men to _____ the wrongs of slavery, with abolition as the first step.

11. Jan tried to capture the _____ beauty of sunrise over the lake but said

    that her skill with paint on canvas was inadequate.

LIST 5 The Incredible Hunk
Prefixes that Give Meaning

This is the second time around for a few of these prefixes. Remember Unit I? We repeat, because the brief group of letters called a prefix really is an incredible hunk. A prefix may give positive or negative meaning to a word. It can indicate size, place in time or space, number—even specific information such as *orth-*, meaning *right* or *straight*. Knowledge of prefixes plus intelligent use of context often give you the meaning of a word you've never seen before.

POSITIVE PREFIXES

1. **Bene- and bon-**   **good, well**

   A *benediction* is a blessing, literally meaning *good speech.*
   A *bonbon* is a delicious chocolate- or fondant-coated candy.
   (Refer to Roots, List 2.)

2. **Eu-**   **good, well**

   The *euphony* (sweet, pleasing sound) of her voice appeals to every listener.
   His eloquent funeral *eulogy* profoundly affected the audience.

3. **Pro-**   **for, in favor of, forward**

   His work with the *pro-liberal* cause gained wide recognition.
   Mike's *proclivity* for sweets led to cavities in his teeth.
   The modern world believes in *progress.*

NEGATIVE PREFIXES

1. **A-**   **no, not**

   Twain's "mysterious stranger" was an *amoral* youth without a sense of right or wrong.
   An *atypical* high jump differs from the normal, expected jump.
   His *apathy* toward schoolwork is probably a form of "senioritis."

2. **Anti-, ant-**   **against, opposite**

   Her idea is the *antithesis* (direct opposite) of mine.
   You'll need an immediate *antidote* (remedy to counteract bad effects) for that poison.
   Helen's *antipathy* (hatred, strong dislike) toward snakes is obvious.
   Antarctic (region of the South Pole, opposite of the arctic, North Pole) wildlife is a fascinating study.

3. **Counter-, contra-**   **against, opposing**

   A successful *counterattack* wiped out the enemy.
   Those statistics *contradict* commonly held beliefs.
   His *contrary* nature leads him into frequent arguments.

4. **Dif-, dis-** negative, not

Although twins, Jan and I *differ* with each other often.
Jan was *distraught* when she thought she'd lost the car keys.
Her *dismay* changed to joy when she found the keys.

5. **For-** against, away

Andy will *forgo* (renounce, give up) the egg hunt in favor of an Easter party.
She *forbade* her son to swim alone.
Naturally, athletes agree to *forsake* smoking in order to remain healthy.

6. **Il-, im-, in-, ir** not

The *infidel* (unbeliever) knew better than to attack the shrine.
An *illiterate* person cannot read or write.
His *impassive* expression revealed nothing.
Whistling during a sermon would be *irreligious* behavior.

7. **Non-, un-** not

Gandhi exhibited *nonviolent* resistance.
A *nonentity* is a nobody—someone seeming to lack personality.
Her *unfeigned* (genuine, not pretended) approval was shown by the magnificant prize she awarded to the winner.

8. **Ob-, oc-, of-, op-** against, opposing

Sally announced her *objections* loudly.
The *offensive* (or *opposing*) team has impressive tackling skills.

9. **Mal-, mis-** bad, wrong

A *malcontent* is always stirring up trouble.
Misbehavior comes naturally to Andy when he's tired.
Someone who dislikes mankind is a *misanthrope*.

PREFIXES OF SIZE OR AMOUNT

1. **Macro-** big, large

Macroeconomics concerns economic systems, not one sector of the economy.
Universe is a synonym for *macrocosm*.

2. **Micro-, min-** small

A *microcosm* is a tiny segment of the world representative of the larger whole.
Antique dollhouse *miniatures* appeal to modern collectors.

3. **Pan-, panto-, omni-** all, entire

A *panacea* is a universal cure-all.
The Greek *pantheon* included dozens of different gods and goddesses.
The old Roman *pantomine* featured one dancer with a narrative chorus. (Now means *all mime*.)
Unlike most carnivorous cats, Marigold is *omnivorous;* she especially likes the blend of meat and vegetables in Mexican tacos.

PREFIXES OF NUMBER

Number prefixes were covered in Unit I, "What You Already Know." They are briefly listed here as memory joggers.

half	hemi-, demi-, semi-, med-	**ten**	dec-, deca-
one	uni-, mono-, sol-	**twelve**	duodec-, dodeca-
one and a half	sesqui-	**hundred**	cent-, hect-, hecato-
two	di-, bi-, du-, duo-, diplo-	**thousand**	milli-, kilo-
three	tri-, ter-	**ten thousand**	myria-
four	quadr-, tetr-	**million**	meg-, mega-
five	quinque-, quint-, penta-	**first**	arch-, prim-, prin-, proto-
six	sex-, hexa-	**both**	ambi-, amphi-
seven	sept-, hepta-	**equal**	equi-, iso-, par-
eight	oct-, octa-, octo-	**few**	oligo-, pauci-
nine	nona-, novem-, ennea-	**many**	multi-, poly-, myria-

Remember also the number *suffixes,* **-teen** (and ten) and **-ty** (times ten).

PREFIXES INDICATING TIME (SOMETIMES PLACE)

1. **Ante-, anti-** **before**

   Those Roman artifacts *antedate* (go before in time) Julius Caesar.
   Anticipation is half the joy of birthdays or holidays.
   The intimate *anteroom* (small room leading to, or coming just before, a larger main room) was ornately decorated.

2. **Ex-** **former**

   Often it is difficult for *ex-convicts* to find jobs.
   My aunt's *ex-husband* continues to visit us frequently.

3. **Fore-** **before**

   The old proverb says, *"Forewarned is forearmed."*
   Can you *foresee* any difficulty?

4. **Pre-** **before**

   We should *predetermine* the desired color before mixing our paint.
   Mozart was *predestined* by his genius for musical fame.
   The PSAT, or *preliminary* SAT exam, is composed of ex-SAT questions.

5. **Post-** **after**

   Twain's novelette, "The Mysterious Stranger," was published *posthumously* (after his death).
   When I *postpone* homework, I begin to worry about it.
   Postpartum care refers to the care of a mother after child delivery.

Using the Prefixes (Part 1)

Review Words Using Prefixes (Part 1)

benediction	antipathy	illiterate	macroeconomics
bonbon	antarctic	impassive	macrocosm
euphony	counterattack	irreligious	microcosm
eulogy	contradict	nonviolent	miniatures
pro-liberal	contrary	nonentity	panacea
proclivity	differ	unfeigned	pantheon
progress	distraught	objection	pantomime
amoral	dismay	offensive	omnivorous
atypical	forgo	opposing	antedate
apathy	forbade	malcontent	anticipation
antithesis	forsake	misbehavior	anteroom
antidote	infidel	misanthropist	
	ex-convicts	predestined	
	ex-husband	predetermine	
	forewarned	preliminary	
	forearmed	posthumously	
	foresee	postpone	
		postpartum	

Exercise I. Antonyms.

Clues on the left will point to the desired antonym on the right. Each dash indicates a missing letter. The first one is shown as an example.

	CLUE	ANTONYM
1.	do on time or ahead of time	post *p o n e*
2.	following, coming after	pre __ __ m __ __ __ __ __
3.	prenatal	post __ __ __ __ __ __
4.	postdate	pre __ __ __ __ or
		ante __ __ __ __
5.	dread	anti __ __ p __ __ __
6.	universe	micro __ __ __ __
7.	many, a great number	pauci __ __
8.	huge, extremely large	minia __ __ __ __
9.	literate	il __ __ __ __ r __ __ __
10.	defense	of __ __ __ __ __

Exercise II. Chart Fill-Ins.
Add the missing items in the chart.

PREFIX	WORD	DEFINITION
1. mis-	_____	someone who dislikes or hates people
2. _____	object (v.)	_____
3. un-	_____	genuine, not pretended
4. _____	impassive	_____
5. fore-	_____	to look into the future, expect
6. _____	pantheon	_____
7. _____	_____	equally skilled with both hands
8. _____	forsake	_____
9. non-	_____	someone without significance, a nobody
10. _____	omniscient	_____

Exercise III. Definitions.
Use your knowledge of roots and prefixes to define the words.

1. bonny (adj.) _____.

2. discredit (v.) _____.

3. invalidate (v.) _____.

4. irrational (adj.) _____.

5. atheism (n.) _____.

6. eurythmic (adj.) _____.

7. proclivity (n.) _____.

8. antithesis (n.) _____.

9. apolitical (adj.) _____.

10. counteract (v.) _____.

Exercise IV. Find the Oddball.

In each word group, one word is *pretending* to have a number prefix, but it is an impostor. Select the oddball by writing its letter in the blank beside each number.

_____ 1.	(a) pentagon	(b) pentathlon	(c) quinquereme	(d) quinine	(e) quintet
_____ 2.	(a) semantic	(b) demitasse	(c) hemisphere	(d) semifinal	(e) demigod
_____ 3.	(a) decalogue	(b) decant	(c) decathlon	(d) December	(e) decennial
_____ 4.	(a) monotone	(b) unit	(c) monetary	(d) solitary	(e) unilateral
_____ 5.	(a) octopus	(b) October	(c) octogenarian	(d) octave	(e) oculist
_____ 6.	(a) triad	(b) trip	(c) equitable	(d) ambivalent	(e) primitive
_____ 7.	(a) principal	(b) primitive	(c) protozoa	(d) prim	(e) archetype
_____ 8.	(a) centennial	(b) hecatomb	(c) hector	(d) hectometer	(e) century
_____ 9.	(a) November	(b) novena	(c) ennead	(d) nonagon	(e) novel
_____ 10.	(a) multitude	(b) polymath	(c) multiply	(d) myriad	(e) mulct
_____ 11.	(a) septet	(b) heptavalent	(c) hepatoma	(d) September	(e) heptagon
_____ 12.	(a) quadruped	(b) squadron	(c) quadrangle	(d) tetralogy	(e) tetrarchy
_____ 13.	(a) sexton	(b) sextuplets	(c) hexagon	(d) hexameter	(e) sextet
_____ 14.	(a) omnipresent	(b) pandemic	(c) pantomime	(d) ominous	(e) panacea

Exercise V. Missing Prefixes.

English would be hilarious—but not very clear—without prefixes. In the following story, underline the thirty-two words that are missing their prefixes. Then write the correct words on the lines at the end of the tale.

1 "Oh, I am so cited!" Jan said, with a cipatory smile on her face. "I've been looking

2 ward to this party for ages."

3   Sently, Dad strode to the room, a frown wrinkling his head. "Well, Jan, you have

4 ritated me gain," he toned solemnly. "You knew I was posed to your driving downtown

5 less you had a(n) perienced driver side you. There'll be no party for you tonight."

6   Comprehending, Jan blinked in fusion. "But I didn't" she torted quickly, may written

7 all over her features. "And I ject to being cused!"

8   "Then who stroyed the front fender?" Dad plied.

9   Traught, Jan shook her head and turned to look out the window at their mobile.

10 Standing, plus a grin, placed the fusion as she cognized the car. "Dad," she said slowly,

11 poning the moment of truth in her joyment, "that's not our car. It's actly like ours, but it

12 longs to Aunt Dolly. You made a teensy take."

_____

_____

_____

_____

PREFIXES DETERMINING PLACE/RELATIONSHIP

1. **Com-, co-, col-, con-, cor-** and
   syn-, syl-, sym-, sys-, sy-   **with, together**

   A *complex* process *compresses* many layers into a wafer-thin chip.
   Let's *coordinate* our jobs, *collaborating* on the work whenever possible.
   Our leaving on time is *contingent* upon your prompt arrival.
   His expert *synthesis* (*combination* into a *coherent* whole) combined the various parts of a
       complex speech into a set of simpler ideas we could understand.
   The *symmetrical* design of Greek temples appeals to those who like regularity and order.

2. **Amphi-, circum-, peri-**   **around**

   They enjoyed the perfect acoustics in the ancient Greek *amphitheater* at Epidaurus.
       (Note: *Amphi-* also means *both,* as in *amphibian.*)
   Circumnavigating the globe in a small yacht sounds exciting, but risky, too.
   Up went the submarine's *periscope* to inspect the neighboring seascape.

3. **Epi-, ecto-**   **on, outer, outside**

   The *epidermis* (outer skin layer) of an elephant looks like heavy gray leather.
   In the *epilogue,* the author explained the main events in her character's lives for the five-year
       period following the story.
   Unlike the round endormorph, the slender *ectomorph* is a lightweight.

4. **Ab-, abs-** and **apo-, ap-**   **from, away, out, down**

   A cat with many *aberrations* (actions straying from right or normal) in behavior, Marigold
       gobbles all her food quickly like a dog.
   Absconding with (taking away illegally) company funds proved to be the accountant's downfall.
   Although attributed to Charlemagne, many of "his" famous sayings may be *apocryphal* (of
       doubtful authorship).
   Future historians will judge at which point twentieth-century life reached its *apogee* (highest
       point, culmination).

5. **E-, ex-, ec-, ef-**   **out, away**

   The old steam engine *emitted* clouds of steam.
   To *exhale* is the opposite of to inhale.
   His *eccentric* (away from normal) behavior attracts much attention.
   The new prison governor *effected* (brought about) many reforms.
   Old designs in the stone had been *effaced* (worn away, erased) by weather and time.

6. **De-** and **cata-**   **away, down, negative**

   Anne Boleyn, second wife of Henry VIII, was *decapitated* at age twenty-nine. (Maybe it's
       apocryphal, but she is supposed to have said, "My neck is very slender," as she placed her
       head upon the block.)
   Deciduous trees shed their leaves each autumn.
   Oscar Wilde's sensational London trial *defamed* him for the rest of his short life.
   Catacombs, with their natural recesses for tombs, form many underground cemeteries.

7. **Se-** away, apart

I always hunt a *secluded* place to study for exams.
At our vet's office, well animals are *segregated* from sick ones.

8. **A-, ad-, af-, ag-, al-, an-, ap-, as-, at- and ob-, oc-, of-, op-** to, toward, against

Please *adhere* (stick) to school rules during all trips.
He was *alleged* (avowed to be) guilty even before the trial.
Annealed (toughened, strengthened) in the fire of war, the character of many Indian chiefs
    seemed hard as steel.
I was breathless after running the new *obstacle* course.
Offensive weapons such as claws, talons, and quills are part of nature's armor for certain animals.
Andy is *opposed* to the idea of homework.

9. **In-, il-, im-, ir- and endo-, en-, em-** in, into, within

A tiny *incision* was made to remove the mole on her arm.
Twain's writings *illuminate* mid-American life in the nineteenth century.
The tumor was *irradiated* after its partial removal by surgery.
The thyroid and pituitary are two *endocrine* glands of the body.
Carrie can *empathize* with anyone who's lost something special, as she remembers how she felt
    when she lost her watch.

10. **Intro-, intra-** in, among, within

Introductory is often a synonym for preliminary.
After her operation, Millie was put on an *intravenous* (entering the body by way of a vein)
    feeding system.
Intramural (within the system, e.g., between class groups) games are normally scheduled after
    classes.

11. **Ana-, re-, retro-** back, over, again

Anastrophe is the inverted order of words in a phrase or sentence to achieve a special effect; e.g.,
    Going to the store for the first time he was—and excited about it, too.
A *reversal* of word order is another way to explain anastrophe.
Hal's behavior *retrogressed* (or *regressed*) after he was released from the asylum.

12. **Inter-** between

"*Interrupt* me during my speech," Jan warned the cast, "and I'll forget my lines!"
She *interjected* her opinion before I had finished speaking.

13. **Tele-** far, distant

Telepathy (communication of thoughts without speech) between sympathetic individuals remains a
    mystery to science.
Telecourse is the modern word for a study course taught by *television*.

14. **Sub-, suc-, suf-, sug-, sum-, sup-, sus-** and **hyp-, hypo-**   **beneath, under**

Dolphins and whales *submerge* below water for long periods.
A blush *suffused* her face with color as Jan stood up to speak.
Witnesses are formally *summoned* to appear in court.
A *hypodermic* needle is inserted under the skin.
A victim of *hypochondria* focuses on ailments real and imagined.

15. **Over-, super-, ultra-, hyper-**   **over, beyond** (sometimes **excessive, exceeding**)

Send any *overabundance* of chocolate chip cookies to my house.
For a few years, my studying will have to *supersede* other things.
Ultraconservative measures are needed to preserve endangered wildlife.
A *hyperactive* student often has difficulty in school.

16. **Exter-, extra-, extro-**   **outside, beyond**

External forces sometimes control our lives.
Extramundane means outside the normal, material world.
The shy introvert often longs to be the outgoing *extrovert*.

17. **Trans-, tra-**   **across**

Modern, exciting fabrics are often created by *transferring* ancient designs to new materials.
Astronomers understand the *trajectory* of Halley's comet well enough to predict its return.
    (Roughly every seventy-five years. It apeared in 1835 when Mark Twain was born, again in
    1910 when he died, and most recently in 1985–86.)

18. **Dia-, di-** and **per-**   **through, between**

Dialogue, diameter, and *diagonal* are just a few words sharing the same prefix.
A *diaphanous* gown is ethereal in effect, floating delicately around the form of its wearer. (Note:
    Often, you can see through something diaphanous.)
As Mom fixed spaghetti, the smell of garlic *permeated* the house.

MORE SPECIFIC PREFIXES

1. **Alter-** and **hetero-**   **different, other**

Plan B is our *alternative* strategy.
A *heterodox* opinion differs from an orthodox, accepted opinion.

2. **Homo-**   **same**

Homogeneous grouping puts like individuals together.
Homonyms sound alike and are spelled alike but have different meanings, e.g., *quail* (v.), to
    shrink in terror, and *quail* (n.), a species of bird.

3. **Meta-**   **change, beyond**

Andy's *metamorphosis* from grubby kid to scrubbed student amazed us all.
One stage of meiosis and mitosis is *metaphase,* when the chromosomes change their arrangement.
(Remember *prophase* [early stage] and *anaphase* [later]?)

4. **Para-, par-**   **beside, variation**

Any exceptionally clear pattern or archetype that may stand as a model for others is a *paradigm*.
A *paradise* is any heavenly, perfect place.
Paralegal and *paramedical* assistants aid the professionals.

5. **Orth-**   **right, straight**

The *orthodontist's* goal is to straighten teeth and align them correctly in the mouth.
The correction or prevention of skeletal deformities is called *orthopedics*.

6. **Wri-, wro-**   **make, work, twist, wring**

An OE and Ger. prefix, **wri-, wro-** begins many words basic to our language: *wring, wrench, wrist, wrinkle, writhe, wrong, wreath, wrath, wrought,* and *wry*. It is the root in *playwright, cartwright,* and *wheelwright,* which refer to people who make plays, carts, and wheels, respectively.
Mom's *wrath* (extreme anger) was something to behold when she realized that Andy had lost her car keys.
Carrie's *wry* (twisted out of shape) expression made us wonder if she liked the tart apple.
The critic's *wry* (ironic, grimly humorous) remarks made the audience laugh.

USING THE PREFIXES (PART 2)

Review Words Using Prefixes (Part 2)

complex	exhale	empathize	hyperactive
compress	eccentric	introductory	external
coordinate	effect (v.)	intravenous	extramundane
collaborate	efface	intramural	extrovert
contingent	decapitate	anastrophe	transfer
synthesis	deciduous	reversal	trajectory
symmetrical	defame	retrogress	dialogue
combine	catacombs	regress (v.)	diameter
coherent	seclude	interrupt	diagonal
amphitheater	segregate	interject	diaphanous
circumnavigate	adhere	telepathy	permeate
periscope	allege	telecourse	alternative (adj.)
epidermis	anneal	submerge	heterodox
epilogue	obstacle	suffuse	homogeneous
ectomorph	offensive	summon	homonym
aberration	oppose	hypodermic	metamorphosis
abscond	incision	hypochondria	metaphase
apocryphal	illuminate	overabundance	paradigm
apogee	irradiate	supersede	paradise
emit	endocrine	ultraconservative	paralegal
paramedical	wrist	playwright	wrinkle
orthodontist	writhe	cartwright	wrong
orthopedics	wrath	wheelwright	wreath
wring	wry	wrench	wrought

Yes, a *big* list. You probably know over half of these words already, but don't stew over the strangers. Hitch each prefix to a word that you *do* know as a memory device. The "must" words are taught again in later lessons.

Exercise I. Chart Fill-Ins.
Add the missing items to the following chart.

	PREFIX	ROOT	WORD	DEFINITION
1.	_____	fame	_____	to destroy someone's reputation
2.	_____	greg	_____	to set one group apart from another
3.	_____	_____	empathy	_____
4.	_____	mit	_____	to give out, give off
5.	homo	_____	_____	similar in type or kind
6.	_____	ge	_____	highest point, culmination
7.	_____	_____	adhere	_____
8.	trans	_____	_____	to move from one place to another
9.	_____	digm	_____	model, archetype
10.	_____	_____	anachronism	_____

Exercise II. Antonyms.
Change the prefix, and voilà! an opposite word. Match these absurdly easy antonyms.

_____ 1. **heterodox**   (a) extramundane

_____ 2. **ectoderm**   (b) asymmetry

_____ 3. **submerge**   (c) reject

_____ 4. **prologue**   (d) emerge

_____ 5. **exclude**   (e) extramural

_____ 6. **irrefutable**   (f) orthodox

_____ 7. **mundane**   (g) include

_____ 8. **inject**   (h) epilogue

_____ 9. **intramural**   (i) synthesis

_____ 10. **symmetry**   (j) endoderm

_____ 11. **thesis**   (k) refutable

_____ 12. **analysis**   (l) antithesis

Exercise III. Analogies.

Complete each analogy with the best pair possible.

_____ 1. disaster : catastrophe ::

    (a) malformation : limb
    (b) prophase : anaphase
    (c) permeation : seepage
    (d) heterodoxy : religion
    (e) introversion : reversion

_____ 2. submarine : periscope ::

    (a) car : sedan
    (b) turtle : amphibian
    (c) slide : microscope
    (d) tank : turret
    (e) ship : deck

_____ 3. apocryphal : doubtful ::

    (a) eccentric : odd
    (b) wry : straight
    (c) orthodox : religious
    (d) interdependent : aware
    (e) maladroit : artful

_____ 4. orthopedist : skeleton ::

    (a) pharmacist : people
    (b) astronomer : moon
    (c) accountant : papers
    (d) orthodontist : teeth
    (e) internist : physician

Exercise IV. Add-a-Prefix.

To the Latin root *jac, jact, ject* (meaning to throw, cast, or hurl), add the necessary prefix to create the word defined on each numbered line. (Some of these are tough. Don't hesitate to ask for help.)

	PREFIX	+ ROOT	= WORD	DEFINITION
1.	_____	+ ject	= _____	to oppose firmly, disapprove
2.	_____	+ ject(ory)	= _____	the path of an object
3.	_____	+ ject	= _____	to refuse to accept
4.	_____	+ ject	= _____	to throw or toss out, usually with some force
5.	_____	+ ject(ure)	= _____	a guess or surmise
6.	_____	+ jac(ulation)	= _____	an impromptu, heartfelt remark
7.	_____	+ ject	= _____	to cast into the future, make a prediction
8.	_____	+ ject(ive)	= _____	a describing or modifying word
9.	_____	+ ject(ed)	= _____	depressed in spirit, downcast
10.	_____	+ ject	= _____	downcast, sad, woeful

Exercise V. Fill-Ins.

Select the most appropriate word from the choices offered, based on clues in context. (This is a hard exercise again—but you can get help from a friend, parent, or teacher.)

contingent	effected	writhed	diaphanous
correlation	effaced	wrought	metamorphosis
aberration	alleged	suffused	annealing

1. The outcome of our game against East High is _____ upon our players' performance more than anything else.

2. The _____ perpetrator of the crime said that he was innocent.

3. Her normally pale complexion _____ with color, Shelley

   _____ on the floor as laughter overcame her.

4. The (n.) _____ (v.) _____ upon the nymph

   Daphne as she fled from Apollo's embrace caused her to change into a laurel tree.

5. After Mom locked him in his room, Andy _____ a rapid escape through his open window onto the porch roof.

6. Time has _____ many handsome murals on interior as well as exterior walls, leaving us to guess at their former beauty.

7. As a freshman, I discovered a direct _____ between the quality of my class notes and my score on quizzes.

8. The heating and cooling process called _____ serves to soften glass or steel, making it tougher as it cools and less brittle.

9. "A bit of a(n) _____ for me," Mom confessed as she stroked her new gown, a filmy, _____ creation resembling gossamer.

Note: Congratulate yourself if you survived this lesson. It is long—and difficult in spots—but you need this knowledge *early* in your vocabulary study. You will use it over and over in the subsequent lessons. Now, how about treating yourself to some time out with friends as a reward??

LIST 6 An Eldritch Cry
Adjectives, The Describing Words

In Context. Before studying the definitions, try reasoning out the meaning of each word, using context as your guide.

1. Jan says that her *astringent* lotion tightens facial skin and dries excess oil.

    Key: Synonyms   **Astringent** means _____.

2. Andy's new friend came into our kitchen, "*brazen* as you please," said Mom, "and announced that it was his birthday so I should bake him a cake."

    Key: Logic   **Brazen** means _____.

3. Mom usually explains things slowly and carefully, as she deplores a *brusque* approach.

    Key: Opposite phrase   **Brusque** means _____.

4. A woman of *catholic* tastes, Aunt Dolly rummages happily in hardware stores, spends hours in art museums, and enjoys hiking on weekends.

    Key: Logic   **Catholic** means _____.

5. "We haven't a *diffident* person in this family," Dad remarked. "No one lacks confidence around here, even when he's wrong!"

    Key: Definition   **Diffident** means _____.

6. "That's really creepy," Andy said, shivering as he listened to the *eldritch* moan of Gollum in the TV version of *The Hobbit*.

    Key: Synonym   **Eldritch** means _____.

7. Dad and I did errands in an *expedient* manner, as he wanted, but that allowed me no time to window-shop.

    Key: Logic   **Expedient** means _____.

8. In spite of repeated scolding and punishment, Marigold has proved *incorrigible*. She insists on fishing in our aquarium.

    Key: Logic   **Incorrigible** means _____.

9. As we divided chores for opening the lake cabin, Dad said that it was *incumbent* on Jan and me to clean windows and floors.

    Key: Logic   **Incumbent** means _____.

10. "Not exactly a *lithe*, quick devil, is he?" Jan said, grinning at the somnolent hippo in his pool at the zoo.

    Key: Opposing idea   **Lithe** means _____.

11. I've formed only one definite plan for college—to major in science. Which particular science is still *nebulous*.

    Keys: Antonym, logic   **Nebulous** means _____.

12. Our parents like the *pastoral*, slow-paced life of summer at the lake, but Jan and I get restless after a month away from the city.

    Keys: Contrast, logic   **Pastoral** means _____.

13. "That's a *plausible* theory," the chem teacher agreed when I explained my experiment, "but we'll need scientific proof of your beliefs."

    Key: Logic   **Plausible** means _____.

14. Mom barred the door to the cabin. "Now that it's spotless, I hate to let anyone ruin the *pristine* appearance with actual living!"

    Keys: Synonym, logic   **Pristine** means _____.

15. "Big guys are fine," the coach told our football team, "but the *requisite* skills for my teams happen to be determination and cooperation."

    Key: Logic   **Requisite** means _____.

16. The most difficult part for my spitfire sister Carrie was playing the role of a *stolid* servant who spoke little and moved woodenly.

    Keys: Contrasting idea, example   **Stolid** means _____.

WORD STUDY

Adjectives make sentences both specific and colorful. An *ancient car*, for instance, gives a more definite picture than just a *car*. A *dilapidated pea green car* is even more specific, giving the reader or listener further information. Specific sentences are usually quite interesting, whereas general statements are almost always dull and lifeless. When you write, try to be precise. Rather than flooding your material with descriptive words, select carefully and let a *few* well-chosen adjectives carry the paragraph.

1. **astringent** (ə-'strin-jənt) adj.   Severe, drily austere, as *an astringent remark*; drawing together soft tissues, as a styptic pencil dries facial cuts; puckery, like a sour lemon; from L. *ad* + *stringere*, to bind fast (tightly)

   The critic's *astringent* comments on the play were humorous but extremely negative.

     Relatives: *astringent* (n), *astringently*
   Synonyms: *dry, tonic; puckery*

2. **brazen** ('brāz-ᵊn) adj.   Unduly bold, forward, or "pushy"; having the color of sound of brass; from OE *brass*, brass

   Newscaster of the Trojan War, Stentor was described by the blind poet Homer in *The Iliad*: "Great-hearted Stentor with *brazen* voice, who could shout as loud as fifty other men."

     Relatives: *brazen*(v.), *as to brazen it out* (be boldly defiant); *brazenly, brazenness*
   Synonyms: *impudent, insolent*
   Antonyms: *timid, timorous, diffident, shy*

3. **brusque** ('brəsk) adj.   Abruptly short and blunt of speech or manner (even rude); from L. *bruscus*, butcher's broom

   We were put off at first by the manager's *brusque* manner, but we learned later that he was merely a man in a hurry.

   Relatives: *brusquely, brusqueness*
   Synonyms: *curt, bluff, terse*
   Antonyms: *unctuous, bland, voluble*

4. **catholic** ('kath-[ə-]lik) adj.   All-encompassing, comprehensive (in interest or tastes), universal; referring to the old, undivided Christian church; when capitalized, means Roman Catholic; from Gr. *katholikos*, universal, general

   Ben Franklin, a man of *catholic* interests, bent his mind to writing and printing, town and federal government, optometry, the nature of electricity, and international diplomacy.

   Relatives: *catholically, catholicize, catholicity*
   Synonyms: *comprehensive, broad, wide-ranging*
   Antonyms: *narrow, limited, parochial, provincial*

5. **diffident** ('dif-ə-dent) adj.   Shy, withdrawn, and lacking confidence, hesitant; from L. *dis + fidere*, to trust

   Determined to get the job, Bob masked his normal *diffident* personality with a firm handshake and an outwardly confident manner.

   Relatives: *diffidence* (n.), *diffidently*
   Synonyms: *shy, reserved, unassertive*
   Antonyms: *confident, bold, brazen*

6. **eldritch** ('el-drich) adj.   Weird, unnatural, and eerie; possibly from OE *elfrice*, fairy realm

   As one of the witches in *Macbeth*, Carrie mastered an *eldritch* cackle that made our hair stand on end.

   Synonyms: *weird, eerie, unearthly*

7. **expedient** (ik-'spēd-ē-ənt) adj.   Suitable, practical; opportunistic or advisable (but not necessarily admirable); from L. *ex + ped, pes*, foot

   We hurled our luggage from the burning hotel, which was *expedient* under the circumstances but hard on the luggage.

   Relatives: *expediency* (n.), *expediential, expediently*
   Synonyms: *advisable, politic*
   Antonym: *inexpedient*

8. **incorrigible** (['ˌ]in-'kȯr-ə-jə-bəl) adj.   Uncontrollable or uncorrectable, not manageable; determined; depraved or not reformable; from L. *in + corrigere*, to correct

   The *incorrigible* behavior of many criminals ensures their return to prison.

   Relatives: *incorrigibility, incorrigible* (n. person), *incorrigibly*
   Synonyms: *uncontrollable, depraved, delinquent* (none exact)
   Antonyms: *docile, amenable, complaisant, compliant, submissive*

9. **incumbent** (in-'kəm-bənt) adj.   Referring to a duty or obligation, used with *on*; from L. *in* + *cumbere,* to lie down

   When I have house guests, it is *incumbent* on me to see that they have clean bedding and towels, plus a place to hang their clothes.

   Relatives: *incumbent* (n., holder of an office); *incumbency*
   Synonym: *obligatory*

10. **lithe** ('līth) adj.   Gracefully and easily flexible; easily bent; from L. *lentus,* slow, through OE *lithe,* gentle

    Jan works to achieve the *lithe,* supple movements necessary for any serious ballet student.

    Relatives: *lithely, litheness, lithesome (lissom)*
    Antonyms: *rigid, inflexible*

11. **nebulous** ('neb-yə-ləs) adj.   Vague, unclear, indistinct; from L. *nebulosus,* misty

    Andy wanted to take the bus home, but his *nebulous* ideas of bus stop locations led him down several wrong streets.

    Relatives: *nebulously, nebulousness, nebula* (galaxy)
    Synonyms: *indistinct, cloudy, vague*
    Antonyms: *distinct, clear*

12. **pastoral** ('pas-t[ə-]rəl) adj.   Referring to the countryside or rural areas; peaceful, with a suggestion of innocence and simplicity; of a minister's (pastor's) job or duties; from L. *pastor,* herdsman

    Turner is noted for painting idyllic *pastoral* scenes of the English countryside.

    Relatives: *pastor* (a clergy person), *pastorally*
    Synonyms: *rural, bucolic, idyllic*
    Antonyms: *urban, metropolitan*

13. **plausible** ('plȯ-zə-bəl) adj.   Believable; from L. *plausibilis,* worthy of applause

    Dad said, "I'm afraid that your reasons for coming home late are neither *plausible* nor acceptable."

    Relatives: *plausibility, plausibly*
    Synonyms: *credible, believable*
    Antonyms: *implausible, incredible, unbelievable*

14. **pristine** ('pris-ˌtēn) adj.   Fresh and clean, pure and uncorrupted; from L. *pristinus,* early, an early riser

    Dad appreciates the *pristine* glories of dawn.

    Relative: *pristinely*
    Antonyms: *impure* or *imperfect, tainted* (none exact)

15. **requisite** ('rek-wə-zət) adj.   Necessary or essential; from L. *requirere,* to seek or ask

Carrie will take any part in any play in order to learn the *requisite* acting skills for her future.

    Relatives: *requisite (n.), prerequisite, requisition (v.)*
Synonyms: *essential, necessary, vital*
Antonyms: *nonessential, unnecessary*

16. **stolid** ('stäl-əd) adj.   Revealing little (or no) emotion; from L. *stolidus,* dull, stupid

The typically *stolid* facial expression of the old cigar store Indian statue probably helped to create a stereotype.

    Relatives: *stolidly, stolidity*
Synonyms: *impassive, phlegmatic, unemotional*
Antonym: *sensitive*

ROOT STUDY

Two of these roots are found in List 6 adjectives (**fid** and **string, strict**). The other two have contributed many vital words to English—words that you depend upon.

1. **AGOG** means *lead* or *leader.*

demagogue—a leader who says what people want to hear, who identifies with popular causes and prejudices
synagogue—a Jewish house of worship
pedagogue—instructor, teacher; originally, a Greek slave who led children to school

2. **FID** means *faith* or *trust.*

fidelity—faithfulness
infidel—one who does not share a set of particular beliefs, especially religious beliefs
confidential—shared between friends or associates as a secret is shared; referring to any information given on trust

3. **GREG** means *flock* or *herd.*

gregarious—enjoying the company of others; sociable, convivial, friendly
congregate—to gather together or crowd together
egregious—highly noticeable in a negative way, as *an egregious error;* outstandingly bad

4. **STRING** and **STRICT** mean to *tie* or *bind fast.*

constrict—to draw together closely, even uncomfortably, as *throat muscles constrict with nervousness;* to contract or squeeze; to inhibit
stringent—strict, rigorous, or rigid, as *stringent rules at the academy;* also referring to credit strictness when money is scarce, as a *stringent budget*
strictures—restrictions, limitations

USING THE WORDS

List 6 Review

astringent	diffident	incumbent	plausible
brazen	eldritch	lithe	pristine
brusque	expedient	nebulous	requisite
catholic	incorrigible	pastoral	stolid

Exercise I. Fill-Ins.
Select the most appropriate word from List 6, based on clues in context.

1. a(n) _____ character, never revealing his emotions

2. careful listing of the _____ items for the lab experiment

3. a strangely _____ figure, hovering vaguely out of reach

4. wanting _____, not ridiculous, reasons for action

5. the graceful, _____ motions of a leaping gazelle

6. realized that it was _____ on me to give clear directions

7. heard in the night the _____ cry of a hoot owl

8. aware that her _____, hesitant manner lacked impact

9. rubbed us the wrong way with his _____ approach

10. a sour apple, nearly as _____ as some lemons

Exercise II. Synonyms.

Each word on the left has *two* synonyms in the right-hand column. Enter both synonyms on the appropriate lines.

Choice of Synonyms

1. **pastoral** _____

   _____

2. **pristine** _____

   _____

3. **expedient** _____

   _____

4. **incorrigible** _____

   _____

5. **catholic** _____

   _____

6. **diffident** _____

   _____

7. **eldritch** _____

   _____

8. **astringent** _____

   _____

9. **brusque** _____

   _____

10. **brazen** _____

    _____

advisable
bucolic
dry
weird
forward
fresh
politic
bluff
puckery
unassertive
uncontrollable
shy
comprehensive
curt
rural
uncorrupted
insolent
delinquent
eerie
wide-ranging

Exercise III. Analogies.

Complete each analogy with the best pair possible.

_____ 1. rabbi : synagogue ::

    (a) minister : pastor
    (b) reverend : board
    (c) instructor : camp
    (d) pedagogue : school
    (e) demagogue : market

_____ 2. dog : fidelity ::

    (a) cat : claws
    (b) cheetah : speed
    (c) puma : diffidence
    (d) giraffe : spots
    (e) mouse : stolidity

_____ 3. diffident : gregarious ::

    (a) requisite : necessary
    (b) nebulous : cloudy
    (c) specious : suspect
    (d) stolid : impervious
    (e) timorous : brazen

_____ 4. catholic : parochial ::

    (a) expedient : suitable
    (b) gregarious : convivial
    (c) incredulous : questioning
    (d) plausible : reasonable
    (e) open : restricted

_____ 5. repeat offender : incorrigible ::

    (a) impassive judge : stolid
    (b) awkward dancer : lithe
    (c) legal incumbent : defensible
    (d) nebulous theory : precise
    (e) astringent remark : weak

Exercise IV. Fill-Ins.

Select the most appropriate word from the choices offered. Hint: Read all sentences quickly first and fill in the most obvious answers. Then work by the process of elimination.

expedient	demagogue	astringent	infidel
pristine	egregious	incorrigible	brazen
incumbent	nebulous		

Deliver me from . . .

—a guide dog for the blind who is _____.
                                                        1

—a family room that must maintain a(n) _____ appearance at all times.
                                                                        2

—_____ criticism when I need encouragement.
                    3

—people who feel it _____ on them to point out my faults.
                                            4

—_____ directions that merely suggest the location of your house.
                    5

—making such a(n) _____ blunder that everyone will think I'm a dodo.
                                        6

—any false leader, the _____ who says only what people want to hear.
                                        7

—the _____ clanging of my alarm before I'm ready to get up.
                        8

—the wild-eyed _____ who kills for the sake of his cause.
                                    9

—people who say, "The end justifies the means," to excuse doing the

_____ thing instead of what is right.
                10

Exercise V. Antonyms.

Write an antonym or opposing phrase for each word.

1. **plausible** _____

2. **incorrigible** _____

3. **catholic** _____

4. **diffident** _____

5. **lithe** _____

6. **pastoral** _____

7. **pristine** _____

8. **requisite** _____

9. **stolid** _____

10. **stringent** _____

Exercise VI. Word Analysis.

1. The word *catholic* (small *c*) is often confused with the word *parochial,* yet they are opposites. Why (or how) could this confusion have arisen?

    _____

    _____

2. Originally, a pastoral poem concerned shepherds (pastors). No wonder *bucolic* is still a synonym; *boukolos* is Greek for cowherd. But now a work dealing with idyllic rural life can be termed *pastoral* or *bucolic.* Shakespeare's *As You Like It* is a pastoral play. What poems, stories, or plays do you know that could be called *pastoral?*

    _____

    _____

3. Latinate (or Greek) words are nearly always longer than Anglo-Saxon words. Try to think of shorter or simpler words for the following:*

LATINATE (OR GREEK)	ANGLO-SAXON/OTHER
astringent	_____
diffident	_____
requisite	_____
stringent	_____
pedagogue	_____
congregate	_____
catholic	_____
confident	_____
synagogue	_____

    * Notice that your answers are rarely perfect synonyms, even though their meanings may be close. *That* is why we have so many words in the English language—each word with its connotations, or shades of meaning.

4. What is the appropriate tone for the following dialogue?

    Editor: You infidel! You dared to split an infinitive!
    Journalist: I can't bear to write "significantly to increase" when I could write "to significantly increase," sir. I just can't bear it!
    Editor: Maybe you're right. Don't let it go to your head.

    _____

    Question: Why is *infidel* a good choice of word in this context?

    _____

In Context. Before studying the definitions, try reasoning out the meaning of each word, using context as your guide.

1. "No more following the crowd," Jan announced firmly as she added the final touches to her outfit. "*Avant-garde* from now on," she added, as we eyed her unusual getup with misgivings.

   Keys: Contrasting phrase, logic   **Avant-garde** means _____.

2. "It's an American hotel," Dad told us, "but they've hired a *concierge*. Wonderful fellow! He helped me to hire a car, got tickets for a play, and made dinner reservations for our group."

   Keys: Logic, partial definition   **Concierge** means _____.

3. Mom staggered in the door. "An utter *debacle*," she said, collapsing into a chair. "Three messy road accidents along the way, and none of us on the road went anywhere for 2 hours."

   Key: Logic   **Debacle** means _____.

4. Apparently tired of fighting one another, Marigold and the neighboring calico cat have reached a temporary *détente*. They merely hiss when they pass in the yard.

   Key: Contrasting phrases   **Détente** means _____.

5. If I think of my cumulative school record as my *dossier*, it sounds more impressive.

   Key: Definition   **Dossier** means _____.

6. Newspapers feature stories about government figures in the top *echelon*, and we rarely learn about the millions of federal workers on lower levels.

   Key: Synonym   **Echelon** means _____.

7. Wearily, Jan tapped one bored heel on the weathered planks of our boat dock. "I'm drowning in *ennui*," she moaned. "Where are all the people in the world?"

   Keys: Synonyms, logic   **Ennui** means _____.

8. "The typical *entrepreneur* is a real go-getter," Mom commented. "Anyone eager to start and maintain a business can't be afraid of work."

   Key: Definition   **Entrepreneur** means _____.

9. Nonchalant, cap tilted at a rakish angle, Dad approached his sailing lessons with an *insouciance* that belied his desire to become a competent sailor.

   Keys: Synonym, logic   **Insouciance** means _____.

10. Every spring, our entire *ménage* shifts to the lake on weekends as everyone in the family prepares the cabin for summer living.

    Keys: Definition, logic   **Ménage** means _____.

11. "Don't you think that's a bit *outré*," Mom said, viewing Jan's latest outfit before school. "Avant-garde I understand, but that costume is bizarre."

    Key: Synonym   **Outré** means _____.

12. *Piqued* by Mom's criticism, Jan tossed her head defiantly and went out the door without a word.

    Key: Logic   **Pique** means _____.

13. Our English teacher explained the *précis* as a concise summary. "I will mark you down for wordiness," she warned, "as well as failure to include all of the vital facts."

    Key: Definition   **Précis** means _____.

14. Jan and I don't agree on everything, but our *rapport* as twins is obvious to all who know us.

    Keys: Logic, near synonym   **Rapport** means _____.

15. With three years of French behind her, Jan likes to toss around phrases. "*Quel sangfroid*," she said admiringly as Indiana Jones coolly survived one life-threatening adventure after another in each of his thrilling movies.

    Keys: Near synonym, logic   **Sangfroid** means _____.

16. "Just a *soupçon* of garlic salt," Jan reminded me as I seasoned the pizzas. "I've got a date, and I don't want to paralyze him when he comes in the door."

    Key: Logic   **Soupçon** means _____.

WORD STUDY

Of course you know *ballet* and *bouquet* and *filet*—the last medium rare and the first performed by someone like Mikhail Baryshnikov. We cannot ignore the enormous influence that French (with its Latin roots) has had on English. For example, the word *boil* that means "an inflamed swelling" is Anglo-Saxon, but *boil* meaning "to bubble up" is French. William the Conqueror and his Norman French made a whopping difference in our language, as many English words were booted out in favor of French words.

> *In Paris they simply stared when I spoke to them in French; I never did succeed in making those idiots understand their own language.*
> —Mark Twain

1. **avant-garde** (ˌäv-ˌän[t]-ˈgärd) n.   Someone in the forefront with new developments, often in the arts. adj.   Referring to anything bold, new, or unusually innovative; from F., *vanguard*

    Once thought strangely *avant-garde*, Pablo Picasso is now acknowledged as a master in the art world.

    Relatives: *avant-gardism, avant-gardist*

2. **concierge** (kōⁿ-ˈsyerzh) n.   A representative of the landlord who acts as building manager (especially in France); a hotel staff member who handles guests' needs (tours, luggage, reservations, etc.); pl. *concierges*; from F. through L. *conservus*, fellow slave

    We arranged for three Paris tours through our *concierge*, a multitalented man who spoke several languages.

3. **debacle** (di-ˈbäk-əl) n.   A rout or huge disaster, tremendous disruption; also, a total failure, fiasco, flop; from F. *débacler*, to unbar

    Unfortunately for us, the second basketball game against East High was a *debacle*, because half our team was sick, the other half demoralized.

    Synonyms: *rout, fiasco* (neither exact)
    Antonyms: *success, victory*

4. **détente** (dā-täⁿ[n]t) n.   The lessening of ill feeling or tension, as between two countries; an easing of strain; from L. *des + tendere*, to stretch

    Until recently, the United States struggled for *détente* with succeeding communist regimes in Russia.

    Opposite idea: escalation or heightening (of tension)
       Derivation: The early *destente* mechanism of a crossbow released the bow's string. This literal slackening of the string's tension corresponds well to today's meaning of lessened strain in relations.

5. **dossier** (ˈdȯs-ˌyā) n.   A file of information or group of papers with detailed reports of information; from F. *dossier*, bundle of documents labeled on the back, from L. *dorsum*, back

    Imagine how interesting it would be to read the *dossier* of James Bond, Ian Fleming's fictional master spy.

6. **echelon** ('esh-ə-ˌlän) n.   One of a series of levels or ranks in an organization, as *top echelon*; a corps of people with a certain rank; from F., literally, *rung of a ladder*

"I'm still in the lower *echelon* of workers," Chet said, grinning. "I'm getting pretty good with a broom, though."

   Relatives: *echelon* (v.t.), to arrange or line up a group in an echelon (v.i.), to take your place in an echelon
   Synonyms: *rank, level*

7. **ennui** ('än-'wē) n.   Boredom plus a feeling of tiredness and dissatisfaction; a ho-hum feeling; from OF *enuier*, to annoy

I think it's the *ennui* of a long summer that makes me ready to return to school, where something is always happening.

   Synonym: *boredom* (not exact)

8. **entrepreneur** (ˌäⁿn-trə-p[r]ə-'nər) n.   One who develops a business (or enterprise) and bears its developmental risks; from OF *entreprendre*, to undertake

Dad said he'd rather be an *entrepreneur*—with all the risks involved—than work for a large company.

   Relatives: *entrepreneurial, entrepreneurship*

9. **insouciance** (in-'sü-sē -ən[t]s) n.   Cheerful lack of concern or care; from F. *in* + *souciant*, care

Andy approached the dentist's chair with amazing *insouciance*, forgetting that he munches candy whenever he can.

   Relatives: *insouciant, insouciantly*
   Synonym: *nonchalance*

10. **ménage** (mā -'näzh) n.   A household, domestic setup; from OF *mesnage*, dwelling

Noël Coward's *Design for Living* concerns a humorous love triangle, a *ménage à trois*, with its modern counterpart in TV's "Three's Company."

   Synonym: *household*

11. **outré** (ü-'trā) adj.   Bizarre, far-out; referring to something outside conventional standards; from F. *outrer*, to carry to excess

Summer boredom at the lake was relieved by our new neighbors, a couple whose *outré* clothing and possessions became the talk of our lake community.

   Synonym: *bizarre* (weak)
   Antonyms: *conventional, traditional, classic*

12. **pique** ('pēk) v.   To irritate, annoy, offend; to rouse curiosity, interest, or pride; to provoke into awareness, as by a challenge or intentional snub.   n.   Resentment or slight feeling of injured pride, as *she stamped off in a fit of pique;* from F. *piquer*, to prick

A brief stay in Vienna *piqued* my curiosity about Empress Elizabeth, the Bavarian princess who led a sad, lonely life.

   Synonyms: (v.) *provoke;* (n.) *resentment* (neither exact)

13. **précis** (prā-'sē) n.   A brief summary of vital facts, points, and ideas; pl., *précis*; from F. *precise*

We concentrated on writing last semester, beginning with paragraphs and working toward mastery of the *précis* before embarking on lengthier essays.

14. **rapport** (ra-'pō[ə]r) n.   A state of agreement, closeness of understanding, and harmony; from L. *ad* + *portare*, to bring, through F. *rapporter*, to bring back

The beloved operas of Gilbert and Sullivan are notable for the *rapport* between Gilbert's words and Sullivan's music.

   Antonym: *discord*

15. **sangfroid** ('sän-'f[r]wä) n.   Coolness, calm, and imperturbability, even under stress; self-possession; from *sang* + *froid*, blood, cold

In a fashion show at school, Jan modeled with a *sangfroid* that Carrie openly envied. "Must be the ballet training," she concluded as she watched Jan's smooth, graceful movements.

Synonyms: *equanimity, composure, coolness*

16. **soupçon** (süp-'sōn, 'süp-ˌsän) n.   A tiny bit, trace, or dash of something; from L. *suspicere*, to suspect, through F. *soupçon*, suspicion

"I wish I weren't so conventional," Ellen complained. "A *soupçon* of daring would be a healthy spice in my personality."

Synonyms: *trace, dash* (neither exact)

ROOT STUDY

You will recognize all of these as being roots of words in List 7.

1. **DORS** means *back* (of the body).

   dorsal—at the back or near the back of a major body part
   endorse—to sign (a document); to approve, as *I endorse his candidacy*

2. **PORT** means *to carry* or *bring*.

   portable—able to be carried, lifted, or moved from place to place
   report—anything carried back, such as information or sound, as *the report of a gun*
   deport—to send legally out of a country
   export—to send out of a country, typically products such as cars, clothing, etc.
   import—to bring into a country, as *we import perfume from Paris*

3. **TEND/TENS/TENT** means *to stretch.*

   tendency—an inclination, leaning toward something
   tensile—usually refers to strength and is the measure of how much lengthwise stress a substance
       will take before tearing apart
   attention—observation or notice; applying the mind to a subject or object; consideration of
       others' needs or wants

USING THE WORDS

List 7 Review

avant-garde	dossier	insouciance	précis
concierge	echelon	ménage	rapport
debacle	ennui	outré	sangfroid
détente	entrepreneur	pique	soupçon

Exercise I. Synonyms.

Write the vocabulary word from List 7 on the line next to its synonym or definition.

1. coolness, composure _____

2. helpful hotel staffer _____

3. nonchalance _____

4. file of information _____

5. harmony, accord _____

6. developer of a business _____

7. concise summary _____

8. disruption, rout _____

9. vanguard _____

10. lessened tension _____

11. rung, rank, level _____

12. household _____

13. bizarre _____

14. a tiny bit _____

15. boredom _____

16. provoke _____

Exercise II. Antonyms.

Select the letter of the best antonym or contrasting phrase for each word and enter it on the line next to its opposite.

_____ 1. **sangfroid**
   (a) musical   (b) exhausted   (c) tiny
   (d) agitation   (e) composure

_____ 2. **soupçon**
   (a) trace   (b) dinner's ready   (c) large amount
   (d) bit   (e) spice

_____ 3. **avant-gard**
   (a) civilian   (b) soldier   (c) leader
   (d) oddball   (e) follower

_____ 4. **debacle**
   (a) bangle   (b) rout   (c) success
   (d) strike   (e) achievement

_____ 5. **détente**
   (a) heightened tension   (b) grave difficulty   (c) increased length
   (d) added awareness   (e) brighter vision

_____ 6. **outré**
   (a) inside   (b) boring   (c) common
   (d) bizarre   (e) within

_____ 7. **rapport**
   (a) silence   (b) unwillingness   (c) clarity
   (d) discord   (e) confusion

Exercise III. Fill-Ins.

Write the appropriate words from List 7 in the blank spaces in this Parisian dream.

You are renting un appartement à Paris. Your sink is stopped up, so you trot downstairs pour visitor with the _____. As the renter of this pleasant flat, you adopt two stray

1

pussycats and a homeless poodle. Your old college roommate moves in tout de suite. No longer alone, you now have a(n) _____. With a plugged sink, a pair of felines jealous of ze

2

poodle, and an amused roommate, you never suffer from _____.

3

But poverty is très nearby. Time to dig out the résumé, the college transcript, and tous les papiers needed for hunting ze job. _____ under your arm, you present yourself with

4

confidence, even _____. It will be only a matter of time until someone snaps

5

you up, oui?

Non!

The Parisian employers' interests are not _____ by your application.

6

They do not care a fig, not a(n) _____. "Votre français est terrible!" they cry.

7

Back in votre appartement, you take stock of yourself, noting your good qualities and knowledge—all the vital information in a brief _____ titled "ME." You realize that
8
you must give birth to une bonne idée. You know that you adore cooking.

Magnifique! Un restaurant américain, run by you! Confidently, you present your bonne idée to the banque, which lends ze money to set up your business. You have just become

a(n)_____.
9

Exercise IV. French in Print.

French phrases constantly pop up in books, newspapers, and magazines. It's frustrating not to know what these phrases mean. Scan the key below; then decode a few of the more common French expressions, matching them with the English. If stumped, ask a friend who's studying French.

coterie = clique, set	*fait* = fact, act	*faire* = to do or make
rigueur = strictness	*savoir* = to know	*faux* = false, bad
vis = beside, next to; derives from face	*vu* = seen	*tête* = head

_____ 1. **coterie**

_____ 2. **déjà vu**

_____ 3. **de rigueur**

_____ 4. **faux pas (or gaffe)**

_____ 5. **fait accompli**

_____ 6. **noblesse oblige**

_____ 7. **pièce de résistance**

_____ 8. **protégé**

_____ 9. **savoir faire**

_____ 10. **tête-à-tête**

_____ 11. **tour de force**

_____ 12. **vis-à-vis**

(a) feat of strength, skill, ingenuity

(b) the responsible obligations of those with rank, nobility, position

(c) savvy, know-how, social competence

(d) select group, set

(e) proper, what is required by society's rules of behavior

(f) related to, compared with

(g) unpleasantly familiar, known or seen before

(h) private conversation between two

(i) an accomplished fact, usually unchangeable

(j) special, favored pupil

(k) a social false step, a boo-boo

(l) outstanding item, the showpiece

Note: All of these phrases, and more, occur in standard, abridged *English* dictionaries. Many were favorites of Hawkeye on "M.A.S.H." and of Mork in "Mork and Mindy," and now are voiced by Frasier and Niles Crane on the TV sitcom "Frasier."

Exercise V. Roots of Derived Words.

Write the correct roots on the lines beside their derived words. Roots: *dors, port, tend, tens, tent*. Also, circle the prefixes in the numbered words.

_____	1. retention
_____	2. support
_____	3. détente
_____	4. dossier
_____	5. rapport
_____	6. tension
_____	7. comportment
_____	8. extended
_____	9. endorse
_____	10. deportation
_____	11. dorsal
_____	12. export
_____	13. attention
_____	14. import
_____	15. dorsispinal

Exercise VI. Word Analysis.

1. In French, *souci* means *worry* or *care*. Why, then, is Sans Souci a good name for a seaside resort?

   _____

   _____

2. The Latin root *sang/sangui*, meaning *blood*, has given us several words. What is the difference between *sanguine* and *sanguinary*? Why do you hope not to *exsanguinate* until you're very old?

   _____

   _____

3. Match these well-known French words with their definitions:

_____ a. bourgeois	(1) meeting, usually secret
_____ b. connoisseur	(2) trite remark
_____ c. rendezvous	(3) young woman formally entering society
_____ d. debutante	(4) middle-class, common
_____ e. cliché	(5) an expert, specialist, or professional

4. How do you regard France and all things French if you are a *Francophile*? a *Francophobe*?

   _____

   _____

5. *Canard* means *duck* in French. One English use of this word might read as follows:

   Judge: You are accused of theft!
   Defendant: That, sir, is a base *canard*. I stole nothing.

   Obviously, *canard* doesn't mean *duck* in English. What does *Webster's New Collegiate Dictionary* say about ye olde French duck and today's usage?

   _____

   _____

   _____

6. Looking back over List 7, note how few of the words have clear-cut synonyms in English. Almost none. Likewise, few have good antonyms. *Why* have these words come into our language?

   _____

   _____

   _____

Mrs. Malaprop Is Alive and Well
Words About Language and Speech

In Context. Before studying the definitions, try reasoning out the meaning of each word, using context as your guide.

1. Mom *alleged* that Andy was the most likely thief of the Oreo cookies, but Andy protested, saying that he'd been at a friend's house all afternoon.

   Key: Logic   **Allege** means _____.

2. Our English teacher is a favorite with students because his amusing *anecdotes* offer personal glimpses into authors' lives.

   Key: Partial definition   **Anecdote** means _____.

3. Being an *articulate* speaker is one of Dad's goals. He prepares his material carefully and practices each speech before making a presentation.

   Key: Logic   **Articulate** means _____.

4. Skill at playful *badinage* in social situations is usually an advantage. Anyone who can entertain others with witty talk or who is known for humorous retorts never seems to lack invitations.

   Key: Definitions   **Badinage** means _____.

5. "I hate to see that pie go to waste," Mom murmured, reaching for the last chocolaty wedge. Dad grinned. "Intentional *double entendre*," he teased, "or just a slip of the tongue?"

   Key: Logic (*Waste* and *waist* are
   homophones.)   **Double entendre** means _____.

6. Mark Twain valued both wit and brevity. Perhaps that is why his *epigrams* are so often quoted today.

   Keys: Partial definition, logic   **Epigram** means _____.

7. The *etymology* of "bonfire" tells us it derived from "bone fire," referring to the open burning of old bones saved for a public celebration or display.

   Keys: Example, logic   **Etymology** means _____.

8. We labeled our cousin Gary *garrulous,* or "G-Squared," because he talks nonstop.

   Key: Definition   **Garrulous** means _____.

9. In a recent TV western, we listened to the condemned man *gibber* insanely as he was led toward the hangman's noose.

   Key: Logic   **Gibber** means _____.

10. A last-minute reprieve released the prisoner from both the gallows and his fear. His relief was visible and his *inflection* altered dramatically in tone and clarity as he gave moving thanks for his deliverance.

    Key: Partial definition   **Inflection** means _____.

11. Comedian George Gobel loves *irony*. On a TV program, he once said, "The National Safety Council has predicted 407 accidents due to careless driving over the weekend . . . and so far only 209 have been reported . . . Now, some of you folks just aren't trying."

    Keys: Logic, example   **Irony** means _____.

12. My favorite *laconic* question and reply belong to Victor Hugo and his publisher. Shortly after publication of *Les Misérables*, author Hugo wrote: "?" The reply was, "!" Now that is being succinct.

    Keys: Logic, synonym   **Laconic** means _____.

13. When Aunt Dolly said she needed "an anecdote for pain," we roared with laughter at her *malapropism*—then handed her two aspirin.

    Key: Logic   **Malapropism** means _____.

14. My old friend Bill is a great *raconteur*, able to make all the family grin at his humorous accounts of our escapades at camp years ago.

    Keys: Example, logic   **Raconteur** means _____.

15. Jan taunted me for days about my beet-red sunburn, but I was unable to come back with a *riposte* cutting enough to silence her.

    Keys: Logic, near synonym   **Riposte** means _____.

16. Asked to find examples of *tautology*, or redundancy, in the newspaper, I came up with *visible to the eye, center around, close proximity, past history,* and *each and every one* on just the front page.

    Keys: Synonym, examples   **Tautology** means _____.

17. Much as we enjoy the anecdotes of our English teacher, we don't enjoy his red pencil as it ruthlessly circles every *trite* remark—every single cliché—on our papers.

    Key: Synonym   **Trite** means _____.

WORD STUDY

Language is an ever-changing thing, with new words born daily. Gelett Burgess, an American humorist who loved to coin words, created *blurb,* which is now very common. We have a particularly large number of words to describe language itself and speech. Many are French words—perhaps because the French so love speech and language.

Speaking of languages, did you know that Urdu is Pakistan's official literary language? Prince Philip, Duke of Edinburgh, said once, "I am referred to in that splendid language [Urdu] as 'Fella belong Mrs. Queen.' "

1. **allege** (ə-'lej) v.   To state as truth although not proved or before proof; to give as a reason or excuse; from L. *ad + legare,* to depute, to legate

   For some time, historians *alleged* that Richard III murdered his two nephews in the Tower of London, but now many English scholars believe Henry VII guilty of that crime.

   > Relatives: *alleged* (so-called, assumed), *allegation*
   > Synonyms: *claim, assert* (neither exact)
   > Antonyms: *contravene, traverse* (to deny at law), *contradict, deny*

2. **anecdote** ('an-ik-ˌdot) n.   A brief story that is humorous or unusually interesting, often biographical; from Gr. *anekdota,* unpublished items

   A popular *anecdote* about Mark Twain quotes a cable that he sent from London to the Associated Press after his lengthy absence from the United States: "The reports of my death are greatly exaggerated."

   > Relatives: *anecdotal, anecdotist, anecdotically*

3. **articulate** (är-'tik-yə-ˌlāt) v.   To pronounce clearly and distinctly; to state effectively; to arrange in a systematic whole, as *articulating a music program throughout a school.*
   adj.   Understandable, intelligible, as *an articulate speech;* speaking clearly, easily, and well *(the articulate speaker);* jointed, as the segments of an animal; plainly marked off, as *the articulated parts of a computer program;* from L. *articulus,* joint, division

   Still under anesthetic, the patient was unable to *articulate,* and we couldn't understand his slurred speech.

   > Relatives: *articulately, articulateness, articulative, articulator, articulation, articulatory*
   > Synonym: *jointed* (articulate animals)
   > Antonyms: *inarticulate, unintelligible, mute*

4. **badinage** (ˌbad-ən-'äzh) n.   Playful, light (often humorous) talk or banter; from F. *badin,* fool

   Dating back to thirteenth-century French, *badinage* is an excellent synonym for repartee, another French word from the same era.

   > Synonyms: *repartee, banter, persiflage, raillery*

5. **double entendre** (ˌdüb[-ə]-ˌlän[n]-ˈtän[n]drə) n.   Ambiguity arising from a word or phrase that may be interpreted two ways, one often risqué; from F., literally, *double meaning*; pl., *double entendres*

   Known for her wit, Dorothy Parker once telegraphed an intentional *double entendre* to her friend who had just had a baby: "Congratulations, we all knew you had it in you."

6. **epigram** (ˈep-ə-ˌgram) n.   A brief, typically witty saying that expresses much in few words; from L. *epi* + *gram,* to write

   What is an epigram? *A dwarfish whole,*
   Its body brevity, and wit its soul.
           —Samuel Taylor Coleridge

7. **etymology** (ˌet-ə-ˈmäl-ə-jē) n.   The study of the earliest beginnings of words and idioms and their language histories; from Gr. *etymon,* earliest known true form of a word, + *-ology,* study of

   Willard Espy's research in *etymology* is presented with irresistible wit and impeccable scholarship.

   Relatives: *etymologist (person), etymological, etymologically*

8. **garrulous** (ˈgar-ə-ləs, ˈgar-yə-ləs) adj.   Talkative to an annoying degree, boringly loquacious; from L. *garrire,* to chatter

   It was the best place to be, thought Wilbur, this warm delicious cellar, with the garrulous *geese, the changing seasons, the heat of the sun...*
           —E.B. White, *Charlotte's Web*

   Relatives: *garrulity, garrulously, garrulousness*
   Synonyms: *talkative, loquacious, voluble, prolix, wordy, verbose, long-winded*
   Antonyms: *laconic, taciturn, reticent, silent, reserved*

9. **gibber** (ˈjib-ər) v.   To speak with great speed, little thought, and almost zero clarity; to gabble, chatter; origin uncertain

   The graves stood tenantless and the sheeted dead
   Did squeak and gibber *in the Roman streets.*
           —Shakespeare, *Julius Caesar*

   Relatives: *gibberish (incoherent speech)*
   Synonyms: *gabble, chatter, jabber, babble* (Note all the *b*s.)
   Antonym: *articulate*

10. **inflection** (in-ˈflek-shən) n.   Difference in loudness or pitch of the voice; the spelling change of words to show plurality, possession, tense, gender, voice, case, or mood; from L. *in* + *flectere,* to bend

    The pronoun is our part of speech with the most *inflections,* changing as it does from subject *(I),* to possessive *(my, mine),* to object *(me),* and into the plural as a different form altogether *(our, ours).*

    Relatives: *inflect, inflective, inflectional, inflectionally*

11. **irony** ('ī-rə-nē) n.   The use of words to convey a meaning other than (often opposite to) the literal meaning; ironic expression that implies the opposite of what is said; an outcome or result just the opposite of what would be expected; from Gr. *eiron*, dissembler

    The prophet Elijah gives us an example of direct *irony* when he jeers at the priests of Baal (heathen god) as they invoke their idols. Elijah taunts: "Cry louder! Baal is a god, but perhaps he is talking, or walking or traveling, or perhaps he is sleeping and must be awakened."

    Relatives: *ironic, ironically, ironist* (person)
    Synonyms: *sarcasm, wit* (weak)

12. **laconic** (lə-'kän-ik) adj.   Using as few words as possible, concise almost to the point of rudeness; from Gr. *lakonikos*, spartan

    One hopeful conqueror sent a message to Laconia: "If I come to Laconia, not one brick will stand on another." The *laconic* answer was "If."

    Relatives: *laconically, laconism*
    Synonyms: *terse, concise, pithy*
    Antonyms: *verbose, voluble, garrulous, wordy, talkative, loquacious, prolix*
    Derivation: Laconia and Sparta (its capital city) are synonymous in connotation. The Laconians (Spartans) were physically oriented folk—proud of their skills in games and war but sparing of speech and emotionally self-contained. Anything described as *Spartan* is simple to the point of self-denial, just as *laconic* speech or writing is pared to the bone.

13. **malapropism** ('mal-ə-ˌpräp-'iz-əm) n.   From Mrs. Malaprop, a character in Sheridan's *The Rivals;* a humorous misuse of words, putting a similar-sounding word in place of the correct one; from F. *mal à propos,* inopportune, unseasonable

    Mrs. Malaprop's verbal fumbles include "as headstrong as an allegory on the Nile," "a progeny of learning," and "Illiterate him, I say, quite from your mind!" Each case of language misused in this way is termed a *malapropism.*

    Relatives: *malaprop, malapropian, malapropos*

14. **raconteur** (ˌrak-ˌän-'tər) n.   One who tells stories or jokes with exceptional skill; from F. *raconter,* to tell

    Oscar Wilde, noted *raconteur* and epigrammatist, said on his deathbed as he was offered a glass of champagne: "I am dying beyond my means."

    Synonym: *storyteller* (not exact)

15. **riposte** (ri-'pōst) n.   A quick verbal retort; any retaliatory thrust, as the fencer's rapid return to a thrust following a parry; from L. *respondere* through It. *rispondere* and F. *riposter,* to respond

    Mistress of the cutting *riposte* was Dorothy Parker. When told that President Calvin Coolidge had died, she said, "How can they tell?"

    Relative: *riposte* (v.i., to retort)
    Synonyms: *retort, rejoinder* (neither exact)

16. **tautology** (tȯ-'täl-ə-jē) n.   The unnecessary repetition of words, ideas, statements, as *a young kitten* (kittens, by definition, are always young); from Gr. *tautologos,* to say

    Trite writing cluttered by *tautology* sends readers to bed or to the television set.

    Relatives: *tautological, tautologically, tautologous*
    Synonym: *redundancy*

17. **trite** ('trīt) adj.   Overused to the point of staleness; lacking freshness and originality; from L. *tritus,* rubbed, worn away (past participle of *terere*)

    "My personal opinion" and "first and foremost" are only two of the dozens of *trite* phrases that are also tautologous.

    Relatives: *tritely, triteness*
    Synonyms: *hackneyed, banal, common, ordinary, insipid, stale*
    Antonyms: *novel, fresh, original*

ROOT STUDY

Roots referring to written and spoken language dominate this study group.

1. **FLEX/FLECT** means *bend, turn, curve.*

   flex—to move or bend, as muscles
   inflexible—unyielding, stubborn, unwilling to bend
   reflection—thought (bending the mind back in time or over material again); image reflected to the viewer, as by a pond or mirror
   deflect—to turn away or aside

2. **GRAPH/GRAM** means to *write.*

   biography—written record of a person's life
   graphic—something written, drawn, or transmitted; extremely vivid, clear, expressive, as *a graphic description*
   telegram—message sent rapidly to a distant location
   gramophone—(formerly capitalized) trademark meaning phonograph, record player

3. **LEG** means *law, legal.*

   legacy—anything left by a deceased or absent person to someone else (e.g., personality traits, possessions, privileges, money)
   legality—established law
   legislature—lawmaking body

4. **ROG** means *to ask.*

   interrogate—to question, often repeatedly
   prerogative—a special right, privilege, power
   derogatory—belittling, disparaging, as *a derogatory remark*

USING THE WORDS

List 8 Review

allege	epigram	inflection	raconteur
anecdote	etymology	irony	riposte
articulate	garrulous	laconic	tautology
badinage	gibber	malapropism	trite
double entendre			

Exercise I. Synonyms.
Each word from List 8 has two synonyms in the group of lettered words. Enter the letters of these synonyms on the lines.

_____ 1. **trite**
       (a) ripe   (b) stale   (c) fresh
       (d) hackneyed   (e) used

_____ 2. **tautology**
       (a) redundancy   (b) science   (c) originality
       (d) repetition   (e) usefulness

_____ 3. **allege**
       (a) announce   (b) cite   (c) shelve
       (d) state   (e) set forth as possible

_____ 4. **articulate**
       (a) disjointed   (b) aware   (c) understandable
       (d) arranged   (e) intelligible

_____ 5. **garrulous**
       (a) loquacious   (b) crotchety   (c) voluble
       (d) voluminous   (e) ancient

_____ 6. **laconic**
       (a) grim   (b) terse   (c) concise
       (d) wordy   (e) inner

_____ 7. **riposte**
       (a) remail   (b) redress   (c) redirect
       (d) retort   (e) rejoinder

_____ 8. **gibber**
       (a) chatter   (b) poker   (c) mince
       (d) affirm   (e) babble

_____ 9. **badinage**
       (a) plaster   (b) repartee   (c) ill humor
       (d) banter   (e) wordiness

_____ 10. **irony**
       (a) laundry   (b) confusion   (c) sarcasm
       (d) wit   (e) annoyance

Exercise II. Analogies.
Complete each analogy with the best pair possible.

_____ 1. anecdote : book ::

    (a) novel : history
    (b) epigram : monologue
    (c) script : play
    (d) riposte : thrust
    (e) dialogue : address

_____ 2. laconic : garrulous ::

    (a) verbose : prolix
    (b) wordy : prolonged
    (c) terse : hackneyed
    (d) novel : trite
    (e) ironic : humorous

_____ 3. Oscar Wilde : raconteur ::

    (a) Benjamin Franklin : poet
    (b) William Wordsworth : mayor
    (c) Teddy Roosevelt : actor
    (d) Miles Standish : carpenter
    (e) Mark Twain : satirist

_____ 4. repetition : speech ::

    (a) tautology : writing
    (b) etymology : music
    (c) inflection : voice
    (d) badinage : raillery
    (e) dynamics : medicine

_____ 5. malapropism : words ::

    (a) sculpture : chisel
    (b) composition : music
    (c) extremism : art
    (d) gibbering : speech
    (e) defeatism : theory

Exercise III. Fill-Ins.
Write the words (from List 8 _and its synonyms_) that fit the descriptions on the lines provided. The first letter is given for each answer.

1. trite expression   c _____

2. light banter   r _____

3. double interpretation possible for a word or expression   d _____

4. storyteller   r _____

5. quick rejoinder, retort   r _____

6. humorous misuse of words   **m** _____

7. hackneyed, stale   **b** _____

8. light, witty talk   **p** _____

9. playful talk, banter   **b** _____

10. a clever remark, witticism   **b** _____ **m** _____

(This one is not given here, although it occurs in a previous lesson. Ask a friend who takes French, a parent, or a teacher.)

Exercise IV. Terms in Use.

The following sentences are examples of general types of verbal expression taught in this lesson. Label each example with the word that describes its type. (Two quotes may be more fully described by *two* of the vocabulary words.)

_____ 1. One of the stories told about Elizabeth Taylor concerns her discovery by the film industry. When told she was too short to play the lead role in *National Velvet,* she replied, "I will grow." And grow she did. By the time filming began, she had added just enough height to qualify.

_____ 2. The boy said, "My aunt has bellicose veins, too, and may need an operation just like your mom."

_____ 3. Gazing from a hilltop down onto Washington, D.C., a woman observed, "Much needs doing down there, but I wish they'd begin by managing the traffic better." "Capital improvement!" exclaimed her friend.

_____ 4. "Experience is the name everyone gives to his mistakes," said Oscar Wilde.

_____ 5. **battology** (bætə-lədzi) needless repetition in writing or speech, from Battos, the stammering man in Herodotus's history of the Greco-Persian wars.

_____ 6. Report of an Indian after guiding a visiting Englishman on a hunting shoot: "Our guest shot beautifully, but heaven was very merciful to the birds."
    —Cited by L. Feinberg, *Introduction to Satire*

_____ 7. After a long, boring evening, Dorothy Parker's somewhat stuffy escort remarked to her, "I can't bear fools."
    "That's strange. Your mother could," Miss Parker rejoined.

_____ 8. The frisky young foal romped and gamboled in the pale green meadow fragrant with new spring grass.

Exercise V. Roots.

Match the words (from the section on roots) with their meanings in the lettered column on the right.

_____ 1. **derogatory**   (a) special right or privilege

_____ 2. **legacy**   (b) story of a life

_____ 3. **graphic**   (c) to turn aside or away

_____ 4. **flex**   (d) to question

_____ 5. **inflexible**   (e) study of handwriting

_____ 6. **gramophone**   (f) extremely vivid and clear

_____ 7. **prerogative**   (g) easily bent, yielding

_____ 8. **reflection**   (h) to move or bend

_____ 9. **biography**   (i) unyielding

_____ 10. **deflect**   (j) thought or image

_____ 11. **interrogate**   (k) disparaging

_____ 12. **flexible**   (l) not lawful

_____ 13. **graphology**   (m) inherited trait, possession, privilege

_____ 14. **legislate**   (n) record player

_____ 15. **illegal**   (o) to enact laws

Exercise VI. Word Analysis.

1. Give one or more _antonyms_ for the following words.

   _____ (a) alleged (assumed, so-called)

   _____ (b) articulate (adj.)

   _____ (c) garrulous

   _____ (d) trite

   _____ (e) laconic

2. Several words in List 8 (plus their synonyms) refer to conversation that would contain _bons mots_ (literally, _good words_). How many of these words can you find and list?

   _____

   _____

3. Since *malapropism* refers to the inappropriate use of words, what does its root *apropos* mean?

   _____

   Examples: (a) Her outfit was *apropos* for the occasion.
                 (b) That speech was *apropos* of nothing significant that we could discover.

4. For a bit, think about inflection as it refers to voice. How does the inflection of a person's voice reflect fear? sorrow? joy? a need for secrecy? anger?

   _____

   _____

   _____

   If your voice were incapable of inflection, could you cheer at a ball game? or whisper?

   _____

   How much does inflection in the voice of a character influence your opinion? (Think of the Big Bad Wolf's voice versus those of the three little pigs, as in the Walt Disney cartoon.)

   _____

   _____

Exercise VII. Just for Fun.

Ever played Stinky Pinkies? It's a word game that gives a definition and requests a two-word rhymed response that names the thing defined.

   Q. an Italian robber bug?
   A. mosquito bandito

Here's a Double Stinky Pinky, which is a tougher kind to dream up:

   Q. a fat cat?
   A. a flabby tabby

Try these if the conversation lags over dinner.

a. aviator?	f. rodent's home?
b. fast crowd?	g. childbirth at the North Pole?
c. cheerful father?	h. nervous/stupid fowl?
d. chicken purchaser?	i. one crazy about the theater?
e. rose-colored basin?	j. submerged friar?

Review

This lesson reviews the words and roots in Lists 5, 6, 7, and 8. As you read over these lists, remember to say each word or prefix aloud to help trigger your memory and plant both the meanings and the spellings in your mind.

LIST 5

bene-, bon-
eu-
pro-
a-
anti-, ant-
counter-, contra-
dif-, dis-
for-
il-, im-, in-, ir- (no, not)
non-, un-
ob-, of-, op-
mal-, mis-
macro-
micro-, min-
pan-, panto-, omni-
ante-, anti-
ex-
fore-
pre-
post-
co-, col-, com-, con-, cor-
syl-, sym-, syn-, sys-, sy-
amphi-, circum-, peri-
epi-, ecto-
ab-, abs-, apo-, ap-
wri-, wro-

e-, ec-, ef-, ex-
de-, cata-
se-
a-, ad-, af-, ag-, al-, an-,
ap-, as-, at-
ob-, oc-, of-, op-
il-, im-, in-, ir- (within, into)
endo-, en-, em-
intro-, intra-
ana-, re-, retro-
inter-
tele-
sub-, suc-, suf-, sug-,
sum-, sup-, sus-
hyp-, hypo-
over-, super-, ultra-,
hyper-
exter-, extra-, extro-
trans-, tra-
di-, dia-, per-
alter-, hetero-
homo-
meta-
para-, par-
orth-

LIST 6	LIST 7	LIST 8
astringent	avant-garde	allege
brazen	concierge	anecdote
brusque	debacle	articulate
catholic	détente	badinage
diffident	dossier	double entendre
eldritch	echelon	epigram
expedient	ennui	etymology
incorrigible	entrepreneur	garrulous
incumbent	insouciance	gibber
lithe	ménage	inflection
nebulous	outré	irony
pastoral	pique	laconic
plausible	précis	malapropism
pristine	rapport	raconteur
requisite	sangfroid	riposte
stolid	soupçon	tautology
		trite

ROOTS

AGOG	FLEX/FLECT	LEG	STRING/STRICT
DORS	GRAPH/GRAM	ROG	TEND/TENS/TENT
FID	GREG	PORT	

USING THE WORDS

Exercise I. Antonyms.
Find the antonym or contrasting phrase for each word on the left and enter its letter on the correct line.

_____ 1. **microcosm**

_____ 2. **brazen**

_____ 3. **catholic**

_____ 4. **requisite**

_____ 5. **sangfroid**

_____ 6. **outré**

_____ 7. **debacle**

_____ 8. **tautology**

_____ 9. **articulate** (v.)

_____ 10. **trite**

_____ 11. **pastoral**

_____ 12. **nebulous**

_____ 13. **incorrigible**

_____ 14. **diffident**

_____ 15. **garrulous**

(a) extra, superfluous

(b) ordinary

(c) gibber

(d) shy

(e) original

(f) amenable

(g) macrocosm

(h) definite

(i) parochial

(j) bold

(k) agitation, nervousness

(l) laconic

(m) concise thought

(n) success

(o) urban

Exercise II. Know Those Roots and Prefixes.

Circle any prefixes in the following numbered words. Underline the roots. Then write a synonym or brief definition on the line.

1. bonus _____

2. interrogate _____

3. rapport _____

4. malapropism _____

5. inflection _____

6. epigram _____

7. allege _____

8. détente _____

9. insouciance _____

10. expedient _____

Exercise III. Chart Fill-In.

Add the missing items in the chart.

	PREFIX	**ROOT**	**WORD**	**DEFINITION**
1.	_____	_____	restricted	_____
2.	dem-	agog	_____	popular leader
3.	_____	_____	infidel	_____
4.	_____	dors	_____	to sign; to give support
5.	_____	_____	deport	_____
6.	meta-	morph	_____	a noticeable change of form or personality
7.	_____	rog	_____	disparaging, downgrading
8.	epi-	_____	_____	short witty saying
9.	_____	_____	astringent	_____
10.	_____	greg	_____	to set apart

Exercise IV. Sentence Completion.
Select the most appropriate word from the choices offered, based on clues in context. The word form may change.

brusque	dossier	irony	incumbent
eldritch	anecdote	raconteur	plausible
avant-garde	badinage	précis	pristine

1. As class treasurer, it was _____ on me to keep track of moneys in our account, sign checks, and make a monthly report.

2. Mom viewed Andy's filthy face and jeans, muddy shoes, and torn shirt. "Well," she said with heavy _____, "it'd be a shame to make you clean up and ruin your perfect boy-at-play image."

3. As Jan reeled off the likes, dislikes, and recent comments of the new, good-looking senior, I had to grin. "I didn't know girls kept a _____ like that on each guy's life," I teased.

4. Used to traditional music, Mom and Dad were startled by the _____ piano compositions at a recent recital.

5. The coin collector's album Carrie gave me keeps each new coin in _____ condition in a separate plastic pocket.

6. I sprinkled my speech about Teddy Roosevelt with amusing quotes and _____ to keep everyone's interest high.

7. Mom confessed, "I was so annoyed with the checkout girl that I spoke quite _____ to hurry her along. I hate to be rude, though," she added.

8. Stories can be told in a variety of ways, but the good _____ knows how to interest and hold an audience.

9. With a steely eye Jan glared at our cat Marigold. "I suppose you have a _____ reason for sleeping next to the aquarium," she said, just as though Marigold would reply with a logical answer.

10. After the class read five different versions of life in wartime Britain, the history teacher assigned a _____ on the topic, warning us that four pages would be the maximum allowable length.

11. Nothing wakes our family quicker than the _____ nighttime howl of the neighboring Siamese as he woos Marigold.

12. Dad has a great sense of humor, but he's not much at small talk or casual _____.

Exercise V. Analogies.

Complete each analogy with the best pair possible.

_____ 1. dancer : lithe ::

    (a) singer : graceful
    (b) manager : brusque
    (c) columnist : incumbent
    (d) speaker : laconic
    (e) entrepreneur : resourceful

_____ 2. stolid : impassive ::

    (a) pristine : keen
    (b) expedient : unnecessary
    (c) naughty : incorrigible
    (d) ironic : sarcastic
    (e) insouciant : careful

_____ 3. enthusiasm : ennui ::

    (a) riposte : retort
    (b) plausibility : illogic
    (c) gibberish : confusion
    (d) stricture : tension
    (e) diffidence : provocation

_____ 4. repartee : riposte ::

    (a) détente : compromise
    (b) raconteur : tale
    (c) inflection : anticipation
    (d) rapport : requisition
    (e) echelon : rank

_____ 5. words : etymology ::

    (a) frogs : biology
    (b) mind : psychology
    (c) science : geology
    (d) books : bibliophile
    (e) music : conservatory

Exercise VI. Word Analysis.

1. How and why do words come into the English language? _____

    _____

    Cite some words adopted from France. Other countries? _____

    _____

    _____

2. How does the root meaning of _echelon_ correspond to its present meaning and usage?

    _____

3. Fill in as many prefixes as you can in the following chart:

Good, Well, Favoring	Bad, Negative, Not	Above, Over	Out/Away

Below, Under	With, Together	Indic. Time/Place	Size/Amount

In, Into, With

4. Describe your ménage briefly. _____

_____

_____

5. What is the difference in these two usages of *pique*?

   (a) *Piqued* by her refusal, I strode away.
   (b) My curiosity *piqued* by the painting, I wanted to ask several questions of the artist.

   _____

6. Students like phrases with a double interpretation because they're laughable. Can you recall a recent *double entendre*?

   _____

   _____

7. Would someone crazy about Mexican food like only a soupçon of chili powder?

   _____

A Hirsute Simian
Words from the Animal Kingdom

In Context. Before studying the definitions, try reasoning out the meaning of each word, using context as your guide.

1. I could tell from his foolish grin and generally *asinine* look that Steve wasn't comprehending what I had said.

   Keys: Synonym, logic   **Asinine** means _____.

2. A look of *bovine* contentment spread over Carrie's face as she chewed gum and watched her favorite video. Jan giggled. "You remind me of old Bossie chewing her cud," she said.

   Keys: Logic, example   **Bovine** means _____.

3. A favorite family documentary titled *"Denizens of the Deep"* explores the lives and habits of sea creatures in the Pacific.

   Key: Logic   **Denizen** means _____.

4. The noisy, demanding *fledglings* in our oak tree keep the parent birds frantically hunting food for them all day.

   Keys: Antonym, logic   **Fledgling** means _____.

5. "I've fed enough *fodder* into this computer today. I ought to get quite a report," Jan said, her eyes glued to the screen.

   Key: Logic   **Fodder** means _____.

6. The 1960s brought a great awareness of hair. People who'd never thought much about hair eyed the *hirsute*, bearded young men with amazement.

   Key: Synonym   **Hirsute** means _____.

7. That part calls for a *leonine* actor—someone with a full head of hair and a beard—someone who exudes the power and vitality demanded by the role.

   Key: Definition; look for the root.   **Leonine** means _____.

8. Several beloved *porcine* characters include the Three Little Pigs, Porky Pig, and Wilbur of *Charlotte's Web*.

   Key: Synonymous ideas   **Porcine** means _____.

9. The *prehensile* tail of a monkey is fascinating to watch as the monkey swings nimbly from branch to branch, grasping almost as well with his tail as with his hands and feet.

   Keys: Logic, example   **Prehensile** means _____.

10. Carrie took one look at the cobra and shuddered. "They're just plain icky. *Reptilian* heads and slithery bodies, ugh!"

    Key: Example; look for the root.   **Reptilian** means _____.

11. The faraway, thoughtful look in Jan's eyes told me that she was *ruminating* yet again on her college choices.

    Key: Logic   **Ruminate** means _____.

12. As a play title, Eugene O'Neill's *The Hairy Ape* sounds better than *The Hirsute Simian.*

    Key: Synonym   **Simian** means _____.

13. Caught up in the movie, we followed the *spoor* of a wounded water buffalo with nearly the same intensity as the tracker, alert for any drops of blood, any patches of trampled grass.

    Keys: Examples, logic   **Spoor** means _____.

14. When humane *vivisection* is responsibly practiced, when necessary laboratory experiments on animals lead to cures for humans, when understanding of the animals' physiology is required by veterinary science—only then will the antivivisectionists be quiet.

    Keys: Definition, logic   **Vivisection** means _____.

15. The *vixen* is known for intelligence, cunning, and ferocity—especially when called upon to defend her fox cubs.

    Keys: Synonym, logic   **Vixen** means _____.

16. Our Labrador retriever had nine *whelps* in her last litter, so we had to find nine homes.

    Key: Logic   **Whelp** means _____.

WORD STUDY

Human beings and animals have been interdependent since time began. Animals have fed us, clothed us, worked for us, amused us, and kept us company. They've been an irreplaceable source of medical and behavioral information. And think of the books: *Moby Dick, Watership Down, Black Beauty, A Cricket in Times Square, Charlotte's Web, Lassie Come Home, Born Free, The Incredible Journey—* just for openers. It's impossible to picture our planet without animals.

> *Man is the only animal that blushes.*
> *Or needs to.*
>   —Mark Twain

1. **asinine** ('as-ǝn-ˌīn) adj.   Remarkably stupid or ridiculous; lacking good sense or judgment; from L. *asinus,* ass

   Hoping for an intelligent answer, Hank was both dismayed and annoyed by Jim's *asinine* response.

   Relatives: *asininely, asininity*
   Synonyms: *inane, ridiculous, absurd, asslike, stubborn*
   Antonyms: *wise, judicious, sensible*

2. **bovine** ('bō-ˌvīn, 'bō-ˌvēn) adj.   Referring to cows (and oxen) or cowlike behavior; slow-moving, stolid, not quick-witted; from L. *bov, bos,* ox or cow

   Thelma waited with *bovine* patience—sitting placidly in her chair, knitting one row after another onto the shawl.

   > Relatives: *bovine* (n., cow, ox), *bovinely, bovinity*

3. **denizen** ('den-ə-zən) n.   An inhabitant, either plant or animal; someone who habitually goes to or lives in one place, as *denizens of the shopping mall;* from L. *de + intus,* within (through F. *denz,* within)

   Students of ecology refer to plants, and sometimes animals, that have adapted to a nonnative ecosystem as *denizens.*

   > Synonym: *inhabitant*
   > Antonym: *alien*

4. **fledgling** ('flej-liŋ) n.   A young bird growing flight feathers; anyone young or lacking experience, as the young bird is untried in flight; from OE *fleōgan,* to fly

   In politics, Henderson is a *fledgling,* but someone with his power of oratory is bound to take off sooner than most.

   > Relative: *fledge* (v.)
   > Synonyms: *novice, tyro, beginner, neophyte*
   > Antonyms: *expert, ace, specialist, master*

5. **fodder** ('fäd-ər) n.   Food for domestic animals; anything used regularly like a food, as *fodder for the computer* (being the steady supply of data); from OE *fōdor,* food

   > *O, it sets my heart a-clickin' like the tickin' of a clock,*
   > *When the frost is on the punkin and the* fodder's *in the shock.*
   >   —James Whitcomb Riley, "When the Frost Is on the Punkin"

6. **hirsute** ('hər-ˌsüt, 'hi[ə]r-ˌsüt) adj.   Hairy or bristly with hairs; from L. *hirsutus* and *horrere,* to bristle

   Of baby gorillas, *hirsute* and charming, satirist Will Cuppy said, "Young gorillas are friendly but they soon learn."

   > Relatives: *hirsuteness, hirsutism* (excess hair), *hirsutulous* (very slightly hirsute)
   > Synonym: *hairy*
   > Antonym: *hairless*

7. **leonine** ('lē-ə-ˌnīn) adj.   Resembling a lion; like a lion in appearance (heavy mane of hair) or behavior; from L. *leonis,* lion

   I can still picture my grandfather, his *leonine* head and beard rising above a powerful set of shoulders.

   > Relatives: *Leo* (constellation, fifth zodiacal sign), *Leonid* (one of the shooting stars), *lionize* (to treat as very important), *leopard* (leo + pardos, leopard)

8. **porcine** ('pȯr-ˌsīn) adj.   Referring to a pig or swine; fat, obese; from L. *porcus,* pig

A disagreeable figure, Gouge bulked ominously in his chair, his *porcine* eyes fixed on the doorway.

Relatives: *pork, porker, porcupine* (*porcus* + *spina,* spine)
Synonyms: *fat, obese* (Careful. These don't always work.)

9. **prehensile** (prē-'hen[t]-səl) adj.   Able to grasp or seize quickly and naturally, as *a monkey's prehensile tail grasps a branch* or *a prehensile mind grasps ideas well;* from L. *prehendere,* to grasp

Gifted with a *prehensile,* precocious mind, Mozart was composing music at an age when the rest of us are learning to tie our shoes.

Relatives: *prehensility, prehension* (mental understanding)

10. **reptilian** (rep-'til-ē-ən) adj.   Referring to snakes, reptiles; snakelike; groveling, sneaky, despicable; from L. *reptilis,* creeping

The lyric from *My Fair Lady* that goes, "He oiled his way across the floor, /Oozing charm from every pore," refers to a *reptilian* character whom Professor Higgins despised.

Relative: *reptile*

11. **ruminate** ('rü-mə-ˌnāt) v.   To ponder repeatedly, slowly, thoughtfully, the way a cud-chewing animal deals with its food; to chew again the swallowed food (the cud of a ruminant mammal); from L. *rumen,* gullet

When I hear of a mind like Einstein's, I wonder if he *ruminated* at length to solve knotty problems or if flashes of inspiration came to him like lightning.

Relatives: *rumen* (first compartment of a ruminant's stomach), *ruminant* (cud-chewing mammal), *ruminant* (adj.), *rumination, ruminative, ruminatively, ruminator*
Synonyms: *reflect, ponder, meditate*

12. **simian** ('sim-ē-ən) adj.   Similar to apes or monkeys in character, behavior, or appearance; from L. *simia,* ape

The famous Scopes trial of 1925, known as the Monkey Trial, pitted lawyer Clarence Darrow against William Jennings Bryan, noted orator and religious fundamentalist. Darrow defended Scopes, an instructor who had taught Darwin's theory of evolution, or *"simian* science," as one reporter derided it. (Note: The movie *Inherit the Wind,* from the play of that name, is an excellent dramatization of the Scopes trial.)

Relative: *simian* (n., monkey, ape)

13. **spoor** ('spu̇[ə]r, 'spō[ə]r) n.   The trail, prints, or droppings of a wild animal; akin to OE *spor,* footprint, spoor

Hungry hunters soon learn to follow the *spoor* of animals if the hunters are serious about eating dinner.

Relative: *spoor* (v., to track by following a spoor)
Synonyms: *track, trail* (neither exact)

14. **vivisection** ('viv-ə-'sek-shən) n.   An operation on a live animal, usually for medical or scientific reasons but sometimes for less legitimate experimental reasons (strong negative connotations); from L. *vivus*, life + E. *section*, cutting into sections

    The Plague Dogs, by Richard Adams, is one man's passionate outcry against irresponsible *vivisection.*

    Relatives: *vivisect, vivisector, vivisectional, vivisectionally, vivisectionist*

15. **vixen** ('vik-sən) n.   A female fox; a woman of nasty, shrewish temperament; from Middle E. *fixene,* female fox

    She was a vixen *when she went to school:*
    And though she be but little, she is fierce.
        —Shakespeare, *A Midsummer Night's Dream*

    Relatives: *vixenish, vixenishly, vixenishness*
    Synonyms: *shrew, termagant, scold, virago*

16. **whelp** ('hwelp, 'welp) n.   Offspring of a carnivorous mammal, especially of a dog; youngster; an upstart or unrespected person;   v.   To give birth; from OE *hwelp,* whelp, to bring forth young

    And in that town a dog was found,
    As many dogs there be,
    Both mongrel, puppy, whelp, *and hound,*
    And curs of low degree.
        —Oliver Goldsmith, "An Elegy on the Death of a Mad Dog"

ROOT STUDY

This group of roots relates to animals, the land, and life—basic roots for sure.

1. **CARN** means *flesh, meat.*

    carnivorous—meat-eating
    incarnate—given human nature and form
    carnage—massacre, a bloody slaughter
    reincarnation—a rebirth in a new body or form of life; the rebirth of a soul in a new body

2. **MUT/MUTAT** means *change.*

    mutation—a significant or basic change of genetic material
    transmute—to transform or change to a higher form
    immutable—unchangeable, unvariable
    commute—to change or alter, as a severe penalty may be *commuted* to a lesser one; also to travel regularly between one place and another

3. **TERR/TER** means *land, earth.*

    terrestrial—of the earth or land
    terrier—a small breed of dog originally bred to hunt furred game, carrying the fight underground if needed; literally, *earth dog*
    terra firma—solid ground, dry land
    inter—to bury (in the ground); *disinter,* to dig up from underground
    terrace—to arrange land in levels, as for planting; any paved or planted area near buildings

4. **VITA** and **VIV** mean *life*.

vitality—vigor, liveliness, physical or mental strength
vitamin—an organic substance needed for good nutrition
vivid—extraordinarily clear and lifelike
viviparous—bearing live young

USING THE WORDS

List 9 Review

asinine	fodder	prehensile	spoor
bovine	hirsute	reptilian	vivisection
denizen	leonine	ruminate	vixen
fledgling	porcine	simian	whelp

Exercise I. Definitions.

Review List 9, pronouncing the words out loud, skimming the definitions as a refresher. Then write each word beside its definition or synonym.

1. hairy, bristly   h _____
2. well-adapted for grasping   p _____
3. lacking sense or judgment   a _____
4. lionlike   l _____
5. to reflect, ponder   r _____
6. inhabitant   d _____
7. apelike   s _____
8. food   f _____
9. trail, track   s _____
10. fat, obese   p _____
11. cowlike   b _____
12. operation on a living animal   v _____
13. youngster   w _____
14. young, untried individual   f _____
15. shrewish female   v _____
16. snakelike   r _____

Exercise II. Adjectives.

Some of our most descriptive words are adjectives borrowed from the animal kingdom. Besides the few in List 9, we have *lupine* from **lup,** wolf; *ovine* from **ovus,** sheep; *taurine* from **taurus,** bull; *ursine* from **ursa,** bear; and *piscine* from **pisces,** fish—plus several others that you already know or can guess.

From the choices offered, select the best adjective for each blank. Each word is used only once.

leonine	reptilian	piscatory	feline
lupine	asinine	elephantine	ovine
equine	ursine	simian	canine
taurine	porcine	bovine	

1. Someone familiar with the habits of trout and bass would be a great companion on a(n) _____ expedition.

2. Don't offer your _____ buddy another box of chocolates.

3. The old saying "A dog is man's best friend" refers to the _____ trait of faithfulness.

4. "Hey, Toro, Toro!" is the taunt in Madrid's _____ spectacle.

5. Big Bear and Little Bear are the _____ constellations.

6. Purring is the traditional sign of _____ contentment.

7. The _____ growl of the Big Bad Wolf didn't scare the Little Pig in the brick house.

8. With _____ agility, the tightrope walker scaled the rope ladder and negotiated the high wire like a monkey.

9. An expression you don't want on your face is one of _____ stupidity.

10. The _____ slitherers of the desert often have deadly fangs.

11. A proud conqueror favors the _____ look of command.

12. The phrase "Tiny, angry eyes in a _____, fleshy face" describes someone we don't want to know.

13. Fleet _____ hooves flash across the finish line each May in the Kentucky Derby.

14. Placid, unemotional women may be described as _____ creatures, but that phrase isn't considered a compliment.

15. Following the crowd with _____, unquestioning loyalty should be the behavior only of sheep, not of people.

Exercise III. Antonyms.

Match the words from List 9 and Roots with their antonyms or contrasting phrases.

_____ 1. **terrestrial**   (a) ace

_____ 2. **asinine**   (b) whelp

_____ 3. **denizen**   (c) variable

_____ 4. **adult**   (d) to dig up

_____ 5. **hairless**   (e) intelligent

_____ 6. **fledgling**   (f) nebulous, vague

_____ 7. **immutable**   (g) stable

_____ 8. **vivid**   (h) celestial

_____ 9. **mutable**   (i) hirsute

_____ 10. **inter** (v.)   (j) alien

Exercise IV. Fill-Ins.

Select the most appropriate word from List 9 and Roots to complete each sentence.

1. A sharp-tongued, ill-tempered female is a _____.

2. Lab experiments with white mice to determine genetic transference may be termed
    _____.

3. A sassy, impudent kid is a _____.

4. Animals bearing live young—as opposed to those who lay eggs—are termed
    _____.

5. *Dis + inter* = _____, meaning to dig up.

6. Noun to mean bloody slaughter = _____.

7. If carnivores eat meat (and they do), *omnivores* eat _____.

8. *Termagant, virago,* and *shrew* are synonyms for a _____.

9. Cud-chewing sheep, giraffe, deer, and camels are _____.

10. *Planet of the Apes* depicted future life with the _____ in control.

Exercise V. Word Analysis.

1. What is the *piscatorial* art? _____

2. How do you suppose an astrologer would describe the personality of someone born under the sign of Leo (July 22–23 through August 23)? _____

   _____

   _____

3. Match the young with their parents:

   _____ a. cygnet   (1) cow (bovine)

   _____ b. cub   (2) horse (equine)

   _____ c. whelp   (3) swan

   _____ d. foal   (4) kangaroo

   _____ e. calf   (5) fox

   _____ f. joey   (6) dog (canine)

4. *Aviator, aviatrix* (fem.), *aviary,* and *rara avis* come from the root *avi,* bird. What is an *aviary?* A *rara avis?* (Hint: Old Webster knows . . .) _____

   _____

   _____

5. When a French girl calls for *la poussiquette,* what animal will come?

   _____

6. Match the *-ologies* (studies of) with the subject studied.

   _____ a. etymology   (1) birds

   _____ b. ornithology   (2) mind and behavior

   _____ c. entomology   (3) mammals

   _____ d. psychology   (4) words

   _____ e. mammalogy   (5) insects

7. What is *educational fodder?* _____

8. Generations have repeated adages such as "Every dog has his day," "a bull in a china shop," and "a wolf in sheep's clothing." How many other sayings can you think of that delineate human behavior in animal terms? _____

   _____

   _____

"If man could be crossed with cat, it would improve man, but deteriorate the cat."
    —Mark Twain

LIST 10

Bigots and Bagatelles
Nouns Nice to Know

In Context. Before studying the definitions, try reasoning out the meaning of each word, using context as your guide.

1. "I enjoy the *ambience* at the elementary school," Mom said. "The atmosphere there is charged with excitement about learning and with exceptional warmth."

   Key: Synonym   **Ambience** means _____.

2. We considered the *amenities* of each hotel in town before selecting one for the holiday dance. We chose Blake House because of its large dance floor, outstanding band, and reasonable food prices.

   Keys: Logic, examples   **Amenities** means _____.

3. Carrie is the *anomaly* in our family, as she's the only one of us who doesn't love chocolate.

   Key: Partial definition   **Anomaly** means _____.

4. The work force at Dad's office is reduced by *attrition*. As people resign, die, or retire, no one replaces them.

   Key: Examples   **Attrition** means _____.

5. "If you and Jan want luggage for graduation," Dad said, "I need to start saving now. Sets of good luggage are not *bagatelles*, you know; they are a major purchase."

   Key: Opposing phrase   **Bagatelle** means _____.

6. "He's such a chauvinist—such a *bigot*!" Jan fumed. "He's never hired a girl's lawn service. He told me only boys could have the job. How narrow-minded can you get?"

   Key: Synonyms   **Bigot** means _____.

7. Seniors would be more tolerant of freshmen if their *demeanor* were more adult. Unfortunately, some freshmen behave like fifth graders.

   Keys: Near synonym, logic   **Demeanor** means _____.

8. "I can't stand *duplicity*," Mom said. "Please don't tell me this dress looks good on me if you think I look like a sack of potatoes. I'd rather hear the truth."

   Keys: Antonym, logic   **Duplicity** means _____.

9. Our schools have regular fire drills so that we know how to evacuate the buildings rapidly in any *exigency*—whether it's fire or not.

   Key: Logic   **Exigency** means _____.

10. "It's the *logistics* that get me," confessed the marching band director. "Transportation to the games, seating arrangements till we perform, getting on and off the field properly. . . . All those details wear me out!"

    Keys: Examples, logic   **Logistics** means _____.

11. Jan's favorite era is the Middle Ages, when the humble simplicity and poverty of most lives formed a stark contrast to the *ostentation* and wealth of a privileged few.

    Key: Opposing phrase   **Ostentation** means _____.

12. Mom wants us to get a bulldog. "I grin every time I see one," she said, "and I admire their *pertinacity*. You know I've always respected determination."

    Key: Synonym   **Pertinacity** means _____.

13. "What a *quisling*!" Jan snorted. "Al promised to vote with us, then voted for the other side."

    Keys: Example, logic   **Quisling** means _____.

14. Aware of the *rancor* he'd incurred by being a turncoat, Al tried to win back the classmates he'd deserted, but we were too bitter to listen.

    Key: Near synonym   **Rancor** means _____.

15. As we prepared for the state marching band contest, our director was merciless, marching us up and down the field with no *respite* until he was satisfied.

    Key: Logic   **Respite** means _____.

16. "If Al has the *temerity* to think he can act nice for a while and we'll forget," Jan said, "then he's got more nerve than I thought!"

    Keys: Synonym, logic   **Temerity** means _____.

17. Leaving nothing to the *vagaries* of chance, our band director made us practice until we could execute each number perfectly.

    Key: Logic   **Vagaries** means _____.

WORD STUDY

As a writer and speaker, you will always depend on two parts of speech: nouns and verbs. They convey the center of your meaning. Select them carefully and you'll be an effective user of language. No quantity of adjectives and adverbs can compensate for weak nouns and verbs. The word *house*, for example, gives only a general picture. But if you specify what sort of house by calling it a *mansion*, a *shack*, or a *Cape Cod cottage*, then a more definite picture emerges—and a more interesting one.

Remember that general, overused words are dull. The specific is interesting. The nouns (and verbs) you use should paint a vivid picture in your reader's or listener's mind.

1. **ambience** ('am-bē-ən[t]s) n.   The environment or feeling of a place or area, its atmosphere; from L. *ambi + ire*, to go around

   The excellent food, cheerful waiters, and overall mood of contentment create an *ambience* at Mama Luisa's restaurant that draws customers from a wide area.

   Synonyms: *atmosphere, environment* (neither exact)

2. **amenities** (ə-'men-ət-ēz) pl. n.   The qualities (of a place or of social interaction) that are desirable, pleasant, and agreeable; any qualities that add to the comfort, salability, or desirability of a property or place; sing., *amenity*; from L. *amoenus*, pleasant

   We chose our summer cottage site based on the local *amenities*: a nearby golf course plus an excellent lake for boating, fishing, and swimming.

3. **anomaly** (ə-'näm-ə-lē) n.   An irregularity or deviation from what is normal or expected; pl., *anomalies*; from Gr. *anomalos*, uneven

   The "black sheep" in a family is the *anomaly*—the one who doesn't share the standards of the rest.

   Relative: *anomalous*
   Synonyms: *irregularity, paradox* (neither exact)

4. **attrition** (ə-'trish-ən) n.   Lowering in number (of people) by means of resignation, death, or retirement; annoyance or harassment by frequent attack to the point of exhaustion (derived from the meaning of friction or rubbing together, as stones are smoothed and worn down in water by *attrition*); from L. *ad + terere*, to rub

   Large companies prefer to reduce employee numbers by *attrition*, because firing people or laying them off attracts undesirable publicity.

   Relatives: *attritional, attrited* (worn down by attrition)
   Opposing ideas: *expansion, addition, accretion*

5. **bagatelle** (ˌbag-ə-'tel) n.   A small, unimportant item, a trifle; also, a table game played with balls and a cue; from It. *bagattella*, trifling

   The wealthy woman gestured casually at the bracelet on her wrist. "Only pearls," she murmured. "A mere *bagatelle*, I assure you."

   Synonyms: *trifle, trinket*

6. **bigot** ('big-ət) n.   Someone stubbornly attached to or prejudiced by his own beliefs, sex, political party, church, etc.; a narrow-minded, opinionated person; from Middle F. *bigot*, a religious, overdevout hypocrite, a bigot

    Sinclair Lewis's satiric novel *Babbitt* is the story of George F. Babbitt, a self-satisfied man of the middle class whose name is now synonymous with *bigot*.

    Relatives: *bigoted, bigotry, bigotedly*
    Synonym: *Babbitt, chauvinist*

7. **demeanor** (di-'mē-nər) n.   Manner, appearance, or bearing; behavior; from OF *demener*, to conduct

    I am a courtier grave and serious,
    Who is about to kiss your hand:
    Try to combine a pose imperious
    With a demeanor *nobly bland.*
        —W. S. Gilbert, *The Gondoliers*

    Relative: *demean* (to behave or to degrade, debase)
    Synonyms: *bearing, behavior, conduct*

8. **duplicity** (d[y]ù-'plis-ət-ē) n.   Crafty or underhanded double-dealing; deception by words or actions in order to hide the truth; from L. *duo* + *plex*, double fold

    Not many of us are comfortable with *duplicity*; we expect others to be straightforward and honest.

    Relatives: *duplicitous, duplicitously*
    Synonyms: *double-dealing, hypocrisy*

9. **exigencies** ('ek-sə-jən-sēz, ig-'zij-ən-sēz) pl. n.   The needs or requirements of a given situation; in singular form, any occasion making urgent demands, as *a lifeguard must act quickly in any sudden exigency;* from L. *exigere,* to demand

    The *exigencies* of World War II in England were such that citizens were rationed to 3 ounces of laundry soap and one egg per month.

    Relative: *exigent* (demanding)
    Synonyms: *needs, junctures* (neither exact)

10. **logistics** (lō-'jis-tiks, lə-'jis-tiks) pl. n.   The management of details in any operation or situation; in military life, the administration, management, and ordering of troops, supplies, and facilities; from Gr. *logos*, reason, + *logistikos*, calculation

    Mandy wanted to plan a trip around the United States, but the *logistics* of her excursion seemed daunting.

    Relatives: *logic, logistic, logistician*

11. **ostentation** (ˌäs-tən-ˈtā-shən) n.   Showy, extensive display of wealth, possessions, skills, etc.; from L. *ostentare*, to display excessively

    Modest people deplore *ostentation* because they are embarrassed by any show of material wealth or special skills.

    Relatives: *ostentatious, ostentatiously, ostentatiousness*
    Synonyms: *pretentiousness, showiness*
    Antonyms: *modesty, restraint, humility, reserve*

12. **pertinacity** (ˌpərt-ən-ˈas-ət-ē) n.   The quality of obstinacy, persistence, and determination that makes someone hang on stubbornly, often in the face of great odds; from L. *per + tenere*, cling to

    Anyone who has spent long hours scraping barnacles off a boat understands *pertinacity*.

    Relatives: *pertinacious, pertinaciously*
    Synonyms: *obstinance, stubbornness, tenacity, perseverance*

13. **quisling** (ˈkwiz-liŋ) n.   A traitor who works with invaders in his country, even to the extent of serving in their government (See "Derivation".)

    Once a Norwegian surname, *quisling* has come into the language as a common noun meaning traitor, just as *mesmerize* and *odyssey* were transformed from names of people into common nouns.

    Relative: *quislingism*
    Synonym: *traitor*
    Derivation: As an English word, *quisling* was "born" in 1945 and comes from the Norwegian politician Vidkun Quisling. During World War II he served the Germans who took over Norway and thus earned the scorn of the free world. At war's end he was tried for treason and executed.

14. **rancor** (ˈraŋ-kər) n.   Extreme ill will or bitter feeling, usually deep-rooted; from Late L. *rancor*, rankness

    'Tis not my speeches that you do mislike,
    But 'tis my presence that doth touble ye.
    Rancor will out.
        —Shakespeare, *King Henry the Sixth*, Part II

    Relatives: *rancorous, rancour* (British)
    Synonyms: *enmity, antagonism, hostility, animosity*
    Antonyms: *accord, friendship* (neither exact)

15. **respite** (ˈres-pət) n.   A welcome rest or relief from anything difficult, tiring, or demanding; a reprieve or delay; from L. *respectus*, the act of looking back

    I pray the gods some respite *from the weary task of this long year's watch that lying on the Atreidae's roof on bended arm, doglike, I have kept. . . .*
        —Aeschylus, *Agamemnon*

    Synonyms: *pause, rest, lull*

16. **temerity** (tə-'mer-ət-ē) n.   Extreme, rash boldness beyond what is wise or acceptable; flagrant or foolhardy recklessness; from L. *temere*, randomly, rashly

    When young Oliver asked for "more" at the orphanage meal, he was guilty of *temerity* in the opinion of those who ran the orphanage. (Have you read *Oliver Twist* or seen the musical version? Great story.)

    Relatives: *temerarious, temerariously*
    Synonyms: *effrontery, audacity, chutzpah, rashness, recklessness, nerve, gall*
    Antonyms: *caution, circumspection*

17. **vagaries** ('va-gə-rēz) pl. n.   Unpredictable, whimsical things, ideas, or actions, as *the vagaries of fate*; sing., *vagary*; from L. *vagari*, to wander

    Rather than risk the *vagaries* of a wandering, elderly Newfoundland, our neighbor fenced his yard to confine old Brutus.

    Relatives: *vagarious, vagariously*
    Synonyms: *caprices, whims*

ROOT STUDY

All these roots except **spec, spic,** and **spect** have derived words in List 10. But what would we do without all of our words that refer to *looking*?

1. **LOGOS** means *reason*.

    logic—the science that deals with reasoning and explains a valid (reliable) inference compared with a faulty one
    illogical—not conforming to the principles of sound logic; unreasonable

2. **PLEX, PLIC,** and **PLY** mean *to fold*.

    complex—not simple; involved, complicated; literally, *with folds*
    explicit—precise, exact, clear, straightforward
    multiply—to grow in number; literally, *many fold* (manifold)

3. **SPEC, SPIC,** and **SPECT** mean *to look*.

    spectator—one who looks on (not a participant)
    conspicuous—highly noticeable; outstanding
    inspector—an investigator or examiner who's supposed to notice everything significant
    specimen—sample or example of a kind or type
    perspicacious—keen, shrewd; wisely observant

4. **TEN, TIN, TAIN,** and **TENT** mean *to hold*.

    tenacious—holding on stubbornly, often against great odds; *pertinacious*
    abstinence—refraining from strong drink (or from food, as in a fast); restraint
    retain—to hold back or keep in one place
    contention—belief, opinion "held" in the mind

USING THE WORDS

List 10 Review

ambience	bigot	logistics	rancor	amenities
demeanor	ostentation	respite	anomaly	duplicity
pertinacity	temerity	attrition	exigency	quisling
vagaries	bagatelle			

Exercise I. Synonyms.

From the choices offered, select *two* synonyms for each word in bold type. Write the letters of the synonyms on the appropriate lines.

_____ 1. **vagaries**   (a) whims   (b) chances   (c) trials
                            (d) caprices   (e) opportunities

_____ 2. **rancor**   (a) level   (b) enmity   (c) animosity
                            (d) sergeant   (e) stench

_____ 3. **pertinacity**   (a) appropriateness (b) vivacity   (c) lack of appeal
                            (d) tenacity   (e) perseverance

_____ 4. **duplicity**   (a) multiplication (b) confusion   (c) double-dealing
                            (d) twofold   (e) hypocrisy

_____ 5. **demeanor**   (a) behavior   (b) appearance   (c) lowering
                            (d) nastiness   (e) character

_____ 6. **bagatelle**   (a) tricycle   (b) satchel   (c) trifle
                            (d) trinket   (e) instrument

_____ 7. **perspicacious** (a) keen   (b) thoughtless   (c) shrewd
                            (d) nervous   (e) uneasy

_____ 8. **explicit**   (a) indefinite   (b) precise   (c) lengthy
                            (d) clear   (e) involved

_____ 9. **tenacious**   (a) wary   (b) persistent   (c) timid
                            (d) aware   (e) determined

_____ 10. **ambience**   (a) atmosphere   (b) walkway   (c) thought
                            (d) environment   (e) desire

Exercise II. Antonyms.

Give as many antonyms as you can for these words from List 10.

1. duplicity _____

2. temerity _____

3. rancor _____

4. ostentation _____

5. anomalous (adj.) _____

Exercise III. Fill-Ins.
Select the most appropriate word from the choices given, based on clues in context.

pertinacity	quisling	anomaly	exigency
bigot	ambience	demeanor	attrition
vagaries	respite		

1. the luxurious atmosphere of the Ritz, justifiably known for its _____

2. dismayed by Andy's _____ when he insisted on coming with Jan and me

3. walking with queenly _____ down the aisle

4. in need of _____ from exhausting toil

5. self-righteous, opinionated pronouncements of the neighborhood _____

6. loss of several staff members through _____

7. admirable person who can handle any _____ that arises

8. a(n) _____ who belied his promises

9. didn't want to gamble on the _____ of the spring weather

10. a(n) _____ in our happy midst, conspicuous because of his gloomy expression

Exercise IV. Analogies.
Complete each analogy with the best pair possible.

_____ 1. amenities : desirable ::

  (a) exigencies : admirable
  (b) logistics : understandable
  (c) vagaries : unpredictable
  (d) anomalies : likable
  (e) measles : inevitable

_____ 2. attrition : reduction ::

  (a) ostentation : awareness
  (b) bearing : demeanor
  (c) rancor : station
  (d) quisling : contestant
  (e) spectator : participant

_____ 3. bigoted : tolerant ::

  (a) keen : perspicacious
  (b) duplicitous : two-faced
  (c) logical : plausible
  (d) ostentatious : modest
  (e) foolhardy : reckless

_____ 4. temerity : effrontery ::

  (a) expansion : attrition
  (b) exigency : superfluity
  (c) pertinacity : obstinacy
  (d) respite : continuity
  (e) vagary : rarity

_____ 5. annoyance : rancor ::

  (a) gall : nerve
  (b) logic : reason
  (c) bigotry : prejudice
  (d) amenity : quality
  (e) display : ostentation

(Be careful here. This is a fine distinction.)

Exercise V. In Your Own Words.

Use the given words in sentences that illustrate their meanings. Be as specific as possible.

1. amenities _____

_____

2. anomaly _____

_____

3. logistics _____

_____

4. duplicity _____

_____

5. explicit _____

_____

6. conspicuous _____

_____

7. restrain _____

_____

8. respite _____

_____

Exercise VI. Word Analysis.

1. What *one noun* from List 10 can you use to express the following idea: management of the many details of the operation of a circus (for example, the deployment of circus personnel, the animals, and all equipment; ordering of supplies and foodstuffs for the circus; plus scheduling of performances and transportation from one place to another)?

    _____

    _____

2. This lesson has stressed nouns and the amount of specific information they can convey. For the following common, overused nouns, suggest more specific alternatives.

    a. friend _____

    b. car _____

    c. smell _____

    d. shoes _____

    e. nervousness _____

3. Lesson 10 taught four nouns commonly used in plural form: *amenities, exigencies, logistics,* and *vagaries.* What other, better-known nouns can you think of that always appear in plural form?

    _____

    _____

4. What is the difference between *vagariously* (rarely used) and *vicariously,* which is used a great deal?

    _____

    _____

5. Stones on the seashore or in a rock polisher rub against one another and are worn down, smoothed, and polished through *attrition.* How is this meaning of attrition related to the other meaning of annoyance or harassment?

    _____

    _____

    How is the current, popular usage of attrition (reduction of employee numbers) related to the above uses?

    _____

    _____

6. The roots **plex/plic/ply, spec/spic/spect,** and **ten/tin/tain/tent** are three of the ten special Latin and Greek roots from which we get over 2,500 English words. (Ta da!) How many words can you list that have derived from these three STAR ROOTS?

    _____

    _____

    _____

In Context. Before studying the definitions, try reasoning out the meaning of each word, using context as your guide.

1. Our family enjoys Chinese food, but we always ask the chef not to *adulterate* the fresh meat and vegetables with foreign substances like monosodium glutamate.

   Keys: Partial definition, logic   **Adulterate** means _____.

2. When we *ascertain* which cats are raiding the nest of baby rabbits, we'll put bells on them, but we want to be absolutely certain before we bell any cat.

   Key: Definition   **Ascertain** means _____.

3. We'd like to *conciliate* our neighbors about our cats' behavior, but the neighbors are fonder of birds and young rabbits than they are of cats, so we have little hope of placating them.

   Key: Synonym   **Conciliate** means _____.

4. When no adult was home, Andy *connived* with his friend Billy to make a batch of cookies. In spite of their careful, secret planning, we found out because they spilled flour everywhere.

   Key: Definition   **Connive** means _____.

5. "I can't *discern* any difference in color between the repaired area and the hood," Dad said as he examined the repainted fender.

   Key: Logic   **Discern** means _____.

6. Although Jan and I put bells on Marigold, Poucette, and Figment, we're afraid that we *exacerbated* the problem. Now they stalk their prey so warily that they're more successful hunters than before.

   Key: Logic   **Exacerbate** means _____.

7. "You have only to recognize the nature of cats to be able to *extrapolate* what ours will do now and in the future," Mom said. "Cats are hunters and that's that."

   Key: Logic (Try substituting a
   word you know.)   **Extrapolate** means _____.

8. Fortunately for me, I can *improvise* a talk almost better than I can plan one if I have a week, so I'm not nervous about speaking impromptu.

   Keys: Antonym, synonymous
   phrase   **Improvise** means _____.

9. Mom *inferred* from Andy's cooking messes that he wanted to learn how to cook, and now she's teaching him to be a chef.

    Key: Logic   **Infer** means _____.

10. Since Andy began cooking, we've been *inundated* with cookies, cakes, and pizza—all the foods he loves.

    Key: Logic   **Inundate** means _____.

11. Whenever we see Andy reading, he is *perusing* a cookbook, examining it carefully to see which recipes turn him on.

    Key: Definition   **Peruse** means _____.

12. Andy has discovered the joys of making candy, which *portends* no good for the waistlines and teeth of our family.

    Key: Logic   **Portend** means _____.

13. Proud of his culinary successes, Andy is *promulgating* himself throughout the neighborhood as one of America's best chefs. We're afraid he'll announce that he's giving dinner parties, too.

    Keys: Synonym, logic   **Promulgate** means _____.

14. A handsome ginger tomcat has been pursuing Marigold recently, but so far she has *spurned* all of his advances.

    Key: Logic   **Spurn** means _____.

    (Note how the little word "but" sets up the contrast that follows, altering the direction of the sentence.)

15. Mindful of its promise to be a home for the homeless, America continues to *succor* the less fortunate, offering refuge and assistance to many in need.

    Key: Definition   **Succor** means _____.

16. Marigold appears to have *succumbed* to the blandishments of the ginger tom. Instead of rejecting him, she now strolls with him in our backyard.

    Keys: Antonym, logic   **Succumb** means _____.

17. Journalists who irresponsibly *vilify* citizens may find themselves sued for libel.

    Keys: Synonym, logic   **Vilify** means _____.

WORD STUDY

We turn to *verbs* again, because they are important. They breathe life into your sentences. Also, it is more fun to have a large verb vocabulary. Isn't it more interesting to say that Brent *pigged out* or *gorged* himself at the party rather than saying that he ate a lot?

Each verb has shades of meaning all its own. True synonyms are rare. Dictionaries suggest that *traverse* or *perambulate* or *stroll* may substitute for *walk*, and sometimes they may—but certainly not in all sentences. Always select the verb that most clearly expresses your meaning.

1. **adulterate** (ə-'del-tə-rāt) v.   To render a food or substance impure by adding an inferior or corrupting element to it; to lower or corrupt by the addition of foreign matter; to debase; from L. *ad + alter*, other, else

   Classes about drug abuse warn us that pushers often *adulterate* the drugs they sell with even more dangerous substances.

   Relatives: *adulterator, adulteration*
   Synonyms: *corrupt, debase*
   Antonym: *purify*

2. **ascertain** (as-ər-'tān) v.   To discover or learn with absolute certainty; from L. *ad + certus* (from *cernere*, to sift, decide, discern)

   In order to include that quote, we must *ascertain* who said it so that we can credit it properly.

   Relatives: *ascertainable, ascertainment*
   Synonym: *discover* (not exact)

3. **conciliate** (kən-'sil-ē-āt) v.   To achieve smooth, pleasant relationships by agreeable behavior; to reconcile, appease; from L. *conciliare*, to win over, unite, procure, assemble

   Unable to *conciliate* their captors, the desperate hostages tried to devise a plan for escape.

   Relatives: *conciliation, conciliator, conciliatory, conciliative*
   Synonyms: *appease, pacify, propitiate, mollify, placate*
   Antonyms: *antagonize, oppose*

4. **connive** (kə-'nīv) v.   To conspire, plot, or intrigue secretly; to agree or plan privately; from L. *connivere*, to close the eyes, connive

   When Brutus *connived* with Cassius, the result was the assassination of Julius Caesar.

   Relatives: *connivance, conniver, connivery*
   Synonyms: *intrigue, conspire, collude*

5. **discern** (dis-'ərn) v.   To see, as *he discerned their campfire in the clearing*; to reason, conclude, or detect by more than sight alone, as *she discerned from his behavior that he was exhausted*; to separate one thing/trait/idea from another by careful discrimination, noting differences; from L. *dis*, apart, + *cernere*, to sift

   Through our own recovered innocence we discern *the innocence of our neighbors.*
      —Henry David Thoreau, *Walden*

   Relatives: *discernment, discerner, discernible, discernibly, discerning*
   Synonym: *discriminate*

6. **exacerbate** (ig-'zas-ər-bāt) v.   To worsen or increase in severity, as *a drought always exacerbates a farmer's woes*; from L. *ex* + *acer(bus)*, harsh, bitter, sharp

   Trying to rub away the stain on my car's paint only *exacerbated* the problem, as I rubbed off some of the paint, too.

   Relative: *exacerbation*
   Synonyms: *aggravate, intensify, irritate*
   Antonyms: *alleviate, relieve, allay*

7. **extrapolate** (ik-'strap-ə-lāt) v.   To use previously gathered or known information to formulate new images or ideas, perhaps of the future or an unknown territory; to forecast by using past experience or facts; from L. *ex* + *polate* (from *interpolate*, where *-polate* means polish)

   Based on their training, astronauts are expected to *extrapolate* how they will react physically, mentally, and emotionally to actual travel in space.

   Relatives: *extrapolation, extrapolative, extrapolator*
   Synonym: *deduce* (works sometimes, not always)

8. **improvise** ('im-prə-'vīz) v.   To create or provide by use of whatever is on hand, as *we improvised a bed using pine boughs and a quilt*; to receive or perform impromptu, without rehearsal; from L. *improvisus*, unforeseen

   A tough opponent forced our football team to *improvise* different strategies based on what we learned during the game.

   Relatives: *improvisation, improvisator, improvisatorial, improvisatory, improviser* (or *improvisor*)

   Synonym: *extemporize* (perform impromptu)

9. **infer** (in-'fər) v.   To reach a conclusion or opinion based on facts, experiences, or conditions; to make a logical guess, as *I infer from your recent letter that you are contented*; to hint or suggest, as *a recent survey infers that more women will hold full-time jobs in the future*; from L. *in* + *ferre*, to carry or bear

   Actors playing the role of Shakespeare's Richard III may adopt a crippled posture so that their audience *infers* that Richard was deformed.

   (Note: Many historians refute this concept, as well as the notion that Richard murdered his two nephews in the Tower.)

   Relatives: *inference, inferable, inferrer, inferential, inferentially*
   Synonyms: *deduce, conclude, judge, gather, hint, suggest*

10. **inundate** ('in-[ˌ]ən-ˌdāt) v.   To overflow or overwhelm, washing over in a flood; from L. *in* + *unda*, wave

    The homework for six demanding subjects *inundated* Jerry so that he vowed to schedule a lighter course load next semester.

    Relatives: *inundation, inundator, inundatory*
    Synonyms: *overwhelm, deluge*

11. **peruse** (pə-'rüz) v.   To study thoroughly or examine in a careful, detailed manner; to consider thoughtfully while reading; from L. *per-*, thoroughly, + Middle E. *usen*, to use

    When I peruse *the conquered fame of heroes and the victories of mighty generals, I do not envy the generals.*
          —Walt Whitman, *Leaves of Grass*

     Relatives: *perusal, peruser*
     Synonyms: *study, examine, consider*

12. **portend** (por-'tend) v.   To indicate as a sign or omen of what is to come; to bode, as *those clouds* portend *rain*; from L. *por-*, forward, + *tendere*, to stretch

    These late eclipses in the sun and moon portend no good to us.
          —Shakespeare, *King Lear*

     Relatives: *portent* (omen), *portentous, portentously*
     Synonyms: *foreshadow, bode, forebode, forewarn*

13. **promulgate** ('präm-əl-,gāt) v.   To announce or declare openly, to proclaim; to activate a rule or law; from L. *promulgare*, expose to public view

    Modern teenage literature is realistic. It no longer *promulgates* the idea that ages 12 to 18 are solely years of hilarity and youthful high jinks.

     Relatives: *promulgation, promulgator*
     Synonyms: *declare, proclaim, announce*

14. **spurn** ('spərn) v.   To reject or scorn with contempt; to refuse to accept; from Old High Ger. and OE *spurnan*, to kick

    Fair sir, you spat on me on Wednesday last;
    You spurn'd *me such a day; another time*
    You called me dog; and for these courtesies
    I'll lend you thus much moneys?
          —Shakespeare, *The Merchant of Venice*

     Relative: *spurner*
     Synonyms: *reject, decline, scorn*
     Antonyms: *crave, embrace, hanker for, yearn for, long for*

15. **succor** ('sək-ər) v.   To help in time of need or stress; to aid or relieve; from L. *sub* + *currere*, to run

    The city council decided that it was their duty to *succor* the struggling symphony orchestra through a financial crisis.

     Relatives: *succor* (n.), *succorer*
     Synonyms: *relieve, aid, help*

16. **succumb** (sə-'kəm) v.   To yield to a greater force or give in to a powerful desire or appeal; to give way (as in death) to something overwhelmingly destructive; from L. *sub + cumbere*, to lie down

    When I *succumb* to my yearning for a hot fudge sundae, I have an odd mixture of feelings: delight at the taste mixed with annoyance at my lack of will power.

    Synonym: *yield*
    Antonym: *resist*

17. **vilify** ('vil-ə-fĩ) v.   To defame or malign by strongly negative statements; to slander; from L. *vilis,* of little value, cheap, common

    It is easier to *vilify* an enemy than to create a solution that will ease the enmity.

    Relatives: *vilification, vilifier, vile* (base, contemptible), *vilely, vileness*
    Synonyms: *malign, defame, slander*
    Antonyms: *praise, eulogize*

ROOT STUDY

You will recognize three of these roots, which have derived words in List 11. **Fer** belongs to the Star Roots club (ones that have contributed the most words to English). **Cur** gives us many verbs as well as other frequently used words.

1. **AC/ACR** means *bitter, sharp, sour.*

    acrid—deeply bitter; sharply pungent, as *acrid smoke*
    acute—penetrating, as *acute powers of observation*; sharp or severe, as *acute pain*; needing immediate attention
    acumen—keen mental perception; discernment, shrewdness
    acrimonious—very bitter or caustic in feeling, as *an acrimonious argument*

2. **CUMB** and **CUB** mean *to lie down.*

    incumbent—(n.) one holding an office; (adj.) referring to a duty or obligation (See List 6.)
    incubator—an apparatus in which environment is controlled
    recumbent—resting, leaning, lying down in a relaxed manner, prone
    incubate—to hatch (an egg or an idea); to ponder and develop a concept, answer, or idea

3. **CUR, CURR, CURS,** and **COURSE** mean *to run.*

    recur—to happen again, to *occur* another time
    current—of the present time; timely; (n.) the flow of water, as *a swiftly moving current*
    cursory—hasty, lacking thoroughness
    recourse—a looking to someone (or something) for assistance; the source of help itself, as *the last recourse* (resort) *in our long search*

4. **FER** means *to carry, bear.*

    defer—to postpone, delay; to yield to the wisdom, wishes, or superior position of another
    deference—honor, esteem, or respect due to someone worthy or someone in a superior position
    fertile—able to germinate crops or ideas profitably and well, as *a fertile garden* and *a fertile mind*
    confer—to discuss with another; to consider with someone else

USING THE WORDS

List 11 Review

adulterate	exacerbate	inundate	spurn
ascertain	extrapolate	peruse	succor
conciliate	improvise	portend	succumb
connive	infer	promulgate	vilify
discern			

Exercise I. Synonyms.

The words at the left are synonyms of words taught in Lesson 11. Write the correct study words on the lines. Use the clue letter to jog your memory before looking back at the definitions.

SYNONYM		STUDY WORD
1. conspire	c	_____
2. discriminate	d	_____
3. extemporize	i	_____
4. corrupt	a	_____
5. deduce	e	_____
6. examine	p	_____
7. proclaim	p	_____
8. yield	s	_____
9. aid	s	_____
10. discover	a	_____
11. overwhelm	i	_____
12. foreshadow	p	_____

Exercise II. Antonyms.

The words at the left are antonyms or phrases in contrast to words in List 11. Write the correct study word on the lines.

ANTONYM/CONTRASTING PHRASE	STUDY WORD
1. crave	_____
2. purify	_____
3. alleviate	_____
4. to plan openly	_____
5. antagonize	_____
6. to rehearse or practice repeatedly	_____
7. to review the past	_____
8. eulogize	_____
9. to deny assistance or support	_____
10. resist, stand firm	_____

Exercise III. Switcheroo—*Verbs into Nouns.*
Match the noun forms of Lesson 11 verbs with their meanings.

_____	1. portent	(a) appeasement
_____	2. adulteration	(b) declaration
_____	3. improvisation	(c) discrimination
_____	4. inference	(d) aggravation
_____	5. conciliation	(e) consent to wrongdoing
_____	6. discernment	(f) discovering beyond doubt
_____	7. promulgation	(g) omen
_____	8. succor	(h) deduction
_____	9. connivance	(i) flood
_____	10. vilification	(j) prediction based on past knowledge or experience
_____	11. exacerbation	(k) corruption
_____	12. perusal	(l) relief, help
_____	13. inundation	(m) abuse, defamation
_____	14. ascertainment	(n) spontaneous creation
_____	15. extrapolation	(o) examination

Exercise IV. Analogies.
Complete each analogy with the best pair possible, using words from List 11.

_____ 1. criticism : vilification ::

    (a) discernment : sight
    (b) history : portent
    (c) acumen : perception
    (d) shower : inundation
    (e) succor : concealment

_____ 2. spurn : hanker for ::

    (a) infer : hint
    (b) peruse : study
    (c) alternate : traverse
    (d) promulgate : announce
    (e) exacerbate : relieve

_____ 3. improviser : ingenuity ::

    (a) conciliator : diplomacy
    (b) promulgator : secrecy
    (c) planner : deference
    (d) conniver : publicity
    (e) vilifier : sanity

_____ 4. ascertainment : conclusion ::

    (a) inference : suggestion
    (b) adulteration : invention
    (c) succor : decision
    (d) exacerbation : cure
    (e) perusal : knowledge

_____ 5. discern : differences ::

    (a) peruse : condiments
    (b) infer : conclusions
    (c) defer : positions
    (d) extrapolate : concerns
    (e) portend : worries

Exercise V. Fill-Ins.

Select the most appropriate word from the choices offered, based on clues in context.

deference	defer	acumen	recumbent
cursory	confer	recourse	acrimonious
acrid	incubate		

"I've put your problem into my mental computer," Dad assured me, "but it will have to

_____ awhile before I have a good answer." He stretched out in his
        1

customary _____ position on the couch, and I assumed he was mulling over
          2

my latest worry.

    Minutes later he sat up. "Did you _____ with your teacher about your grade?"
                3

    "Well, sort of. Actually we had a(n) _____ discussion that left both of
                4

us furious. I told him that he'd given my paper only a(n) _____ reading
                  5

instead of reading it carefully. He told me that his mental _____ was
                  6

sufficiently great for him not to have to study every word of a student's paper. Then he said that I

must _____ to his judgment because he was the teacher."
       7

    Dad nodded, "Yes, _____ is due to your instructor, certainly. But you
          8

didn't achieve anything with that sort of discussion. Instead, there's a bad aftertaste, like the

_____ smoke that lingers after a fire."
     9

    Glumly, I nodded agreement. "I guess I have no _____ except talking to
           10

him again."

Dad smiled. "I think you just solved your own problem."

Exercise VI. Word Analysis.

1. The word *infer* is often misused because people confuse it with *imply, intimate,* or *impute.* Using a dictionary, sort out the meanings of these separate verbs and use each correctly in a sentence.

   _____

   _____

   _____

   _____

2. How does a *cursory inspection* of a book differ from *perusal*?

   _____

3. The Latin root *fer* is one of the Star Roots used to form so many English words. Aside from the ones already given, how many words can you list that derive from *fer*?

   _____

   _____

   _____

4. Substitute a few of your new verbs for the everyday words and expressions that follow:

   a. to find out   _____

   b. make up something on the spot   _____

   c. study carefully   _____

   d. to plot secretly   _____

   e. to overwhelm   _____

   f. to reject   _____

   g. to give in or up   _____

   h. to talk with someone else   _____

   i. to put off, postpone   _____

   j. to ruin the purity of something by adding an   _____
      inferior substance

5. A nearly perfect synonym for *exacerbate* is *aggravate* because both share the meaning element of making an already-existing problem worse or increasing its severity. How have *you* heard the word *aggravate* used? Is it being correctly used in everyday speech?

   _____

   _____

6. How does the phrase *coursing with hounds* relate to the root meaning of the word *course*? Is coursing still a popular sport?

_____

_____

7. Using the original prefix and root meanings, can you deduce the current meanings of *defer, refer,* and *confer*? If so, explain.

_____

_____

LIST 12 Mind and Matter
Psychological and Medical Terms

In Context. Before studying the definitions, try reasoning out the meaning of each word, using context as your guide.

1. "I made a super suggestion," Carrie told us, "but you wouldn't believe the *anemia* of their response. No excitement, no vitality, just blah. I don't get it!"

   Keys: Antonyms, colloquial
   synonym   **Anemia** means _____.

2. The neighbors' young collie that we were "puppy-sitting" ate something mildly poisonous. We rushed him to the vet to see if an *antidote* was needed.

   Key: Logic   **Antidote** means _____.

3. "Saccharin's supposed to cause cancer, and repeated suntans are asking for skin cancer. If those are *carcinogens,* how can I ever stay thin and look gorgeous?" Jan moaned.

   Key: Definitive phrases   **Carcinogen** means _____.

4. Exhausted from putting in the boat dock, Dad and I flopped down on the beach. Andy danced around us, pretending we'd had heart attacks yelling, *"Cardiac* arrest! *Cardiac* arrest!"

   Key: Synonym   **Cardiac** means _____.

5. When our old cat, Napoleon, had a terminal case of feline leukemia, we opted for *euthanasia,* reasoning that an easy death was kinder than a long illness.

   Key: Definition   **Euthanasia** means _____.

6. Mom examined Andy's cut daily to be sure that it didn't ooze pus or become inflamed. "If it *festers,*" she told him, "we'll see the doctor."

   Key: Definition   **Fester** means _____.

7. "I just have to smell a charcoal fire," Dad said with a grin, "and the *gastric* juices in my stomach churn in anticipation."

   Keys: Logic, synonym   **Gastric** means _____.

8. "We'll keep an eye on that *lesion,*" Dad said. "A gash of that size in the bark could cause us to lose our favorite maple tree."

   Keys: Near synonym, logic   **Lesion** means _____.

9. "The body's *lymph* system discharges its fluid into the blood through the thoracic duct," our biology teacher explained. "This lymphatic fluid is like blood plasma but normally contains only white blood cells. Lymph nodes trap bacteria to prevent their passage into the blood."

    Key: Definition   **Lymph** means _____.

10. "Andy's concern about these cupcakes is almost *paranoia*," Mom told me. "He's convinced that we're going to eat them all before he's finished his dinner and can have one."

    Key: Logic   **Paranoia** means _____.

11. We have sympathy for a neighbor whose *phobia* about heights prevents him from hiking the local mountains and skiing.

    Key: Logic   **Phobia** means _____.

12. Knowledge of CPR, cardiopulmonary resuscitation, is necessary when you live by a lake. Last summer we had to *resuscitate* a visitor who nearly drowned.

    Key: Logic   **Resuscitate** means _____.

13. "Nothing like a *salutary* swim to make you feel invigorated," Jan announced as she toweled her hair. "I always feel so strong and healthy after swimming across the lake and back."

    Key: Logic   **Salutary** means _____.

14. Aunt Dolly came home from the hospital with a list of *therapeutic* exercises, which she did faithfully to restore muscle tone.

    Keys: Logic, example   **Therapeutic** means _____.

15. In art class Jan studied Greek and Roman sculptured *torsos*, concentrating on the proportions of the body's trunk without the distraction of head, arms, and legs.

    Key: Definition   **Torso** means _____.

16. All of the *toxic* substances in our house have been labeled "Poison" to prevent any disastrous errors.

    Key: Synonym   **Toxic** means _____.

17. The *vascular* system of higher plants is comparable to the human blood vessel system in that both conduct vital body fluids through a series of channels.

    Keys: Definition, example   **Vascular** means _____.

WORD STUDY

Medical science seems to interest more people than any other science. Naturally, we are concerned with our health. Medical programs on TV abound, as do medical books. *Arrowsmith* by Sinclair Lewis, *Dear and Glorious Physician* by Taylor Caldwell, and the Robin Cook novels *Coma* and *Brain* are only a few of the hundreds of popular titles. Stephen King has capitalized on our fascination with the powers of the mind in books like *Firestarter.* Medical movies and psychological thrillers draw millions of viewers.

Obviously, we need to learn the medical lingo—not only for the TV programs, books, and movies but also to communicate intelligently with our own physicians.

1. **anemia** (ə-'nē-mē-ə) n.   A condition resulting from insufficient red blood cells or reduction of hemoglobin content in these cells; a lack of sparkle, verve, or liveliness; from Gr. *anaimia,* bloodlessness

   Anemia may result from iron deficiency, loss of blood, excessive destruction of red corpuscles, or a malfunction of the liver or bone marrow.

   Relatives: *anemic, anemically*
   Synonyms: *dullness, apathy* (second meaning)
   Antonyms: *sparkle, verve, vitality, liveliness* (second meaning)

2. **antidote** ('ant-i-ˌdōt) n.   A counteracting remedy that minimizes or eliminates a poison's effects; anything that behaves as a counteracting force, as *an antidote to the materialism of our time;* from Gr. *anti + didonai,* to give against, to give as a counteragent

   Macbeth asked his doctor:
   Canst thou not minister to a mind diseased,
   Pluck from the memory a rooted sorrow,
   Raze out the written troubles of the brain,
   And with some sweet oblivious antidote
   Cleanse the stuffed bosom of that perilous stuff
   Which weighs upon the heart?
       —Shakespeare

   Relatives: *antidotal, antidotally*

3. **carcinogen** (kär-'sin-ə-jən, 'kärs-ᵊn-ə-ˌjən) n.   Anything that causes cancer (a malignant tumorous disease); from Gr. *karkinos,* cancer, + *gen,* kind, type, cause

   One *carcinogen* currently under heavy attack by doctors and laymen alike is tobacco.

   Relatives: *carcinogenic, carcinogenesis, carcinoid* (usually benign tumor), *carcinoma* (malignant tumor), *carcinomatosis* (multiple tumors developing simultaneously)

4. **cardiac** ('kärd-ē-ˌak) adj.   Referring to the heart or its bodily region or to heart disease; from Gr. *kardia,* heart

   Known as an EKG or ECG, an electrocardiogram is the paper tracing that shows changes of electrical potential during the heartbeat; thus, it is useful for diagnosing *cardiac* abnormalities.

   Relatives: *cardiology, cardiogram, cardiograph, cardiopulmonary* (referring to heart and lungs), *-cardium* (suffix = heart), *cardialgia* (heartburn)

5. **euthanasia** (ˌyü-thə-'nā-zh[ē-]ə) n.   The killing or allowing to die, for merciful reasons, of a person or animal ill or injured beyond hope of recovery; from Gr. *eu,* good or easy, + *thanatos,* death

   Determined not to linger through a hopeless illness, many people have signed living wills, which authorize their *euthanasia* when the doctor agrees that death is preferable to living.

   Relatives: *euthanasic*

6. **fester** ('fes-tər) v.   To form pus or to make inflamed, as *a wound that festers is not healing;* to rankle, irritate, or worry, as *his insult festered in my mind;* from Middle F. *festre* and L. *fistula,* pipe, fistulous ulcer

   Her cruel remark still *festers* in my brain, infecting it with an anger I dare not release.

   Relative: *fester* (n.), an oozing sore
   Synonyms: *rankle, inflame*
   Antonyms: *soothe, alleviate*

7. **gastric** ('gas-trik) adj.   Referring to the stomach; from Gr. *gastr-,* belly

   A man whose *gastric* juices probably did double duty was actor Orson Welles, who confessed, "Gluttony is not a secret vice."

   Relatives: *gastrectomy, gastral, gastrin, gastritis, gastronome* (epicure, gourmet), *gastronomy* (study of fine eating or cooking customs)

8. **lesion** ('lē-zhən) n.   A change (for the worse) in bodily tissue due to injury or disease, especially one clearly defined area of injury like a cut; from L. *laedere,* to injure

   While the dolphin was suspended in a canvas sling, the veterinarian treated two separate *lesions* in the heavy, glistening skin.

9. **lymph** ('lim[p]f) n.   The nearly colorless bodily fluid that bathes tissues, has its own system of channels and ducts, and passes into the blood; from L. *lympha,* water goddess, water

   One indication of infection is enlargement of the *lymph* nodes, as in Hodgkin's disease, which typically progresses to severe anemia.

   Relatives: *lymphatic, lymphocyte, lymphoma* (tumor of lymphoid tissue)

10. **paranoia** (ˌpar-ə-'nȯi-ə) n.   An illogical, persistent feeling of distrust or suspicion of others, the "everybody's out to get me" syndrome; the mental state characterized by delusions of being picked on *or* of being greater than everyone else; from Gr. *paranous,* demented

    A modern song lyric rhymes "may destroy you" with *paranoia,* which certainly is a self-destructive mind-set.

    Relatives: *paranoid, paranoiac*

11. **phobia** ('fō-bē-ə) n.   An extreme fear, usually illogical and inexplicable; from Gr. *phobos,* fear, flight

    Some of the more common *phobias* include *claustrophobia* (fear of enclosed spaces), *acrophobia* (fear of heights), and *agoraphobia* (fear of open, limitless spaces).

    Relatives: *phobic* plus the names of all recognized phobias, as above

12. **resuscitate** (ri-ˈsəs-ə-ˌtāt) v.   To revive or bring back to life (from near death or unconsciousness); to give new life or revitalize; from L. *resuscitare,* to stir up again

    For three years, out of key with his time,
    He strove to resuscitate *the dead art*
    Of poetry; to maintain "the sublime":
    In the old sense.
        —Ezra Pound, *Hugh Selwyn Mauberley*

    Relatives: *resuscitation, resuscitative, resuscitator*
    Synonyms: *revive, revitalize*

13. **salutary** (ˈsal-yə-ˌter-ē) adj.   Having a good effect on health; curative or remedial; from L. *salut,* health

    Taking the dog for a brisk walk is a *salutary* exercise for both human and animal.

    Relatives: *salutarily, salutariness*
    Synonym: *healthful*

14. **therapeutic** (ˌther-ə-ˈpyüt-ik) adj.   Beneficial to recovery from an ailment, disease, or problem, as *hospitals prescribe therapeutic diets for patients with special ailments;* medicinal, curative; from Gr. *therapeuein,* to attend or treat

    "After studying all week, I find a weekend of friends and fun is positively *therapeutic,*" Jan announced.

    Relatives: *therapy, therapist*

15. **torso** (ˈtȯr-[ˌ]sō) n.   The human trunk or main body portion, as in a statue whose head, arms, and legs have been broken off; anything that is minus parts or unfinished, as *the torso of a manuscript;* pl., *torsos* or *torsi;* from L. *thyrsus,* stalk

    Michelangelo's *David,* a larger-than-life sculpture, depicts the *torso* of an ideal man, with head, arms, and legs of equal perfection.

    Synonym: *trunk*

16. **toxic** (ˈtäk-sik) adj.   Poisonous; influenced by a poison or toxin; from L. *toxicum,* poison

    A skull and crossbones label *toxic* substances to warn of their danger.

    Relatives: *toxin, antitoxin, toxicity, toxicant, toxicogenic, toxicological, toxicology, toxicosis, toxemia*
    Synonym: *poisonous*

17. **vascular** (ˈvas-kyə-lər) adj.   Referring to a channel system conveying fluids; the blood of animals and people or the sap of plants; composed of these channels, as *a vascular area;* from L. *vasculum,* small vessel

    Vascular surgery to relieve the problem of varicose veins has become increasingly sophisticated, to the joy of many.

    Relatives: *vascularity, vascularization, vasculature*

ROOT STUDY

All of these roots fit tidily into a lesson about physical and mental health.

1. **CIDE** and **CIS** mean *to cut* or *to kill.*

   incision—a cut, usually made in surgery
   incise—to cut, engrave, or carve
   incisive—clear-cut, biting, crisp, as *an incisive remark*
   homicide—the killing of another person

2. **DERM** means *skin.*

   dermatitis—irritation or disease of the skin
   dermatologist—physician specializing in skin and its diseases
   epidermis—the outer skin layer
   pachyderm—an elephant, rhinoceros, or pig; literally, *thick-skinned*

3. **MANIA** means *craving* or *insanity.*

   maniac—a deranged, demented person; someone wildly enthusiastic about something
   pyromaniac—someone who feels compelled to start fires
   manic-depressive—describing a mental state that varies from wild enthusiasm to deep depression
   megalomania—mental illness characterized by delusions of grandeur and a conviction of great
      personal power

4. **PATH** means *feeling, suffering, disease.*

   pathology—study of the nature of disease
   sympathy—a feeling of pity or concern for another
   empathy—an identical, shared feeling when you know exactly how another feels
   apathy—lack of feeling, indifference

5. **VIRUS** means *poison.*

   virus—the cause of an infectious disease
   virulent—malignant; unusually strong, rapid, or destructive
   viricide—a substance that kills viruses
   virology—scientific study of viruses

USING THE WORDS

List 12 Review

anemia	fester	paranoia	therapeutic
antidote	gastric	phobia	torso
carcinogen	lesion	resuscitate	toxic
cardiac	lymph	salutary	vascular
euthanasia			

Exercise I. Substitution.

Cross out the words in italics and substitute the correct terms from List 12.

1. We had to make a tracing of the human *blood* system for advanced biology class.

2. Has your lifesaving class learned the CPR method of *reviving* an accident victim?

3. Bobbie has a noticeable *fear* of cats; she won't even go near a kitten.

4. I have excellent salve for this *wounded area* on my arm.

5. Tobacco has been implicated as a *cancer-causing agent* in several organs of the body.

6. Physicians are understandably wary, but veterinarians have long practiced *a good death* for hopelessly ill or suffering animals.

7. *Stomach* ulcers tend to flare up in times of stress.

8. Jack's *feeling of persecution* overwhelms him at times, and he sounds quite deranged.

9. We've given up sugar, caffeine, and animal fats. How's that for a *healthful* diet?

10. On the day our neighbor collapsed, he was rushed to the hospital for care by a team of *heart* specialists.

Exercise II. Matching.

From the choices listed below, select the specialist who could best treat or diagnose the symptoms you have. (Note: *Neur* means nerve; *ophthalm* means eye.) These are not the simplest decisions. Ask a friend, teacher, or parent if you need help.

oculist/ophthalmologist	obstetrician	toxicologist
pediatrician	physical therapist	pathologist
internist	neurologist	vascular specialist
psychiatrist	orthodontist	podiatrist/chiropodist
dermatologist	cardiologist	

1. Your baby's on the way. _____

2. You have pains around your heart. _____

3. You drank something out of a bottle decorated with a skull and crossbones.

_____

4. You are continually depressed.

_____

5. You are unable to see distant objects.

_____

6. You have a weird rash on your legs.

_____

7. Mysterious symptoms need diagnosis.

_____

8. You need a vein transplant.

_____

9. Your ingrown toenails are "killing" you.

_____

10. You don't want to be with people anymore.

_____

11. You have recurrent gastric pain.

_____

12. Now that the baby's born, it's colicky.

_____

13. Your muscles are weak from disuse.

_____

14. You suffer from flat feet and aching ankles.

_____

15. Your teeth are crooked.

_____

16. You've had two seizures and fear a brain tumor.

_____

Exercise III. Chart Fill-In.
Add the missing items in the following chart.

	PREFIX	ROOT	WORD	DEFINITION
1.	_____	_____	incision	
2.	_____	path	_____	knowing exactly how someone else feels
3.	hypo-	_____	_____	injection under the skin
4.	_____	didonai	_____	counteracting remedy
5.	_____	_____	fratricide	_____
6.	_____	virus	_____	unusually strong, rapid, or destructive
7.	mega-	_____	_____	delusions of power
8.	_____	_____	euthanasia	_____
9.	re-	_____	_____	to revive, revitalize
10.	_____	toxicum	_____	remedy to counteract a poison

Exercise IV. Antonyms.
Select two antonyms for each word in bold type and write their letters on the appropriate lines.

_____ 1. **indecisive**   (a) incisive   (b) vague   (c) shallow   (d) marginal   (e) clear-cut

_____ 2. **salutary**   (a) worthy   (b) toxic   (c) farewell   (d) harmful   (e) greeting

_____ 3. **fester**   (a) bother   (b) soothe   (c) rankle   (d) slower   (e) alleviate

_____ 4. **anemic**   (a) lackluster   (b) profound   (c) vivacious   (d) sparkling   (e) acidic

_____ 5. **maniacal**   (a) sane   (b) wild   (c) composed   (d) unruly   (e) disturbed

Exercise V. Definitions.
Some words don't have synonyms or antonyms but require explanation instead. If you had to explain the following words to a younger person, what would you say?

1. Anemia _____

   _____

2. Lymph _____

   _____

3. Paranoia _____

   _____

4. Torso _____

   _____

5. Therapeutic _____

   _____

Exercise VI. Word Analysis.
1. What is a *carcinoma?* _____

   _____

2. *Homeopathy*, derived from the root *path,* is an alternative to traditional medical practice. Check your dictionary for a brief explanation of homeopathy. Why might patients abandon the customary medical treatment and seek an alternative? _____

   _____

3. Statistics say that the average man has 2.21 phobias. The average woman is reputed to have 3.55. See how many of the more common phobias you can match correctly.

    _____ a. acrophobia   (1) dreadful fear of thunder

    _____ b. pyrophobia   (2) dreadful fear of confined places

    _____ c. aquaphobia   (3) dreadful fear of lightning

    _____ d. agoraphobia   (4) dreadful fear of fire

    _____ e. claustrophobia   (5) dreadful fear of heights

    _____ f. keraunophobia   (6) dreadful fear of wide-open spaces

    _____ g. astraphobia   (7) dreadful fear of water

4. What is a *salutation?* Does that word have the same root as *salutary?* _____

    _____

    _____

5. Pretend that you're the surgeon who will perform the operations listed below. In each case, tell what organ or part of the body you are removing or operating on. (**-tomy** = *to cut.*)

    a. Tonsillectomy _____

    b. Lobotomy _____

    c. Appendectomy _____

    d. Hysterectomy _____

    e. Gastrectomy _____

    f. Mastectomy _____

6. Remember the root *sang* from List 7? What word is used to mean death through excessive loss of blood?

    _____

7. What is the subject of William Cullen Bryant's famous poem titled "Thanatopsis"? (Check that root against words in this list.)

    _____

8. Match the words at the left with their synonyms or definitions. Remember to use the process of elimination. Do the ones you know first.

_____ a. incision   (1) optimistic, cheerful

_____ b. epidermis   (2) cause of infectious disease

_____ c. kleptomania   (3) division into two parts

_____ d. apathy   (4) science of the nervous system

_____ e. virus   (5) surgical cut

_____ f. dermatitis   (6) lack of feeling or interest

_____ g. virology   (7) compulsion to steal

_____ h. sanguine   (8) irritation or disease of the skin

_____ i. neurology   (9) outer skin layer

_____ j. dichotomy   (10) scientific study of viruses

This lesson reviews the words and roots in Lists 9 through 12, with the hope of planting each one in your mind for all time. As you read over the lists, please pronounce each word out loud. The sound of a word is often an excellent memory aid.

LIST 9	LIST 10	LIST 11	LIST 12
asinine	ambience	adulterate	anemia
bovine	amenities	ascertain	antidote
denizen	anomaly	conciliate	carcinogen
fledgling	attrition	connive	cardiac
fodder	bagatelle	discern	euthanasia
hirsute	bigot	exacerbate	fester
leonine	demeanor	extrapolate	gastric
porcine	duplicity	improvise	lesion
prehensile	exigency	infer	lymph
reptilian	logistics	inundate	paranoia
ruminate	ostentation	peruse	phobia
simian	pertinacity	portend	resuscitate
spoor	quisling	promulgate	salutary
vivisection	rancor	spurn	therapeutic
vixen	respite	succor	torso
whelp	temerity	succumb	toxic
	vagaries	vilify	vascular

ROOTS

AC/ACR	DERM	PATH	TEN/TIN/
CARN	FER	PLEX/PLIC/PLY	TAIN/TENT
CIDE/CIS	LOGOS	SPEC/SPIC/	VIRUS
CUMB/CUB	MANIA	SPECT	VITA/VIV
CUR/CURR/	MUT/MUTAT	TERR/TER	
CURS/COURSE			

USING THE WORDS

Exercise I. Antonyms.
Find an antonym for each word on the left. Write its letter in the space provided.

_____	1. **asinine**	(a)	to welcome
_____	2. **duplicity**	(b)	variable
_____	3. **adulterate**	(c)	honesty
_____	4. **exacerbate**	(d)	hairless
_____	5. **spurn**	(e)	to mollify, appease
_____	6. **whelp**	(f)	alien
_____	7. **hirsute**	(g)	judicious
_____	8. **denizen**	(h)	parent
_____	9. **immutable**	(i)	to antagonize
_____	10. **conciliate**	(j)	to purify

Exercise II. Analogies.
Complete each analogy with the best pair possible. Remember to clarify the given relationship first before you begin hunting the answer.

_____ 1. rumination : idea ::

    (a) exigency : need
    (b) mutation : anomaly
    (c) lesion : wound
    (d) amenities : niceties
    (e) thought : result

_____ 2. whims : vagaries ::

    (a) trinket : bagatelle
    (b) patriot : quisling
    (c) resuscitate : depress
    (d) inundation : waters
    (e) concepts : conclusions

_____ 3. bovine : herbivorous ::

    (a) simian : monkey
    (b) porcine : multifarious
    (c) ovine : omnivorous
    (d) leonine : carnivorous
    (e) masculine : portentous

_____ 4. dismay : phobia ::

    (a) antidote : poison
    (b) exercise : therapy
    (c) anger : conciliation
    (d) behavior : demeanor
    (e) glance : perusal

_____ 5. spoor : pawprint ::
    (a) fledgling : adult
    (b) adder : cobra
    (c) temerity : backtalk
    (d) inference : deduction
    (e) terrier : animal

_____ 6. grain : fodder ::
    (a) nutrition : food
    (b) anemia : illness
    (c) poison : toxin
    (d) vixen : mare
    (e) life : vitality

_____ 7. duplicity : truth ::
    (a) confusion : logic
    (b) succumbing : yielding
    (c) attrition : reduction
    (d) decision : action
    (e) discernment : understanding

Exercise III. Definitions.

Write each word beside its synonym or definition. The first letter is given as a hint.

1. able to grasp well and quickly   p _____
2. operations on live animals for medical or scientific reasons   v _____
3. referring to the blood channel system   v _____
4. the trunk of the body   t _____
5. beneficial to recovery   t _____
6. persistent feeling of distrust or suspicion of others   p _____
7. the bodily fluid that bathes tissues   l _____
8. referring to the heart   c _____
9. the environment of a place   a _____
10. management of details; strategies   l _____
11. to discover with certainty   a _____
12. project into the future using past experience or facts   e _____
13. extemporize, perform impromptu   i _____
14. referring to the stomach   g _____
15. merciful death to relieve incurable pain in hopeless cases   e _____

Exercise IV. Fill-Ins.

Select the most appropriate word from the choices offered, based on clues in context. The word form may need changing.

salutary	lesion	antidote	discern	resuscitate
fester	succor	connive	carcinogen	vilify
promulgate	attrition	succumb	portend	infer

1. "Red sun at night, sailor's delight," is a well-known adage that _____ a fair day on the morrow.

2. Vidkun Quisling _____ with the Germans in their takeover of Norway during World War II, but his treachery earned him a traitor's death.

3. Hoping to provide _____ for the starving in three neighboring African countries, a group of musicians staged a benefit concert that was broadcast worldwide.

4. Last summer, as a(n) _____ to boredom, we tried teaching Andy and his friends to water ski, but that created problems worse than the boredom.

5. "I _____ from all the arguments," Dad commented dryly, "that the water-skiing lessons aren't going too well."

6. Mom said, "Water sports are supposed to be so _____, but our version is not contributing to my mental health."

7. _____ to parental pleading, Jan and I gladly deferred lessons on the water skis until another time.

8. I am always more suspicious of the politician who _____ an opponent than I am of the individual under attack.

9. To please Mom, Carrie tried to _____ a childhood interest in sewing, but her effort was only halfhearted.

10. The larger the company, the more employees it loses through _____ as men and women leave for other jobs, die, or retire.

11. _____ of extreme or weird ideas is one way to gain attention, but it may not be the sort of attention you want.

12. Substances suspect as _____ are under heavy scrutiny in scientific labs because we need to eliminate as many cancer-causing agents as possible from our lives.

13. Examining the _____ on Andy's leg, Mom said that she could _____ no alarming redness or other sign of infection that would prompt a trip to the doctor's office.

14. "If the wound begins to _____ or fails to heal," Mom assured Andy, "we'll certainly see the doctor."

Exercise V. Remembering Roots.

1. The common root in *speculate, despicable,* and *inspector* is _____, meaning _____.

2. *Explicit, complicated,* and *Plexiglas* share the root _____, meaning _____.

3. The shared root in *incisive, incision, homicidal,* and *genocide* is _____, meaning _____.

4. *Occurrence, cursive, cursory, course,* and *current* share the root _____, meaning _____.

5. The common root in *tenacity, abstinence, retain,* and *retention* is _____, meaning _____.

Circle the roots in the following words and write the root meanings on the lines provided.

6. acrid   acrimonious   acumen   _____

7. transfer   defer   confer   _____

8. terrace   terrier   extraterrestrial   _____

9. vitality   vivacious   vivid   _____

10. apathy   pathology   empathy   _____

Exercise VI. Find the Oddball.
In each numbered group of words, select the **one** unrelated word or phrase. Cross out the oddball.

1. pachyderm   skin   hypodermic   needle   dermatitis
2. recumbent   incubate   cumbrous   incumbent   idea
3. maniac   insanity   paranoia   megalomania   thought
4. poison   viricide   virulent   health   toxin
5. mask   opinionated   bigot   Babbitt   hypocrite
6. bearing   taste   demeanor   manner   conduct
7. display   ostentation   showiness   indigence   pretentiousness
8. timorousness   obstinacy   determination   pertinacity   perseverance
9. relief   alteration   rest   respite   pause
10. ill will   enmity   accord   rancor   bitterness

LIST 13 Accentuate the Positive
Words with a Positive Connotation

In Context. Before studying the definitions, try reasoning out the meaning of each word, using context as your guide.

1. The hearty applause of the audience and the congratulations of her classmates are the sort of *adulation* Carrie enjoys each time she performs in a play.

   Keys: Logic, examples   **Adulation** means _____.

2. Our play director is exceptionally *astute* at casting and is known for making the wisest choice possible for each role in the production.

   Key: Definitive phrase   **Astute** means _____.

3. "Everyone's on time, the stage and lighting crews look alert, and the props are in place—an *auspicious* beginning for our first full rehearsal!" exulted the director.

   Key: Logic   **Auspicious** means _____.

4. Carrie shed her customary *blithe* personality and became Marguerite instead, a glum character of woeful countenance.

   Key: Antonyms   **Blithe** means _____.

5. The director cautioned Carrie to remember that she was no longer a *congenial* girl. "As Marguerite, you distrust people and don't like them at all," he said.

   Keys: Opposing idea, logic   **Congenial** means _____.

6. Carrie is anticipating the *exhilaration* she will feel at the end of their first performance. "It's a real high in emotion—like nothing else," she says.

   Key: Definitive phrase   **Exhilaration** means _____.

7. A play critic hopes that his summation of a play will be a *felicitous* remark—the most fitting or apt comment that could have been made about the play.

   Keys: Synonyms, definition   **Felicitous** means _____.

8. As she left for school on the night of dress rehearsal, we could hear Carrie muttering *fervent* prayers to a host of unseen beings, beseeching their help with her performance.

   Key: Logic   **Fervent** means _____.

9. Mom grinned at Carrie's retreating back. "If I didn't know better, I'd swear she pays *homage* to a group of ancient goddesses."

   Keys: Previous sentence, logic   **Homage** means _____.

10. As an actress, Carrie is extremely particular about her costume and makeup. She works until her appearance is impeccable.

    Key: Logic   **Impeccable** means _____.

11. *The Unsinkable Molly Brown* is a musical about an *indomitable* woman whose innate intelligence and good humor made her truly "unsinkable."

    Key: Synonyms   **Indomitable** means _____.

12. A favorite character in the movie *Mary Poppins* is *jocular* Uncle Albert, whose love of laughter and jokes often causes him to float to the ceiling in high spirits.

    Keys: Definition, logic   **Jocular** means _____.

13. It's a good thing that Dad is *placid* by nature. A nervous or irritable father would go crazy in our house with all the commotion.

    Key: Antonyms   **Placid** means _____.

14. In spite of commotion and occasional flare-ups, Dad remains *sanguine*—ever optimistic about the future of his family.

    Key: Definition   **Sanguine** means _____.

15. Balding now, Dad assures us that he was once a suave lady-killer, a debonair man-about-town whom Mom was delighted to capture.

    Keys: Synonyms, logic   **Suave** means _____.

16. "As for your mother," Dad says, "she was a *zany*, unpredictable character who fascinated me the first time I met her. Crazy girl but just right for me."

    Keys: Synonyms, logic   **Zany** means _____.

WORD STUDY

This list is only a tiny sample of the words we use to describe life when everything is going just right. You know many positive words such as *hilarious, ecstasy,* and *joyful.* Others you can deduce from the context or from knowing roots. If someone has made a *magnanimous* gesture that met with approval, you can guess that it was "a good, big gesture," and you'll be correct. You can also suppose that *euphoria* is an "absolutely wonderful feeling" by examining the context and by knowing the prefix **eu-** means "good."

Some words are trickier to puzzle out and may not appear as often as the ones you know well. Instead of using the same old vocabulary, try adding these to your repertoire.

1. **adulation** (ˌaj-ə-ˈlā-shən) n.   Extreme admiration or flattery, sometimes amounting to adoration; from L. *adulari,* to flatter

   People of a shy, retiring nature do not seek the *adulation* of a crowd but prefer to live quiet lives.

      Relatives: *adulate, adulator, adulatory*
   Synonyms: *idolatry, veneration, worship* (none exact)
   Antonyms: *revulsion, repugnance, loathing, abhorrence*

2. **astute** (ə-'st[y]üt) adj.   Wise, perceptive, and shrewd to an acute degree; from L. *astus*, craft, cunning

   Known for his *astute* observations on human nature, Mark Twain is as enjoyable for American readers today as when he began writing in the last century.

   Relatives: *astuteness, astutely*
   Synonyms: *shrewd, discerning, cagey, canny*
   Antonyms: *gullible, credulous, naive*

3. **auspicious** (ȯ-'spish-əs) adj.   Promising good, favorable in outlook, boding success, as *an auspicious beginning;* from L. *auspic-,* diviner by birds (See "Derivation.")

   Being born a turkey is not an *auspicious* start in life, as most turkeys end up on holiday platters.

   Relatives: *auspice* (favorable prophetic sign), *auspiciously, auspiciousness, inauspicious*
   Synonyms: *favorable, promising, propitious*
   Antonyms: *inauspicious, ill-omened*
   Derivation: *Auspicious* derives literally from the Latin *avis* (bird) and *specere* (look at). The ancients depended upon an *auspex* or *augur* to divine the future by careful examination of birds in flight or birds feeding. Nearly everything of importance depended on the augur's report. If the *auspices* were bad, elections could be declared invalid. Likewise, auspices were read before a commander set forth in battle and before any important ceremony, such as marriage.

4. **blithe** ('blīth or 'blīth) adj.   Joyous and lighthearted; casual or careless, as *with blithe disregard;* from OE *blithe,* joyous

   Hail to thee, blithe *spirit!*
   Bird thou never wert,
   That from heaven or near it,
   Pourest thy full heart
   In profuse strains of unpremediatated art.
       —Percy Bysshe Shelley, "To a Skylark"

   Relatives: *blithely, blithesome, bliss* (n., state of joy)
   Synonyms: *merry, cheerful, joyful*
   Antonyms: *morose, downcast, glum, sulky, sullen*

5. **congenial** (kən-'jēn-yəl) adj.   Sharing like tastes, kindred; pleasant, sociable, harmoniously agreeable; from L. *con-* + *genius,* inclination

   To me more dear, congenial *to my heart,*
   One native charm, than all the gloss of art.
       —Oliver Goldsmith, *The Deserted Village*

   Relatives: *congeniality, congenially*
   Synonyms: *consonant, kindred; genial, sociable*
   Antonyms: *uncongenial* (of persons), *abhorrent* (of jobs or required duties)

6. **exhilaration** (ig-ˌzil-ə-ˈrā-shən) n.   The feeling of being cheerful, stimulated, and exceedingly positive in outlook; from L. *ex + hilarare*, to gladden

   As we went ahead of our traditional football rival, the wild *exhilaration* in the stands was audible for several blocks around the school.

   > Relatives: *exhilarate, exhilarating, exhilarative, exhilaratingly, hilarious, hilarity*
   > Synonym: *invigoration*
   > Antonyms: *dullness, deadness, stupefaction*

7. **felicitous** (fi-ˈlis-ət-əs) adj.   Aptly expressed, fitting or well chosen (of remarks); pleasant; from L. *felicitare,* to make happy

   Sometimes, when we're most eager to make a *felicitous* remark, we suffer from the "foot-in-mouth" disease that plagues everyone now and then.

   > Relatives: *felicitate, felicitation, felicitator, felicitously, felicitousness, felicity*
   > Synonyms: *apt, fit, appropriate, delightful, pleasant*
   > Antonyms: *infelicitous, inappropriate*

8. **fervent** (ˈfər-vent) adj.   Showing sincere and heartfelt emotion, impassioned; from L. *fervere,* to boil, glow

   The effectual fervent *prayer of a righteous man availeth much.*
       —*The Holy Bible,* James 5:16

   > Relatives: *fervor, fervently, fervency, fervid, fervidly, fervidness*
   > Synonym: *impassioned*
   > Antonyms: *apathetic, emotionless*

9. **homage** (ˈ[h]äm-ij) n.   Respectful deference as tribute to someone or something deemed worthy; any act of respectful admiration; from L. *homin,* man

   The idea of paying *homage* dates back to feudal days when a man swore allegiance to his lord and was then bound to his service by sacred honor.

   > Relative: *homager* (vassal)
   > Synonym: *honor* (not exact)

10. **impeccable** (ˈim-ˈpek-ə-bəl) adj.   Without fault or blame; free from error or sin; from L. *in + peccare,* to sin

    Confident that he spoke *impeccable* English, Jason moved to London, only to discover that American English was somewhat different from English as spoken in England.

    > Relatives: *impeccability, impeccably, peccadillo* (Sp. *pecadillo,* a small sin, slight offense)
    > Synonyms: *flawless, faultless*
    > Antonyms: *flawed, faulty, imperfect*

11. **indomitable** (in-'däm-ət-ə-bəl) adj.   Unconquerable, dauntless, incapable of being overcome; from L. *in* + *domitare*, to tame or daunt

    I love Vermont because of her hills and valleys, her scenery and invigorating climate, but most of all because of her indomitable *people.*
    —Calvin Coolidge, 1928

    Relatives: *indomitability, indomitableness, indomitably*
    Synonyms: *unconquerable, dauntless*

12. **jocular** ('jäk-yə-lər) adj.   Normally happy, witty, and merry, fond of jesting and joke making; from L. *jocus*, joke

    Len once wanted to be a comedian, but his nature became more serious than *jocular* as he aged.

    Relatives: *jocularity, jocularly, jocose, jocund*
    Synonym: *witty*
    Antonym: *humorless*

13. **placid** ('plas-əd) adj.   Of a peaceful nature, serene, calm, and quiet; from L. *placere*, to please

    I think I could turn and live with the animals,
        they are so placid *and self-contained . . .*
    They do not sweat and whine about their condition . . .
    Not one is dissatisfied, not one is demented
        with the mania of owning things.
        —Walt Whitman, *Leaves of Grass*

    Relatives: *placidity, placidly, placidness, placate*
    Synonyms: *calm, unruffled, serene, quiet*
    Antonyms: *ruffled, choleric, jittery*

14. **sanguine** ('saŋ-gwən) adj.   Optimistic, positive, and confident in outlook; cheerful; from L. *sanguin*, blood

    Around the fourteenth century, four main humors of the body were believed to determine personality: blood, phlegm, choler, and melancholy. In *sanguine* folk, the healthy red blood predominated, giving them their positive, confident outlook on life.

    Relatives: *sanguineness, sanguinely, sanguinity, sangfroid* (equanimity), *sanguinary* (blood-thirsty), *exsanguinate*
    Synonyms: *confident, optimistic*
    Antonyms: *pessimistic, melancholic*

15. **suave** ('swäv) adj.   Smoothly sophisticated and polite in social situations, socially polished or finished (said of men); from L. *suavis*, sweet

    Macavity, Macavity, there's no one like Macavity,
    There never was a Cat of such deceitfulness and suavity.
        —T.S. Eliot, *Old Possum's Book of Practical Cats*

    Relatives: *suavity, suavely, suaveness*
    Synonyms: *urbane, smooth, bland, politic, diplomatic*
    Antonyms: *bluff, boorish, ill-mannered, unrefined*

16. **zany** ('zā-nē) adj.   Wildly, usually humorously, silly or funny; crazy, but likeable; from It. *zanni*, traditional masked clown

    Always a highlight at circuses, the clowns with their *zany* antics amuse both young and old.

      Relatives: *zany* (n., clown or buffoon), *zanily, zaniness*
    Synonyms: *crazy, nonsensical, absurd* (none exact)
    Antonyms: *sensible, sober, practical, logical*

ROOT STUDY

Only one of these roots occurs in List 13. The others are still worth knowing, though. One of them may earn you a correct answer on a test someday. (Remember—not all tests occur in schoolrooms.)

1. **BELL** means *beautiful*.

   belle—a girl popular because of looks and charm
   embellish—to adorn, to decorate
   belles lettres—sophisticated, entertaining literature

2. **BELL** means *war*.

   bellicose—inclined to fight or dispute
   belligerence—an aggressive attitude, prone to argument
   rebellious—hard to manage or discipline, refractory
   postbellum—usually referring to the period following the U.S. Civil War; literally, *after war*

3. **DOC/DOCT** means *to teach*.

   docile—easily taught, managed, or led
   doctrine—teaching or belief
   doctor—originally, one who taught
   document—to furnish with documents or proof (v.); informative writing, official paper (n.)

4. **HOM** means *man, human being*.

   Homo sapiens—the species name of human beings; literally, *wise man*
   homicide—the killing of a human being
   hombre—Eng., fellow, guy; Sp., man
   homburg—man's hat with a firm, curled brim and a high crown with a lengthwise crease

5. **LEV** means *to raise* and *light in weight*.

   levity—humor, lightness of approach (to a subject)
   levitate—to float in air, seemingly defying gravity
   alleviate—to relieve the severity of a condition, as pain or sorrow; to lessen in severity
   elevator—a mechanism that lifts or raises something

USING THE WORDS

List 13 Review

adulation	congenial	homage	placid
astute	exhilaration	impeccable	sanguine
auspicious	felicitous	indomitable	suave
blithe	fervent	jocular	zany

Exercise I. Antonyms.

Select the word or phrase most nearly opposite in meaning to the word in bold type in each question.

_____ 1. **zany**   (a) insane   (b) sober   (c) dull
   (d) wild   (e) sleepy

_____ 2. **impeccable** (a) external   (b) normal   (c) rich
   (d) mistaken   (e) flawed

_____ 3. **blithe**   (a) morose   (b) lengthy   (c) down
   (d) casual   (e) uncaring

_____ 4. **adulation**   (a) reduction   (b) revulsion   (c) praise
   (d) confusion   (e) subtraction

_____ 5. **suave**   (a) cool   (b) uncomfortable   (c) cultured
   (d) boorish   (e) aged

_____ 6. **jocular**   (a) dull   (b) quiet   (c) humorless
   (d) dry   (e) unathletic

_____ 7. **fervent**   (a) apathetic   (b) disorganized   (c) eager
   (d) distraught   (e) peaceable

_____ 8. **felicitous**   (a) well-spoken   (b) ill-timed   (c) ill-bred
   (d) well-endowed   (e) ill-fitting

_____ 9. **astute**   (a) careful   (b) reluctant   (c) eager
   (d) credulous   (e) native

_____ 10. **auspicious**   (a) unimportant   (b) discouraging   (c) vital
   (d) ill-omened   (e) bad

Exercise II. Analogies.

Complete each analogy with the best pair possible, using words from List 13 and Roots.

_____ 1. friend : congenial ::

(a) doctor : medicinal
(b) Daffy Duck : zany
(c) hombre : prompt
(d) enemy : placid
(e) parent : professional

_____ 2. temperament : sanguine ::

(a) water : vital
(b) gaiety : blithe
(c) document : belligerent
(d) writing : belles lettres
(e) chemistry : studious

_____ 3. happiness : exhilaration ::

(a) depression : worry
(b) conviction : determination
(c) panic : fear
(d) naughtiness : rebellion
(e) humor : levity

_____ 4. homage : respectful deference ::

(a) sanguinity : pessimism
(b) calmness : placidity
(c) fervency : lack of passion
(d) levity : noted seriousness
(e) alleviation : exacerbation

_____ 5. fortress : indomitable ::

(a) warrior : bellicose
(b) classroom : cozy
(c) cottage : accessible
(d) guard dog : timorous
(e) office : embellished

Exercise III. The Right Word

From List 13 and Roots select the word that most aptly illustrates the following. The word form may need changing.

1. the girl everyone wants to be with at the ball _____

2. the well-mannered, well-behaved, _____ kid who always sits in the front row in class

3. a Georgia mansion built after the Civil War _____

4. the human species of today _____

5. what your teacher *won't* appreciate in the middle of an angry lecture about late homework

_____

6. what laughter causes Uncle Albert to do in the film *Mary Poppins*

_____

7. the best attitude to have before a test _____

8. the way you want your room to look before a parental inspection tour

_____

9. what you look for in a close friend _____

10. what many rock stars seem to crave _____

11. one word you'd love to have applied to your solution of a tough math problem

_____

12. the feeling you want when you see your test score _____

13. the adjective describing a particularly apt comment _____

14. the honor and respect we give our country _____

15. a _____ plea to be allowed one more hour of sleep on weekend

mornings

Exercise IV. Switcheroo.

The words in this lesson appear in several forms, not just as taught. Match the words at the left with their correct synonyms or definitions.

_____ 1. **inauspicious**   (a) teach with a definite opinion/point of view

_____ 2. **bliss**   (b) merry, jolly

_____ 3. **exhilarate**   (c) boding ill

_____ 4. **indomitably**   (d) adorned, decorated

_____ 5. **jocund**   (e) state of delight

_____ 6. **placidly**   (f) relief

_____ 7. **suavely**   (g) enliven, excite, refresh

_____ 8. **alleviation**   (h) unconquerably

_____ 9. **indoctrinate**   (i) in a polished manner

_____ 10. **embellished**   (j) serenely

Exercise V. Truth or Fiction.

Mark the statements below (**T**) for truth and (**F**) for fiction.

_____ 1. A *homburg* is best kept in the refrigerator.

_____ 2. *Homicide* can refer to killing a woman.

_____ 3. With the proper *leverage* you can lift more than you would think possible.

_____ 4. *Euphonious* music is apt to give you a headache.

_____ 5. A *sanguine* person would be bloodthirsty in battle.

_____ 6. When "the roll is called up yonder," you hope to be found *impeccable* . . . or nearly so.

_____ 7. *Blithe* is an appropriate name for a shy, rather solemn girl.

_____ 8. Misplacing the wedding ring prior to the ceremony will get the day off to an *auspicious* start.

_____ 9. At the funeral of your little brother's gerbil, noticeable *levity* on your part will be comforting.

_____ 10. *Truculence* is a synonym for *belligerence,* and neither is recommended in polite society.

Exercise VI. Word Analysis.

1. Both *bell* (beautiful) and *bell* (war) are spelled the same. How can you distinguish the separate meanings when you are trying to figure out a strange word?

    _____

    _____

2. (a) Words ending in *-or* and *-er* are often persons or at least live beings. Think of *idolator, adulator, professor, performer, dancer,* and so on. How many others can you remember?

    _____

    _____

    (b) In what way can this knowledge of a suffix help you on a verbal test such as the **PSAT, SAT,** or **ACT**?

    _____

    _____

3. (a) *Repugnance* (strong distaste, abhorrence) is the opposite of *adulation* or *admiration.* What does the root in question—**pug, pugn**—mean? (See Webster's handy book.) What or who is a *pugilist?* Is he *pugnacious?* Can *pugnacious* be a synonym for *belligerent* and *truculent?*

    _____

    _____

    _____

    (b) And did the *pug dog* get his name from this root? _____

4. Girls' names have changed considerably over time. To what personalities would you give the names Blithe, Felicity, Faith, Patience, Prudence, and Charity?

    _____

    _____

    _____

    _____

5. When you *placate* someone, what are you doing? _____

6. Just for the heck of it, consider the roots **stupere** and **-fy.** Together they make *stupefy,* which literally means *to make senseless, benumbed,* or *astonished.* What other words come from **stup,** according to Webster?

    _____

    _____

LIST 14 Eliminate the Negative
Words with a Negative Connotation

In Context. Before studying the definitions, try reasoning out the meaning of each word, using the context as your guide.

1. Our family enjoys scary novels; the more grisly the theme or horrifying the outcome, the better we like it, as long as all of the *atrocious* details are pure fiction.

   Keys: Synonyms, logic   **Atrocious** means _____.

2. We don't enjoy the *captious* critic who writes book reviews for our newspaper, because he delights in finding fault with every book that's published.

   Key: Definition   **Captious** means _____.

3. The *choleric* nature of this book critic permeates his work, making us wonder if he's irascible in real life, too, venting his spleen on anyone within range.

   Keys: Synonyms, definition   **Choleric** means _____.

4. Dad agreed with the critic on one book, however, saying that it was an *execrable* piece of work, with the most wretched philosophy of any he'd read in a long time.

   Key: Synonym   **Execrable** means _____.

5. "I hope I wasn't seen returning that book to the library," Dad said. "I slipped it into the return slot in a *furtive* manner and got out of there fast."

   Key: Logic   **Furtive** means _____.

6. Jan took her cue from Dad. "I've had it with *heinous* crimes and ghoulish ideas," she confessed. "Time to read something uplifting and admirable for a change."

   Key: Antonyms   **Heinous** means _____.

7. "I'm with Jan," Mom said. "All that gore is *inimical* to my nature. It's beginning to rub me the wrong way."

   Key: Logic   **Inimical** means _____.

8. The more proficient equestrians laughed at Jan and me, awkwardly astride our horses for the first time. "We must look pretty *ludicrous* to people who've ridden all their lives," I whispered to Jan.

   Key: Logic   **Ludicrous** means _____.

9. I listed all the gruesome things that could happen to us if our mounts bolted, but Jan begged me to spare her the *lurid* details.

   Key: Synonym   **Lurid** means _____.

10. I laughed when Jan accused me of being a *macabre* person who liked to contemplate the most gruesome possibilities.

    Key: Definition   **Macabre** means _____.

11. Pressed to defend myself, I reminded Jan that I really wasn't the *morbid* sort, who brooded about death or gloomy things, but that I believed in being prepared for the worst, especially when riding a horse.

    Key: Partial definition   **Morbid** means _____.

12. "You have a point," Jan admitted. "I'm sure my horse has a *nefarious* plan to scrape me off under a low-hanging branch—or some equally evil idea."

    Key: Synonym   **Nefarious** means _____.

13. As we set off down the horse trail, I could hear Jan's *plaintive* cries behind me as she pleaded with her horse to stay on the path.

    Key: Logic   **Plaintive** means _____.

14. Fortunately, our trail guide wasn't a *pompous* sort, impressed by his own experience or importance, and he gave us a great deal of friendly, useful advice.

    Key: Partial definition   **Pompous** means _____.

15. An intriguing sidelight to our ride was the flood of *scurrilous* talk that poured from the mouth of one of the riders, who apparently knew every obscenity in the book and used them all on his horse.

    Keys: Logic, near-synonym   **Scurrilous** means _____.

16. Jan gestured at the loudmouth and whispered to me. "There goes one of life's more *sordid* characters. He must be the meanest mouth in these here parts, eh, podner?"

    Keys: Logic, synonym   **Sordid** means _____.

17. It is probably *specious* logic to think that everyone who seeks the company of animals will become basically good and innocent like the animals. That idea seems plausible on the surface but lacks proof in real life.

    Keys: Definition, example   **Specious** means _____.

WORD STUDY

An old popular song by Johnny Mercer and Harold Arlen goes, "You've got to accentuate the positive, eliminate the negative, latch on to the affirmative, and don't mess with Mister In-Between." Besides being tuneful, the song expresses an admirable philosophy: We'd all like to eliminate what is negative or depressing from our lives.

But an ever-happy state is elusive, and so our vocabulary abounds with negative words. Some, like *defunct* and *putrid*, give themselves away by sounding utterly negative. Others, like **dis**consolate, **ig**noble, and **in**famous, tell us what they mean with a negative prefix, plus context to point the way to meaning. If someone shows us a picture of a starving child, asking that we note "the pitiful emaciation of the figure," we can deduce that *emaciated* means *physically wasted away*.

The problem is what to do when context gives no clue. The answer is a line you've heard before—*learn more words*.

1. **atrocious** (ə-'trō-shəs) adj.   Absolutely revolting, appalling, or wicked; of extremely low or bad quality, as *atrocious cooking;* from L. *atroc-,* gloomy, atrocious

    One of my brother Andy's most *atrocious* habits is listening in on other people's phone conversations.

    > Relatives: *atrocity, atrociously, atrociousness*
    > Synonyms: *outrageous, barbaric, appalling, revolting, horrifying, abominable*
    > Antonym: *admirable*

2. **captious** ('kap-shəs) adj.   Excessively critical, inclined to object or point out faults; designed to embroil in argument or dispute; from L. *captio,* the act of taking or deceiving

    Snow White could never please her *captious* stepmother, who delighted in finding fault with her.

    > Relatives: *captiously, captiousness*
    > Synonyms: *critical, faultfinding*
    > Antonym: *appreciative*

3. **choleric** ('käl-ə-rik or kə-'ler-ik) adj.   Easily irritated, annoyed, or made angry; hot-tempered, irate; from L. *cholera,* bilious disease

    A reader seldom peruses a book with pleasure until he knows whether the writer of it be . . . of a mild or choleric *disposition, married or a bachelor.*
    —Joseph Addison, *The Spectator*, No. 1

    > Relatives: *choler, cholera* (the disease)
    > Synonyms: *irascible, splenetic*
    > Antonyms: *placid, imperturbable*

4. **execrable** ('ek-si-krə-bəl) adj.   Detestable, evil, thoroughly reprehensible; extremely bad or wretched, as *execrable handwriting;* from L. *ex + sacr-,* sacred

    That execrable *sum of all villanies, commonly called the Slave Trade.*
    —John Wesley, *Journal,* 1772

    > Relatives: *execrate, execrableness, execrably, execrator*
    > Synonyms: *detestable, evil; wretched, foul* (second meaning)
    > Antonyms: *noble, admirable, praiseworthy*

5. **furtive** ('fərt-iv) adj.   Stealthy or sly in manner, hoping not to be discovered, surreptitious; also, stolen, as *furtive goods;* from L. *fur,* thief

Some nocturnal blackness, mothy and warm,
When the hedgehog travels furtively *over the lawn.*
    —Thomas Hardy, *Afterwards*

    Relatives: *furtively, furtiveness*
    Synonyms: *secret, stealthy, surreptitious; stolen* (second meaning)
    Antonyms: *forthright, brazen, straightforward*

6. **heinous** ('hā-nəs) adj.   Outrageously evil or appalling, shocking in the extreme; from Middle F., *haineus,* hateful

A famous rhyme about a double murder (murderer still unknown) accuses the murder victims' own daughter, Lizzie Borden, of a *heinous* crime:

Lizzie Borden took an axe,
And gave her mother forty whacks;
When she saw what she had done,
She gave her father forty-one.
    —Author unknown

    Relatives: *heinously, heinousness*
    Synonyms: *outrageous, abominable, odious, villainous*
    Antonyms: *admirable, praiseworthy*

7. **inimical** (in-'im-i-kəl) adj.   Hostile, as an enemy would be, distinctly unfriendly and uncongenial; adverse or contrary to, as an enemy; from L. *inimicus,* enemy

The *inimical* relationship between neighboring nations like Israel and the Arab countries, or England and Ireland, creates tension worldwide.

    Relative: *inimically*
    Synonyms: *hostile; adverse*
    Antonyms: *friendly, congenial; favorable*

8. **ludicrous** ('lüd-ə-krəs) adj.   Laughable because of oddness, ineptitude, foolishness, or absurdity; deserving of scornful laughter for the same reasons; from L. *ludus,* play or sport

Andy's early attempts at cooking were so *ludicrous* that I'm amazed we didn't discourage him altogether with our laughter.

    Relatives: *ludicrously; ludicrousness*
    Synonyms: *ridiculous, laughable, comical*

9. **lurid** ('lùr-əd) adj.   Arousing horror or undue sensation by being gruesome or revolting; formerly, exceedingly pale in appearance; from L. *luridus,* sallow or pale yellow

Seen in the eerie stage lighting, the phantom's make-up appeared *lurid* and foreboding.

    Relatives: *luridly, luridness*
    Synonyms: *gruesome, sensational*

10. **macabre** (mə-'käb(-rə) or mə-'käb-ər) adj.   Dwelling on death; gruesome or extremely horrible in aspect; from F. *danse macabre,* dance of death

The logical literary predecessor of Stephen King was Edgar Allan Poe, who penned *macabre* short stories.

Derivation: The danse macabre (macaber) was supposed to be danced by all those who were dead and was presided over by Death himself. This allegory on the mortality of mankind was a favorite subject of medieval artists and poets.

What are these paintings on the wall
around us? The danse macaber.
    —H. W. Longfellow, *The Golden Legend*

11. **morbid** ('mȯr-bəd) adj.   Preoccupied with unwholesome, gloomy, or macabre feelings; referring to or typical of disease; causing disease; from L. *morbus,* disease

Not everyone is drawn by *morbid* curiosity to scenes of fire, accident, or disaster.

  Relatives: *morbidity, morbidly, morbidness*
Synonyms: *grisly, gruesome* (neither exact); *diseased*
Antonym: *wholesome*

12. **nefarious** (ni-'far-ē-əs) adj.   Noticeably evil, wicked, or impious; from L. *nefas,* crime

What Hitler tried to disguise with rhetoric was actually a *nefarious* plan to exterminate the Jewish people.

  Relatives: *nefariously, nefariousness*
Synonyms: *vicious, wicked, evil, sinful*
Antonyms: *benevolent, pious, kind, charitable* (none exact)

13. **plaintive** ('plānt-iv) adj.   Revealing misery, woe, or suffering; melancholy or dismal; from L. *plangere,* to beat one's breast or lament

Jan had to sing a brief solo for the holiday concert and, although she began in a *plaintive* treble, she gained true soprano tone and confidence as she sang.

  Relatives: *plaint* (wail, lamentation), *plaintively, plaintiveness, complain, complaint*
Synonyms: *woeful, melancholy, lugubrious* (none exact)
Antonyms: *cheerful, merry, buoyant*

14. **pompous** ('päm-pəs) adj.   Full of self-importance, often arrogant in manner; high-flown or ornate, as *pompous speech or writing;* from L. *pompa,* procession, pomp

I am no lover of pompous title, but only desire that my name may be recorded in a line or two, which shall briefly express my name, my virginity, the years of my reign, the reformation of religion under it, and my preservation of peace.
    —Elizabeth I, discussing her epitaph with her ladies

  Relatives: *pomp, pomposity, pompously, pompousness*
Synonyms: *self-important, pretentious*
Antonyms: *self-effacing, unpretentious, modest*

15. **scurrilous** ('skər-ə-ləs) adj.   Abusive, coarse, or vulgar, as *scurrilous language;* base and evil, as *scurrilous liars;* from L. *scurra,* buffoon

It takes a pretty gullible person to believe the often-*scurrilous* innuendo in the weekly pulp newspapers.

   Relatives: *scurrility, scurrilously, scurrilousness*
Synonyms: *blasphemous, obscene* (neither exact)

16. **sordid** ('sȯrd-əd) adj.   Base, gross, or vile, mean and dishonorable in intent; marked by squalor or wretchedness, as *the sordid village huts;* from L. *sordes,* dirt

The world is too much with us; late and soon,
Getting and spending, we lay waste our powers;
Little we see in Nature that is ours;
We have given our hearts away, a sordid *boon!*
     —William Wordsworth, "The World Is Too Much with Us"

   Relatives: *sordidly, sordidness*
   Synonym: *mean* (meaning low, base, vile)
   Antonyms: *honorable, noble*

17. **specious** ('spē-shəs) adj.   Appearing truthful or genuine on the surface, plausible but false; from L. *speciosus,* beautiful, plausible

To murder thousands takes a specious *name,*
War's glorious art, and gives immortal fame.
     —Edward Young, *Love of Fame* (satire)

   Relatives: *speciosity, speciously, speciousness*
   Synonym: *plausible*

ROOT STUDY

Three of these roots have representatives in List 14. The fourth (**dur**) has not only contributed many words to English but has also lived up to its promise by being *durable* and *lasting.*

1. **CAP, CAPT, CEIVE, CEPT,** and **CIP** mean to *take.*

   captivate—to influence or attract by means of special charm or appeal
   intercept—to take, stop, or interrupt in progress or prior to arrival
   deceive—to give a false appearance, mislead, delude
   anticipate—to foresee or act ahead of time; to expect

2. **DUR** means *hard, lasting.*

   endurance—the capability of lasting a long time, even under stress
   obdurate—firm-minded, stubborn
   duration—the time that something lasts or exists
   duress—restraint through force; threat for the purpose of gaining a desired end

3. **MOR/MORT** means *death*.

   moribund—nearly dead
   mortician—the professional who prepares the dead for burial
   mortal—human *(our mortal failings);* awful or dreadful *(a mortal shame);* fatal *(a mortal wound);* conceivable *(every mortal day);* trying to the spirit or long-lasting *(four mortal hours)*
   mortify—to embarrass severely

4. **SACR** and **SACER** mean *sacred*.

   sacrilege—a serious lack of reverence toward a sacred place, person, or thing; profanation
   desecrate—to profane or defile a holy place, person, memory, or thing
   consecrate—to affirm as sacred, holy; to dedicate to a purpose solemnly

USING THE WORDS

List 14 Review

atrocious	heinous	macabre	pompous
captious	inimical	morbid	scurrilous
choleric	ludicrous	nefarious	sordid
execrable	lurid	plaintive	specious
furtive			

Exercise I. Definitions.

Please review List 14, pronouncing the words out loud, skimming the definitions as a refresher. Then write each word beside its definition or synonym. The first letter for each word is given.

1. overly concerned with gloomy thoughts or grisly details; diseased   **m** _____

2. self-important, arrogant   **p** _____

3. base, low, vile   **s** _____

4. plausible on the surface   **s** _____

5. noticeably evil, shocking, appalling   **h** _____

6. hostile, uncongenial; adverse   **i** _____

7. surreptitious, secretive   **f** _____

8. irascible, splenetic   **c** _____

9. overly critical, fault-finding   **c** _____

10. wretched, exceedingly bad   **a** _____
        e _____

11. laughable, ridiculous   **l** _____

12. woeful, melancholy   **p** _____

Exercise II. Fill-Ins.

Select the most appropriate word from the choices offered for each sentence. Write your choice on the line in each sentence.

1. Revolted by the inclusion of so many _____ details about the crime, I turned off the TV set.

    (a) heinous   (b) pompous   (c) inimical   (d) lurid

2. I read about the spy's _____ plan to infiltrate our foreign service and sell secrets to our enemies.

    (a) captious   (b) atrocious   (c) nefarious   (d) morbid

3. The _____ conditions in many prisons have been the subject of several TV documentaries.

    (a) sordid   (b) scurrilous   (c) macabre   (d) inimical

4. "The Masque of the Red Death" by Edgar Allan Poe has the appropriate setting of a masked ball, to which a particularly _____ figure comes disguised as the Red Death.

    (a) morbid   (b) macabre   (c) ludicrous   (d) choleric

5. With luck you can _____ the phone call so that you hear the information before anyone else does.

    (a) interrupt   (b) intercept   (c) interview   (d) execrate

6. "I've been worried every _____ moment all evening long," she explained. (Refer to Root Study.)

    (a) morbid   (b) putrid   (c) mortal   (d) mortifying

7. He would never admit that, unless he were under extreme _____

    (a) durability   (b) infamy   (c) morbidity   (d) duress

8. She can _____ any boy with her personality, but when you add those homemade chocolate chip cookies—wow!

    (a) endure   (b) consecrate   (c) captivate   (d) anticipate

9. If he weren't so _____, he'd have given in a long time ago.

    (a) obdurate   (b) durable   (c) scurrilous   (d) inimical

10. When the coach promised that strenuous exercise would prevent all colds and illnesses, I suspected that that was an example of _____ reasoning.

    (a) ignoble   (b) specious   (c) sacrilegious   (d) mortal

Exercise III. Antonyms.

Select the word or phrase most nearly opposite to the word in bold type. Write the letter of the antonym you select on the blank provided.

_____ 1. **choleric**   (a) placid   (b) irritable   (c) quiet
                                          (d) healthy   (e) heated

_____ 2. **execrable**   (a) wretched   (b) admirable   (c) well
                                          (d) sanguine   (e) interior

_____ 3. **disconsolate**   (a) emaciated   (b) plaintive   (c) buoyant
                                          (d) introspective   (e) euphonious

_____ 4. **mortal**   (a) unready   (b) untried   (c) not in time
                                          (d) not fatal   (e) inseparable

_____ 5. **specious**   (a) suspect   (b) flawed   (c) positive
                                          (d) uplifting   (e) genuine

_____ 6. **pompous**   (a) direct   (b) pretentious   (c) self-effacing
                                          (d) self-rewarding   (e) optimistic

_____ 7. **plaintive**   (a) whiny   (b) cheerful   (c) unbraided
                                          (d) healthful   (e) forewarned

_____ 8. **furtive**   (a) self-starting   (b) forward-looking   (c) sly
                                          (d) aboveboard   (e) external

_____ 9. **inimical**   (a) congenial   (b) warm   (c) sanguine
                                          (d) fake   (e) comical

_____ 10. **captious**   (a) accepting   (b) creditable   (c) not taken
                                          (d) intercepted   (e) free

Exercise IV. Analogies.

From List 14 and Roots enter the word that best completes the analogy. The first letter of each answer is given as a clue.

1. pollute : waterway :: d _____ : temple

2. slander : scurrilous :: enemy : i _____

3. sacrilege : heinous :: squalor : s _____

4. deed : n _____ :: motion : furtive

5. moribund : sick :: a _____ : misdeed

Exercise V. Matching.

Match each sentence to the noun it best represents. Write the correct letter on each line.

_____	1. **endurance**	(a) I did it in stealth.
_____	2. **mortification**	(b) I solemnly dedicated myself.
_____	3. **furtiveness**	(c) I rarely find anything I like.
_____	4. **morbidity**	(d) He looked so silly I roared with laughter.
_____	5. **consecration**	(e) You can't do anything for me.
_____	6. **ludicrousness**	(f) I reveled in every gruesome detail.
_____	7. **captiousness**	(g) I can withstand anything.
_____	8. **pomposity**	(h) We gasped as he destroyed the icon.
_____	9. **luridness**	(i) I nearly died of embarrassment.
_____	10. **sacrilege**	(j) I'm fascinated by accidents.

Exercise VI. Word Analysis.

1. Can the theft of someone's pencil be considered a *heinous crime?* Explain.

   _____

   _____

2. Laughter comes in many forms. What element is present in *derisive* laughter (e.g., at something ludicrous) that is missing when we laugh at our favorite comedians?

   _____

   _____

3. Your knowledge of negative words is probably greater than you think. Match these frequently used negatives with their definitions. If in doubt, shout for assistance.

_____	a. destitute	(1) utter shame or disgrace
_____	b. dissolute	(2) base, low, contemptible
_____	c. disconsolate	(3) lacking necessary possessions or resources
_____	d. infamous	(4) worn out, useless, dead
_____	e. ignominy	(5) morally loose, unrestrained
_____	f. defunct	(6) unable to be consoled, downcast
_____	g. putrid	(7) foul, rotten, malodorous
_____	h. ignoble	(8) notorious

4. What is the difference between a crime and an *atrocity?*

   _____

   _____

5. What connotation has the word *furtive* that the word *wary* lacks?

   _____

   _____

LIST 15 Test Tubes and Dinosaurs
Terms from Science

In Context. Before studying the definitions, try reasoning out the meaning of each word, using context as your guide.

1. We're always nervous when Aunt Dolly comes to stay because her ideas about teenagers are *antediluvian*. Only Noah and other parents from the time before the Flood share her opinions.

   Keys: Logic, partial definition   **Antediluvian** means _____.

2. "Let's face it," Jan said glumly. "We always think just the opposite of Aunt Dolly. We love her, but our viewpoints are like the North and South Poles—absolute *antipodes*."

   Keys: Logic, example   **Antipodes** means _____.

3. Carrie said that we should form an *axis*—like that of Germany, Italy, and Japan during World War II—as a united front against our aunt. Scornfully Andy replied, "An *axis* is what the earth rotates around!"

   Keys: Examples, logic   **Axis** means _____.

4. The cars on one ride at our amusement park whirl rapidly, pressing the riders in the cars back against their seats by *centrifugal* force. I tried to lean into the center of the car, but the force was stronger than I was.

   Keys: Logic, example, prefix clue   **Centrifugal** means _____.

5. Jan made an oval silver pendant in jewelry class with a slightly *concave* surface. In the hollow, or concavity, she inscribed her initials.

   Key: Synonym   **Concave** means _____.

6. "I don't want you kids in the *doldrums*," Mom said briskly as she prepared to leave on her trip. "You know Aunt Dolly loves cheerfulness, not the blues."

   Keys: Antonym, synonym   **Doldrums** means _____.

7. Someone once advised me to throw out life's *dross* and concentrate instead on what was purely good and true.

   Key: Antonyms   **Dross** means _____.

8. Nuclear *fission*, the splitting of an atomic nucleus that results in the release of large amounts of energy, is not unlike Andy in action.

   Key: Definition   **Fission** means _____.

9. The *fusion* of a tiny silver clasp to the chain Jan made to hold her pendant took only seconds. She dripped a liquid called the "fixer" onto the silver, added a bit of solder, and melted them together in the heat of a bluish flame.

   Keys: Logic, example   **Fusion** means _____.

10. On our trip West, we collected samples of *igneous* rock left by the volcanic eruption of Mount Saint Helens.

    Key: Logic   **Igneous** means _____.

11. After a cross-country race, I succumb to *inertia* and refuse to do anything for a few hours.

    Keys: Logic, partial definition   **Inertia** means _____.

12. Once an acronym meaning "**l**ight **a**mplication by **s**timulated **e**mission of **r**adiation," *laser* is now accepted as a word, like the acronyms "sonar" and "bacitracin."

    Key: Definition   **Laser** means _____.

13. Until astronomers understood *refraction*, the bending of light rays as they pass through the atmosphere, they must have had difficulty placing celestial bodies correctly in space.

    Key: Definition   **Refraction** means _____.

14. At an archaeological dig, Jan and I were shown how each artifact, each tiny *shard* of pottery, is meticulously numbered and located within the site.

    Key: Logic   **Shard** means _____.

15. Under the lab's high-power microscope, we were able to examine plant *spores* responsible for reproduction.

    Key: Logic   **Spore** means _____.

16. "The *velocity* of change in my department makes me wonder if I can keep up," Dad said. "Things are moving fast."

    Key: Logic   **Velocity** means _____.

WORD STUDY

Aristotle could have avoided the mistake of thinking that women have fewer teeth by the simple device of asking Mrs. Aristotle to open her mouth.
   —Bertrand Russell

Science has come a long way since the days of Aristotle. A time traveler from a past century would be agog at what science has created—and what it threatens to destroy if we are not vigilant. Only a few decades ago, science was a comparatively minor subject in America's schools. Today, everyone needs a strong, working vocabulary in several sciences in order to understand what is happening around us.

1. **antediluvian** (ˌant-i-də-ˈlü-vē-ən) adj.   Referring to the time prior to the biblical Flood; antiquated or out of date; from L. *ante* + *diluvium*, deluge

    There was silence supreme! Not a shriek, not a scream,
    Scarcely even a howl or groan,
    As the man they called "Ho!" told his story of woe,
    In an antediluvian *tone.*
       —Lewis Carroll, *The Hunting of the Snark*

      Relative: *antediluvian* (n.)
      Synonym: *antiquated*
      Antonyms: *modern, up-to-date*

2. **antipodes** (an-ˈtip-ə-ˌdēz) pl. n.   Parts of the earth exactly opposite one another; any exact opposites; from Gr. *antipod*, with feet opposite

    Common sense is the very antipodes *of science.*
       —E. B. Titchener, *Systematic Psychology: Prolegomena*

      Relatives: *antipodal, antipodean*

3. **axis** (ˈak-səs) n.   The straight line about which a body such as the earth revolves or is symmetrically arranged; the pivotal neck vertebra; a plant stem; alliance, union, or partnership; (pl. *axes*) from L. *axis*, axle

    The axis *of the earth sticks out visibly through the center of each and every town or city.*
       —Oliver Wendell Holmes, *The Autocrat of the Breakfast Table*

      Relatives: *axial, axially, axillary, axile*
      Synonyms: *partnership, alliance* (last meaning)

4. **centrifugal** (sen-ˈtrif-yə-gəl) adj.   Directed away from an axis or center; employing this force, as *a centrifugal machine*; moving away from centralization, as *a centrifugal culture*; from L. *centre-* + *fugere*, to flee (from the center)

    The centrifuge employs *centrifugal* force to separate substances or different densities, to simulate the effects of gravity, and sometimes, as in a washing machine, to remove moisture.

      Relatives: *centrifuge, centrifugally, centrifugation*
      Synonym: *separatist* (last meaning)

5. **concave** (kän-'kāv, 'kän-kāv) adj.   Resembling the inside of a bowl by being rounded inward, arched or curving inward; from L. *com* + *cavus*, hollow, cave

   Have you not made a universal shout,
   That Tiber trembled underneath her banks,
   To hear the replication of your sounds
   Made in her concave *shores?*
        —Shakespeare, *Julius Caesar*

   > Relatives: *concave* (n.), *concavity*
   > Antonym: *convex* (bulging or rounded outward)

6. **doldrums** ('dol-drəmz, 'däl-drəmz) pl. n.   The blues; also a state of inactivity, listlessness, or collapse; the area near the equator known for its variable winds and squalls alternating with total calm; perhaps from OE *dol*, foolish

   Sailors aboard old-time vessels dreaded the *doldrums*, where a ship could be tossed by squalls or becalmed for days without wind.

   > Synonyms: *blues, slump*
   > Antonyms: *euphoria, sanguinity, cheerfulness* (none exact)

7. **dross** ('dräs, 'dros) n.   The scummy waste occurring on the surface of molten metal; an impurity, a waste product, or foreign matter, like the dregs in the bottom of a bottle of wine; from OE *dros*, dregs

   What men call treasure and the gods call dross.
        —James Russell Lowell, ode recited at Harvard Commemoration, 1865

   > Relative: *drossy*
   > Synonyms: *dregs, impurity*

8. **fission** ('fish-ən, 'fizh-ən) n.   Separation into parts, usually by splitting; the splitting of an atomic nucleus to release large amounts of energy; from L. *findere*, to split

   Although we have recently joined the word nuclear to *fission*, the older meaning of *fission*—the spontaneous splitting of a body into two or more parts, each capable of growing into a complete organism—has been recognized by scientists for years.

   > Relatives: *fissile, fissionable, fissionability, fission* (v.), *fission bomb* (atom bomb)

9. **fusion** ('fyü-zhən) n.   A merging or partnership, a coalition; a joining or union by heat, as in melting; the union of certain atomic nuclei, resulting in the release of vast amounts of energy; from L. *fusus*, poured, melted

   Space scientist Merton E. Davies predicts that by the year 2050, advances in nuclear *fusion* power plants will facilitate inexpensive travel through space in reasonably priced rockets.

   > Relatives: *fusionist, fusible, fusion bomb* (hydrogen bomb)
   > Synonym: *coalition* (first meaning)
   > Antonym: *dissolution* (first meaning)

10. **igneous** ('ig-nē-əs) adj.   Like fire, fiery; referring to a substance formed in great heat, as the magma from volcanoes is *igneous* rock; from L. *ignis*, fire

    In fifth grade science class we studied the three major types of rock: *igneous*, metamorphic, and sedimentary.

    Relatives: *ignite, ignition, ignitron, ignescent*
    Synonym: *fiery*

11. **inertia** (in-'ər-shə) n.   The tendency of a thing not to change but to remain in the state it is in, as of a body to remain in motion or at rest, until acted upon by an external force; inertness; from L. *inert-*, unskilled, idle

    Science has given us the knowledge needed to save our wildlife and our environment, but we must still combat mankind's old enemy: *inertia*.

    Relatives: *inert, inertly, inertness, inertial, inertially*

12. **laser** ('lā-zər) n.   The acronym of **l**ight **a**mplification by **s**timulated **e**mission of **r**adiation; a device that generates electromagnetic radiation in the visible, infrared, or ultraviolet areas of the spectrum

    Writing in the late seventies for *The People's Almanac*, a theoretical physicist named Freeman J. Dyson predicted that we would be able to send vehicles into space on *laser* highways in just a few decades.

    Relative: *lase* (v., back formation from laser)

13. **refraction** (ri-'frak-shən) n.   The supposed "bending" of light that we observe when light or energy waves pass from one medium (such as air) into another (such as water); the correction we must apply to the location of a body (e.g., a planet) because of this deflection from a straight path; from L. *re + frangere*, to break

    Because the lake by our cabin is crystal clear, we often dive for quarters as a game. I can spot the coin from the surface; but *refraction* is confusing, and, once I am underwater, that quarter is never exactly where I thought it would be.

    Relatives: *refract, refractive, refractively, refractiveness, refractivity, refractometer*

14. **shard** ('shärd), also **sherd** n.   A fragment or piece of pottery or (sometimes) shell, as a remnant of a pottery-making civilization; from OE *sceard*, cut, notch

    For heathen heart that puts her trust
    In reeking tube and iron shard,
    All valiant dust that builds on dust,
    And, guarding, calls not Thee to guard,
    For frantic boast and foolish word—
    Thy mercy on Thy People, Lord!
            —Rudyard Kipling, "Recessional"

    Synonym: *potsherd*

15. **spore** ('spō[ə]r) n.   A normally one-celled reproductive or resistant body in plants and some invertebrates capable of developing into a new organism; from L. *spora*, seed, spore

Organisms that produce reproductive *spores* may also reproduce by fission or by budding, whereas the nonreproductive, resistant *spore* is in a resting-cell stage and typically found in bacteria.

   Relatives: *spore* (v.), *sporicide, sporiferous, sporulation*

16. **velocity** (və-'läs-ət-ē) n.   Speed or rapidity of motion; the rate of occurrence, especially when rapid, as *the velocity of architectural change*; also the rate of turnover; from L. *veloc-*, quick

"I don't think Andy needs a bike," Mom observed. "He has a natural *velocity* of his own that hurtles him from place to place."

   Relatives: *velocimeter, velocipede, velodrome*
   Synonyms: *speed, rapidity*

ROOT STUDY

This is a brief collection of roots often used in scientific contexts.

1. **BIO** means *life*.

   biology—the science that studies living organisms and life processes
   biophysics—the study of physical principles as they may be applied to biological problems
   biomedicine—the branch of medicine concerned with human survival in stressful environments
   antibiotic—substance capable of killing or inhibiting a microorganism (used in weak solution so
       as to preserve the host)

2. **FRAG** and **FRACT** mean *to break*.

   fragile—something easily broken
   fragmentation—separation into smaller parts
   refractory—unmanageable, unruly, stubborn
   infraction—a violation or breaking of a law or rule

3. **IGN** and **PYR** mean *fire*.

   ignition—kindling, setting alight
   ignis fatuus—a misleading goal or hope; literally, *foolish fire*
   pyre—any pile to be burned, usually a *funeral pyre*
   pyrite—often called "fool's gold," actually FeS_2, iron disulfide
   pyretic—referring to fever

4. **LAV** and **LU** mean *to wash*.

   lave—to wash, as *he laved his body with the soap*
   lavatory—a place for washing, bathroom
   deluge—a flood; anything washing over someone in excessive amount, such as a deluge of work
   alluvial—referring to sand, silt, gravel, or similar substances deposited by running water

5. **-LOGY/-OLOGY** means *study, discourse.*

anthropology—the study of humankind's development, origin, and civiliations
criminology—the study of criminal behavior and motives
paleontology—the study of fossil remains to learn about life in past geological periods
petrology—the study of rocks and everything about them

USING THE WORDS

List 15 Review

antediluvian	concave	fusion	refraction
antipodes	doldrums	igneous	shard
axis	dross	inertia	spore
centrifugal	fission	laser	velocity

Exercise I. Synonyms.
Write a synonym or brief definition for each word.

1. velocity _____
2. shard _____
3. antediluvian _____
4. concave _____
5. doldrums _____
6. inertia _____
7. dross _____
8. igneous _____
9. fusion _____
10. fission _____

Exercise II. Substitution.
Substitute words learned in List 15 for the words or phrases in italics. Cross out the italics and write the study word above.

1. The *unicellular reproductive bodies* of that mushroom are particularly interesting to examine with a microscope.

2. Leaders of different countries often epitomize *diametric opposites*: One may be informal and congenial, the other, formal and cold in manner.

3. Because of *bending of light*, I know that the North Star is not where it appears to be when seen from Earth.

4. In certain phases of World War II, the *alliance* formed a redoubtable adversary to England and her allies.

5. Our ear, nose, and throat doctor, who calls himself an otolaryngologist, is studying the latest techniques in *electromagnetic radiation* surgery.

6. Although my brain knows that The Mad Spinner at our amusement park will plaster me against its carpeted walls by an irresistible *away-from-the-center* force, my emotions suffer when the floor of the whirling canister drops away.

7. Jan and I totally lost our cool at the archaeological dig when we uncovered a layer of brightly colored *bits of broken pottery* and a partial skeleton.

8. Because of its *natural tendency to remain motionless*, Bill and I had to push with all our strength to get the stalled car rolling toward the curb.

9. The expression "separating the wheat from the chaff" reminds us to sort out what is worthwhile and to leave the *impurities* behind.

10. We were all amazed by the *coalition* of those three different officers into a cohesive unit for class leadership.

Exercise III. Analogies.
Complete each analogy by selecting the best pair possible.

_____ 1. washing machine : centrifuge ::
- (a) doldrums : dregs
- (b) physics : biomedicine
- (c) plant stem : axis
- (d) velocity : change
- (e) cable : twine

_____ 2. biology : life systems ::
- (a) science : facts
- (b) petrology : transportation
- (c) anthropology : humankind's development
- (d) paleontology : apatosaurus
- (e) graphology : law

_____ 3. wine : dregs ::
- (a) metal : dross
- (b) food : cabbage
- (c) liquid : water
- (d) automobile : cart
- (e) orange : fruit

_____ 4. Dark Ages : unenlightened ::
- (a) period : medieval
- (b) time : fleeting
- (c) era : Mesozoic
- (d) tyrannosaurus : antediluvian
- (e) fossil : interred

_____ 5. concave : convex ::
- (a) inner : within
- (b) invigorated : inert
- (c) porcine : obese
- (d) terrestrial : earthly
- (e) refracted : bent

_____ 6. axis : periphery ::
- (a) junction : highway
- (b) animal : fur
- (c) bicycle : transportation
- (d) cell : spore
- (e) tree heart : twig

_____ 7. shower : deluge ::

    (a) velocity : speed
    (b) pause : doldrums
    (c) trickle : drop
    (d) dew : moisture
    (e) linkage : fission

_____ 8. medicine : antibiotic ::

    (a) alluvium : sedimentary
    (b) lavatory : building
    (c) laser : beam
    (d) rock : igneous
    (e) biology : ecology

Exercise IV. Matching.

Match each word on the left with its best synonym or definition.

_____ 1. **infraction**	(a) resistant single cell
_____ 2. **antipodal**	(b) hollow, depression
_____ 3. **fission**	(c) violation
_____ 4. **refraction**	(d) opposite
_____ 5. **spore**	(e) unruly
_____ 6. **petrology**	(f) bending of light
_____ 7. **ignition**	(g) separatist
_____ 8. **refractory**	(h) rapidity
_____ 9. **lave**	(i) splitting into parts
_____ 10. **velocity**	(j) the study of rocks
_____ 11. **concavity**	(k) kindling
_____ 12. **centrifugal**	(l) to wash

Exercise V. Completion.

Select the best word from List 15 and Roots to complete the sentences. (See Root Study for 1–4.)

1. The medical science studying human survival and adaptation in stressful environments is

_____.

2. A good adjective to apply to the detritus left in the streambed of a dried-up creek is

_____.

3. The man next door who studies fossils, who told you all about the pterodactyl, is probably a

_____.

4. The large ceremonial pile that Rajiv Gandhi solemnly lit with a torch was his mother's funeral

_____.

5. Not to be confused with metamorphic rocks, which have undergone change over time, rocks formed by volcanoes are termed _____.

6. Unlike fission, which involves the splitting of atoms, _____ is the union of atomic nuclei to make heavier nuclei, resulting in the creation of huge amounts of energy when certain elements are joined.

7. The vertebra in your neck on which your head pivots is called the

   _____.

8. That period in August when the sun is too hot and there's no beach in sight, when everyone you enjoy is on vacation and you're home alone, can be called the _____.

9. Attending a party that turns into a brawl is usually the very _____ of what you had hoped for.

10. In the movie *Goldfinger*, James Bond lay strapped to a table, perspiring with fear as he watched a beam of light advancing to dissect him. We in the audience assumed that the beam was a

   _____.

Exercise VI. Word Analysis.

1. What is a *velocipede?* A *velodrome?* _____

2. Do you agree with E. B. Titchener that "commonsense is the very antipodes of science?" George Santayana says, "Science is nothing but developed perception, integrated intent, common sense rounded out and minutely articulated." With which comment are you more comfortable and why?

    _____

    _____

    _____

3. One of the newer *-ologies* is *ecology.* What is this science the study of?

    _____

    _____

4. Match some of the better-known *-ologies* with their definitions. Ask someone for help if you run aground, but remember to use elimination as your ally, as well as prefixes.

_____ a. geology	(1) the study of birds
_____ b. criminology	(2) the study of mammals
_____ c. archaeology	(3) the study of the nature and cause of diseases
_____ d. bacteriology	(4) the study of civilizations' artifacts or remains
_____ e. pathology	(5) the study of Earth's history, makeup, etc.
_____ f. virology	(6) the study of crime and criminal behavior
_____ g. mammalogy	(7) the study of the origin and history of words
_____ h. entomology	(8) the study of insects
_____ i. ornithology	(9) the study of viruses
_____ j. etymology	(10) the study of bacteria

    The universe is full of magical things patiently waiting for our wits to grow sharper.
    —Eden Phillpots

LIST 16 Presto, a Bonanza!
Words from Italy and Spain

In Context. Before studying the definitions, try reasoning out the meaning of each word, using context as your guide.

1. When tired of winter, our family gathers for an indoor picnic by the fireplace, but we prefer to eat *alfresco* with the birds and bugs.

   Keys: Logic, antonym   **Alfresco** means _____.

2. Our high school's art show drew not only parents and students but also the local *cognoscenti*, eager to share their expert knowledge with any willing listener.

   Key: Partial definition   **Cognoscenti** means _____.

3. Mom said the art show drew its share of *dilettantes*, too, and she was particularly amused by one of our local dabblers in the arts who repeatedly misused artistic terms.

   Key: Definition   **Dilettante** means _____.

4. Our most outspoken local art critic got into a regular *imbroglio* with a member of the press. They had a complicated and heated dispute that attracted quite a crowd.

   Keys: Logic, partial definition   **Imbroglio** means _____.

5. One of our classmates has spent the last three years adding to his art *portfolio*, which is required for admission to a nearby school of design.

   Key: Logic   **Portfolio** means _____.

6. When the band fails to keep up the tempo of a piece, the whole school can hear our director shouting, "*Presto, presto!* Move it along, for heaven's sake!"

   Key: Logic   **Presto** means _____.

7. After a recent band concert, we were overjoyed at the *salvos* of praise fired our way by the two town newspapers.

   Key: Logic (note the verb)   **Salvo** means _____.

8. "Tone it down," whispered the band director. "This part is like a lullaby and we want it pianissimo, *sotto voce*.

   Key: Synonym   **Sotto voce** means _____.

9. Twain's satire on feuding in the American South featured two families and their bitter *vendetta*, which Huckleberry Finn witnessed in all its horror.

   Key: Synonym   **Vendetta** means _____.

10. Aficionados of bullfights might not appreciate the fictional bull Ferdinand, who preferred to sit quietly and smell the flowers under his cork tree.

    Key: Logic   **Aficionado** means _____.

11. We heard Carrie muttering, "*Bonanza* Steak House—a box office *bonanza*—a regular *bonanza* of gold," and we decided that she was learning the word for a vocabulary test.

    Key: Examples   **Bonanza** means _____.

12. When we first bought our run-down lake property, Mom had visions of a beach *cabana* for guests' use down by the lakeshore. That's pretty funny because the cabin itself is only 40 feet from the lake.

    Key: Logic   **Cabana** means _____.

13. A visiting student from Spain told us that her mother had never been allowed to go on dates alone with her father; a *duenna* had always been their chaperone, according to custom.

    Key: Synonym   **Duenna** means _____.

14. Our Spanish guest referred to a recent upheaval in South America by a group of political plotters that she termed the worst *junta* yet.

    Key: Definition   **Junta** means _____.

15. We asked Dad when we could have some kids over for a party, and he jokingly began humming an old song, "*Mañana, mañana, mañana* is soon enough for me." He broke off to ask, "How do you feel about sometime in the next century?"

    Keys: Logic, example   **Mañana** means _____.

16. Sometimes Jan's *quixotic* nature is at real odds with my down-to-earth realism and practicality, but at least she's never boring to be around.

    Key: Antonyms   **Quixotic** means _____.

17. Probably influenced by our Spanish-speaking neighbors in the Southwest, we named our saw-toothed western mountains the *Sierras*.

    Key: Synonym   **Sierra** means _____.

18. Heat makes us drowsy, but the first two seasons we owned the lake property we had no time for a pleasant afternoon *siesta*.

    Key: Logic   **Siesta** means _____.

WORD STUDY

One of the reasons English is considered to be a rich language is its willingness to adopt words from other languages. Usually we do so because there is no precise English equivalent. Lovers of words love precision. We want to say exactly what we mean. We are particularly happy with an adopted word when it expresses a concept that would take many English words to encompass, like *quixotic* or *salvo*.

Without the healthy, interesting additions from Italian and Spanish cuisine like pasta, spaghetti, pizza, tacos, and enchiladas, we would be lonely and bored at the table. (When you're hungry for pizza or a taco, nothing else will do.) Also, most of our musical terms have come from Italy, home of song. And where did Italian and Spanish come from? *Latin, the major source of our language.*

1. **alfresco** (al-'fres-(ˌ)kō) adj., adv.   Outdoors, in the open air; from It. *al fresco*

   Hiking and mountain climbing take place in the great out-of-doors, but an outdoor picnic or musical entertainment with buildings adjacent is said to be held *alfresco*.

   Synonym: *outdoors*
   Antonym: *indoors*

2. **cognoscenti** (ˌkän-(y)-ə-'shent-ē) pl. n.   Experts or connoisseurs, especially in fashion or the arts; sing., *cognoscente*; from It.

   Mom, who pays little attention to clothing, had to sit through a fashion show surrounded by *cognoscenti*, all keenly interested in the latest feminine attire.

   Synonyms: *connoisseurs, experts*
   Antonyms: *amateurs, tyros, dilettantes, dabblers*

3. **dilettante** ('dil-ə-ˌtänt) n.   Someone who dabbles in the arts (or another field of knowledge) and has a little information but lacks serious commitment; pl., *dilettantes* or *dilettanti*; from It.

   In this strange, terrible world war there is a place for everyone, man and woman, old and young, hale and halt; service in a thousand forms is open. There is no room now for the dilettante, *the weakling, for the shirker, or the sluggard.*
   —Winston Churchill, speech in Canada, December 30, 1941

   Synonyms: *amateur, dabbler, tyro*
   Antonyms: *connoisseur, expert, professional*

4. **imbroglio** (im-'brōl-[ˌ]yō) n.   A complex, often bitter argument or dispute; a complicated situation or entanglement, as in a play or book; pl., *imbroglios*; from It.

   Watching Abbott and Costello or Laurel and Hardy weave their dexterous way through a hilarious *imbroglio* always sends me into gales of laughter. (Rent these oldies for fun sometime.)

   Synonym: *embroilment* (off the mark)

5. **portfolio** (pōrt-'fō-lē-ˌō) n.   A loosely fastened case for carrying pictures, papers, artwork, etc.; the duties of a cabinet member or state official; securities, as *his stock portfolio* (meaning his investments in stocks or bonds); from It.

   Dad gave Andy five shares of stock in a growing company as an encouragement to begin saving. He had no idea that Andy would mention his stock *portfolio* whenever the opportunity arose.

6. **presto** ('pres-(,)tō) adv., adj.   Right away, quickly; in music, at a rapid tempo; from It.

   To the Duchess of Shrewsbury, a foreigner to the English language, the satirist Jonathan Swift was *Presto*, which meant the same thing as far as she was concerned.

   Relatives: *prestissimo* (music, faster than presto), *presto* (n., musical passage, movement)
   Synonyms: *quick(ly)*, *rapid(ly)*
   Antonyms: *slow(ly)*; (music) *lento, andante*

7. **salvo** ('sal-[,]vō) n.   The shooting of guns, either in fighting or as a salute; the firing of a number of pieces (weapons) in rapid succession; any salute in tribute to an achievement, as *they welcomed the salvo of praise from the* Daily Tribune; a spontaneous and sudden burst, as *surprised by the salvos of the excited fans;* from It.

   Unnerved by repeated *salvos* from the enemy's bunker, the new recruit perspired heavily.

   Relatives: *salvo* (v.), *salve!* (hail!)

8. **sotto voce** (,sät-ō-'vō-chē) adv., adj.   Whispered or in a soft undertone, usually in a private way; in music, very softly, pianissimo; literally, *under the voice;* from It.

   Andy asked me *sotto voce* if Mom had said anything about his little before-dinner snack that had polished off the last of the brownies.

   Antonyms: (music) *forte* (loud), *fortissimo* (very loud)

9. **vendetta** (ven-'det-ə) n.   A lengthy blood feud, typically marked by revenge; from It., *revenge*

   The idea behind a *vendetta* is that the nearest kin of a murdered man is obligated to kill the murderer—a self-perpetuating vicious circle prevailing in Sicilian, Corsican, Druse, and Arab societies.

   Synonym: *blood feud*

10. **aficionado** (ə-'fish-[ē]-ə'näd-[,]ō) n.   Fan, anyone keenly devoted to something, as *an aficionado of wrestling;* from Sp.

    No one in our family is more attached to our VCR than Carrie, a true *aficionada* of old movies.

    Relative: *aficionada* (feminine)
    Synonym: *devotee*

11. **bonanza** (bə-'nan-zə) n.   A great amount, as *a bonanza of attention;* something financially rewarding or valuable, as *a show-biz bonanza;* an unusually large vein of gold or silver ore; literally, *fair weather;* from Sp.

    America's fondness for the chocolate chip cookie has been a *bonanza* for cookie-baking entrepreneurs.

    Synonym: *gold mine* (colloquial)

12. **cabana** (kə-'ban-[y]-ə) n.   A small shelter by a pool, lake, or sea, with one open side usually facing the water; a rather tiny, not too substantial, live-in cabin; literally, *hut;* from Sp.

    Movie scenes of the 1920s depict girls clothed in voluminous swim costumes emerging shyly and self-consciously from beach *cabanas.*

     Relative: *cabin*

13. **duenna** (d[y]ü-'en-ə) n.   An older female chaperone, companion, or governess for younger women in Spanish and Portuguese families; chaperone (or chaperon); from Sp. *dueña*

    There is no duenna *so rigidly prudent and inexorably decorous as a superannuated coquette.*
     —Washington Irving, "Spectre Bridegroom"

14. **junta** ('hün-tə, 'jənt-ə) n.   A political faction or group of plotters (pl., juntas); from Sp.

    One historically famous *junta* consisting of Russell, Somers, Montagu, and others exercised enormous influence over the English nation during the reign of William III.

     Relative: *junto* (group with a common purpose)

15. **mañana** (mən-'yän-ə) n., adv.   Some unspecified time in the future; literally, *tomorrow;* from Sp.

    My friend Juan Carlos replies, "Oh, *mañana,*" if I ask him when he will finish a job, but this casualness is only a mask for his serious attitude about work.

16. **quixotic** (kwik-'sät-ik) adj.   Idealistic, lacking practicality; noble or lofty in motive, yet unrealistic; from Sp. literature

    Cervantes's novel, *Don Quixote,* a satire on the chivalric romances of the Middle Ages, gave us the word *quixotic* from its hero and marked the end of knight-errantry.

     Relatives: *quixotically, Quixote* (n.), *quixotical, quixotism*
     Derivation: In the Cervantes novel, Don Quixote was a lovable, idealistic, impractical, rather ridiculous older man who imagined himself a knight. Sancho Panza was his faithful companion and Dulcinea was his sweetheart. *Man of La Mancha* is the musical based on this book, and both works contrast idealism with reality. A quixotic scheme is noble in purpose but impossible to realize.

17. **sierra** (sē-'er-ə) n.   A range of saw-toothed or jagged mountains; the area near a sierra; literally, *saw;* from Sp.

    I should be judged as a captain who went from Spain to the Indies to conquer a people numerous and warlike, whose manners and religion are very different from ours, who live in sierras *and mountains, without fixed settlements . . .*
     —Christopher Columbus, letter, 1500

     Relatives: *Sierra* (code word for letter S), *sierran*

18. **siesta** (sē-'es-tə) n.   A rest or nap in the afternoon; literally, *sixth hour;* from Sp.

    Mad dogs and Englishmen go out in the mid-day sun;
    The Japanese don't care to, the Chinese wouldn't dare to;
    Hindus and Argentines sleep firmly from twelve to one,
    But Englishmen detest a siesta.
     —Noël Coward, *Mad Dogs and Englishmen*

ROOT STUDY

This tiny group of roots has contributed hundreds of words to our language. (**Duc** and **fac** are two of the Star Roots mentioned earlier.)

1. **CAPIT** means *head.*

    capital—punishable by death, as *a capital crime*
    　　　—uppercase (refers to a letter of the alphabet)
    　　　—of major importance or influence
    　　　—excellent, fine, as *a capital idea*
    　　　—major city or site, the seat of government of a state or country
    　　　—money stake or accumulated goods
    recapitulate—to summarize, repeat the main points
    decapitate—to cut off the head

2. **COGN** means *to know.*

    recognize—to realize as known
    　　　—to acknowledge, as *he was recognized for his part in the play with a special award*
    cognition—known through awareness and judgment
    cognizant—aware, informed
    incognito—with identity concealed
    connoisseur—expert, cognoscente

3. **DUC/DUCT** means *to lead.*

    ductile—malleable, easily molded or led
    inductive—leading on, referring to logical induction, as in *inductive reasoning*
    traduce—to betray or violate by lying or deliberate misrepresentation; also, to malign, defame
    abduct—to take or lead away, usually by force

4. **FAC, FECT, FIC, FICT,** and **-FY** mean *to do, make, create.*

    factitious—produced by special effort or artificial means, as *a factitious demand for the product created by advertising*, sham
    affect—to make a difference, influence
    artificial—not genuine; false or imitative
    factotum—servant with diverse duties, skills
    fiction—something created, as a story
    magnify—to make larger, increase in size

USING THE WORDS

List 16 Review

alfresco	presto	bonanza	mañana
cognoscenti	salvo	cabana	quixotic
dilettante	sotto voce	duenna	sierra
imbroglio	vendetta	junta	siesta
portfolio	aficionado		

Exercise I. Fill-Ins.
Select the best word for each phrase from the choices given.

cabana	salvo	siesta	portfolio
imbroglio	sotto voce	presto	bonanza
quixotic	mañana	vendetta	sierra

1. a beach _____ complete with shower and dressing rooms

2. caterwauling that interrupted my afternoon _____

3. "... on the double, I mean _____!" hollered Dad

4. papers bulging out the sides of her dilapidated _____

5. various utopias, each a _____ yearning for perfection

6. Hatfields—9, McCoys—10: score in a famous _____

7. *Peter Rabbit*, a _____ for author Beatrix Potter

8. don't want to be involved in an embarrassing _____

9. in _____ country, where the peaks cast long shadows

10. might mention that _____, but certainly not now

11. the resounding _____ fired over the hero's casket

12. hinted, _____, that we keep quiet about it

Exercise II. Synonyms and Definitions.
Choose the two lettered answers that best define or clarify each word in bold type.

_____ 1. **alfresco**   (a) wall mural   (b) outdoors   (c) in the open air
    (d) under the trees   (e) new soft drink

_____ 2. **junta**   (a) coalition with a definite purpose   (b) administrative body   (c) plotters
    (d) casual get-together   (e) political party

_____ 3. **dilettante**   (a) loser   (b) idler   (c) dabbler
    (d) one lacking commitment   (e) a devotee

_____ 4. **aficionado**   (a) friend   (b) fan   (c) swain
    (d) devotee   (e) partner

_____ 5. **duenna**   (a) wife   (b) relative   (c) chaperone
    (d) companion   (e) buddy

_____ 6. **cognoscenti**   (a) experts   (b) persons learning an art   (c) critics
    (d) connoisseurs   (e) persons versed in diplomacy

_____ 7. **capital**   (a) okay   (b) outstanding   (c) of major importance
    (d) building   (e) insignificant

_____ 8. **ductile**   (a) referring to pipes   (b) easily molded   (c) referring to reason
    (d) concerning water   (e) malleable

_____ 9. **factitious**   (a) sham   (b) genuine   (c) artificial
    (d) hypocritical   (e) handmade

_____ 10. **imbroglio**   (a) Italian umbrella   (b) pasta dish   (c) embroilment
    (d) broiling instructions   (e) hostile, confusing argument

Exercise III. Logic.
Enter the word from List 16 that fits best with each of the following comments.

_____ 1. "There'll be no stolen kisses while *I'm* around."

_____ 2. "I'm gonna get him. He wasted my brudder!"

_____ 3. "I just love art, don't you? I mean, being around artists is so thrilling. They're such interesting people, and I feel so interesting myself when I hang out with them."

_____ 4. "I've seen every Paul Newman film ever made. Did you know he has an apartment in New York and a house in Westport? I have the labels from his marinara sauce and his salad dressing on my bulletin board."

_____ 5. "I think that if we all decided to be really nice to each other, no matter what, all our problems would go away."

Exercise IV. Contrasting Ideas.

Match the antonyms or contrasting ideas. Take your time. Fill in answers by remembering what a word does *not* represent as well as what it does.

_____	1. **alfresco**	(a) meager amount
_____	2. **cognoscenti**	(b) yesterday
_____	3. **sotto voce**	(c) mansion
_____	4. **presto**	(d) reduce
_____	5. **bonanza**	(e) desert
_____	6. **cabana**	(f) tyros
_____	7. **junta**	(g) single shot
_____	8. **mañana**	(h) fortissimo
_____	9. **sierra**	(i) indoors
_____	10. **cognizant**	(j) introduce
_____	11. **recapitulate**	(k) fact
_____	12. **traduce**	(l) andante
_____	13. **fiction**	(m) entire political party
_____	14. **magnify**	(n) honor, praise
_____	15. **salvo**	(o) unaware

Exercise V. Logic.

Answer the questions using common sense and logic. Your answers may differ from your neighbor's.

1. For whom would a leather portfolio be a handsome present?

   _____

2. Why might a Latin American require a siesta while Noël Coward's Englishmen "detest a siesta"?

   _____

3. Why are the words *mountain* and *sierra* not exactly interchangeable?

   _____

4. What sort of person is the antithesis of a quixotic soul?

   _____

5. What major change in social attitudes spelled the doom of the formal duenna?

   _____

6. Where, and in what form, does our society continue to endorse the "duenna concept"?

   _____

7. Why is a vendetta appropriately described as a vicious circle?

    _____

8. How does the altercation termed an *imbroglio* differ from an ordinary argument?

    _____

9. What old Christian ethic, still highly respected, does the dilettante flout?

    _____

10. Why might your father or mother say, "Without the general office factotum, our business would fall apart?"

    _____

Exercise VI. Word Analysis.

1. With the help of a dictionary, explain the difference between *junto* and *junta*.

    _____

    _____

    _____

2. The Spanish word *pecadillo*, respelled as *peccadillo*, has full acceptance in the English language and appears in our dictionaries just as do the other words in this lesson. Do you remember (from a few lessons back) what it means?

    _____

3. We have only to read a quote from a "classic" author like Washington Irving to notice the wealth of vocabulary he had and expected his readers to have. Rephrase Irving's quote (under no. 13, *duenna*) in current language.

    _____

    _____

4. *Deductive reasoning* is somewhat different from *inductive reasoning*. Try to explain both (with the aid of dictionary definitions) so that you see the difference between them.

    _____

    _____

    _____

    _____

This lesson reviews the words and roots in Lists 13–16. As you read over each word, try to remember a synonym or definition. Forgotten any? Recheck, fixing each in your mind before you begin the review exercises.

LIST 13	LIST 14	LIST 15	LIST 16
adulation	atrocious	antediluvian	aficionado
astute	captious	antipodes	alfresco
auspicious	choleric	axis	bonanza
blithe	execrable	centrifugal	cabana
congenial	furtive	concave	cognoscenti
exhilaration	heinous	doldrums	dilettante
felicitous	inimical	dross	duenna
fervent	ludicrous	fission	imbroglio
homage	lurid	fusion	junta
impeccable	macabre	igneous	mañana
indomitable	morbid	inertia	portfolio
jocular	nefarious	laser	presto
placid	plaintive	refraction	quixotic
sanguine	pompous	shard	salvo
suave	scurrilous	spore	sierra
zany	sordid	velocity	siesta
	specious		sotto voce
			vendetta

ROOTS

BELL	DUC/DUCT	LAV, LU
BIO	DUR	LEV
CAP, CAPT, CEIVE, CEPT, CIP	FAC, FECT, FIC, FICT, -FY	-LOGY/-OLOGY
CAPIT	FRAG/FRACT	MOR/MORT
COGN	HOM	PYR
DOC/DOCT	IGN	SACR/SACER

USING THE WORDS

Exercise I. Analogies.
Complete each analogy with the best pair possible.

_____ 1. connoisseur : dilettante ::

    (a) neighbors : antipodes
    (b) fight : imbroglio
    (c) splitting : fission
    (d) blues : doldrums
    (e) impeccable : neat

_____ 2. sanguine : exhilarated ::

    (a) discerning : astute
    (b) choleric : testy
    (c) satisfied : pompous
    (d) adulation : scorn
    (e) silent : furtive

_____ 3. sluggish : inert ::

    (a) axis : pivot
    (b) alfresco : indoors
    (c) fission : fusion
    (d) bad : heinous
    (e) gold mine : bonanza

_____ 4. presto : music ::

    (a) unusual : salvo
    (b) indomitable : spirit
    (c) zany : star
    (d) congenial : friendship
    (e) rushing : current

_____ 5. saleswoman : portfolio ::

    (a) professional : code
    (b) lawyer : client
    (c) desperado : crime
    (d) writer : instrument
    (e) aficionado : scrapbook

_____ 6. plaintive : sentence ::

    (a) nefarious : ideal
    (b) morbid : outlook
    (c) disinterested : homage
    (d) auspicious : value
    (e) lurid : menu

_____ 7. shard : pottery ::

    (a) ethic : doctrine
    (b) metal : dross
    (c) concavity : hollow
    (d) fragment : portion
    (e) atrocity : disease

_____ 8. sophistication : suavity ::

    (a) chaperone : duenna
    (b) beam : sight
    (c) peace : captiousness
    (d) junto : party
    (e) naiveté : knowledge

_____ 9. stance : ludicrous ::

    (a) action : delicious
    (b) attitude : inimical
    (c) velocity : repetitive
    (d) behavior : sotto voce
    (e) belief : blithe

_____ 10. cognoscente : respect ::

    (a) doctor : understanding
    (b) amateur : admiration
    (c) professor : felicitations
    (d) murderer : execration
    (e) expert : compassion

Exercise II. Chart Fill-In.

Add the missing items in the chart. If you get stuck, refer to the Root Study sections for Lists 13–16.

	PREFIX	**ROOT**	**WORD**	**MEANING**
1.	_____	bell	_____	to adorn, decorate
2.	_____	_____	rebellious	_____
3.	in-	doc	_____	to teach beliefs
4.	_____	lev	_____	to relieve, lessen
5.	_____	cip	_____	to foresee, expect
6.	_____	_____	obdurate	_____
7.	im-	_____	_____	living forever
8.	de-	sacr	_____	to profane, defile
9.	_____	bio	_____	medication to kill or inhibit microorganisms
10.	re-	fract	_____	stubborn, unruly
11.	_____	_____	reignite	_____
12.	petr-	ology	_____	_____
13.	_____	lu	_____	a flood
14.	_____	_____	recapitulate	_____
15.	tra-	_____	_____	to betray or malign

Exercise III. Affect and Effect.
Although both *affect* and *effect* come from the same root, their meanings are quite different. Because these words are often confused or misused, they are worth some time and thought.

Remember that **affect** means *to influence, to make a difference to,* or *to assume as a pretense.* **Effect** means to *cause to happen, to bring about*—or *the result,* when used as a noun. Using the correct form of *affect* or *effect,* fill in the blanks in the following sentences.

1. Rainy weather _____ my temperament, and I may become moody and quiet.

2. The prisoner _____ his escape from jail by disguising himself in order to slip past the guards.

3. We know some of the _____ of acid rain, and we may be doomed to learn others.

4. For her part in the play, Carrie _____ the halting gait of a deranged old woman.

5. Mom hopes that Carrie can use her dramatic talents to good _____ in college drama productions.

6. _____ to be exhausted from homework, Jan pulled a pillow over her head and hoped no one would ask her to do anything around the house.

7. One _____ of the chemistry experiment was the creation of a new compound.

8. Having _____ a cure for the animal's disease, the veterinarian sent his detailed results to a scientific journal.

Exercise IV. Antonyms.

Select the lettered word or phrase most nearly opposite in meaning to the word in bold type.

_____ 1. **induce**
(a) return   (b) distress   (c) recite
(d) discourage   (e) uphold

_____ 2. **quixotic**
(a) stable   (b) practical   (c) thoughtful
(d) kind   (e) unrealistic

_____ 3. **vendetta**
(a) disbelief   (b) acceptance   (c) incorporation
(d) imbroglio   (e) accord

_____ 4. **antediluvian**
(a) postwar   (b) predated   (c) foresight
(d) antisocial   (e) current

_____ 5. **furtive**
(a) open   (b) inner   (c) noteworthy
(d) frequent   (e) loud

_____ 6. **macabre**
(a) morose and   (b) religious and   (c) cheerful and
    downcast   uplifting   jocular
(d) zany and   (e) regular and
    ludicrous   accepted

_____ 7. **scurrilous**
(a) fair   (b) noble   (c) caring
(d) acceptable   (e) valuable

_____ 8. **honorable**
(a) lurid   (b) inimical   (c) sordid
(d) choleric   (e) captious

_____ 9. **specious**
(a) above suspicion   (b) under the table   (c) beneath contempt
(d) from the heart   (e) beside the point

_____ 10. **apathetic**
(a) lazy   (b) fervent   (c) blissful
(d) placid   (e) astute

_____ 11. **centrifugal**
(a) in opposite   (b) toward   (c) with little motion
    directions   separation
(d) toward a center   (e) tending to
                         disperse

_____ 12. **agitated**
(a) withdrawn   (b) involved   (c) auspicious
(d) placid   (e) congenial

Exercise V. Story Fill-In.

Select the best word for each blank in the following story. The word form may need changing.

auspicious	nefarious	shard	pompous
impeccable	velocity	sanguine	felicitous
choleric	fusion	inimical	placid

A CAT TALE

Marigold's entrance into our household had a most _____ beginning. As

1
a young cat, she touched our hearts with her pathetic "meow." Cats know that a judicious meow is as
effective for a feline as any _____ remark for a human. We were too naive as

2
pet owners to suspect Marigold of any _____ motives. At first, her behavior

3
was _____, absolutely above reproach, and our viewpoint on pets in general

4
became _____ in the extreme. "I cannot believe that other people have so

5
much trouble with their pets," Dad would declare rather_____, as if no more

6
need be said on the subject.

Marigold thrived under our care, gaining weight at a rapid pace. This weight transformed itself
into six kittens overnight, or so it seemed. On that same night, Dad developed an

_____ attitude toward pet owning and eyed Marigold askance. Moreover, our

7
cat's once-_____ temperament became _____, and

8   9
she nipped us testily if we tried to inspect her litter.

Still, the rest of us banded together—a familial type of _____—to

10
defend poor Marigold and her babies. As the kittens grew, they needed our defense, for they rocketed
through the house with remarkable _____ and agility. One day we saw Mom

11
sadly picking up the _____ of her favorite pot, knocked off the counter in an

12
exuberant kitten spree. Of the kittens, we kept Poucette and Figment, who have taught us more about
pets than we needed to know.

Exercise VI. Substitution.

Replace each italicized phrase with the most appropriate word from the following list. Write your selections above the italicized phrases.

cabana	spore	captious	ludicrous
fission	siesta	homage	zany
execrable	salvo	mañana	exhilarating
indomitable	plaintive	dilettante	fusion

1. I am always disturbed by the *woeful, unhappy* sounds of animals in the Rescue League shelter.

2. One of the best weekends of my life was spent in a run-down *hut by the beach* in Florida, where two guys and I camped out.

3. We asked one boy if we could borrow his surfboard. He waved, hollered, "Sure, *in a little while,*" and began paddling out to sea again, which made us think that we'd never see that surfboard.

4. None of us had ever surfed, so I suppose we looked *pretty silly* the first time we tried; but we didn't care what people thought.

5. Bob made breakfast the first morning on the beach, but his food was the most *wretched and disgusting* stuff I'd ever seen or eaten.

6. A good cook, I decided, deserves all the *respectful deference* in the world from those who gather at the table.

7. Our mom's no *dabbler* in the art of cuisine; she often spends hours trying out new recipes or bettering old ones.

8. Unfortunately, Andy's hard to please, and Mom often gets annoyed by his *nitpicky, negative* criticism at mealtime.

9. One night when it was Jan's turn to cook dinner, she served *a crazy, off-the-wall* meal composed of foods that everybody liked but that didn't blend well together.

10. Dad didn't criticize Jan's meal but rubbed his stomach in an odd manner and said, "I think I'll just lie down for a *little nap.*"

11. Jan got Dad's subtle message, but with her customary *dauntless* spirit, she quoted old Ben Franklin: "Experience keeps a dear school, but fools will learn in no other." She grinned. "I guess I was the fool, but it certainly was *exciting for the mind and spirit* fixing that meal!"

12. Carrie's earth science class held a formal three-way debate on energy sources, one team favoring development of *the splitting of atomic nuclei,* one championing *the union of certain atomic nuclei,* and one promoting the use of fossil fuels.

13. My cousin, a botany major in his sophomore year, told me that he had spent a long time isolating one group of *reproductive cells* in order to make an acceptable slide.

14. Each cry of "¡Olé!" from the crowd, each *salute in tribute* of admiration, must be music to the ears of a matador.

LIST 17 Pardon the Pun
More Words About Language and Speech

In Context. Before studying the definitions, try reasoning out the meaning of each word, using context as your guide.

1. Ben Franklin was a natural with *aphorisms.* He sprinkled the pages of *Poor Richard's Almanac* with many adages, such as *Three may keep a secret, if two of them are dead.*

   Keys: Synonym, example   **Aphorism** means _____.

2. One of Dad's former bosses, despised for his *bombast,* has taken his pompous, inflated style to another company.

   Key: Definition   **Bombast** means _____.

3. Eyeing the essay lying face down on my desk, the teacher pointed to it and asked, "Should I *construe* that as a finished piece of work?"

   Key: Logic   **Construe** means _____.

4. "All ayes and no nays?" the principal asked our committee. "Good. Since no one wishes to *dissent* on this issue, we can present a united front."

   Keys: Contrasting phrase, logic   **Dissent** means _____.

5. "Her answer was a trifle *glib* to suit me," Mom explained. "I don't think she had thought about the matter at all. I've always distrusted a slick response like that."

   Key: Definition   **Glib** means _____.

6. The exaggeration of comedians like Helen Hunt or Eddie Murphy may be dismissed as *hyperbole,* but their humor is often close to truth.

   Key: Synonym   **Hyperbole** means _____.

7. "She insinuated that I was out to get her boyfriend," Jan fumed. "You wouldn't have believed the *innuendo!* One nasty hint right after the other, so I just left."

   Keys: Definition, logic   **Innuendo** means _____.

8. Jan and I had great hopes for the lecture on Mark Twain, but the speaker *prated* on at such length, chattering about whatever came to mind, that we left after half an hour.

   Key: Synonym   **Prate** means _____.

9. Once I asked Granddad, who's addicted to *puns,* to explain what wise meant. He said, "It means a kid's question—like 'Wise the night dark?' 'Wise the moon white?' "

   Key: Example   **Pun** means _____.

10. Aunt Dolly, never one to be *reticent,* talked at great length about her newest discovery.

    Key: Contrasting phrase   **Reticent** means _____.

11. "Just so much empty *rhetoric,*" Dad said disgustedly as he tossed the paper on the floor. "You can't disguise lack of knowledge with a bunch of fancy words."

    Keys: Logic, partial definition   **Rhetoric** means _____.

12. Although Huck Finn's speech is filled with *solecisms,* such as "I seen him" or "He knowed what was comin'," I enjoy what he has to say and how he says it.

    Key: Examples   **Solecism** means _____.

13. Carrie practiced so long on her *soliloquy* for the play—giving that lengthy, reflective speech a dozen different interpretations—that we weren't sure we ever wanted to hear it again.

    Key: Definition   **Soliloquy** means _____.

14. The sideshow barkers at a circus have developed such compelling *spiels* that I am lured in by their extravagant promises in spite of myself.

    Key: Logic   **Spiel** means _____.

15. Just once, instead of her usual garrulousness, I would like to get a *terse* reply from Aunt Dolly.

    Key: Contrasting phrase   **Terse** means _____.

16. It's impossible to ignore Marigold, Poucette, and Figment at dinnertime, when their *vociferous* meows can be heard throughout the house.

    Key: Logic   **Vociferous** means _____.

WORD STUDY

Language is the light of the mind.
—John Stuart Mill

You know the old adage, *The pen is mightier than the sword.* In other words, language has tremendous power. Nearly everything you do is influenced by your use of language or someone else's. According to the experts, about 90 percent (or more) of college study depends on reading comprehension. Many jobs are similarly dependent on reading and writing skills. Ideally, your proficient use of words will someday win you the career you want. Ask any person now in midcareer about the importance of language and accurate communication, and you're apt to hear an impassioned speech.

Even if it is extremely difficult for you, you need to master English grammar and as much vocabulary as possible. *Your language will shape your life.*

1. **aphorism** ('af-ə-ˌriz-əm) n.   A pithy saying that expresses an acknowledged truth or shared feeling; from Gr. *aphorismos,* definition, aphorism

   An aphorism *is never exactly truthful. It is either a half-truth or a truth and a half.*
       —Karl Kraus, *Aphorisms and More Aphorisms*

   Relatives: *aphorist, aphoristic, aphoristically, aphorize*
   Synonyms: *adage, saying*

2. **bombast** ('bäm-ˌbast) n.   Pompous, high-flown, pretentious writing or speech; from L. *bombac-,* cotton, especially cotton-wool used for padding

   . . . He [Shakespeare] is many times flat, insipid; his comic wit degenerating into clenches, his serious swelling into bombast. *But he is always great, when some occasion is presented to him.*
       —John Dryden, *Essay of Dramatic Poesy*

   Relatives: *bombastic, bombaster, bombastically*
   Synonyms: *pomposity, grandiloquence, lucubration, fustian*

3. **construe** (kən-'strü) v.   To interpret or understand the intention of, as *he construed my attitude as favorable;* to analyze the construction of a sentence, especially when translating; from L. *construere,* to construct

   I take the official oath to-day with no mental reservations, and with no purpose to construe *the Constitution or laws by any hypercritical rules.*
       —Abraham Lincoln, First Inaugural Address

   Relative: *construe* (n., piecemeal translation)
   Synonyms: *interpret, understand, infer*

4. **dissent** (dis-'ent) v.   To hold a different opinion, to differ, disagree.   n. A difference of opinion; from L. *dis* + *sentire,* to feel

   We must learn to welcome and not to fear the voices of dissent. *We must dare to think about "unthinkable things" because when things become unthinkable, thinking stops and action becomes mindless.*
       —James W. Fulbright, speech in the Senate, 1964

   Relatives: *dissenter, dissension, dissentient*
   Synonyms: v., *differ, disagree* (n.), *disagreement, difference*
   Antonyms: v., *assent, accord, agree* (n.), *agreement, accordance*

5. **glib** ('glib) adj.   Easily fluent in speech or writing, often slick and superficial; revealing lack of serious thought, as *a glib reply to my important question;* probably from Low Ger., *glibberig,* slippery

   I want that glib *and oily art,*
   To speak and purpose not.
       —Shakespeare, *King Lear*

   Relatives: *glibly, glibness*
   Synonyms: *slick, superficial*
   Antonyms: *thoughtful, considered* (of responses, opinions)

6. **hyperbole** (hī-'pər-bə-[ˌ]lē) n.   Extremely exaggerated speech or writing; from Gr. *hyper* + *ballein,* to throw

   Although the word *hyperbole* may have predated the person, a man named Hyperbolus (far-throwing) lived in Athens around the fourth century B.C. and was known for his colorfully exaggerated figures of speech.

   Relatives: *hyperbolist, hyperbolic, hyperbolically*
   Antonym: *understatement*

7. **innuendo** (ˌin-yə-'wen-[ˌ]dō) n.   An indirect hint or unpleasant insinuation about someone's reputation or character; a veiled, unflattering comment; in law, the person nodded at or indirectly referred to; pl., innuendos or innuendoes; from L. *in* + *nuere,* to nod

   Political campaign speeches can feature obvious mud-slinging or the subtler *innuendo,* both designed to put an opponent on the defensive.

   Synonym: *insinuation*

8. **prate** ('prāt) v.   To chatter, usually at length and to little purpose; from Middle Du., *praten,* to prate, akin to prattle

   . . . Thou sure and firm-set earth,
   Hear not my steps, which way they walk, for fear
   The very stones prate *of my whereabout. . . .*
       —Shakespeare, *Macbeth*

   Relatives: *prate* (n.), *prater, pratingly, prattle*
   Synonyms: *chatter, babble, prattle*

9. **pun** ('pən) n.   The humorous or unusual use of a word or words to suggest a new/different meaning; from It. *puntiglio,* fine point, quibble

   Some of my favorite *puns* use names of animals, as "He otter go fishing," "There's pandamonium in the bears' den," and "Ostrich in time saves nine."

   Relative: *pun* (v.)

10. **reticent** ('ret-ə-sənt) adj.   Reserved in speech, tending to be silent; restrained in appearance or manner, as *the hall has an aspect of reticent grandeur;* from L. *re + tacere,* to be silent

    When asked what a minister preaching on sin had said, the *reticent* Calvin Coolidge replied, "He said he was against it."

    Relatives: *reticence, reticency, reticently*
    Synonyms: *silent, reserved, restrained, taciturn, uncommunicative, close-mouthed*
    Antonyms: *garrulous, talkative, voluble, loquacious*

11. **rhetoric** ('ret-ə-rik) n.   Insincere or high-flown writing or speech; originally, the study of effective communication or written composition; from Gr. *rhetorike,* art of oratory

    In his book *On Language*, William Safire reminds us that *rhetoric* once meant "the science of persuasion." Safire regrets the degeneration of this word to its current meaning of empty talk.

    Relatives: *rhetorical, rhetorically, rhetoricalness, rhetorician*
    Synonyms: *grandiloquence, bombast*

12. **solecism** ('säl-ə-,siz-əm) n.   An ungrammatical combination or use of words; also an impropriety in etiquette, decorum; from Gr. *soloikos,* an inhabitant of Soloi

    A writer who is concerned about accuracy may write many a *solecism* as his characters move through the narrative; each character's speech must be distinctive and realistic rather than grammatically perfect.

    Relative: *solecistic*
    Derivation: Soloi was a city in ancient Cilicia (near present-day Syria) inhabited by colonists from Athens. The Athenian Greeks considered the colonists' speech to be corrupt and beneath them. Thus, *solecism* came to refer to an error in grammar or usage.

13. **soliloquy** (sə-'lil-ə-kwē) n.   A typically lengthy speech intended as someone's thoughts or reflections (usually in a play); from L. *solus,* alone, + *loqui,* to speak

    Written in the form of a *soliloquy,* Robert Browning's poem "Soliloquy of the Spanish Cloister" gives the thoughts of a spiteful monk jealous of a fellow monk, whom he tries to lead into sin.

    Relatives: *soliloquist, soliloquize*

14. **spiel** ('spēl[ə]l) n.   A loquacious, well-rehearsed line of talk, as a salesman's pitch; from Ger. *spielen,* to play

    I wanted to buy something from a door-to-door salesman once, but his *spiel* was so long and so obviously full of hyperbole that I turned him away in anger.

    Relatives: *spiel* (v.), *spieler*
    Synonym: *pitch*

15. **terse** ('tərs) adj.   Succinct, pithy, concise, brief (of speech or writing); from L. *tersus,* clean, neat

    Former President Harry Truman could be nicely *terse* at times, willing us at least two pithy sayings worth remembering: *If you can't stand the heat, get out of the kitchen* and *The buck stops here* (sign on his desk).

    Relatives: *tersely, terseness*
    Synonyms: *concise, succinct, pithy*
    Antonyms: *verbose, wordy, prolix*

16. **vociferous** (vō-'sif-[ə]rəs) adj.   Loudly and clamorously insistent; literally, *carrying the voice*; from L. *voc, vox,* voice, + *ferre,* to carry or bear

    It is nearly impossible to ignore the *vociferous* cries of a baby determined to be fed.

    Relatives: *vociferate* (v., to shout), *vociferously, vociferant, vociferation, vociferousness*
    Synonyms: *clamorous, strident*

ROOT STUDY

All of the following roots have contributed mightily to our vocabulary. Notice how many of the derived words refer to language and speech.

1. **LUC** and **LUX** mean *light.*

    lucid—sane, intelligible, as *a lucid argument*
    elucidate—to make clear through explanation
    translucent—allowing light through; genuine and open, as *her translucent charity and goodness*
    lucubration—a pompous expression in writing or speech, often purposely so; also, meditation
    Lucifer—the morning star, Venus; the fallen archangel known as the Devil

2. **PON** and **POS** mean *to place* or *put.*

    posit—to postulate, assume that something exists
    postpone—to delay, put off until another time
    interpose—to insert or place in between; to toss in between parts of a conversation; to intervene
    propose—to set forth an idea

3. **SENS** and **SENT** mean *to feel.*

    sensation—a feeling; sometimes a great amount of feeling, as *her costume created a sensation at the ball*
    sentient—keenly aware/sensitive in feelings or perceptions
    sentiment—an emotion, usually deeply felt
    presentiment—a premonition that something will happen

4. **VOC** and **VOKE** mean *voice* and *to call.*

    vocal—referring to the voice
    vocation—career, job; literally, *one's calling*
    revoke—to call back, annul, rescind
    irrevocable—beyond the point of being called back; unchangeable, irremediable, irreversible
    invoke—to call upon for aid; to solicit or to cause

USING THE WORDS

List 17 Review

aphorism	glib	pun	soliloquy
bombast	hyperbole	reticent	spiel
construe	innuendo	rhetoric	terse
dissent	prate	solecism	vociferous

Exercise I. Identification.

Identify the following examples by writing the most appropriate term from List 17 on each of the lines.

_____ 1. "I seed where he was jittery, so I jest set back and waited."

_____ 2. "What's the opposite of wealth?" "Illth."

_____ 3. "I'm so exhausted I could sleep for a year."

_____ 4. "Children begin by loving their parents. After a time they judge them. Rarely, if ever, do they forgive them."
—Oscar Wilde

_____ 5. "That stranger's been eyeing the jewelry on the counter. Do you think he's contemplating something, perhaps?"

Exercise II. Definitions.

Write the correct word from List 17 beside its definition or synonym.

_____ 1. pompous language

_____ 2. empty talk; literally, *the art of oratory*

_____ 3. loud and clamorous

_____ 4. a pitch or well-rehearsed flow of words

_____ 5. to interpret, understand

_____ 6. succinct, laconic, pithy

_____ 7. to chatter

_____ 8. long, reflective speech

_____ 9. to differ in opinion

_____ 10. silent, withdrawn, uncommunicative

_____ 11. suspiciously fluent

Exercise III. Aphorisms.

You know the following aphorisms, but they have been elaborated upon by someone with *bombastic* tendencies or pretensions to impressive *rhetoric*. How many can you return to their original, uncluttered state by writing the real adage on the lines?

1. Members of an avian species possessing identical plumage congregate. _____

   _____

2. Pulchritude possesses solely epidermal profundity. _____

   _____

3. The stylus possesses more potency than the cutlass. _____

   _____

4. Neophyte's serendipity. _____

   _____

5. Individuals who domicile in vitreous abodes ought to refrain from catapulting petrous missiles.

   _____

6. Ligneous and petrous projectiles can potentially fracture my osseous structure, but pejorative

   appellations will forever remain innocuous. _____

   _____

7. It is bootless to indoctrinate a superannuated member of the canine species with innovative

   artifices. _____

8. Male cadavers refrain from elucidation. _____

   _____

9. A plethora of persons inclined toward culinary excellence vitiate the potable concoction created

   by simmering certain comestibles. _____

   _____

10. A revolving sample of petrous material accumulates no aggregation of bryophytes.

   _____

Exercise IV. Antonyms.
Match words from List 17 and Roots with their antonyms or contrasting phrases.

_____ 1. **assent/consent**

_____ 2. **glib**

_____ 3. **understatement**

_____ 4. **innuendo**

_____ 5. **garrulous**

_____ 6. **terse**

_____ 7. **soft, quiet**

_____ 8. **lucid**

_____ 9. **sentient**

_____ 10. **revoke**

(a) accusation

(b) vociferous

(c) reticent

(d) establish

(e) unintelligible

(f) dull, insensitive

(g) dissent

(h) wordy, verbose

(i) hyperbole

(j) lacking fluency

Exercise V. Analogies.
Complete each analogy with the pair that expresses the same relationship as the beginning pair. Remember to clarify the relationship of the first pair *before* hunting its mate.

_____ 1. construe : gesture ::

(a) designate : building
(b) repeat : pattern
(c) interpret : language
(d) reverse : law
(e) insist : obedience

_____ 2. prate : speak haltingly ::

(a) eat : hurriedly
(b) run : stumble
(c) ask : with confusion
(d) gibber : distractedly
(e) talk : with inflection

_____ 3. play on words : pun ::

(a) satire : tragedy
(b) anecdote : speech
(c) raconteur : guest
(d) playful badinage : discussion
(e) grammatical error : solecism

_____ 4. demagogue : rhetoric ::

(a) politician : analysis
(b) door-to-door salesperson : spiel
(c) lawyer : client
(d) manager : products
(e) minister : parsonage

_____ 5. bombast : lucubration ::

    (a) innuendo : insinuation
    (b) sentiment : warning
    (c) voice : vociferation
    (d) posit : inundation
    (e) problem : elucidation

_____ 6. compassion : Lucifer ::

    (a) understanding : parent
    (b) comfort : hotel
    (c) mortality : deity
    (d) leniency : judge
    (e) affability : host

_____ 7. presentiment : future ::

    (a) hope : dream
    (b) precursor : harbinger
    (c) absent : present
    (d) measurement : time
    (e) review : past

_____ 8. thespian : soliloquy ::

    (a) director : sales
    (b) clerk : records
    (c) minister : invocation
    (d) mother : recreation
    (e) artist : proposition

Exercise VI. Word Analysis.

1. Your vocation is your career or job. What is your _avocation?_ _____

2. When we say that an author's book is _marred by sentimentality,_ what do we mean? (Puzzled? Ask any librarian or knowledgeable friend.) _____
_____

3. The nurse tiptoes out of a patient's room and informs the police that they cannot interview the injured person. "He's not _lucid,_" she says. What does she mean? _____
_____

4. A flood of words derive from the root **pon/pos.** How many can you list?
_____
_____
_____
_____

5. What is a _rhetorical question?_ _____
_____

6. Create your own high-flown aphorisms from the following:

   a. Silence is golden. (Hint: Use a word in List 17's definitions to begin this one.)

   _____

   b. Talk is cheap. (Guess what? You can begin this one with a word from List 17, too.)

   _____

   c. Never put off until tomorrow what you can do today.

   _____

7. Far from being the lowest form of humor, a well-made pun is a form that is highly respected. One of the best is biblical, in Matthew 16:18: *Thou art Peter* (Greek form, **Petros**), *and upon this rock* (Greek, **petra**) *I will build my church.*

   Shakespeare loved puns, even at strange times in a drama. After the murder of Duncan, Lady Macbeth says to Macbeth, "Give me the daggers . . . If he do bleed, I'll *gild* the faces of the grooms withal, For it must seem their *guilt* [gilt]."

   The fancy name for puns is *paronomasia*. Check the dictionary definition of this term (especially its derivation) and write that definition here.

   _____

   _____

Latina Vivit
Common Latin Words and Phrases

In Context. Before studying the definitions, try reasoning out the meaning of each word, using context as your guide.

1. When our senior adviser said we needed an *ad hoc* committee for graduation, we weren't sure what he meant until he explained that this would be a special committee to handle graduation details and arrangements.

   Key: Definition   **Ad hoc** means _____.

2. Because I'd expected him to be just the opposite of me, I was astonished when my cousin Brad, who's lived half his life abroad, turned out to be my *alter ego*.

   Key: Contrasting phrase   **Alter ego** means _____.

3. One little difference between Brad and me is his brain; the guy's a *bona fide* genius compared with me.

   Key: Logic   **Bona fide** means _____.

4. *"Caveat emptor,"* Dad commented regretfully as he examined a newly purchased tool that had broken on first use. "Some stores sell shoddy merchandise, and today's consumer had better beware."

   Key: Synonymous phrase   **Caveat emptor** means _____.

5. "If we consider the *corpus delicti* in this case," Mom said, grimly viewing the mess around our aquarium, "we'll see that the evidence points to one mama pussycat with two feline accomplices."

   Key: Synonym   **Corpus delicti** means _____.

6. "We should never have allowed those cats in the same room as the aquarium," Dad said, "but to forbid them now is *ex post facto*, just like locking the barn door after the horse has been stolen."

   Key: Logic   **Ex post facto** means _____.

7. The new speech and drama teacher expects students to be able to speak *extempore* whenever called upon, as she believes that most of life's speeches are impromptu rather than planned.

   Keys: Synonym, antonym   **Extempore** means _____.

8. "Can you issue a writ of *habeas corpus* on a pussycat?" Dad asked, trying not to grin. "I'd like to have that individual here right now to face our family court."

   Key: Definition   **Habeas corpus** means _____.

9. On cleaning up the aquarium disaster, we found one tetra *in extremis* behind the tank, and although we put him back in the water, he failed to survive.

   Key: Logic   **In extremis** means _____.

10. Andy got a little carried away with *Charlotte's Web*. After reading about that spider and her egg sac, Andy began claiming that his every accomplishment or good deed was his *magnum opus*, too.

    Keys: Example, logic   **Magnum opus** means _____.

11. Noted for her hilarious *non sequiturs*, Aunt Dolly often has us laughing at comments that appear totally irrelevant to what we've been discussing.

    Key: Definition   **Non sequitur** means _____.

12. Like unwelcome diplomats or students with too many demerits, Marigold, Poucette, and Figment were *persona non grata* for a while after their raid on the aquarium.

    Keys: Synonym, examples   **Persona non grata** means _____.

13. Jan and I have a *quid pro quo* arrangement about tapes; I lend mine to her, and she does the same for me.

    Key: Example   **Quid pro quo** means _____.

14. After Dad restocked the aquarium with tropical fish, he shut the door to the family room. "That closed door is vital," he announced. "It is the *sine qua non*. Otherwise, we'll lose this batch just as we lost the last ones."

    Keys: Synonym, logic   **Sine qua non** means _____.

15. So far, with the door shut, we have preserved the *status quo* in the fish tank. We have every single fish that was put in there two weeks ago.

    Key: Logic   **Status quo** means _____.

16. When the family-room door was left open by mistake, Dad joked about issuing *subpoenas* for every member of the family to make us appear before him to give testimony.

    Key: Definition   **Subpoena** means _____.

WORD STUDY

Want to see an adult cry? Just tell a Latin teacher that Latin is a dead language.

Although Latin **per se** (as such) is *not spoken*, its roots form 60–70 percent of the English language and are the base of all the Romance languages—those modern languages going back to Latin through uninterrupted oral tradition: Portuguese, Spanish, Catalan, Provençal, French, Rhaeto-Romanic, Italian, Sardinian, and Romanian.

Latin is especially lively in medicine and law, ensuring your acquaintance with it sooner or later. You refer to your old school as your **alma mater,** literally "fostering mother" for education. One female graduate or former student is an **alumna** and all the girls, **alumnae.** A male is an **alumnus** and all the boys, **alumni.** You read the list of the **dramatis personae** in your play program to see who's in the cast. New words like **computerist, space station,** and **biomedicine** are coined from ageless Latin roots. In altered form perhaps, but . . . *Latina definitely vivit.*

1. **ad hoc** ([']ad-'häk or [']äd-'hōk) adv., adj.   For a specific, particular purpose; literally, *for this*

    The Student Council created an *ad hoc* judiciary board to deal with student misbehavior after school hours.

2. **alter ego** (ȯl-tə-'rē[ˌ]gō) n. phrase.   The person most like you in temperament and tastes; literally, *another I*

    The business tycoon had hoped for an *alter ego* in his brother, but he was disappointed by the younger man's involvement with the arts.

    Synonymous phrase: *kindred soul*

3. **bona fide** ('bō-nə-ˌfīd) adj.   Sincere; genuine or authentic; literally, *in good faith*

    Jan's attraction to good jewelry was intensified when Aunt Dolly gave her a pendant watch that was a *bona fide* antique more than 150 years old.

       Relative: *bona fides* (n., lack of fraud or deceit)
    Synonyms: *genuine, authentic*
    Antonyms: *bogus, counterfeit, fraudulent*

4. **caveat emptor** ('kav-ē-ˌät-'em[p]-tər) n. phrase   In marketing, the buyer must assume the risk of anything purchased without a guarantee of quality; literally, *let the buyer beware*

    Familiar Latin phrases include *Cave canem* (Beware of the dog), *Errare humanum est* (To err is human), and *Caveat emptor.*

       Relative: *caveat* (n., any warning or prohibition; also an explanation necessary to prevent misunderstanding)

5. **corpus delicti** ('kȯr-pəs-di-'lik-ˌtī) n. phrase   The essential fact or facts necessary to prove a crime; the body of a murder victim; literally, *the body of the crime;* pl., *corpora delicti*

    Snatching the dead mouse from Marigold, Jan said to the cat, "I'm putting the *corpus delicti* in the trash, if you don't mind."

       Relative: *corporeal* (referring to the physical or material elements in life, not the spiritual)

6. **ex post facto** (ˌek-ˌspōst-ˈfak-[ˌ]tō) adj., adv. phrase   After the fact, as *an ex post facto law;* literally, *from a thing done afterward;* adv., retroactively

   Not always popular but sometimes necessary, the *ex post facto* law is one enacted after a crime to ensure justice.

7. **extempore** (ik-ˈstem-pə[ˌ]rē) adv.   On the spur of the moment, impromptu; literally, *of or at the time*

   Addressing a group *extempore* becomes quite normal for any celebrity besieged by reporters.

      Relatives: *extemporize, extemporaneous, extemporaneously*
   Synonyms: *impromptu, extemporaneously*

8. **habeas corpus** (ˌhā-bē-ə-ˈskȯr-pəs) n. phrase   A legal writ or paper ordering someone before a judge or into court; literally, *you should have the body* (words beginning the legal writ); also your citizen's right to get a writ of *habeas corpus* to prevent illegal imprisonment

   One of our most protective judicial devices is the writ of *habeas corpus,* which dates back to the English Magna Carta (1215).

9. **in extremis** (ˌin-ik-ˈstrē-məs) adv. phrase   The last stages of life, near death; literally, *at the extremity*

   Far from being *in extremis,* the butterfly struggled free of the net and fluttered away.

10. **magnum opus** (ˌmag-nə-ˈmō-pəs) n. phrase   The chief or most significant work of a writer (or artist in any field); literally, *great work*

    I believe that *The Adventures of Huckleberry Finn* was Twain's *magnum opus,* but I often wonder what Twain thought was his greatest work.

11. **non sequitur** ([ˈ]nän-ˈsek-wat-ər) n. phrase   A response that fails to follow the logic or sense of what has just been said and therefore seems ludicrous or inappropriate; literally, *it does not follow*

    One of our school newspaper's humorous *non sequiturs* concerned a new teacher. "Tall, of hefty build and smiling face, Mr. Smith has introduced some exciting lab skills to the chemistry department."

    (What, you may well ask, do Mr. Smith's height and appearance have to do with his lab skills in the chem department?)

12. **persona non grata** (pər-ˌsō-nə-ˌnän-grät-ə) adj. phrase   Unacceptable or unwelcome; literally, *person not acceptable*

    Andy's early attempts at cooking were so messy that Mother considered him *persona non grata* in her kitchen until he learned to clean up after himself.

    Synonymous ideas: *outcast, pariah*
            Antonym: *persona grata* (personally welcome)

13. **quid pro quo** (ˌkwid-ˌprō-ˈkwō) n. phrase   Like trade or barter, one thing given in exchange for something else; literally, *this for that* or *something for something*

    To those of us on the outside, high-level disarmament talks seem to be merely *quid pro quo,* a tense form of international barter.

    Synonymous idea: *tit for tat*

14. **sine qua non** (ˌsin-i-ˌkwä-ˈnōn) n. phrase   An essential, vital thing considered to be indispensable; literally, *without which not*

    At the cooking school, Mom, Jan, and Andy asked the famous chef what had flavored the soup. "Ah," he replied quickly, "the spices. They are the *sine qua non* for this recipe."

15. **status quo** (ˌstāt-ə-ˈskwō or ˌstat-ə-ˈskwō) n. phrase   The state of things as they now exist; literally, *the state in which*

    Eager to preserve the *status quo,* our town passed strict zoning laws to prohibit inappropriate or dangerous developments within town limits.

        Relative: *status* (condition, position, rank)

16. **subpoena** (sə-ˈpē-nə) n. phrase   A formal writ ordering the person named to appear in court or face penalty; literally, *under penalty.*   v. To serve the writ of subpoena.

    Subpoenaed to appear in court, Mother calmed herself by writing down every detail of the accident she had witnessed so that she was sure about her evidence.

ROOT STUDY

In keeping with a Latinate lesson, here are four Latin roots that have contributed a vast number of words to English. Can you find the one *Greek* root, the oddball?

1. **CEDE**, **CEED**, and **CESS** mean *to go* or *to yield.*

    precede—to go before or ahead in time or place
    succeed—to follow in time or place
    secession—withdrawal, retirement, as *the secession of the South at Civil War time*
    intercede—to go between parties with the goal of reconciling differences; to interpose

2. **LOC** means *place.*

    location—a distinct place or area
    dislocate—to place or put out of position, as *a dislocated bone*
    locomotion—movement from place to place

3. **MORPH** means *form, shape.*

    morpheme—a meaningful language unit, e.g., *pin, bit,* that cannot be divided into smaller units
        containing meaning
    amorphous—lacking definite shape, unformed
    metamorphosis—a change of form, style, personality
    morphology—the biological study of the form and structure of animals and plants

4. **PEN** (from *poena*) means *punishment.*

   penalize—to punish
   penance—an act or feeling of sorrow for a wrong
   penitentiary—a state or federal prison
   penitent—regretful or sorrowful, *repentant* of some sin or wrong, contrite

5. **TEMPOR** means *time.*

   temporary—not permanent, for the time being
   temporize—to compromise; to delay, thereby drawing out a discussion or negotiation to gain time
   contemporary—of the current time, modern; of the same period in time, as *a contemporary of mine*
   temporal—earthly (as opposed to heavenly or spiritual concerns); chronological

   (Did you guess that the Greek root was **morph?** *Ph* is a common Greek letter combination.)

USING THE WORDS

List 18 Review

ad hoc	corpus delicti	in extremis	quid pro quo
alter ego	ex post facto	magnum opus	sine qua non
bona fide	extempore	non sequitur	status quo
caveat emptor	habeas corpus	persona non grata	subpoena

Exercise I. Definitions.
Write the Latin phrase from List 18 next to its definition or synonym. The first letter is a gift.

1. order to appear in court or face a penalty   s _____

2. for a particular purpose   a _____

3. near to death   i _____

4. supreme achievement   m _____

5. essential thing   s _____

6. other self, one's double   a _____

7. illogical response   n _____

8. tit for tat   q _____

9. buyer beware   c _____

10. retroactive(ly)   e _____

11. impromptu, unrehearsed   e _____

12. authentic   b _____

Exercise II. Fill-Ins.
Select the most appropriate word from List 18, based on clues in context.

1. A fair trade or barter arrangement is _____.

2. Learning to buckle your seat belt after having been pitched out of the car in a nasty collision is learning _____.

3. A commission was established _____ to investigate compliance with government safety regulations.

4. As long as no new kids join our class, we'll keep the same old _____.

5. Our band director, who finished the march he's been composing for four years, refers to it as his _____.

6. The way Andy carried on about writing his first book report, you'd have thought he was _____ and in need of an ambulance and stretcher.

7. Our motto for the garage sale had to be _____, as most of the sale items were pretty dilapidated.

8. Those who saw Yul Brynner in *The King and I* believe that his inspired performance was the _____; he will never be replaced exactly.

9. It looks as though little Poucette will be Marigold's _____, and we will have two pets of equally strong personality in the house.

10. Fearful that he would be accused of a crime he had not committed, the nervous citizen obtained a writ of _____.

11. In front of all our friends at the lake, Dad began to declaim _____ on the joys of living far away from noisy traffic and hectic schedules.

12. Dad's business lawyer _____ employees to appear in court to testify to the sorry condition in which the latest merchandise had arrived. (Hint: Use the verb form.)

13. Agatha Christie's detective named Miss Marple is skilled at unearthing the _____, which convicts the guilty party.

14. "I doubt that this is a _____ gemstone," Aunt Dolly said, peering at the old ring Jan and I had found. She added, "It's an excellent counterfeit, however."

15. Jan was rhapsodizing about her new boyfriend when Dad broke in and asked if she'd completed her homework. In Jan's mind, Dad's question was a total _____.

16. Dad was serious about the homework, of course, and told Jan that the new boyfriend was

_____ at our house unless her schoolwork was up to date.

Exercise III. Logic.
Using information from this lesson, answer the questions as completely as possible.

1. When might you be served a writ of habeas corpus? _____

_____

2. When would you want to secure a writ of habeas corpus as protection? _____

_____

3. Who in our government (general types/groups) would be considered *persona grata*?

_____

4. How do corporeal beings differ from spiritual beings? _____

_____

5. In what way is progress the enemy of the status quo? _____

_____

Exercise IV. Matching.
Match the words learned in Roots with their meanings.

_____ 1. **precede**   (a) change of form, type

_____ 2. **intercede**   (b) withdrawal

_____ 3. **penance**   (c) earthly

_____ 4. **amorphous**   (d) language unit

_____ 5. **temporize**   (e) movement

_____ 6. **contemporary**   (f) contrite

_____ 7. **metamorphosis**   (g) to interpose

_____ 8. **temporal**   (h) to play for time

_____ 9. **secession**   (i) to go before

_____ 10. **morpheme**   (j) current

_____ 11. **penitent**   (k) an act of repentance

_____ 12. **locomotion**   (l) unformed, vague, shapeless

Exercise V. Useful Latin Bits.

1. Little bits of Latin pop up everywhere, and some of the most useful are abbreviations. Remember these?

    e.g. = *exemplia gratia* = for example
    (Introduces an example or several examples.)

    et al. = *et alia* = and other
    (Used, like *et cetera* or *etc.,* to eliminate a longer list of items.)

    ibid. = *ibidem* = the same
    (Used to avoid repetition of a reference, as in footnotes or in a reference volume.)

    i.e. = *id est* = that is
    (Introduces a statement to clarify what has just been said.)

    N.B. = *nota bene* = mark well
    (Calls attention to an important point.)

    Enter the appropriate Latin abbreviation required by the following situations.

    _____ a. Footnote 3 in your term paper or report refers to a quote from the book cited in footnote 2.

    _____ b. You have written a fine general statement in an essay, but you wish to clarify with a more specific statement that will help to make your point.

    _____ c. After a major Latin root, you want to list several examples of words derived from it.

    _____ d. At the end of a paragraph on the English language, you want readers to remember one significant point.

    _____ e. You have compiled a book list and listed one or two titles by your favorite authors, but you haven't room for more. How will you indicate that these authors have written other titles?

2. Using *per annum* (each year), *per capita* (each head or person), *per diem* (each day), and *per se* (as such), complete the story.

    In sixteen years, I have had only sixteen incredibly wonderful boxes of cookies, one box

    _____. And while chocolate chip cookies _____

    are not worth anything, still everyone loves me when I share them. I have 10 friends and 200

    cookies, so I can lavish 20 cookies _____ on my friends. But then they

    will be all gone. If I give each friend only 5 cookies _____, they will

    last four days.

3. Match the words or phrases that directly *contrast* with one another.

_____ a. bona fide   (1) rehearsed, planned

_____ b. in advance   (2) ex post facto

_____ c. extemporaneous   (3) welcome

_____ d. persona non grata   (4) sine qua non

_____ e. nonessential thing   (5) bogus

4. You have heard of people graduating *cum laude,* with honor or distinction. Might you rather graduate *magna cum laude,* _____, or perhaps *summa cum laude,* _____? (Write the English meanings in place.)

Exercise VI. Word Analysis.

1. We speak of someone who is chairman *pro tem* and understand that the position is held only temporarily. For what Latin phrase is *pro tem* the abbreviation?

   _____

   (The word you need is part of a word is List 18.)

2. Deduce the meaning of the Latin phrases in italics in the following sentences and write it in.

   a. We are acting *in loco parentis* for the orphan until adoptive parents can be found.

   _____

   b. We discovered fourteen major kinds of insects *in toto,* just in our backyard.

   _____

   c. And, *mirabile dictu,* among the insects was a pair of praying mantises.

   _____

   (N.B. Think of *miracle* and *dictate* to lead you to correct roots here.)

   d. Arms raised, the priest said, *"Pax vobiscum,"* at the end of mass.

   _____

   (N.B. *Pacifist* and *pacific* come from *pax.*)

   e. The entire plot was conducted *sub rosa* to ensure total secrecy.

   _____

   f. *"Tempus fugit,"* the teacher warned, eyeing the clock.

   _____

   (N.B. You know *tempus* from *tempore.* What does a *fugitive* from the law have to do?)

   g. Our captured insects seemed delighted to set their many feet on *terra firma* again after having been imprisoned in a jar for hours.

   _____

3. In *The Rime of the Ancient Mariner,* Samuel Taylor Coleridge writes, "The man hath penance done, And penance more will do." How would you explain this line to someone who had no idea of the word *penance*?

_____

_____

4. The Bible refers often to "a contrite heart." What word from Roots means *contrite?*

_____

5. Latinate words tend to be longer—sometimes much longer—than Anglo-Saxon words. What reasons can you give for this?

_____

_____

_____

LIST 19 Call My Lawyer!
Legal Terms

In Context. Before studying the definitions, try reasoning out the meaning of each word, using context as your guide.

1. Our new principal announced that he plans to *abrogate* some of the school rules and institute others, which has us all wondering what will be abolished and what established.

   Key: Synonym   **Abrogate** means _____.

2. When a sad-eyed holstein cow was discovered in school the morning after Halloween, certain sophomores were accused then later *acquitted* when the guilty juniors confessed.

   Keys: Logic, antonym   **Acquit** means _____.

3. The principal encouraged our student Disciplinary Review Board to *adjudicate* the Holstein Affair and later told us how pleased he was with our judicial process.

   Key: Near definition   **Adjudicate** means _____.

4. The *advocate* for the sophomores' defense was the biology teacher, who'd hosted a party for the sophomores at his house on Halloween.

   Key: Logic   **Advocate** means _____.

5. After hearing our sentence for the juniors, their advocate asked that we *commute* it to only one week of floor scrubbing instead of two because the guilty ones had come forth voluntarily—and had returned the cow intact.

   Keys: Logic, example   **Commute** means _____.

6. One of the messiest cases our Disciplinary Review Board had to settle concerned upperclass students who were *extorting* exam questions and answers from two frightened freshmen who worked part-time in the school office.

   Key: Logic   **Extort** means _____.

7. Students from other schools who are found misbehaving on our school property are *extradited* to their own schools for disciplinary action.

   Keys: Logic, example   **Extradite** means _____.

8. Our student court would never deal with a crime as serious as a *felony*.

   Key: Logic   **Felony** means _____.

9. We had always known that our biology teacher was a skilled debater, but we were especially impressed with his *forensic* skills when he defended the sophomores.

   Key: Logic   **Forensic** means _____.

10. The innocent sophomores in the Holstein Affair realized that their own reputations had *indicted* them before trial. Since their acquittal, they have all been model students.

    Key: Logic   **Indict** means _____.

11. The juniors were relieved that the owner of the holstein did not charge them with *larceny*. As his cow was worth several hundred dollars, their theft would have been considered grand larceny had the animal died or disappeared.

    Key: Synonym   **Larceny** means _____.

12. We were able to assign fair punishment for the offenders in the Holstein Affair within the confines of our school, whereas formal *litigation* in court would have embarrassed everyone.

    Keys: Logic, contrast   **Litigation** means _____.

13. Our local mayor had been suspected of wrongdoing for several months, so it was actually a relief to the town when he was brought to court on a charge of *malfeasance*.

    Keys: Synonym, example   **Malfeasance** means _____.

14. Not wishing to be convicted of malfeasance, the mayor lied under oath, but he was caught at that as well, and *perjury* was added to his list of offenses.

    Key: Definition   **Perjury** means _____.

15. The *sanction* attached to smoking on our school grounds is a three-day suspension, which, as Dad said, "Certainly puts teeth into that rule."

    Keys: Near definition, example   **Sanction** means _____.

16. In government class we discussed the law of *torts*, which came to us from England with the colonists. A tort is a legal wrong committed on the person or property of another, independent of contract—such as trespass, nuisance, and defamation of character.

    Keys: Definition, examples   **Tort** means _____.

17. Unlike New York City—vast, impersonal home of the bag ladies—our town is so small that a *vagrant* is immediately noticed and cared for.

    Keys: Logic, example   **Vagrant** means _____.

WORD STUDY

After a Latin lesson, you are in fine etymological shape for learning legal terms. Like *habeas corpus* and *corpus delicti*, many have come *verbatim* from Latin into the English language. Not long ago, a list of law terms would rarely have appeared in a text like this. Now, the number of legal suits has greatly increased, as has our awareness of human rights, so that everyone needs to understand legal terminology.

> *A state is better governed which has but few laws,*
> *and those laws strictly observed.*
> —René Descartes (1596–1650)

1. **abrogate** ('ab-rə-ˌgāt) v.   To annul, abolish, or legally do away with; from L. *ab* + *rogare*, to ask, propose a law

    The word *abrogate* comes directly from the old Roman senate that asked the people *abrogare legem* (to speak or solicit against the law) when they wished to repeal a law.

    >   Relative: *abrogation*
    > Synonyms: *annul, nullify*
    >   Antonym: *establish*

2. **acquit** (ə-'kwit) v.   To free of blame or obligation entirely; to behave well or acceptably, as *the novice class acquitted itself with distinction at the tournament;* from L. *ad* + *quite*, free of

    We had blamed Marigold for attracting a stray black cat, but she was *acquitted* when we realized that the stray was wooing young Poucette.

    >   Relatives: *acquittal, acquittance* (legal document/receipt)
    > Synonyms: *exonerate, exculpate; behave* (second meaning)
    >   Antonyms: *accuse, inculpate*

3. **adjudicate** (ə-'jüd-i-ˌkāt) v.   To settle by legal process as a judge does or to act as judge; from L. *ad* + *judicare*, to judge

    Newly elected members of the Disciplinary Review Board think they will be able to *adjudicate* students' problems with ease, but they learn otherwise.

    >   Relatives: *adjudicator, adjudge, adjudicative, adjudication, adjudicatory*

4. **advocate** ('ad-və-kət, 'ad-və-ˌkāt) n.   One who pleads a case or represents the accused, as a lawyer; anyone who defends or acts as champion for a cause or proposal.   v.   To speak or write in favor of, as *his essay advocates fewer elections for longer terms of office;* from L. *ad* + *vocare,* to call, summon

    At the famous Scopes trial in 1925, the respected *advocate* for the defense, Clarence Darrow, said, "I do not pretend to know where many ignorant men are sure—that is all that agnosticism means."

    >   Relatives: *advocator, advocation, advocative*
    > Synonyms: n., *lawyer, solicitor* (Brit.); v., *support*
    >   Antonym: v., *decry*

5. **commute** (kə-'myüt) v.   To reduce or change a penalty or punishment to something less demanding; in law, to commutate; also to go back and forth with regularity, as *he commutes from New Jersey to New York every day;* from L. *commutare,* to exchange

The felon's sentence was *commuted* to twenty years when his rehabilitation became obvious to everyone.

   Relatives: *commutation, commutate, commutable, commuter, commute* (n., the trip)

6. **extort** (ik-'stȯ[ə]rt) v.   To get something from another by force, power, intimidation, wits, etc.; to wring, as *he extorted a confession from the accused man;* from L. *ex + torquere,* to twist, wring

When more of the people's sustenance is exacted through the form of taxation than is necessary . . . such exaction becomes ruthless extortion *and a violation of the fundamental principles of a free government.*
   —Grover Cleveland, 2nd annual message, 1886

   Relatives: *extortion* (gross overcharge, usually of money), *extorter, extortive, extortioner, extortionate, extortionately*
   Synonyms: *educe, extract; elicit* (second meaning)

7. **extradite** ('ek-strə-ˌdīt) v.   To hand over an accused person to the authority with proper jurisdiction to try the case; from L. *ex + tradition-, traditio,* act of handing over

International criminals are often *extradited* to their home countries, but exceptions have occurred when a victimized country refuses to *extradite* terrorists.

   Relatives: *extradition, extraditable*

8. **felony** ('fel-ə-né) n.   A crime serious enough to be legally declared a felony, usually incurring a severe penalty such as imprisonment for longer than a year or death; from L. *fellon-, fello,* villain, evildoer

There shall be in England seven halfpenny loaves sold for a penny; the three-hooped pot shall have ten hoops; and I will make it felony *to drink small beer.*
   —Shakespeare, *King Henry VI,* Part II

(Note: Said by rebel Jack Cade. The normal three-hooped drinking mug held a quart, so a ten-hooper would hold more than 3 quarts. Small beer was weak beer.)

   Relatives: *felon* (criminal), *feloniously, felonry* (the convict population)

9. **forensic** (fə-'ren[t]-sik) adj.   Referring to or used in law courts or discussion and debate; argumentative or rhetorical; from L. *forensis,* public, from *forum*

The aim of forensic *oratory is to teach, to delight, to move.*
   —Cicero, *De Optimo Genere Oratorum*

   Relatives: *forensic* (n., an exercise in argument), *forensically*

10. **indict** (in-'dīt) v.   To accuse or charge with a wrong; to charge with a crime by due process of law; possibly from L. *in + dicere*, to pronounce, utter

Injustice is difficult to bear, and we remember times when we were unfairly *indicted*.

Relatives: *indictment, indicter (-or), indictable*
Synonyms: *accuse, inculpate*
Antonyms: *absolve, exculpate*

11. **larceny** ('lärs-ən-ē) n.   Theft; any offense by which property is gotten illegally; from L. *latrocinium*, robbery

"You're a mouse studying to be a rat," Wilson Mizner said, just as we might say that *petit larceny* differs from *grand larceny* only in size.

Relatives: *larcenist, larcenous, larcenously*
Synonym: *theft*

12. **litigation** ('lit-ə-'gā-shən) n.   A legal suit in a court of law, a lawsuit; from L. *lit-, lis,* lawsuit, + *agere*, to drive

Large, wealthy corporations must employ numerous lawyers for *litigation*, some of which is justifiable and some surely reprehensible for its waste of court time and everyone's money.

Relatives: *litigant (n., one party to a lawsuit), litigant (adj.), litigate, litigable, litigious*
Synonym: *lawsuit*

13. **malfeasance** ([']mal-'fēz-ən[t]s) n.   Official misconduct or wrongdoing, usually by someone in charge of public affairs; from AN *malfaisance*, doing evil

The governor's shady dealings in the awarding of public contracts came to light and resulted in his trial and eventual conviction of *malfeasance*.

14. **perjury** ('pərj-[ə-]rē) n.   Lying under oath, either by saying something untrue or by failing to do what was promised in the oath; from L. *per + jurare*, to swear

An oath, an oath, I have an oath in heaven:
Shall I lay perjury *upon my soul?*
No, not for Venice.
     —Shakespeare, *The Merchant of Venice*

Relatives: *perjure (v.), perjurer, perjurious, perjuriously*

15. **sanction** ('saŋ[k]-shən) v.   To confirm or authorize; to endorse, approve, or support. n. Authorization, support, or approval; that which gives force to a law, such as the penalty for breaking that law or the reward for upholding it or enforcing it; used in pl.: forceful, coercive measures to ensure compliance with law (usually international sanctions); from L. *sancire*, to make sacred

I cannot *sanction* your attendance at a street gathering that is apt to become dangerous. It will take the pressure of international *sanctions* to preserve many sea creatures from extinction.

Relatives: *sanctioner, sanctionable*
Synonyms: v., *authorize, endorse, approve*; n., *authorization, support, approval*
Antonyms: v., *disapprove, interdict*; n., *disapproval*

16. **tort** ('tȯ(ə)rt) n.   With the exception of breach of contract, a wrongful act against another that results in injury or damage and for which satisfaction can legally be obtained; from L. *torquere,* to twist

Our U.S. law of *torts,* developed to protect a wide range of human interests against wrong, has its roots in the Norman Conquest of England in 1066, when the English common law was born.

17. **vagrant** ('vā-grənt) n.   Someone lacking a definite home who wanders from place to place; a wanderer, rover; someone whose behavior is socially unacceptable, e.g., a drunkard, who can legally be classified a vagrant.   adj. Roving, wandering, or fleeting, with no set course, as *a vagrant thought;* random; from AN *vagaraunt,* vagrant

Gifted actress-comedian Lucille Ball no doubt enjoyed her challenging role as a New York *vagrant* in the television play *Stone Pillow.*

   Relatives: *vagrancy, vagrantly*
   Synonyms: n., *wanderer, rover, vagabond, tramp*; adj., *random, roving, wandering, errant*

ROOT STUDY

This collection of roots deals mainly with people and the law.

1. **DEM** and **PLEB** mean *people.*

   democracy—system of government wherein the people rule directly or through their elected
       representatives; literally, *rule by the people*
   endemic—confined within a specific, local area; native, as opposed to *epidemic*, which refers to
       something affecting many people at the same time, or *pandemic*, referring to anything
       occurring throughout a large area and affecting a high proportion of the population
   demagogue—a false leader of people who says what the people want to hear
   plebiscite—a vote by all people in a country/district
   plebeian—rude, common, low, coarse, or crude, as *plebeian tasks;* literally, *of the common people*

2. **DIC/DICT** means *to speak, say.*

   verdict—the official ruling of a court or authority
   interdict—n., a prohibition, a formal decree that forbids something; v., to forbid with authority,
       refuse to sanction
   malediction—a curse, execration
   dictator—one whose word is law, who exercises total control and authority
   jurisdiction—the power and authority to apply/interpret law; literally, *speaking in judgment*

3. **JUD, JUR,** and **JUS** mean *judge.*

   judicial—referring to a judge; in a considerate, deliberate, and thoughtful manner
   jurisprudence—the body of law with its working system; science/philosophy of law
   justice—a person, as *a chief justice* (judge); the acknowledged fair result, fairness
   abjure—to reject, renounce, or forswear, as *people on diets abjure desserts.* (Sigh.)
   adjure—to charge or command solemnly, to order, as *I adjure you to ignore that chocolate cake.*

4. **JUNCT, JUG,** and **JOIN** mean *to join, to marry, mating.*

junction—a place of meeting or joining
injunction—a court order requiring you to do or to refrain from doing something; an order or admonition
conjugal—referring to marriage, matrimonial
joint—adj., combined, united, as *joint effort*; n., a skeletal point of contact, as *the elbow or knee joint;* large piece of roasting meat; anywhere two things or parts are joined

(Note: The root LEG, meaning law, was in List 8. Remember *legislate, legal, illegal, legacy?* A *paralegal* employee is one who works with the law but lacks a degree in law.)

USING THE WORDS

List 19 Review

abrogate	extort	indict	perjury	acquit
extradite	larceny	sanction	adjudicate	felony
litigation	tort	advocate	forensic	malfeasance
vagrant	commute			

Exercise I. Definitions.

Feeling comfortable with this list of words requires practice. Writing is a superb memory aid. Write a brief definition or synonym for words from List 19 and Roots.

1. **vagrant** _____

2. **acquit** _____

3. **tort** _____

4. **abrogate** _____

5. **sanction** _____

6. **adjudicate** _____

7. **perjury** _____

8. **malfeasance** _____

9. **advocate** (v.) _____

10. **litigation** _____

11. **commute** _____

12. **larceny** _____

13. **extort** _____

14. **indict** _____

15. **extradite** _____

16. **forensic** _____

17. **felony** _____

18. **annul** _____

19. **verdict** _____

20. **injunction** _____

Exercise II. You're the Lawyer.

Using *all* of the information in List 19 and Roots, complete the following with the correct expressions or words on the lines.

1. A model prisoner hopes that his five-year sentence may be _____ to only two or three years.

2. I trespassed on your property in such a disorderly, noisy manner that your flock of turkeys panicked and several died in the crush. Under what law may you take me to court?

   _____

3. On the witness stand, I failed to mention that the accused had been at the scene of the crime on the fatal night. When this critical omission was discovered, I was charged with

   _____.

4. The final pronouncement of innocence or guilt is known as the _____.

5. The marriage of King Henry VIII and Anne of Cleves was not consummated, and Henry had their marriage abrogated by court order. This is commonly called _____.

6. The noise of my building crew exceeded that allowed by local ordinance, and I was prohibited from further building by a court _____ until the situation could be rectified.

7. I didn't have enough money to pay for the gas put in my tank. I took money from the gas station's cash box and was caught red-handed with the stolen 5-dollar bill. The station owner prosecuted, charging me with _____.

8. On a dare, I dressed in rags, pretended to be sozzled, and loitered conspicuously around the bus station. Luckily, the policeman who questioned me believed my story and didn't haul me to the station as a _____.

9. Having watched lots of cops and robbers on television, I know that when taken to the police station I have the right to call my _____, who will act as _____ for my defense.

10. At an international meeting, members voted on _____ prohibiting excessive fishing of dolphins and whales and establishing mileage limits within which the creatures would be safe from all fishing.

11. Although jaywalking and speeding may be classified as _____, homicide is definitely a major crime, a _____. (Hint: See sentence 8 of "In Context.")

12. I am a famous person—a household name, in fact—when my daughter is kidnapped and held for an enormous ransom. This particularly ugly form of _____ is legally a felony with severe penalties. (Clue: Check out word 6.)

13. The kidnapper of my daughter will need a lawyer with awesome _____ skills if he hopes to be imprisoned the minimum number of years required by law.

14. As elected treasurer of the Latin club, I deposited the dues in my personal bank account so that I could collect the interest. The dues were spent over the year but I kept the interest and am guilty of _____.

15. My car rammed your car, which I maintain was crossing illegally in front of me. Neither of us will admit blame. We've hired lawyers and are now embroiled in _____.

16. Pity the judge who _____ the foregoing disputes. He must have some long days.

17. Everyone in our community is talking and reading about a much-publicized local murder. In order to ensure a fair trial, the governor of our state has agreed to _____ the alleged murderer to his home state to stand trial in a less emotionally charged atmosphere.

18. In his home state the alleged murderer was _____ by a grand jury on a charge of homicide.

19. Months later we heard that our alleged murderer was just that: alleged. He was innocent of the crime and _____ by a jury of his peers.

20. The Head Resident of our dorm explained that what went on in the dorm was under her _____. She said that she was required to enforce the college rules.

    (Hint: Hunt through Root Study.)

Exercise III. Antonyms.
Find an antonym (or opposing phrase) for each word on the left.

_____ 1. **interdict**   (a) to indulge in

_____ 2. **establish**   (b) to absolve, acquit

_____ 3. **advocate** (v.)   (c) to sanction

_____ 4. **abjure**   (d) stable, fixed

_____ 5. **indict**   (e) dictatorship

_____ 6. **sanction** (v.)   (f) to abrogate

_____ 7. **vagrant**   (g) separation

_____ 8. **democracy**   (h) to disapprove of

_____ 9. **adjure**   (i) to discourage, go against

_____ 10. **junction**   (j) to beg, plead with

Exercise IV. Analogies.
Complete each analogy with the best pair possible.

_____ 1. felony : indictment ::

    (a) misdemeanor : wrong
    (b) democracy : rule
    (c) libel : litigation
    (d) slander : libel
    (e) acquittal : accusation

_____ 2. death : legacy ::

    (a) advocate : lawyer
    (b) trial : verdict
    (c) commute : trip
    (d) jurisdiction : territory
    (e) law : tort

_____ 3. noble : plebeian ::

    (a) fixed : vagrant
    (b) illicit : illegal
    (c) civil : polite
    (d) joint : shared
    (e) larcenous : timid

_____ 5. oath : perjury ::

    (a) tort : nuisance
    (b) junction : corner
    (c) adjudication : justice
    (d) public office : malfeasance
    (e) theft : larceny

_____ 4. curse : malediction ::

    (a) sanction : disapproval
    (b) epidemic : health
    (c) abrogation : establishment
    (d) prisoner : extradition
    (e) interdict : prohibition

Exercise V. The Root of It All.

Answer the questions as fully as possible. If the dictionary cannot assist you, ask a helpful soul.

1. _Extort_ and _tort_ come from _torquere,_ to twist or wring. What other words can you think of that derive from **tor-?** _____

2. DIC/DICT has many derivatives. How many can you list? _____

_____

3. Why is a first-year student called a _plebe_ at the U.S. Military Academy, West Point?

_____

4. Why is the part of speech termed a _conjunction_ well named? (Famous, beloved conjunctions include _and, but, or, nor, although, as, because, unless,_ and _than._)

_____

5. Distinguish between _pandemic_ and _epidemic._ _____

_____

Exercise VI. Word Analysis.

1. What is the difference between a civil lawsuit and a criminal one? _____
    _____
    _____
    _____

2. Do you agree or disagree with René Descartes' assertion about the government of a state? Why? (See "Word Study," p. 272.)
    _____
    _____

3. The television program *Quincy* was about a medical doctor in the police department whose specialty was forensic medicine. Briefly, what is forensic medicine?
    _____
    _____

4. *Vagabond, rover, vagrant, wanderer,* and *tramp* can, at times, be synonymous, but their connotations are quite different. Which ones are positive or neutral in meaning, and which negative?
    _____
    _____

    Which one(s) suggest(s) a carefree, independent person? _____
    _____

    Of the five words, which one could you accept as a description of yourself? _____
    _____

5. What is a *larcenous* thought? _____

    And last, some "laws" to make you smile.

    Calvin Coolidge: "A lost article invariably shows up after you replace it."

    Sam Levenson: "Insanity is hereditary—you can get it from your children."

    Joan Carris: The day you're proudest of your homework is the day the teacher decides not to collect it.

LIST 20   Jane and Spot Grow Up
Verbs Yet Another Time

In Context. Before studying the definitions, try reasoning out the meaning of each word, using context as your guide.

1. "This spring vacation," asserted Carrie, "I'm *abstaining* from everything that's good for me. Instead, I'm going to indulge myself: sleep late, avoid work, and eat goodies."

    Key: Contrasting phrase   **Abstain** means _____.

2. "But Carrie, you'll wipe out all you accomplished by dieting and exercise!" Jan exploded. "You just couldn't *annihilate* all those great results, could you?"

    Key: Definitive phrase   **Annihilate** means _____.

3. Often, Carrie won't *condescend* to reply when Jan explodes; she just stalks out of the room. But this time she unbent enough to snort, "Rubbish!"

    Key: Synonym   **Condescend** means _____.

4. "I hate to *divulge* anyone's secrets," Mom said with a big grin, "but Carrie has told me she's running away from home if we serve so much as one more lettuce salad."

    Key: Logic   **Divulge** means _____.

5. Carrie added, "I think that all recipes using lettuce should be *expurgated* from every cookbook in the world so that people on diets could eat something else for a change!"

    Key: Logic   **Expurgate** means _____.

6. Hoping to *extricate* herself from the discussion, Mom said she was going for a walk, but Jan and Carrie tagged after her, so that Mom was still entangled in their argument.

    Key: Contrasting phrase   **Extricate** means _____.

7. "I haven't *imbibed* a thing worth swallowing for weeks," Carrie continued. "Just tea and water and diet soda, ugh!"

    Key: Logic   **Imbibe** means _____.

8. "You've *imputed* much of your hatred of dieting to the foods," Mom told Carrie. "Instead of attributing your dislike to the same old foods, you might consider trying new recipes."

    Key: Synonym   **Impute** means _____.

9. "I didn't mean to provoke you, Carrie," Jan volunteered at last, "and I didn't want to *instigate* an argument, so let's drop it, okay?"

   Keys: Synonym, logic   **Instigate** means _____.

10. "I'm not arguing!" Carrie *remonstrated*. "I said I'm going to do what I want now, and I'm not ever eating another bite of lettuce, and then you two got all excited."

    Key: Logic   **Remonstrate** means _____.

11. "You should eat something you really love," Mom conceded, "and I don't mean one bite. Just *sate* yourself with a forbidden treat, and then you can forget about it."

    Key: Contrasting phrase   **Sate** means _____.

12. Jan nodded. "That usually *suffices*. After a gooey hot fudge sundae I can be a noble dieter for weeks."

    Key: Logic   **Suffice** means _____.

13. Carrie's face *suffused* with color as she poked Jan and Mom in the ribs. "Hush up about dieting. Don't you see those two cute guys walking right ahead of us?"

    Key: Logic   **Suffuse** means _____.

14. Immediately, a discussion of the weather *supplanted* that of diets, and Carrie hissed, "Now we sound just plain stupid!"

    Keys: Logic, previous sentence   **Supplant** means _____.

15. Mom sighed. "Carrie, I know that parents are supposed to *temper* their love with wisdom, discipline, and patience, but my patience with you today is wearing thin."

    Key: Logic   **Temper** means _____.

16. I've always thought that Jan and Carrie needed a live-in referee to give the rest of us peace. I felt *vindicated* in this opinion when Mom reported their talk to me.

    Key: Logic   **Vindicate** means _____.

WORD STUDY

The verb is the sine qua non—the heart—of every sentence. Choose the verb carefully, and your reader or listener will know exactly what you have in mind.

Many of your best adjectives are past participles of verbs: *stooped, exhausted,* and *withered,* for example. Other descriptive adjectives are present participles like *whirring, stomping,* and *truckling.* Each of these adjectives gives a vivid picture because of the action feeling that the verb buried within it confers on the adjective. Likewise, great nouns are born from verbs: *condescension, instigation,* and *satiety,* to name just three from this lesson.

Author E. B. White—creator of Charlotte, Wilbur, Louis the trumpeter swan, Stuart Little, and several volumes for adults—is the final word on language. In *The Elements of Style,* he and the original author, William Strunk, remind us to "Write with nouns and verbs."

1. **abstain** (əb-'stān) v.   To refrain from an action or indulgence by exerting willpower; to refrain from voting; literally, *to hold back;* from L. *ab + tenere,* to hold

   Part of the Hippocratic oath taken by all physicians reads: "I will keep pure and holy both my life and my art. . . . In whatsoever houses I enter, I will enter to help the sick, and I will *abstain* from intentional wrongdoing and harm. . . ."

   Relatives: *abstainer, abstention, abstentious, abstinence, abstinent, abstinently*
   Synonym: *refrain*
   Antonym: *indulge*

2. **annihilate** (ə-'nī-ə-ˌlāt) v.   To wipe out, destroy, or vanquish completely; to rout, as *we annihilated the opposition;* to abolish; from L. *ad + nihil,* nothing

   Hoping not to *annihilate* ourselves, we still develop weapons capable of doing just that.

   Relatives: *annihilation, annihilative, annihilator, annihilatory*
   Synonyms: *nullify, destroy, vanquish, rout*
   Antonym: *create*

3. **condescend** (ˌ-kän-di-'send) v.   To bend or stoop to a less formal or exalted level; to put on a superior air, as *she condescended to grant me an interview;* from L. *com + descendere,* to descend

   'Tis an old maxim in the schools,
   That flattery's the food of fools;
   Yet now and then your men of wit
   Will condescend *to take a bit.*
        —Jonathan Swift, *Cadenus and Vanessa*

   Relatives: *condescension, condescendence*
   Synonyms: *stoop, unbend*

4. **divulge** (də-'vəlj, dī-'velj) v.   To reveal something held in confidence or secret; literally, *to make known;* from L. *dis + vulgare,* make known

   Further in the Hippocratic oath, the physician swears, "And whatsoever I shall see or hear in the course of my profession in my intercourse with men, if it be what should not be published abroad, I will never *divulge,* holding such things to be holy secrets."

   > Relative: *divulgence*
   > Synonym: *reveal*
   > Antonym: *conceal*

5. **expurgate** ('ek-spər-ˌgāt) v.   To clean or purge of something objectionable, wrong, or harmful, as *the offensive lines in the play were expurgated before production;* from L. *ex + purgare,* to purge

   A Shakespearean play may be *expurgated* not because its material is offensive but because the original is deemed too lengthy for modern audiences.

   > Relatives: *expurgation, expurgator, expurgatory*
   > Synonym: *purge*

6. **extricate** ('ek-strə-ˌkāt) v.   To free from an entanglement or awkward situation; from L. *ex + tricae,* trifles, perplexities

   The ancient "tricae" were hairs or strings tied around the feet of birds as fetters to prevent their wandering; a wily bird who escaped his fetters had quite literally *extricated* himself.

   > Relatives: *extrication, extricable*
   > Synonyms: *disentangle, untangle, disencumber*
   > Antonyms: *entangle, encumber, enmesh*

7. **imbibe** (im-'bīb) v.   To drink; to take in or soak up, as *our new bath towels imbibe moisture;* from L. *in + bibere,* to drink

   Jason *imbibed* philosophical principles as though he were dying of thirst; his entire education, he felt, had been preparing him for the study of philosophy.

   > Relatives: *imbiber, imbibition, imbibitional*
   > Synonym: *absorb*
   > Antonyms: *exude, ooze*

8. **impute** (im-'pyüt) v.   To attribute or credit, as *their success has been imputed to their determination;* to charge or blame, often unfairly; from L. *in + putare,* to consider (Note: *Impute* is used with *to.)*

   Andy *imputed* his failure at soccer to hatred of the game, but we told him that his muscle coordination would improve with age, and then he'd have more success even if he still disliked the game.

   > Relatives: *imputation* (n., insinuation), *imputable, imputability*
   > Synonyms: *ascribe, attribute, charge*

9. **instigate** ('in[t]-stə-ˌgāt) v.   To egg on or urge forward; to goad or provoke; from L. *instigare*, to incite

Huck Finn decided to "light out for the territory," unsure of what had *instigated* his departure, knowing only that he needed to escape civilization for a time.

   Relatives: *instigator, instigation, instigative*
Synonyms: *incite, provoke, goad*
Antonyms: *deter, inhibit*

10. **remonstrate** (ri-'män-ˌstrāt, 'rem-ən-ˌstrāt) v.   To raise objections or argue in protest; to plead pro or con, as *she remonstrated gently, reminding her son of his manners;* from L. *re + monstrare*, to show

In the manner of a cat, Figment *remonstrated* with me vigorously as I fastened his new and detested collar. He stalked off when I finished, leaving his *remonstrances* behind in the form of several scratches on my hands and wrists.

   Relatives: *remonstrance, remonstrant, remonstration, remonstrator, remonstrative, remonstra-tively*
Synonyms: *object, expostulate*

11. **sate** ('sāt) v.   To stuff or glut yourself to a point beyond satisfaction; to indulge to the point of satisfaction; probably an alternative form of *satiate*, from L. *satis*, enough

When she had *sated* herself with sleep, Jan said she was finally ready to write her term paper.

   Relatives: *satiate* (adj.), *satiable, insatiable, satiation, satiety*
Synonyms: *satiate* (v.), *surfeit, glut, gorge*
Antonym: *starve*

12. **suffice** (sə-'fīs) v.   To be enough or sufficient for a need; from L. *sub + facere*, make or do

I think I know enough of hate
To say that for destruction ice
Is also great
And would suffice.
    —Robert Frost, *Fire and Ice*

   Relatives: *sufficer, sufficiency, sufficient, sufficiently, insufficient*

13. **suffuse** (sə-'fyüz) v.   To spread throughout, as liquid or light spreads; to blush, flush; from L. *sub + fundere*, to pour (under)

Edgar Allan Poe's writing was *suffused* with gloom and foreboding, sadly befitting an author who expected to die both tubercular and insane.

   Relatives: *suffusion, suffusive*
Synonym: *infuse* (off the mark)

14. **supplant** (se-'plant) v.   To take the place of or replace because of superiority or by force or treachery; to erase and offer a substitute for, as *their attempts to supplant local slang met with no success;* from L. *sub + planta,* sole of the foot

In a coup d'état, one ruler or government *supplants* another.

  Relatives: *supplanter, supplantation*
  Synonym: *replace*

15. **temper** ('tem-pər) v.   To moderate or adjust as conditions require, as *she tempered discipline with love;* to strengthen through hardship, as *a ballet corps tempered by a worldwide tour;* to soften steel or cast iron or to toughen steel by definite heating/cooling processes; from L. *temperare,* to moderate, mix, temper

Let the word go forth from this time and place, to friend and foe alike, that the torch has been passed to a new generation of Americans, born in this century, tempered *by war, disciplined by a hard and bitter peace, proud of our ancient heritage....*
    —John F. Kennedy, Inaugural Address

  Relatives: *temper (n.), temperament, temperamental, temperance, temperate, temperature*
  Synonyms: *moderate, toughen*

16. **vindicate** ('vin-də-ˌkāt) v.   To confirm or justify, as *my confidence in them was vindicated by their performance;* to free from blame, absolve, as *he was vindicated by the tribunal;* to avenge, as *only by his death will I be vindicated;* from L. *vindicare,* to lay claim to, avenge

An old Roman method of settling a serious argument was to give each litigant a rod. The two crossed rods as if to fight. The person *vindicated* by the judge then broke his opponent's rod, called a *vindiciae,* from which we get the meaning *to justify* for vindicate.

  Relatives: *vindicator, vindicable, vindication, vindicatory*
  Synonyms: *justify, substantiate, confirm* (first meaning); *absolve, exonerate, exculpate, acquit* (second meaning); *avenge* (third meaning)

ROOT STUDY

From these four roots come dozens of English words, all strongly influenced by the verbs from which they sprang.

1. **FLU, FLUCT,** and **FLUX** mean *to flow.*

   fluctuate—to move one way, then another, at random
   effluent—outflowing material, e.g., the branch of a waterway or pollutants as waste
   influx—a flowing in, as *the influx of holiday crowds*
   mellifluous—richly smooth and flowing (of voice)

2. **GRAD** and **GRESS** mean *to step.*

   graduate—to move to another level or step within a process, like education; n., *graduate,* a
        person who has completed one level or step in a process
   gradual—step by step in measured progression
   regress—to move backward or to a former level
   egress—an exit; the act of going or coming out

3. **MONI** means *to advise, remind, warn*.

   monitor—one who advises, warns, reminds, oversees others
   admonish—to warn or advise; to urge to good behavior through warning or advice; n., *admonition*
   premonition—a foreboding of ill; literally, *prewarning*

4. **PEL** and **PULS** mean *to push*.

   compel—to force compliance or urge in an irresistible way, as *the author felt compelled to write;*
       n., *compulsion;* adj., *compulsive*
   repel—to arouse strong dislike; to push backward or drive away or apart, *repulse*
   pulsate—to beat, throb; n., *pulsation*
   impulse—a sudden push or incentive; inspiration; whim or caprice

USING THE WORDS

List 20 Review

abstain	expurgate	instigate	suffuse
annihilate	extricate	remonstrate	supplant
condescend	imbibe	sate	temper
divulge	impute	suffice	vindicate

Exercise I. Substitution.

Substitute the best word from List 20 for the phrase or word in italics in each question. Write the word above its italicized counterpart.

1. her face *filled* with color at his compliment

2. glad to see my evaluation *justified* by her exam score

3. won't *purge* any of the beautiful, poetic lines

4. afraid that will have to *do* for today

5. strange that she had *ascribed* all the movie's flaws to one cause when there'd been many

6. no need to *object* so forcibly

7. steel being *strengthened* by the annealing process

8. better if you didn't *incite* ill will within the class

9. a way to *disentangle* Poucette from this ball of yarn

10. can't *soak up* any knowledge in all this commotion

Exercise II. Fill-Ins.

Select the most appropriate word from List 20 and Roots based on clues in context.

1. Dad _____ Jan and me about drinking as soon as we passed our
   driver's tests, warning us that unless we _____ from alcohol we would
   never be allowed to use the family car.

2. Carrie took Mom's advice and _____ herself on a rich chocolate cake, eating
   so much of it that she had a _____ she would be sick before very long.

3. Carrie's foreboding became grim truth. Although she never _____ how much
   cake she had gobbled, she did _____ to admit that she'd really overdone it.

4. When our archrival is scheduled for a basketball game, we dream of absolutely
   _____ them. We know that a narrow win gives less satisfaction than
   a rout.

5. The _____ of people from neighboring islands or oppressive regimes
   has _____ some natives of Florida, who have chosen to move to less
   populous states. (Hint: Check out Roots to fill the first blank.)

Exercise III. Switcheroo.

Although List 20 consists of verbs, most can be *adjectives* as well. Match these adjectives with their
correct *antonyms* or *contrasting phrases*.

_____ 1. **abstemious**	(a) exuded
_____ 2. **condescending**	(b) drained
_____ 3. **divulged**	(c) fulfilled or satisfied
_____ 4. **sufficient**	(d) unaffected, natural, not superior in manner
_____ 5. **imbibed**	(e) agreeable
_____ 6. **insatiable**	(f) unavenged
_____ 7. **suffused**	(g) concealed
_____ 8. **tempered**	(h) self-indulgent
_____ 9. **remonstrative**	(i) weakened
_____ 10. **vindicated**	(j) lacking

Exercise IV. Rhyme Completion.

Complete the following verses with the appropriate *noun form* of words taught in this lesson. This is a bit tough. You really should review all the Relatives for List 20 words before beginning your career in poesy.

1. Her diet revolting, she yearned for variety;

   Offered some fudge, she succumbed to _____.

2. My cohort in writing is Reverend Kemper,

   A fellow who's loved for agreeable _____.

3. Tim flouted the rules about drink; thus, detention.

   He wrote fifty times, "I believe in _____.

4. Bowdler's been scorned for notorious translation.

   The classics sure suffered from his _____.
   (Note: Early in the 1800s, Dr. Thomas Bowdler decided to "clean up" the classics. *Bowdlerize* means *to rewrite to the detriment of the original.)*

5. How motley a group was that team's delegation!

   They quickly departed at our _____.

6. A spider's web's a dainty fabrication,

   But not to flies concerned with _____.

7. The notion of jogging fills Jan with revulsion,

   Yet her exercise is one form of _____.
   (Clue: Look among the Roots.)

8. There's just one trait I'd like to mention:

   I can't abide your _____.

9. On nuclear weapons he has reservations;

   To him they threaten mass _____.

10. My friend esteems his witty reputation.

    He'd choke at any other _____

Exercise V. Find the Oddball.

In each numbered group, select and cross out the one *unrelated* word or phrase.

1.	exchange	supplant	imbed	replace	oust
2.	object	defy	argue	remonstrate	expostulate
3.	maintain	bowdlerize	expurgate	cleanse	purge
4.	reveal	disclose	tell	discuss	divulge
5.	expel	avenge	justify	vindicate	absolve
6.	spread	suffuse	suffice	flush	infuse
7.	incite	foment	instigate	annoy	egg on
8.	imputation	innuendo	hint	suggestion	remonstrance
9.	go back	regress	retreat	revile	relapse
10.	beat	throb	palpitate	precipitate	pulsate
11.	free	extricate	tricae	trickle	disentangle
12.	dispute	toughen	moderate	soften	temper

Exercise VI. Word Analysis.

1. Within *annihilation* is the root *nihil*, meaning *nothing*. What sort of doctrine is *nihilism?* (You know which book will help you if you're stuck.) _____

   _____

   If you are a believer in nihilism, what might be your viewpoint of war? _____

   _____

2. What is the *confluence* of rivers? _____

   What word derived from JUNCT, JUG, JOIN is a synonym for confluence? _____

3. How is a *vindictive* remark different from a *vindicatory* statement? (Same root, but note the difference.) _____

   _____

   _____

4. How does *precognition* differ from *premonition?* _____

   _____

5. Knowing the root TRICAE, can you explain the meaning of *intricate?* _____

   _____

6. AMAZING THING! Each word in this lesson comes from Latin, many almost *verbatim,* which happens to be a Latin word unchanged in 2,000+ years. (All but three in List 20 have Latin prefixes.) That's not so amazing, but . . . we have hundreds of everyday words that are spelled exactly as they were when Caesar and Antony walked the earth. How many can you think of? Take a peek at List 18, "Latina Vivit," for starters.

   _____

   _____

Review

This lesson reviews the words and roots in Lists 17–20. Read over all the words and roots, one by one, to see how many you remember. Forgotten a couple? Recheck, fixing each in your mind before you begin the review exercises.

LIST 17	**LIST 18**	**LIST 19**	**LIST 20**
aphorism	ad hoc	abrogate	abstain
bombast	alter ego	acquit	annihilate
construe	bona fide	adjudicate	condescend
dissent	caveat emptor	advocate	divulge
glib	corpus delicti	commute	expurgate
hyperbole	ex post facto	extort	extricate
innuendo	extempore	extradite	imbibe
prate	habeas corpus	felony	impute
pun	in extremis	forensic	instigate
reticent	magnum opus	indict	remonstrate
rhetoric	non sequitur	larceny	sate
solecism	persona non grata	litigation	suffice
soliloquy	quid pro quo	malfeasance	suffuse
spiel	sine qua non	perjury	supplant
terse	status quo	sanction	temper
vociferous	subpoena	tort	vindicate
		vagrant	

ROOTS

CEDE, CEED, CESS	JUNCT, JUG,	PEN
DEM	JOIN	PLEB
DIC, DICT	LOC	PON, POS
FLU, FLUCT, FLUX	LUC, LUX	SENS, SENT
GRAD, GRESS	MONI	TEMPOR
JUD, JUR, JUS	MORPH	VOC, VOKE
	PEL, PULS	

USING THE WORDS

Exercise I. Antonyms.
Select the word or phrase most nearly opposite to the word or phrase in bold type.

_____ 1. **terse**
   (a) short   (b) vivacious   (c) loquacious
   (d) patient   (e) hasty

_____ 2. **abrogate**
   (a) establish   (b) deny   (c) ascertain
   (d) acquit   (e) adjudicate

_____ 3. **sanction**
   (a) legalize   (b) disapprove   (c) end
   (d) disturb   (e) equate

_____ 4. **bona fide**
   (a) honest   (b) spurious   (c) nauseous
   (d) similar   (e) unpleasant

_____ 5. **innuendo**
   (a) slur   (b) interrogation   (c) private
   (d) open statement (e) vindication   comment

_____ 6. **bombast**
   (a) regeneration (b) peace   (c) reticence
   (d) sympathy   (e) secession

_____ 7. **glib remark**
   (a) hasty retort (b) anxious question (c) indecisive
   (d) witty saying (e) judicious statement comment

_____ 8. **fluctuation**
   (a) ex post facto (b) extrication   (c) status quo
   (d) infiltration (e) mirabile dictu

_____ 9. **abstain**
   (a) release   (b) adjure   (c) divulge
   (d) indulge   (e) misinterpret

_____ 10. **dissent**
   (a) concur   (b) advise   (c) implicate
   (d) egress   (e) instigate

Exercise II. Truth or Fiction.
Mark **T** for statements that express truth and **F** for those that are fiction.

_____ 1. Your advocate in court will present the case for the county, city, or state.

_____ 2. Zack's term in prison may be commuted for good behavior.

_____ 3. Fearing illegal imprisonment, you may ask your lawyer to obtain a writ of habeas corpus to prevent such an unfortunate circumstance.

_____ 4. If you have a pressing engagement, you may ignore a subpoena.

_____ 5. Each carefully written, well-thought-out piece of creative writing can be thought of as your magnum opus.

_____ 6. A humorous non sequitur will help your listener to grasp the point you are trying to make.

_____ 7. If you deliberately omit something from your testimony in a trial, you have perjured yourself.

_____ 8. *Corpus delicti* can refer either to the victim of a murder or to the vital facts that prove the crime.

_____ 9. The term *rhetoric,* which historically refers to the art of writing and speech, is an example of a word whose meaning has degenerated.

_____ 10. *Either the players or the coach calls time out* is an example of a solecism.

Exercise III. Chart Fill-In.

Add the missing items to the chart.

	PREFIX	**ROOT**	**WORD**	**DEFINITION**
1.	voc-	fer	_____	clamorously insistent
2.	_____	_____	extemporaneous	_____
3.	mal-	_____	_____	illegal use of public office
4.	_____	purg-	_____	to purge offensive matter
5.	pre-	_____	_____	foreboding, fear of what is to come
6.	_____	_____	amorphous	_____
7.	_____	tricae	_____	to disentangle
8.	sol-	_____	_____	long, reflective speech
9.	in-	satis	_____	incapable of being satisfied or fulfilled
10.	_____	_____	endemic	_____

Exercise IV. Analogies.

Complete each analogy with the best pair possible.

_____ 1. rootless : vagrant ::

    (a) regrettable : annihilation
    (b) fortunate : junction
    (c) likely : alter ego
    (d) handy : impulse
    (e) glib : spiel

_____ 2. felon : persona non grata ::

    (a) imbiber : satiated
    (b) adjudicator : impartial
    (c) president : reticent
    (d) punster : pathetic
    (e) extortionist : lithe

_____ 3. fondness : sentimentality ::

    (a) talk : prating
    (b) larceny : theft
    (c) understatement : hyperbole
    (d) felony : crime
    (e) hint : suggestion

_____ 4. legal code : law of torts ::

    (a) building : construction
    (b) medicine : profession
    (c) barter : quid pro quo
    (d) judgment : verdict
    (e) trees : maple

_____ 5. condescend : stoop ::

    (a) impose : put down
    (b) dictate : plead
    (c) secede : join
    (d) ascribe : impute
    (e) supplant : begin anew

_____ 6. progress : regress ::

    (a) instigate : discourage
    (b) acquit : exonerate
    (c) imbibe : inhale
    (d) extort : pressure
    (e) advocate : sponsor

_____ 7. suffice : sate ::

    (a) prate : chatter
    (b) abstain : refrain
    (c) suggest : dictate
    (d) indict : accuse
    (e) plead : remonstrate

_____ 8. sine qua non : essential ::

    (a) caveat emptor : trivial
    (b) in extremis : early
    (c) non sequitur : vital
    (d) extortion : intimidating
    (e) extradition : illegal

Exercise V. Fill-Ins.

Select the most appropriate word from the choices offered, based on clues in context.

construed	annihilate	in extremis	larceny
aphorism	ad hoc	pun	divulging
hyperbole	reticent	forensic	litigation
alter ego	caveat emptor	remonstrated	vindicated

DOUBLE TROUBLE

Horace and Maurice were identical twins, that is, identical in appearance, but one was certainly

not the _____ of the other in personality. As someone who enjoyed creating

                     1

an effect, Horace was given to _____; he loathed understatement. By

                                 2

contrast, Maurice was the strong, silent type, _____ in the extreme, rarely

                                 3

_____ even his name. Horace would say or do anything, which involved the

               4

two in constant _____. Poor Maurice was forever being dragged into court

                       5

for something Horace had said or done.

Horace raised and sold turkeys with little regard for either his turkeys or his customers.

_____ was his motto, and many an unwary customer had purchased a turkey

               6

_____ who died en route to its new home. When neighbors teased Maurice,

               7

telling him he had "double trouble," their _____ was painfully true.

                                 8

Maurice decided that he needed a lawyer with powerful _____ skills to

                                 9

defend him in court, since he seemed doomed to spend much of his time there. A perceptive fellow,

Maurice's lawyer sized up the twins' situation and accurately _____ it as one

                                 10

of constant tension. Vowing to _____ Horace in court at the first opportunity,

                       11

the lawyer advised his distraught client to have patience and repeated his favorite

_____: "Experience keeps a dear school, but fools will learn in no other."

               12

"We'll nail the fool next time," the lawyer promised. The lawyer created

a(n) _____ team of teenagers to keep an eye on Horace and told another

                 13

group of kids to keep Maurice company. Thus, he'd have witnesses to the actions of both men.

Maurice's lawyer _____ with both of his investigative teams, urging

                      14

them to behave professionally.

Maurice's worst fears were realized when he was accused of the theft of forty turkey hens, a(n)

_____ he would never even have contemplated. Horace had stolen the
                    15
turkeys, of course, but this time Maurice was _____ in court by his resource-
                                                                16
ful attorney, who had witnesses to both men's actions.

Exercise VI. Matching.

Match the words on the left with the best possible synonym or definition on the right.

_____	1. **ex post facto**	(a)	take the place of
_____	2. **acquit**	(b)	repentant, contrite
_____	3. **extradite**	(c)	low or common
_____	4. **imbibe**	(d)	withdraw, go back
_____	5. **suffuse**	(e)	continued flow, movement
_____	6. **supplant**	(f)	postulate
_____	7. **temper**	(g)	clear, sane
_____	8. **recede**	(h)	urge forward
_____	9. **flux**	(i)	exonerate, free
_____	10. **conjugal**	(j)	absorb, take in
_____	11. **lucid**	(k)	surrender to another authority
_____	12. **posit**	(l)	retroactively, after the fact
_____	13. **penitent**	(m)	marital
_____	14. **plebeian**	(n)	flush, fill, infuse
_____	15. **impel**	(o)	moderate

Here's to You, Simon and Garfunkel
Terms from Music and the Arts

In Context. Before studying the definitions, try reasoning out the meaning of each word, using context as your guide. By now you should be good at finding key words, so no more hints.

1. When the full-length opera *Porgy and Bess* was produced in New York, Clamma Dale as Bess sang one memorable *aria* after another, to the delight of her audiences.

    Aria means _____.

2. The execution of many *bravuras*, those always-difficult musical passages, requires the skill of someone like Segovia if Spanish guitar music is to sound its best.

    Bravura means _____.

3. After their art appreciation course, Mom and Jan enjoyed using words like *chiaroscuro* to describe an artist's technique of depicting light and shade.

    Chiaroscuro means _____.

4. Our school's music director explained that the *concerto* we'd be performing was typical: a lengthy orchestral composition with one or more instrumental solos.

    Concerto means _____.

5. The caricature of a Wagnerian opera *diva* is a familiar cartoon figure. She is shown as a statuesque prima donna with a magnificent chest (presumed necessary to house her powerful voice).

    Diva means _____.

6. Although we'd learned the concerto's notes, we had trouble mastering the *dynamics*. Instead of varying the force and loudness of contrasting passages, we played them much the same.

    Dynamics means _____.

7. I adopted a *falsetto* voice in my attempt to be a soprano for the track team's skit. While the high-pitched singing was funny, it was a strain on my normally baritone voice.

    Falsetto means _____.

8. After Jan had studied remnants of some old Roman *frescoes* in a museum, she was able to explain the technique of painting on moist, fresh plaster with water-based paints.

    Fresco means _____.

9. Jan copied the design in a richly ornamented band of sculpture for a bracelet she made in art class. Her bracelet was displayed under the title "Grecian *Frieze*."

    Frieze means _____.

10. Our family's favorite librettist is William Gilbert, who wrote the *librettos* for the well-known Gilbert and Sullivan operas, like *The Pirates of Penzance* and *H. M. S. Pinafore*. Sullivan's music is made twice as memorable by its marriage with Gilbert's words.

    Libretto means _____.

11. We think of the Statue of Liberty as being green, but her color is the natural *patina* that forms on copper and bronze after long exposure, just as long wear and many polishings impart a satiny silver *patina* to sterling.

    Patina means _____.

12. Gershwin's *Rhapsody in Blue* stands for all that is glorious about the *rhapsody*—a highly melodic composition that appeals to our emotions.

    Rhapsody means _____.

13. Beethoven's *Moonlight Sonata* (No. 14 in C-sharp minor) is typical of the *sonata* form: it has three distinct movements, each one different in style.

    Sonata means _____.

14. One of the band's more difficult pieces had many *staccato* sections with short, sharp breaks between the notes, which forced each instrumentalist to pay close attention.

    Staccato means _____.

15. During Book Week, each English class wrote brief skits based on the class's favorite titles. These *vignettes* were then combined for an all-school assembly.

    Vignette means _____.

16. The violin *virtuoso* for the movie of *Fiddler on the Roof* was Isaac Stern, a Russian-born musician supremely skilled and perfectly appropriate for a musical set in Russia.

    Virtuoso means _____.

WORD STUDY

If you are in high school or your early college years, familiarity with classical music and the arts may not seem important. But people change as they grow, and their minds reach out for new knowledge, often in the arts. If you were once dragged protesting through museums, you will find yourself seeking them out as an adult. Later, clutching another reluctant young hand, you will take your child to see the wonders of the past. Some day you may prefer classical music to the modern, popular tunes.

No doubt you know what an *opera* is, what *lyrics* are, and when the *overture* is played. You can tell the difference between a picture painted in *oil* and one done in *pastels* or *charcoal*. But you'll enjoy knowing even more about the arts. For instance, one student taking a recent SAT would love to have known the meaning of *diva* to earn herself points for a correct answer. These words most definitely appear on standardized tests.

1. **aria** ('är-ē-ə) n.   A melody, usually somewhat elaborate, sung by one person with musical accompaniment; an operatic solo; from It. *aria*, atmospheric air

   Dad said that he preferred the *aria* of a bird, accompanied by the great outdoors, to any operatic performance he had ever heard.

2. **bravura** (brə-'v[y]ür-ə) n.   A musical passage requiring skill to execute well; a display of bravery, brilliance, or daring; from It. *bravura*, bravery

   For the Dinkey-Bird's bravuras,
   And staccatos are so sweet—
   His roulades, appoggiaturas,
   And robustos so complete,
   That the youth of every nation—
   Be they near or far away—
   Have especial delectation,
   In that gladsome roundelay.
      —Eugene Field, "The Dinkey-Bird" (children's poem)

3. **chiaroscuro** (kē-,är-ə-'sk[y]ü[ə]r-[,]ō) n.   The treatment of light and dark in a work of art; a picture rendered as light and shade, not in actual colors; a woodcut print using different tones of one color; from It. *chiaro*, clear, light + *oscuro*, dark, obscure

   Often called "black and white," *chiaroscuro* was conceived by Leonardo da Vinci to create the illusion of space by turning a two-dimensional canvas into something appearing to have three dimensions.

4. **concerto** (kən-'chert-[,]ō) n.   A musical piece with three different movements performed by an orchestra and featuring one or more soloists; from It. *concerto*, concert

   A very famous *concerto* is Richard Addinsell's *Warsaw Concerto*, written for the British film *Dangerous Moonlight* and featuring the piano as solo instrument.

   Relatives: *concert, concertina, concertize*

5. **diva** ('dē-və) n.   The lead female singer or prima donna (first lady); from It. *diva*, goddess

   Literally *goddess* in Italian, *diva* is akin to many words in other languages, all referring to a deity with only four letters: *dieu* in French, *dios* in Spanish, *deus* in Latin, and *diva* again in Sanskrit.

6. **dynamics** (dī-'nam-iks) n. pl.   The variation in loudness or force (music); the forces operating in any matter subject to change or variation, as *the dynamics of the marketplace* or *the dynamics of personality;* that branch of physics concerned with matter in motion; from Gr. *dynamis,* power

   When we say that a pianist can produce tremendous volume and variety of tone, we are commenting on the artist's mastery of *dynamics.*

   Relatives: *dyne* (unit of force), *dynamic, dynamism, dynamite, dynamo*

7. **falsetto** (fȯl-'set-[ˌ]ō) n.   The artificially high voice, mainly above normal range.   adv. In an artificially high voice, as *he sang amusingly falsetto;* from It. *falso,* false

   Many male comedians have used their voices to good effect, adopting the *falsetto* to indicate sudden terror or nervousness, as Richard Pryor did in the film *Silver Streak.*

8. **fresco** ('fres-[ˌ]kō) n.   Painting with water-based paints on fresh, moist plaster; a painting done by this technique; pl., frescoes, frescos; from It. *fresco,* fresh

   At Fontainebleau in France, sixty different *frescoes* depict the travels of Ulysses.

   Relative: *fresco* (v.)

9. **frieze** ('frēz) n.   The decorative band on a building, often sculptured to have three dimensions; the same ornamented band around the walls of a room; from L. *frisium,* embroidered cloth

   On ancient buildings in Europe, as well as some from the last century, the eye is drawn up the columns of a structure to the richly ornamented *frieze* depicting gods, battles, or memorable heroes.

10. **libretto** (lə-'bret-[ˌ]ō) n.   The words (text) that go with a piece of music, such as an opera or operetta (light opera); from L. *liber,* book

    Stephen Sondheim, a famous modern musician, wrote the *libretto* for Leonard Bernstein's classic *West Side Story.*

    Relative: *librettist* (the writer of a libretto)

11. **patina** (pə-'tē-nə, 'pat-ə-nə) n.   The much-admired look that time/weather/acids give to metals, usually a turquoise green on copper and bronze and a dulled satiny finish on sterling; from L. *patina,* shallow dish

    My young aunt used her sterling daily and polished it weekly until its *patina* satisfied her.

    Relative: *patine* (v., to cover with a patina)

12. **rhapsody** ('rap-səd-ē) n.   A musical composition without definite form, improvisational in type, usually expressing strong feeling; something said, written, or sung with fervent emotion, as *the dawn rhapsody of a bird*; from Gr. *rhapsoidia*, a recitation of epic poetry selections, rhapsody

    The well-loved Hungarian Rhapsody No. 2 by Liszt is based on Gypsy sources and is only one of his nineteen Hungarian *rhapsodies* originally written for a solo piano.

    Relatives: *rhaposodist, rhapsodize, rhapsodic, rhapsodical, rhapsodically*
    Derivation: Rhapsody literally means *songs strung together*, as the base roots **rhaptein** (to sew, stitch together) and **aidein** (to sing) tell us. The term rhapsody originally referred to the books of the *Iliad* and the *Odyssey*, which were in fragments until bards collected and sung them as long stories, the way we know them now. Red-robed bards sang the *Iliad*; those in blue robes sang the *Odyssey*.

13. **sonata** (sə-'nä-tə) n.   A fairly lengthy musical piece, usually with several distinct movements that contrast in key and style; from It. and L. *sonare*, to sound

    Three of Beethoven's most famous sonatas are known by the names *Moonlight, Pathétique,* and *Appassionata.*

    Relative: *sonatina* (shorter or simpler sonata)

14. **staccato** (stə-'kät-(ˌ)ō) adj.   Abrupt, clear-cut, short, distinctly separate, as *staccato* notes in music; disjointed, disconnected; from It. *staccare*, to detach

    The sharp, *staccato* manner in which she delivered her orders revealed that she had lost her patience.

    Relatives: *staccato* (n.), *staccato* (adv.), *staccato mark* (the dot or pointed vertical stroke over a musical note to be played staccato)

15. **vignette** (vin-'yet) n.   A succinct verbal or literary sketch; a small segment representative of the whole, i.e, one scene of a play, book, or movie, usually selected for its excellence; from F. *vignette* (little vines, tendrils), diminutive of *vigne*, vine

    Originally a *vignette* was a portrait or small likeness of someone, bordered with vine leaves. (See the root.)

    Relatives: *vignettist* (n.), *vignette* (v., to describe briefly)

16. **virtuoso, virtuosa** (vər-chə-'wō(ˌ)sō and vər-chə-'wō(ˌ)sə) n.   One supremely skilled and knowledgeable in an art; from It. *virtuoso*, virtuous, skilled

    The concertmaster of an orchestra (first violinist) is the *virtuoso* (or *virtuosa*) of the group and the assistant to the conductor.

    Relatives: *virtuoso* (adj.), *virtuosity*
    Antonyms: *beginner, neophyte, tyro, novice*

ROOT STUDY

This is a rather motley assortment of roots, but all are big contributors to our language and worth knowing.

1. **DYN/DYNAM** means *power.*

   dynasty—a hereditary line of rulers, owners, etc.
   dynamo—usually a small generator for electric current; also, someone with astonishing energy or drive
   dynamite—anything that sets off a powerful reaction, as nitroglycerine does in the explosive
   thermodynamics—branch of physics dealing with heat and related energy forms

2. **HAL** and **SPIR** mean to *breathe, breath, life.*

   inhale—to breathe in; *exhale*—to breathe out
   inhalator or *respirator*—machines to aid breathing as means of artificial *respiration*
   expire—to breathe one's last; to die; to reach an end
   aspire—to seek, to hope or long for, as *she aspired to a career in music*

3. **LEG, LIG,** and **LECT** mean *to choose, gather, read.*

   legible—clear enough to be read; antonym, *illegible*
   eligible—capable of being selected because of skills, knowledge, availability, etc.
   select—to choose or pick out of a group
   legumes—peas or beans, which typically have to be chosen for ripeness, then gathered

4. **NOC/NOX** means *night.*

   nocturne—a dreamy musical composition, usually restful
   nocturnal—referring to night, as *nocturnal animals*
   equinox—a time when day and night are equally long; *autumnal equinox* = September 22, *vernal equinox* = March 21

5. **NOC/NOX** means *harm, injury*

   innocent—free from blame, not guilty; unaware, unsophisticated, childlike
   nocuous and *noxious*—harmful, injurious, unpleasant
   innocuous—harmless

USING THE WORDS

List 21 Review

aria	diva	frieze	sonata
bravura	dynamics	libretto	staccato
chiaroscuro	falsetto	patina	vignette
concerto	fresco	rhapsody	virtuoso/a

Exercise I. Definitions.

Write the correct word from List 21 on the line following its definition.

1. short, abrupt, disconnected

2. aged/weathered film or appearance

3. richly ornamented band

4. watercolor painting on damp plaster

5. the lead female singer, prima donna

6. art technique using light and shade to give the illusion of depth

7. tricky musical passage or a show of brilliance, bravery, or daring

8. brief literary sketch

9. skilled, knowledgeable performer

10. demanding musical solo for voice

11. musical piece for a solo instrument, consisting of separate movements contrasting in key and style

12. the text for a musical drama

13. emotional piece of music with no set form, tending to be improvisational

14. variation in force or loudness of music

15. an unnaturally high voice

16. lengthy musical composition featuring one or more solo instruments, usually with three contrasting movements

Exercise II. Fill-Ins.

Words from List 21 are used every day, not solely with reference to the arts. From the choices offered, select the most appropriate word for each sentence.

bravura	rhapsodize	chiaroscuro	diva
frieze	staccato	vignette	patina
aria	dynamics	virtuosa	

1. Because population _____ strongly affect our economy, modern professionals study various trends as people age, relocate, and change habits or attitudes.

2. Breaking up an angry fight between Andy and Carrie, Mom said, "We've witnessed this _____ of family life many times before. Both of you go to your rooms!"

3. Although young, Figment is notable for _____. Not a leaf stirs or a butterfly flutters without an arched back and a warning hiss from our "attack kitten."

4. "You don't need to _____ quite so often about the new guy in your class," Jan told Carrie. "We got the message sometime last week."

5. Mom's an authentic _____ with her food processor, creating delicious foods whose recipes are not in cookbooks.

6. My alarm clock is my dad's morning _____ in the shower as he tortures yet another operatic classic.

7. Andy must have told his entire school about Marigold's new kittens, because a _____ of kids wound its way up our sidewalk and around the house all one afternoon.

8. Although our house was new a few years ago, active living and energetic family members have given it that lived-in look, a _____ of age all its own.

9. In the very early hours on the lake, a dawn _____ emerges that needs no sharp coloration to be memorable.

10. Our neighbor's canary would be aptly named _____, because she spends hours trilling melodious solos.

11. The _____ beat of Jan's high heels as she marched up the sidewalk told us that she was in a hurry.

Exercise III. Logic.
Based on the information given so far in this lesson, answer the following questions.

1. Which type of music might help a baby drift off to sleep? (Hint: Search among Roots.)

   _____

2. Is a rabid dog *innocuous*? _____

3. When applied to people, does the word *dynamo* have positive or negative connotations?

   _____

4. What are *aspirations*? _____

5. What word derived from LEG/LIG/LECT can describe the handwriting of many doctors and 4-year-olds?

   _____

6. What do the words *libretto* and *library* have in common?

   _____

7. The soft drink Fresca™ was not named by accident. What good connotations does its name suggest?

   _____

8. When people act *in concert* with one another, how are they behaving?

   _____

   What is a *concerted effort*? _____

9. Dynamics in music concerns degrees of loudness. Can you arrange the following musical terms in order of increasing loudness? *forte, pianissimo, fortissimo, piano*

   _____

10. How is the word *falsetto* related to *false*?

    _____

    _____

Exercise IV. Analogies.

Complete each analogy with the best pair possible, using words from List 21 and Roots.

_____ 1. wall : fresco ::

(a) sidewalk : art
(b) museum : exhibition
(c) canvas : oil painting
(d) newspaper : advertising
(e) corridor : frieze

_____ 2. Beethoven : sonatas ::

(a) Simon and Garfunkel : literature
(b) Gilbert and Sullivan : operas
(c) Walt Disney : horror films
(d) Vienna Boys' Choir : rock and roll
(e) symphonies : Boston Pops Orchestra

_____ 3. *mountain climbing : bravura ::

(a) Windsor family : dynasty
(b) legumes : soybean
(c) lyrics : libretto
(d) orchestra : concerto
(e) politics : Kennedy family

*Keep calm on this one. Remember to _decide what kind of analogy it is_ before examining answers. Eliminate the impossible answers, one by one.

_____ 4. physics : thermodynamics ::

(a) concerto : rhapsody
(b) song : aria
(c) inhalator : respirator
(d) architecture : designer
(e) play : vignette

_____ 5. overture : finale ::

(a) tempo : time
(b) desires : aspirations
(c) drama : scene
(d) onset : expiration
(e) selection : eligibility

Exercise V. Antonyms.

Find an antonym or contrasting phrase for each word on the left.

_____ 1. **timidity**	(a) dampen, discourage
_____ 2. **chiaroscuro**	(b) sloth
_____ 3. **falsetto**	(c) harmless
_____ 4. **inspire**	(d) bravura
_____ 5. **dynamo**	(e) flowing, connected
_____ 6. **noxious**	(f) diurnal (in the daytime)
_____ 7. **eligible**	(g) lacking emotion
_____ 8. **nocturnal**	(h) full color spectrum
_____ 9. **staccato**	(i) unsuitable
_____ 10. **rhapsodic**	(j) bass

Exercise VI. Word Analysis

1. *Vignette* (root meaning little vines or tendrils) is an example of many words with the suffix **-ette** or **-etta**. You are familiar with *novelette, cigarette, operetta, rosette,* and *sermonette,* to name a few. How does this suffix alter the meaning of the root words in these examples?

   _____

   _____

2. Each person's voice is unique, just like his or her fingerprints. But we have grouped singing voices into categories. Beginning with the word for the lowest (or deepest) singing voice, arrange the voices in order, ending with the highest. *baritone, soprano, contralto* (or *alto*), *tenor, basso, mezzo soprano*

   _____

3. The musical term to describe a *smooth and connected technique* is *legato*. What word in List 21 is its antonym?

   _____

4. A *crescendo* gradually increases in force or loudness. Add a prefix to *crescendo* to change the meaning to a gradual *decrease* in force or loudness.

   _____

5. If you describe an older person as "exhibiting the patina of age," what physical description do your words suggest?

   _____

   _____

6. What would be some differences between a funeral *dirge* and a *rhapsody?*

   _____

   _____

LIST 22 O Ye Gods! Part Two
More Words from Myth and Legend

In Context. Before studying the definitions, try reasoning out the meaning of each word, using context as your guide.

1. After the basketball game Carrie moaned, "That team had nothing but *amazons*, who kept dunking the ball. The girl I guarded ran me all over the floor, and my eyes were about level with her waistband!"

    Amazon means _____.

2. Jan's art class studied *Attic* style before attempting to design a modern building along those Greek lines noted for refined simplicity.

    Attic means _____.

3. Jan and I have ridden horseback several times, but we have little hope of emulating the *centaur* who leads our trail rides and who seems totally at one with his horse.

    Centaur means _____.

4. When instruction on personal *hygiene* entered a school's curriculum years ago, it stressed cleanliness of the body; today's teaching includes moral issues.

    Hygiene means _____.

5. Whenever we can get to an ocean beach, our family walks with eyes down, searching for mussels and other shells with beautiful, *iridescent* shell linings.

    Iridescent means _____.

6. Although the new principal is a strict disciplinarian, we have learned that he's basically a *jovial* person who would rather laugh than frown.

    Jovial means _____.

7. One kid in our school is feared, not only because he is tough but also because he has an ever-present gang of followers, *myrmidons* dumb enough to do whatever he tells them.

    Myrmidon means _____.

8. "The human race would probably pay a fortune if a *panacea* could be discovered for all the cold viruses," Dad said as he reached for a tissue.

    Panacea means _____.

9. The principal decreed that those of us with driver's licenses and parental consent could drive to school, even though he knew he was opening *Pandora's box*, and problems with cars would then plague his administration.

    Pandora's box means _____.

10. In response to our persistent begging, Dad bought an old car that Jan and I could drive. He dubbed the car *Phaeton*, saying it was a rickety jalopy at best but heavy enough to protect us in case of an accident.

    Phaeton means _____.

11. When he visited us at the cottage, Dad's business associate arrived in a small plane with *pontoons*, instead of wheels, for landing on water.

    Pontoon means _____.

12. "Insistence upon conformity no-matter-what is not my style," the principal said. "We won't have *procrustean* discipline in this school. But we will have dress standards that reflect a professional attitude toward our work."

    Procrustean means _____.

13. For a small girl, Carrie has a *stentorian* bellow. "I don't care if you were cheering for the team," Mom told her once. "No lady ever sounds like that!"

    Stentorian means _____.

14. Poets revel in the wealth of words that English offers, but I prefer the poet who writes "wooded glen" to the one who pens "*sylvan* glen."

    Sylvan means _____.

15. Andy was so bored over Easter vacation that he spent hours *tantalizing* the cats, holding catnip mice just out of reach and dangling balls of yarn above their heads.

    Tantalize means _____.

16. "An absolute horde of *Valkyries*," Mom gasped as she burst out the door of the department store. "I've never seen women so ferocious at a sale. Now I know how Carrie felt about the basketball amazons."

    Valkyrie means _____.

17. "No spring *zephyr*, that's for sure," Dad observed as we gathered at the window to watch the trees bent nearly double in a windstorm.

    Zephyr means _____.

WORD STUDY

The words in this list were once proper nouns, and all have come to us from ancient times and legends. So many have survived that you can see what a giant sponge our language is. We refer to *martial arts*, the planet *Mars*, and the month of *March* without ever thinking of the Roman god **Mars** who fathered all these words. But it's interesting to know where the words come from, and a word is always easier to remember if you know its etymology. All these words have a story to tell.

1. **amazon** ('am-ə-ˌzän) n.   A woman taller and stronger than average; literally, *without breast*; from Gr. *amazon*, female warrior

   Predecessor of today's tall, strong women whom we call *amazons* was Hippolyta, daughter of Ares (Greek god of war) and queen of the mythical race of Amazons.

   > Relatives: *amazonian, Amazon* (the river)
   > Derivation: According to Greek mythology, the Amazons were a ferocious race of African warrior-women. Men were not part of their nation; a baby boy was either killed at birth or sent to his father in a neighboring state. All girls had their right breast cut or burned off so that they could better draw a bow in battle. Near the end of the Trojan War, they came to help Priam, the king of Troy.

2. **Attic** ('at-ik) adj.   Referring to Greece or Athens; noted for Grecian refinement and purity, as *an Attic architectural style*; from Gr. *attike*, Attica or Greece

   As a small, topmost story of a home, the attic gets its name from classical *Attic* architecture, which featured a small order (design form) placed above a much larger order.

   > Relatives: *Attic salt* (delicate, elegantly refined wit); *Attic faith* (unassailable, sacred faith)

3. **centaur** ('sen-ˌtȯ[e]r) n.   A member of a legendary race—half man, half horse—that lived in the part of ancient Greece known as Thessaly; a rider so attuned to his horse that they seem one; from Gr. *Kentauros*, centaur

   Why don't they knead two virtuous souls for life
   Into that moral centaur, man and wife?
       —Lord Byron, *Don Juan*, c. III

   > Relative: *Centaurus* (southern constellation)

4. **hygiene** ('hī-ˌjēn) n.   Habits or conditions that promote good health, such as cleanliness; from Gr. *Hygeia*, goddess of health

   After many of us got plantar warts on our feet, we became extremely conscious of *hygiene* and everyone wore thongs into the showers in the boys' locker room.

   > Relatives: *hygienist, hygienic, hygienically*
   > Derivation: Health goddess Hygeia was the daughter of Asclepius, the Greek god of healing who was a son of Apollo. Hygeia's symbol was a serpent drinking from a cup in her hand. Her sister was Panacea, meaning "all-heal." Today's physicians still take the oath of Hippocrates, a famous Greek doctor, which begins: "I swear by Apollo, the Asklepios, and Hygeia and Panacea and all the gods and goddesses . . ."

5. **iridescent** (ˌir-ə-ˈdes-ᵊnt) adj.   Having the colors of the rainbow or a play of these colors when position is changed, as with a glass prism or a soap bubble; glittering, brilliant, as *a memorable and iridescent performance in a demanding role*; from L. *irid-*, iris, and *Iris*, goddess of the rainbow

The purification of politics is an iridescent *dream. Government is force.*
    —John James Ingalls, newspaper article, 1890

    Relatives: *iridescence, iridescently, iridium* (the element)
    Synonyms: *glittering, brilliant, shining* (none exact)
    Derivation: Iris, goddess of the rainbow, carried messages for Zeus and Hera, rulers of the Greek gods. She has left her name to a part of the eye and a flower, and as a synonym for rainbow. In later Greek poetry, Iris is the wife of Zephyrus and the mother of Eros.

6. **jovial** (ˈjō-vē-əl) adj.   Merry and good-humored, jolly and convivial; from L. *Jovem*, Jove or Jupiter

It's of three jovial *huntsmen, and a-hunting they did go;*
And they hunted and they holloed, and they blew their horns also...
    —"The Three Jovial Huntsmen," Old English ballad

    Relatives: *joviality, jovially, Jovian* (of Jove, or Jupiter)
    Synonyms: *mirthful, merry, jolly, convivial*
    Antonyms: *dour, choleric, testy, gloomy, irritable*
    Derivation: The Roman (Latin) name of Zeus was Jove, or Jupiter, generally a merrier sort than Zeus. From the ancient root (**Ju = Ze**) we get the words *Tuesday, diva, deity, adieu, Diana, journey, adjourn, sojourn,* and *July*. It is said that Sagittarians born under Jupiter's sign are jolly folk.

7. **myrmidon** (ˈmər-mə-ˌdän) n.   Faithful follower, especially one who executes any order, no matter how distasteful, issued by his leader; from Gr. *Myrmidon*, a member of a Thessalian people

In *West Side Story*, both gang leaders have a band of *myrmidons* who will "rumble" when their leaders name the time and place.

    Derivation: The Thessalian Myrmidons went with their king Achilles to the Trojan War. Although they did not figure prominently in mythology, their name lives on. Once, *myrmidon* meant loyal follower, but the word has degenerated in meaning.

8. **panacea** (ˈpan-ə-ˈsē-ə) n.   A universal cure-all or absolute remedy; from Gr. *pan*, all + *akos*, remedy, and Panacea, "all-heal"

Those who know it consider the English traffic circle, while not a *panacea*, to be a far better method of regulating traffic flow than the ubiquitous American stoplight.

    Relative: *panacean*
    Synonym: *cure-all*
    Derivation: See *hygiene*.

9. **Pandora's box** (pan-,dōr-əz-'bäks) n.   A seemingly endless source of problems and difficulties; from Gr. *pan* + *dora*, all-gifted, plus the myth

Motivated by security reasons and/or idealism, the United States has taken several struggling countries under its wing—perhaps a modern version of *Pandora's box*, with the expected accompanying problems.

Derivation: Prometheus stole fire from the gods to benefit the human race, which made Zeus (Jupiter) furious. In retaliation, he ordered Hephaestus (Vulcan) to make the first mortal woman—Pandora—an exquisite creature to whom Zeus gave a box containing all the ills of the world with which he planned to punish human beings. When the box was opened—some say by Pandora, others by her husband, Epimetheus—the evils were let loose, but so was Hope, the last to fly out of the box.

10. **phaeton** ('fā-ət-ən) n.   Either a lightweight, rather unstable carriage drawn by horses or a touring car; from Gr. *Phaëthon*

We yelled with excitement as the *phaetons* raced round the last curve and each driver flicked his whip at his horse's flanks.

Derivation: When a young man, Phaeton (Phaëthon) begged to be allowed to drive his father's chariot of the sun. Tired of listening to him, Apollo (Helios) finally gave in, but poor Phaeton was unable to keep the magnificent chariot and powerful horses in their usual track. He reduced Libya to barren sands and scorched most of Africa, turning its inhabitants black and nearly ruining its vegetation. Zeus was forced to thunderbolt him from the sky, and the boy plunged into a river.
(Note: One major purpose of a myth is to explain things. This one explains why your parents are reluctant to hand over the car keys.)

11. **pontoon** (pän-'tün) n.   A float used to support an airplane, raft, boat, or similar structure on water; from L. *pont*, bridge

At our lake cottage we have a dock supported by *pontoons* as well as a swimming raft with oil barrels as *pontoons* underneath its wooden planks.

Relatives: *ponton* (pontoon), *pontonier* (one who builds a pontoon bridge)
Synonym: *float* (n.)
Derivation: Pontus was the ancient name for sea, and Uranus meant the sky. Pontus has left his name in many words referring to bridges, as the Greeks viewed the sea as a bridge from one land to another. A *pontiff* was once a high Roman priest in charge of bridge construction, although a modern pontiff is a bishop or pope.

12. **procrustean** (p[r]ə-'krəs-te-ən) adj.   Marked by insistence upon conformity no matter what, with total disregard for extenuating circumstances; from G. *Procrustes*

The anger and questions aroused by the Vietnam War forced Americans to reevaluate the military draft, that *procrustean bed* that conscripted youth regardless of temperamental fitness.

Relative: *procrustean bed* (pattern into which one is thrust arbitrarily)
Derivation: Procrustes was a giant Greek robber who redesigned wayfarers to fit his iron bed. He either stretched the victim to fit, or lopped off any excess length of leg. His nickname was "The Stretcher," and he was eventually killed by the hero Theseus.

13. **stentorian** (sten-'tōr-ē-ən) adj.   Exceedingly loud; from Gr. *Stentor*

Seven hundred years B.C. the poet Homer wrote of the *stentorian* sound of "Great-hearted Stentor with brazen voice, who could shout as loud as fifty other men."

   Relatives: *stentor* (one with a loud voice; also a protozoan with a trumpet-shaped body), *stentorophonic* (extremely loud)
   Synonyms: *booming, thunderous, bellowing* (none exact)
   Derivation: Stentor was a Greek herald, known in the time of the Trojan War for his incredibly loud voice.

14. **sylvan** ('sil-vən) adj.   Referring to the woods or forest, wooded; from L. *sylva,* wood

Thou still unravished bride of quietness,
Thou foster-child of silence and slow time,
Sylvan *historian, who canst thus express*
A flowery tale more sweetly than our rhyme:
What leaf-fringed legend haunts about thy shape?
   —John Keats, "Ode to a Grecian Urn"

   Relative: *sylvan* (n., one who hangs out in the woods)
   Synonym: *wooded*
   Derivation: Silvanus was a good-natured god who lived mostly in the woods and left his name behind to the joy of poets, who find the Latin *sylvan* infinitely more melodious than the Old English *wooded.*

15. **tantalize** ('tant-əl-ˌīz) v.   To bedevil or tease by pretending to offer something, yet keeping the offering beyond reach; from Gr. *Tantalus*

The smell of our neighborhood pizza parlor *tantalizes* us with a nearly irresistible fragrance each time we go by.

   Relatives: *tantalizing, tantalizingly, tantalus* (a glass cabinet displaying wine decanters unobtainable without a key)
   Derivation: A wealthy king and son of Zeus, Tantalus did a sinful thing by serving up his own son Pelops as a dinner for the gods. His punishment in Hades put him in the middle of a lake. As thirst consumed him he bent to drink but the water always receded, while over his head hung luscious fruits, forever beyond his reach.

16. **Valkyrie** (val-'kir-ē, 'val-kə-rē) n.   A woman even tougher than an amazon; literally, *chooser of the slain;* from ON *valkyrja*

One of the most stirring pieces of orchestral music is the *Ride of the Valkyries,* a wild and soaring composition by Richard Wagner.

   Derivation: Odin was king of the Norse gods, and the Valkyries were his beautiful-but-awful nymphs in Valhalla, heavenly home of warriors killed in battle. When a battle raged on earth, the Valkyries rode swift horses through the fray and chose the men destined to die. Back home in Valhalla, these nymphs served the heroes tasty drinks in the evenings and let them play at war all day long.

17. **zephyr** ('zef-ər) n.   A soft, gentle breeze, often westerly; from Gr. *Zephyros*, god of the west wind

    Fair laughs the morn, and soft the zephyr *blows,*
    While proudly riding o'er the azure realm
    In gallant trim the gilded vessel goes;
        —Thomas Gray, *The Bard*

    Opposing Idea: *boreal* (adj.) (from Boreus, god of the north wind; used to describe something chillingly cold)

    Derivation: Zephyrus, god of the west wind, led a more interesting life than most. With the Harpy named Podarge, he fathered Achilles' favorite horses, Xanthus and Balius. Meanwhile, he was married to Chloris, with whom he had a son, and somehow he was also married to Iris, and thereby the father of Eros—not Cupid, but another Eros.
    (Doesn't this sound like an ancient soap opera?)

ROOT STUDY

These four roots are the parents of dozens of our most common and useful English words.

1. **GNOS** and **GNOM** mean *to know*.

    prognosis—a prospect or forecast, as *the prognosis in severe cases of the disease is poor*
    agnostic—one who doubts or says he cannot know for sure, usually regarding the existence of God
    gnome—a sometimes-deformed dwarf of folklore who lives underground and guards treasure

2. **MANU** means *hand*.

    manuscript—originally something written by hand
    manacle—handcuff, shackle, or similar restraint for the hands or wrists
    manage—to handle, supervise, oversee, conduct

3. **PEND** and **PENS** mean *to hang, weigh,* or *pay*.

    pendant—an ornament that hangs or is *suspended*, as on a chain
    compensation—payment or remuneration, emolument; a thing that makes up for something else or takes its place satisfactorily
    suspense—anxiety or pleasurable excitement

4. **TANG, TING, TACT,** and **TIG** means *to touch.*

    tangible—concrete, substantial, as opposed to *intangible,* not definite or concrete
    contingent—adj., dependent upon; n., group, as *the contingent from the office*
    tactile—referring to the sense of touch
    contiguous—adjacent, touching along a boundary

USING THE WORDS

List 22 Review

amazon	jovial	phaeton	sylvan
Attic	myrmidon	pontoon	tantalize
centaur	panacea	procrustean	Valkyrie
hygiene	Pandora's box	stentorian	zephyr
iridescent			

Exercise I. Multiple Choice.

In the blank for each word on the left, write the letter of the best definition or synonym.

_____ 1. **Valkyrie**   (a) shopper   (b) ferocious female   (c) fighter

_____ 2. **stentorian**   (a) unpleasant   (b) rigorous   (c) booming

_____ 3. **panacea**   (a) goddess   (b) cure-all   (c) answer

_____ 4. **jovial**   (a) merry   (b) pleasant   (c) shy

_____ 5. **Attic**   (a) Grecian   (b) ancient   (c) upper story

_____ 6. **zephyr**   (a) wind   (b) gust   (c) gentle breeze

_____ 7. **procrustean**   (a) irritable   (b) of arbitrary uniformity   (c) of serious trouble

_____ 8. **phaeton**   (a) carriage   (b) wagon   (c) vehicle

_____ 9. **centaur**   (a) beast   (b) warrior   (c) skilled rider

_____ 10. **amazon**   (a) African   (b) tall, strong woman   (c) basketball player

_____ 11. **tantalize**   (a) tease   (b) torture   (c) tenderize

_____ 12. **pontoon**   (a) rope   (b) float   (c) wheel

_____ 13. **Pandora's box**   (a) source of trouble   (b) answer to problems   (c) origin of questions

_____ 14. **myrmidon**   (a) subordinate   (b) leader   (c) unquestioning follower

_____ 15. **iridescent**   (a) roseate   (b) glassy   (c) glittering

_____ 16. **hygienic**   (a) healthful   (b) dental   (c) hopeful

_____ 17. **sylvan**   (a) outdoor   (b) wooded   (c) grassy

Exercise II. Who Said That?

Using information from Word Study, write the name of the probable speaker for each of the following comments.

1. "He's uncommonly brave. He deserves to live in Valhalla." _____

2. "What harm could one little peek do—just to see what's inside? We could close the lid if we had to." _____

3. "Whatever you say, Chief, whatever you say." _____

4. "All I want is one sip, just one itsy-bitsy sip!" _____

5. "No sweat, Dad, just watch me. See you at sundown." _____

6. "I can ride anything, anywhere." _____

7. "Give me the shade of the woods anytime." _____

8. "CAN EVERYBODY HEAR ME?" _____

9. "I can cure anything." _____

10. "Hmm, a trifle short. You'll have to stretch." _____

11. "Ho, ho, ho!" _____

12. "Black is for funerals. I love color." _____

13. "I am the bridge." _____

14. "No hurricanes or gusts for me." _____

15. "Remember to brush your teeth and wash your face." _____

16. "What's that man doing here? Show him the way to go home." _____

Exercise III. Analogies.

Complete each analogy with the best pair possible, using words from List 22 and Roots.

_____ 1. Attic salt : wit ::

    (a) stentor : leader
    (b) pontoon : plane
    (c) compensation : emolument
    (d) Procrustes : lord
    (e) hygiene : body

_____ 2. suspense : denouement ::

    (a) research : panacea
    (b) zephyr : gale
    (c) health : hygiene
    (d) tangent : angle
    (e) phaeton : race

_____ 3. pleasant : jovial ::

    (a) unruly : manageable
    (b) agnostic : doubting
    (c) tangible : accessible
    (d) bright : iridescent
    (e) appended : attached

_____ 4. amazon : gnome ::

    (a) Valkyrie : nymph
    (b) stentor : whisperer
    (c) hygienist : aide
    (d) giant : titan
    (e) listener : recorder

_____ 5. manage : conduct ::

    (a) prognosticate : inspect
    (b) contact : repel
    (c) abide : adhere
    (d) diagnose : reveal
    (e) tantalize : bedevil

Exercise IV. Fill-Ins.
Select the most appropriate word from the choices offered, based on clues in context.

Attic	sylvan	myrmidon	manacled
centaur	pontoons	pending	hygienic
zephyr	Pandora's box	intangible	agnostic

1. stepped out of the police car, _____ and defiant

2. real can of worms, a classic _____

3. keep that decision _____ until we know more

4. _____ habits instilled by medical training

5. typical Mafia _____ who does what he's told

6. classically elegant _____ prose style

7. the secret _____ silence the forest

8. _____, yet definite; unthinkable, but true

9. his webbed feet gliding briefly on the surface of the water like intelligent

   _____

10. her sigh, a gentle _____ in my ear

11. unspoken desire of the _____ to know for sure

12. a veritable _____, at home in the saddle

Exercise V. Word Analysis.
1. What parallels do you see between the story of Pandora and the story about Adam and Eve?

   _____

   _____

2. In the Ingalls quote illustrating *iridescent* in Word Study, what word might be substituted for *iridescent?* Is this substitution fully satisfactory? _____

   _____

3. The words in List 22 are extremely old. Can you think of one overriding reason for their continued, useful existence? _____

   _____

4. Why does the term *Valkyrie* have a more negative impact than the word *amazon?*

   _____

5. Vahalla was the Norse home for slain warriors. Where did the American Indian warriors go after death in battle?

   _____

   And does anyone know where the women of these two societies went after death?

   _____

   The Greeks went to the Elysian fields or the Isles of the Blessed after death.
   What is the Christian equivalent? _____

6. If you knew only mythology, and not the words themselves, what could you say about the aurora borealis? (Hint: Check the dictionary for *aurora* only, and take it from there.)

   _____

   _____

In Context. Before studying the definitions, try reasoning out the meaning of each word, using its context as your guide.

1. Looking at Jan and me in our formal prom clothes, Dad said slowly, "Toddlers one minute, adults the next." Mom nodded. "Childhood is all too brief, an *evanescent* thing . . . at least to parents."

   Evanescent means _____.

2. "Your kittenhood is an *extenuating* circumstance," Dad told Poucette and Figment. "But that excuse works for only a short time, you know."

   Extenuating means _____.

3. "Down to fifty cents," Jan moaned as she peered into her purse. "I wish I were the *frugal* sort, not someone who loved to spend money."

   Frugal means _____.

4. My English term paper earned a good grade, even though I added material that wasn't exactly *germane* to the topic.

   Germane means _____.

5. Marigold stares out the window with an *inscrutable* expression on her face that none of us can interpret.

   Inscrutable means _____.

6. Are all cats *intransigent* creatures? Ours refuse to compromise on the subject of an evening stalk . . . or any other subject, for that matter.

   Intransigent means _____.

7. The upper regions of our sloping yard are carefully tended, but we let the *nether* regions turn to meadows because they're out of sight.

   Nether means _____.

8. At an early age, Poucette displayed a *palpable* interest in hunting, made even more noticeable in contrast to Figment's preference for lying in the sun.

   Palpable means _____.

9. The kids in our youth group at church are a fairly *pious* bunch, but we tend to be quiet about our beliefs.

   Pious means _____.

10. Figment has always been a *prodigious* eater. Marigold and Poucette eat sparingly, perhaps because they're good hunters who have a tasty morsel outdoors from time to time.

    Prodigious means _____.

11. Our cousin Frank talks for hours on *recondite* subjects. Jan and I listen politely, although his obscure topics are usually beyond our comprehension.

    Recondite means _____.

12. It's impossible to be *remiss* in our duties toward any of Marigold's family. Each cat meows loudly to remind us of attention due or meals that are behind schedule.

    Remiss means _____.

13. A man in our town wears a *sardonic* expression on his face that clearly expresses his disdain of fellow human beings.

    Sardonic means _____.

14. Jan sighed as she peered into the travel bureau's display window. "The *torrid* sands of Torre-molinos look so romantic." I said that in summer those Spanish sands would be way too torrid for me.

    Torrid means _____.

15. The travel bureau's salesman slithered out the door and began recounting the joys of Torremoli-nos in *unctuous* tones, unaware that his ingratiating, overly sincere approach would turn Jan off.

    Unctuous means _____.

16. As we left the salesman, Jan hissed, "I can't stand people like that!" in a *vehement* whisper.

    Vehement means _____.

WORD STUDY

The surest way to arouse and hold the attention of the reader is by being specific, definite, and concrete.
    —William Strunk Jr. and E. B. White, *The Elements of Style*

Adjectives can be used with telling effect, or they can be squandered as excess fillers. A sentence loaded with adjectives overwhelms us and thereby loses effectiveness. Still, it's important to know many adjectives so that you can choose the one that is exactly right. And one is usually enough to describe the noun (or nounlike word) that you want your reader or listener to imagine.

1. **evanescent** (ˌev-ə-ˈnes-ᵊnt) adj.   Short-lived, fleeting, transient; apt to disappear like vapor; from L. *evanescere,* to vanish

    And what are these fluxions? The velocities of evanescent *increments . . . And may we not call them ghosts of departed quantities?*
        —George Berkeley, *The Analyst*

    Relatives: *evanescence, evanesce*
    Synonyms: *transient, ephemeral*
    Antonyms: *eternal, long-lived, lasting, enduring*

2. **extenuating** (ik-ˈsten-yə-ˌwā-tiŋ) participial adj.   Tending to lessen the seriousness of by offering excuses or reasons; reducing in strength or effectiveness; literally, *to thin,* as *extenuating the broth;* from L. *ex + tenuis,* thin

    Team members are to swim in every meet unless *extenuating* circumstances, such as illness, prevent their participation.

    Relatives: *extenuate, extenuator, extenuatory*

3. **frugal** (ˈfrü-gəl) adj.   Sparing, careful, economical in the use of resources; from L. *frugalis,* virtuous, frugal

    O'erjoyed was he to find,
    That, although on pleasure she was bent,
    She had a frugal *mind.*
        —William Cowper, "John Gilpin"

    Relatives: *frugality, frugally*
    Synonym: *sparing*
    Antonym: *wasteful*

4. **germane** (ˌjer-ˈmān) adj.   Both fitting and appropriate, relevant; literally, *having the same parents;* from Middle E. *germain*

    We excluded the problems with nuclear energy as they were not *germane* to our debate.

    Relative: *germanely*
    Synonyms: *relevant, material*
    Antonyms: *foreign, alien, immaterial*

5. **inscrutable** (in-'skrüt-ə-bəl) adj.   Difficult to grasp, understand, or interpret, as *the Mona Lisa's inscrutable smile;* from L. *in + scrutari,* to search

   Cruel, but composed and bland,
   Dumb, inscrutable *and grand,*
   So Tiberius might have sat,
   Had Tiberius been a cat.
      —Matthew Arnold, "Poor Matthias"

   Relatives: *inscrutability, inscrutableness, inscrutably*
   Synonyms: *mysterious, enigmatic*

6. **intransigent** (in-'tran[t]s-ə-jənt) adj.   Unwilling to compromise or alter an opinion or custom, even though it may be extreme; uncompromising; from L. *in + transigere,* to transact

   Mom and Dad are absolutely *intransigent* on the subject of drinking and driving; if we drink, we don't drive.

   Relatives: *intransigent* (n., person), *intransigence, intransigently*
   Synonym: *uncompromising*

7. **nether** ('ne<u>th</u>-ər) adj.   Placed below or under something else, lower; beneath the earth's surface, as *the nether world;* from OE *nither,* down

   Alas! why gnaw you so your nether *lip?*
   Some bloody passion shakes your very frame;
      —Shakespeare, *Othello*

   Relatives: *nethermost, netherworld* (world of the dead or the criminal underworld)

8. **palpable** ('pal-pə-bəl) adj.   Noticeable or readily perceived; able to be felt or touched, tangible; from L. *palpare,* to stroke, feel

   These lies are like the father that begets them; gross as a mountain, open, palpable.
      —Shakespeare, *King Henry IV,* Part I

   Relatives: *palpability, palpably, palpate, palpation*
   Synonym: *perceptible*
   Antonyms: *impalpable, imperceptible*

9. **pious** ('pī-əs) adj.   Devout or worthy; self-consciously virtuous or religious in a hypocritical or conspicuous way, as *that pious soul who cheats when not in church;* from L. *piare,* to appease

   The pious *ones of Plymouth, who, reaching the Rock, fell first upon their own knees and then upon the aborigines.*
      —William M. Evarts, in Louisville's *Courier-Journal*

   Relatives: *piously, piety, piousness*
   Synonym: *devout*
   Antonym: *impious*

10. **prodigious** (prə-'dij-əs) adj.   Impressively large, enormous; calling forth wonder or amazement; from L. *pro-, prod-,* forth, + *agere,* to drive

    All cultures have created heroes of *prodigious* strength, from Atlas, Hercules, and Samson to the more modern Paul Bunyan, Superman, Rocky, or Rambo.

    Relatives: *prodigiously, prodigiousness*
    Synonym: *awesome* (off the mark)
    Antonyms: *tiny, insignificant, puny, infinitesimal* (none exact)

11. **recondite** ('rek-ən-,dit, ri-'kän-,dīt) adj.   Difficult to understand, deep, as a *recondite subject;* of something obscure, generally unknown; from L. *recondere,* to conceal

    The Druidic priests of old kept their knowledge secret, and so the *recondite* mysteries of their time have been lost forever.

    Relatives: *reconditeness, reconditely*
    Synonym: *abstruse* (first meaning)

12. **remiss** (ri-'mis) adj.   Showing lack of attention and care; lax, negligent, careless; from L. *remittere,* to send back

    "I think we'd be *remiss* in our duty as friends if we failed to visit a classmate who's in the hospital," our adviser suggested.

    Relatives: *remission, remissly, remissness, remissible*
    Synonyms: *negligent, careless*
    Antonyms: *attentive, dutiful, careful*

13. **sardonic** (sär-'dän-ik) adj.   Mocking or sarcastic; scornfully humorous or derisive, as *a sardonic expression of contempt;* from Sardinia (See Derivation.)

    The *sardonic* smile on the terrorist's face told the captives that they had no hope of compassion from their captor.

    Relatives: *sardonically, sardonicism*
    Synonyms: *derisive, sarcastic* (neither exact)
    Derivation: If you taste an acrid herb from Sardinia, it will cause convulsive facial movements that look like a terribly painful and nasty grin. The accompanying bitter laugh has been termed *rire sardonique* by the French, from whom we get our word. The Greek poet Homer was supposedly the first to use *sardonic* to describe an ugly smile of contempt.

14. **torrid** ('tòr-əd) adj.   Intensely hot or parched by the heat, scorching; full of passion, ardent, as *torrid love scenes;* from L. *torrere,* to parch, burn

    Give me more love or more disdain;
    The torrid *or the frozen zone:*
    Bring equal ease unto my pain;
    The temperature affords me none.
        —Thomas Carew, "Mediocrity in Love Rejected"

    Relatives: *torridness, torridly, torridity*
    Synonyms: *scorching; passionate, ardent* (second meaning)
    Antonyms: *gelid, icy, frigid*

15. **unctuous** ('eŋ[k]-chə[-wə]s) adj.   Showing a false warmth or sincerity in an oily-smooth way; being self-consciously virtuous, earnest, or spiritual; from L. *unctum,* ointment

   If you want to describe an *unctuous* fellow, these lyrics from *My Fair Lady* are tough to beat: "He oiled his way across the floor, / Oozing charm from every pore . . ."

   Relatives: *unctuousness, unctuously*

16. **vehement** ('vē-ə-mənt) adj.   Full of emotion, feeling, passion; fervid, intense; expressed with force or animosity, as *a vehement denial;* from L. *vehement-,* impetuous, violent

   James Michener's book *The Drifters* concerns the youth of the late sixties and early seventies who turned their backs on society in *vehement* protest against a system they believed to be fatally flawed.

   Relatives: *vehemence, vehemently*
   Synonyms: *impassioned, fervid, fervent*

ROOT STUDY

You will probably know most of these words derived from four of our most useful language roots.

1. **HER** and **HES** means to *stick, cling to.*

   inherent—inborn, alive, innate
   adhere—to stick to, abide by
   coherent—logically consistent, as *a coherent speech*

2. **IT** means *to go.*

   exit—v., to go out; n., a place of departure
   itinerary—planned outline of where you will go
   reiterate—to repeat, go over again; to restate
   initiative—drive, enthusiasm, colloquially "git up and go"

3. **MISS** and **MIT** mean *to send.*

   missive—a letter or note
   missionary—one sent to another place, usually with religious, educational, or medical knowledge
   remission—a period when something, usually a disease process, is inactive (not virulent)
   transmit—to send or give; literally, *to send across*

4. **NOMEN, NOMIN, -ONYM,** and **ONOMA** mean *name.*

   nomenclature—system of names, terms, or symbols
   nominal—small or insignificant, as *a nominal sum;* in name only, as *nominal head of the group*
   anonymous—literally, *without name*
   onomatopoeia—use of words that sound the same as the words' meanings, e.g., hiss, buzz, ding

USING THE WORDS

List 23 Review

evanescent	inscrutable	pious	sardonic
extenuating	intransigent	prodigious	torrid
frugal	nether	recondite	unctuous
germane	palpable	remiss	vehement

Exercise I. Synonyms and Definitions.

Write a synonym or brief definition beside each word, using your memory as much as possible, before referring to Word Study.

1. **unctuous** _____

2. **sardonic** _____

3. **recondite** _____

4. **prodigious** _____

5. **palpable** _____

6. **inscrutable** _____

7. **frugal** _____

8. **evanescent** _____

9. **extenuating** _____

10. **germane** _____

11. **intransigent** _____

12. **remiss** _____

13. **pious** _____

14. **nether** _____

15. **torrid** _____

16. **vehement** _____

Exercise II. Antonyms.
Find an antonym or contrasting phrase for each word in bold type.

_____ 1. **remiss**
(a) confused
(b) dutiful
(c) angry
(d) energetic
(e) prompt

_____ 2. **evanescent**
(a) eternal
(b) steamy
(c) dire
(d) solid
(e) amorphous

_____ 3. **frugal**
(a) meaty
(b) wasteful
(c) placid
(d) weak
(e) extreme

_____ 4. **germane**
(a) local
(b) vague
(c) immaterial
(d) essential
(e) international

_____ 5. **palpable**
(a) obvious
(b) intriguing
(c) vast
(d) loathesome
(e) imperceptible

_____ 6. **prodigious**
(a) monumental
(b) indescribable
(c) serene
(d) fraudulent
(e) insignificant

_____ 7. **recondite**
(a) somewhat mistaken
(b) not suspicious
(c) unrecoverable
(d) readily compre-
hensible
(e) vaguely contemptuous

_____ 8. **vehement**
(a) willy-nilly
(b) complacent
(c) dull
(d) repentant
(e) lukewarm

_____ 9. **torrid**
(a) gelid
(b) acid
(c) fervid
(d) tepid
(e) rabid

_____ 10. **intransigent**
(a) difficult to explain
(b) easily swayed
(c) readily available
(d) hard to convince
(e) eagerly anticipated

_____ 11. **inscrutable**
(a) tired yet exhilarated
(b) tough but not
impossible
(c) open and easily
understood
(d) discreet and
secretive
(e) visible and real

_____ 12. **nether**
(a) either
(b) positive
(c) extreme
(d) upper
(e) escalated

Exercise III. Famous Descriptions.
Use the words in List 23 to complete the following descriptions.

1. In Barrie's *Peter Pan*, the _____ fairy was Tinker Bell, who was on stage one second, gone the next.

2. Scrooge McDuck is a _____ fowl with every buck.

3. Fat Albert might be Skinny Albert if he didn't have a(n) _____ appetite.

4. Henry Clay, known as the Great Compromiser, could never be called

    _____.

5. Ruler of Hades was Pluto, god of the _____ regions.

6. A dastardly enemy of Batman and Robin was the Joker, who perfected a sneering laugh and

    _____ smile.

7. Who has a more _____ face than the Sphinx?

8. Our forebears, the Puritans, known for their _____,

    dressed with a sober regard for propriety.

    (This rhyme requires a noun form, not an adjective.)

Exercise IV. Know Those Roots.
Knowledge of the roots in this lesson should enable you to match the words on the left with their meanings.

_____ 1. **adhesive**	(a) false, assumed name
_____ 2. **circuit**	(b) inborn, innate
_____ 3. **incoherent**	(c) drive, enterprise
_____ 4. **remit**	(d) projectile
_____ 5. **pseudonym**	(e) follower, believer
_____ 6. **itinerant**	(f) a course or route
_____ 7. **initiative**	(g) sticky
_____ 8. **adherent**	(h) name derived from a father or paternal ancester

_____ 9. **nominate**   (i) going from place to place, roving, wandering

_____ 10. **patronymic**   (j) babbling, illogical

_____ 11. **missile**   (k) to send back

_____ 12. **inherent**   (l) to name, suggest, propose

Exercise V. Analogies.

Complete each analogy with the best pair possible, using words from List 23 and Roots.

_____ 1. warm : torrid ::

    (a) difficult : recondite
    (b) tepid : lukewarm
    (c) nominal : insignificant
    (d) local : particular
    (e) coherent : distraught

_____ 2. unctuous : sincerity ::

    (a) upper : society
    (b) prodigious : behavior
    (c) sardonic : sympathy
    (d) frugal : economy
    (e) vehement : feeling

_____ 3. palpable : touch ::

    (a) legible : understand
    (b) credible : debate
    (c) attractive : see
    (d) audible : hear
    (e) distinctive : smell

_____ 4. irreverent : pious ::

    (a) adhesive : clinging
    (b) remiss : attentive
    (c) bitter : sardonic
    (d) great : prodigious
    (e) thinning : extenuating

_____ 5. annoyed : vehement ::

    (a) inherent : innate
    (b) antonym : synonym
    (c) frugal : miserly
    (d) intransigent : compliant
    (e) unctuous : smooth

Exercise VI. Word Analysis.

1. *Scrutinize* is a verb that often pops up on standardized tests. You know its root. Define *scrutinize,* as in *he scrutinized the document at length before he gave an opinion.*

    Scrutinize means _____

2. You know that context can change a word's meaning. In Arnold's poem (with word 5 in Word Study), what does *dumb* mean?

    _____

3. In Virgil's *Aeneid,* which traces the wanderings of Aeneas after the Trojan War, the hero often introduces himself with these words: *"Sum pius Aeneas,"* meaning "I am the pious Aeneas." This phrase—always good for a chuckle in any advanced Latin class—tells us something about the word *pious.* What has happened to its meaning over time?

    _____

    What expression is used to describe a word whose meaning has altered in a negative or disparaging way?

    _____

4. What is a *misnomer?* _____

5. During a physical examination, the doctor may palpate your abdomen. If he says that you have a *palpable spleen,* what do you think he means?

    _____

    _____

6. Can you think of *extenuating* circumstances that might explain why your homework is late? Please be creative!

    _____

    _____

LIST 24 The Low-Down Noun
Nouns with a Negative Connotation

In Context. Before studying the definitions, try reasoning out the meaning of each word, using context as your guide.

1. When we read Dickens's story, Andy wasn't worried by the four *apparitions* that appeared to Scrooge, but he found the TV version of those ghostly figures much more scary.

    Apparition means _____.

2. If I were certain of my eventual career, I could view the next several years with less *apprehension.*

    Apprehension means _____.

3. My cousin referred to his first college roommate as "that *churl.*" When I met him, I agreed that he was quite rude.

    Churl means _____.

4. "What do you do if the roommate you're assigned is a loser?" Jan asked with *consternation.*

    Consternation means _____.

5. True to character as the family *cynic,* our cousin told Jan she could expect the worst. "But you'll have it sorted out by the second semester," he added in an unusually optimistic tone.

    Cynic means _____.

6. Andy was downcast by the *demise* of his entire first litter of gerbils and only recovered his good spirits when the second litter survived.

    Demise means _____.

7. Although a *detriment* to the appearance of the kitchen, Andy's cooking has done wonders for his confidence.

    Detriment means _____.

8. Barry warned us that getting concert tickets required *guile.* "By now I know all the tricks," he said smugly.

    Guile means _____.

9. The *infamy* of that crime was made clear to us by the shocking details related in the paper and on television.

    Infamy means _____.

10. When he discovered that his hidden candy had melted all over his windowsill, Andy's mournful *lament* could be heard throughout the house.

    Lament means _____.

11. We were in high gear for finals and graduation, but afterward we succumbed to lassitude and slept till noon for several days in a row.

    Lassitude means _____.

12. "Miserable *miscreants!*" Mom hollered as she vigorously beat a wool rug infested with moths. "Only criminals would attack a good rug!"

    Miscreant means _____.

13. "I'll never understand *parsimony,*" Dad commented. "We have to be thrifty to make ends meet, but I hope we're never downright stingy."

    Parsimony means _____.

14. Mom sprayed her wool rug for moths, and said she felt not a single *qualm* as one bug after another dropped at her feet.

    Qualm means _____.

15. "Our mother, the *sadist,*" Jan teased as Mom finished spraying the moths. "I swear you enjoyed killing those bugs." Mom nodded without a shred of remorse.

    Sadist means _____.

16. "I'll visit you at school and take you out to dinner," Mom promised, "but college boys live in such *squalor* that I can't bear to see your room. Filth gives me a headache."

    Squalor means _____.

WORD STUDY

As you know, nouns and verbs are the building blocks of our language. *Birds fly* is a sentence. *Birds soar* is a better sentence because it has a more precise verb. *Eagles soar* is better still because both noun and verb evoke distinct images. The more you write and speak, the more you will want to be precise. Being misinterpreted or misunderstood is frustrating. This last lesson gives you more nouns to work with—nouns that will allow you to say **exactly** what is on your mind.

1. **apparition** (ˌap-ə-ˈrish-ən) n.   A specter or ghostly shape; appearance (in the sense that something has become visible); from L. *apparere,* to appear

   She was a phantom of delight
   When first she gleamed upon my sight;
   A lovely apparition, *sent*
   To be a moment's ornament.
       —William Wordsworth, "She Was a Phantom of Delight"
   (Note: Here, *apparition* is a positive idea. Words are so sneaky.)

      Relative: *apparitional*
      Synonym: *ghost, phantom, specter* (none exact)

2. **apprehension** (ˌap-ri-ˈhen-chən) n.   Foreboding or fear of something bad to come; arrest, as *the swift apprehension of the suspect;* understanding or mental comprehension, as *a person of slow apprehension;* from L. *ad* + *prehendere,* to seize

   My apprehensions *come in crowds;*
   I dread the rustling of the grass;
   The very shadows of the clouds
   Have power to shake me as they pass.
         —William Wordsworth, "The Affliction of Margaret"

   Relatives: *apprehend, apprehensive, apprehensible, apprehensively, apprehensiveness*

3. **churl** (ˈchər[ə]l) n.   Rude, loutish male or one typically in a bad mood; originally a peasant; from OE *ceorl,* man

   "Peasant—lout—churl!" Carrie declaimed onstage. "I would rather live in the streets than in your house!"

   Relatives: *churlish, churlishly, churlishness*
   Synonyms: *boor, lout*

4. **consternation** (ˌkän[t]-stər-ˈāa-shən) n.   Surprise, often with dismay, that arouses worry or confusion; from L. *consternare,* to bewilder, alarm

   We watched in *consternation* as one of the zoo's gorillas paced back and forth, betraying his distress at confinement.

   Relative: *consternate*

5. **cynic** (ˈsin-ik) n.   A nitpicky critic of human nature who typically believes that people care only about themselves; from Gr. *kynikos,* like a dog (See Derivation.)

   In Oscar Wilde's play *Lady Windermere's Fan,* Cecil asks, "What is a *cynic?*" "A man who knows the price of everything and the value of nothing," replies Lord Darlington.

   Relatives: *cynical, cynically, cynicism*
   Derivation: A student of Socrates began the school of the Cynics, an odd name considering its derivation from *dog.* The Cynics held that the only good was virtue, based in independence and self-control. Over time, this noble doctrine has been totally lost; today's cynics think that people are basely selfish.

6. **demise** (di-ˈmīz) n.   Final end or death; literally, *to send down,* smite; from L. *de* + *mittere*

   The *demise* of ponderous or verbose prose is welcome to modern readers, who are fond of a leaner and cleaner style.

   Relative: *demise (v., to give over, as in a will or lease; to die, pass on by bequest)*
   Synonym: *death*
   Antonym: *life*

7. **detriment** (ˈde-trə-mənt) n.   Harm or damage, as *the difficult work was a detriment to her health* (use with *to*); from L. *deterere,* to impair, wear away

   The heavy rains that turned the flower beds into mud puddles were a *detriment* to our work in the gardens.

   Relatives: *detrimental, detrimentally*

8. **guile** ('gī(ə)l) n.   Clever, artful deceit; duplicity, cunning; from Of *guile,* cunning

   The infernal serpent; he it was, whose guile,
   Stirr'd up with envy and revenge, deceived
   The mother of mankind.
       —John Milton, *Paradise Lost*

   Relatives: *guileful, guilefully, guilefulness, beguile, guileless, guilelessly, guilelessness*

9. **infamy** ('in-fə-mē) n.   Extreme disgrace or evil reputation (usually the result of something shockingly awful); from L. *in* + *fama,* fame

   Yesterday, December 7, 1941—a date which will live in infamy—*the United States of America was suddenly and deliberately attacked by naval and air forces of the Empire of Japan.*
       —F.D. Roosevelt, War Message to Congress, December 8, 1941

   Relatives: *infamous, infamously*

10. **lament** (lə-'ment) n.   A wailing, sorrowful cry or complaint; from L. *lamentum,* lament

    When our dog Ruffles died, her mate uttered pitiful *laments* that we will never forget.

    Relatives: *lament* (v.), *lamentable, lamentableness, lamentably, lamentation, lamented*
       (mourned)

11. **lassitude** ('las-ə-,t[y]üd) n.   Lack of energy, fatigue, weariness; languor; from L. *lassus,* weary

    Overcome by *lassitude,* our cats sleep away the days in preparation for nights of exploration and hunting.

    Synonym: *languor*
    Antonyms: *vigor, dynamism*

12. **miscreant** ('mis-krē-ənt) n.   One who acts in a criminal or vicious way; villain, wrongdoer; from Middle F. *mescroire,* to disbelieve

    To a chicken farmer, a fox in the hen house is a wretched *miscreant* never to be forgiven.

    Relative: *miscreant* (adj., wicked, villainous)
    Synonym: *villain*

13. **parsimony** ('pär-sə-,mō-nē) n.   Extreme thrift, often amounting to stinginess; niggardliness; from L. *parsimonia,* from *parcere,* to spare

    Economy is a distributive virtue, and consists not in saving but selection. Parsimony *requires no providence, no sagacity, no powers of combination, no comparison, no judgement.*
       —Edmund Burke, letter, 1796

14. **qualm** ('kwäm, 'kwälm) n.   A pang of upsetting emotion, such as fear or remorse; an uneasy twinge on a matter of conscience, manners, or ethics; origin obscure

    Poet James Naylor wrote that when King Solomon and King David wrote the Proverbs and the Psalms, they did so "with many, many *qualms.*"

    Relatives: *qualmy, qualmish, qualmishly, qualmishness*
    Synonyms: *scruple, compunction*

15. **sadist** ('sād-əst, 'sad-əst) n.   One who enjoys cruelty or the infliction of pain; from the Marquis de Sade (See Derivation.)

The *sadist,* who delights in cruelty to others, and the masochist, who inflicts physical or mental pain on himself, are the subjects of many books and much psychological study.

Relatives: *sadistic, sadistically, sadism*
Derivation: The Marquis de Sade incurred infamy by torturing the women he loved. The French condemned him to death in 1772, but he escaped and fled to Italy, where he resumed his nasty old habits. He eventually landed back in France, in the Bastille. There he began writing lurid prose and never stopped, even when he was removed to the lunatic asylum where he died years later.

16. **squalor** ('skwäl-ər) n.   A state of disgusting filth, degradation, or both; from L. *squalidus,* squalid

In Port au Prince, Haiti, the contrast between the opulent homes of the wealthy and the appalling *squalor* of the poor has to be seen to be believed.

Relatives: *squalid, squalidly, squalidness*

ROOT STUDY

Let's hear it for the last roots to be learned!

1. **DOL** means *grief.*

   doleful—sorrowful, full of grief, *dolorous*
   condole—to express sympathy in time of sorrow or grief
   Dolores—Spanish name honoring St. Mary of the Sorrows

2. **MAL** means *bad, badly.*

   malady—ailment or illness
   dismal—gloomy or depressing; without merit
   abysmal—incredibly great or profound, as *their abysmal ignorance*
   malfunction—to fail to function, to function improperly

3. **MOB, MOT,** and **MOV** mean to move.

   mobile—capable of being moved, *movable*
   motive—an impulse or incentive causing you to act; a recurrent theme or *motif* in a piece of music
   emote—to express emotion, especially when acting
   immovable—firm, fixed, stable

4. **PHON** means *sound*

   phonograph—record player; literally, *written sound*
   phonetics—the system of spoken sounds of a language
   homophone—one of two (or more) words that sound the same but have different meanings and spellings, e.g., *to, too, two*

5. **PREHEND**, **PREHENS**, and **PRIS** mean
    to take or *seize*.

    apprehend—to seize, as you would a criminal; to grasp, perceive, understand, *comprehend*
    reprehensible—deserving blame or censure
    prison—place of confinement for those seized as criminals
    predatory—seeking to gain at the expense of others, as a predatory animal *preys* on others for its
      food and a predatory company may take over other companies for its own gain

    (Note: Remember *prehensile* from List 9?)

USING THE WORDS

List 24 Review

apparition	cynic	infamy	parsimony
apprehension	demise	lament	qualm
churl	detriment	lassitude	sadist
consternation	guile	miscreant	squalor

Exercise I. Knowing the Words.
Answer as many of these as you can before referring back to Word Study for help.

1. Write an *antonym* for each of the following words:

    a. **demise** _____

    b. **guile** _____

    c. **lassitude** _____

    d. **parsimony** _____

    e. **squalor** _____

2. Write a one-word *synonym* for each of the following words:

    a. **apparition** _____

    b. **churl** _____

    c. **lament** _____

    d. **miscreant** _____

    e. **detriment** _____

3. Write a brief *explanation* of each of the following words:

a. **sadist** _____

b. **qualm** _____

c. **infamy** _____

d. **cynic** _____

e. **apprehension** _____

f. **consternation** _____

Exercise II. Switcheroo.

Some words in List 24 frequently appear as verbs or adjectives, not just nouns. Match these other forms with their meanings or synonyms.

_____ 1. **apprehensive**   (a) to understand or to seize

_____ 2. **infamous**   (b) wantonly cruel

_____ 3. **parsimonious**   (c) to bemoan, regret exceedingly

_____ 4. **apprehend**   (d) sadly regrettable

_____ 5. **churlish**   (e) innocent, free of artifice

_____ 6. **sadistic**   (f) boorish

_____ 7. **lamentable**   (g) fearful of something ahead

_____ 8. **cynical**   (h) to please by charming

_____ 9. **guileless**   (i) stingy, niggardly

_____ 10. **detrimental**   (j) notorious

_____ 11. **beguile**   (k) harmful

_____ 12. **lament** (v.)   (l) distrustful of human nature

Exercise III. Chart Fill-In.

Add the missing items to the chart. The first is done as an example.

	WORD	ROOT	DEFINITION	WORDS IN THE FAMILY
1.	telephone	phon	instrument to transmit distant sound	phonics, phone, phonetics, homophone
2.	predatory	_____	_____ _____	prey, apprehend, comprehensive
3.	_____	mot	impulse or incentive	_____ _____
4.	_____	mal	excessively great, profound	_____ _____
5.	condole	_____	_____ _____	dolorous, doleful, condolence
6.	_____	fama	utter disgrace	_____ _____
7.	_____	kynikos	_____ _____	cynical, cynicism, cynically
8.	_____	mis, mit	an ending, death	_____ _____
9.	squalor	_____	_____	squalid, squalidly
10.	_____	prehens	deserving of blame or criticism	_____ _____

Exercise IV. Substitution.

Substitute words learned in List 24 and Roots for the phrases in italics. Write your words above the italicized word or phrase.

1. Knowing that I didn't have permission to take the car, I had *twinges of guilt* as I drove out of the driveway.

2. "Rotten little *villain*'s been in my cosmetics again," Jan grumbled as she pawed through her bureau drawer.

3. Mom explained that she'd had to give up jogging because the jarring of her feet against the pavement had been *harmful* to both her knees. (Hint: Use the adjective form.)

4. One night, to Marigold's *great confusion and dismay,* both of her kittens ran into the woods and stayed there.

5. Jan and Carrie confessed that they disliked being alone in the house at night. "We imagine there are strange *ghostly figures* lurking around outdoors," Jan said.

6. In spite of wanting to see the movie, I yielded to the *relaxed and languorous feeling* that overcame me.

7. If it weren't for the *cessation of publication* of that magazine, I'd have renewed my subscription.

8. Carrie doled out her candy so *stingily* that I could barely see the tiny pieces in my hand.

9. In *Four Seasons,* Stephen King tells a ghoulish story of a teenage boy whose morbid fascination with Nazi war criminals led him to become a *person who enjoys inflicting cruel suffering on others* and a murderer.

10. What may appear as *incredible filth* to a sanitized Westerner is apt to represent normal living conditions for some destitute people who lack modern conveniences.

Exercise V. Find the Oddball.

Select the one word in each group that does not fit with the others. Write its letter on the line.

_____	1.	(a) prehensile	(b) apprehend	(c) appreciate
		(d) prey	(e) predatory	
_____	2.	(a) impolite	(b) churl	(c) lout
		(d) fool	(e) peasant	
_____	3.	(a) impious	(b) evildoer	(c) villain
		(d) miscreant	(e) criminal	
_____	4.	(a) pang	(b) wound	(c) qualm
		(d) twinge	(e) scruple	
_____	5.	(a) drowsiness	(b) unease	(c) lassitude
		(d) weariness	(e) languor	
_____	6.	(a) terror	(b) amazed concern	(c) consternation
		(d) worry	(e) alarm	
_____	7.	(a) emotion	(b) mobility	(c) immovable
		(d) locomotion	(e) motley	
_____	8.	(a) cynical	(b) sadistic	(c) satiated
		(d) squalid	(e) lamentable	

_____ 9. (a) Dolores (b) guileless (c) promote
             (d) dismal   (e) life
             (Tip: Check connotations.)

_____ 10. (a) ailment (b) malady (c) medical
             (d) illness (e) sickness

Exercise VI. Word Analysis.

1. What might you suspect of someone wearing a determinedly guileless smile?

_____

2. If the police have apprehended a suspect, where is that person apt to be?

_____

3. How many homophones can you think of? _____

_____

_____

4. What sort of person would you describe as _maladroit?_ _____

_____

5. Oscar Wilde's definition of a cynic—"A man who knows the price of everything and the value of nothing"—falls into a distinct category in the list of literary terms. What is the term that classifies this witticism of Wilde's?

_____

_____

This final lesson reviews the words and roots in Lists 21–24. Read over all the words and roots, one by one. If a few have become fuzzy—not surprising at this point in the book—reread their definitions and example sentences before beginning the review exercises.

LIST 21	LIST 22	LIST 23	LIST 24
aria	amazon	evanescent	apparition
bravura	Attic	extenuating	apprehension
chiaroscuro	centaur	frugal	churl
concerto	hygiene	germane	consternation
diva	iridescent	inscrutable	cynic
dynamics	jovial	intransigent	demise
falsetto	myrmidon	nether	detriment
fresco	panacea	palpable	guile
frieze	Pandora's box	pious	infamy
libretto	phaeton	prodigious	lament
patina	pontoon	recondite	lassitude
rhapsody	procrustean	remiss	miscreant
sonata	stentorian	sardonic	parsimony
staccato	sylvan	torrid	qualm
vignette	tantalize	unctuous	sadist
virtuoso/a	Valkyrie	vehement	squalor
	zephyr		

ROOTS

DOL	MAL	-ONYM and ONOMA
DYN/DYNAM	MANU	PEND/PENS
GNOS/GNOM	MISS and MIT	PHON
HAL	MOB, MOT, and MOV	PREHEND, PREHENS, and PRIS
HER and HES	NOC/NOX	SPIR
IT	NOMEN and NOMIN	TANG, TING, TACT, and TIG
LEG, LIG, and LECT		

USING THE WORDS

Exercise I. Antonyms.

Select the word or phrase most nearly opposite in meaning to the word in bold type.

_____ 1. **dynamic**
(a) soft
(b) undecided
(c) lethargic
(d) striated
(e) pianissimo

_____ 2. **parsimony**
(a) stability
(b) philanthropy
(c) detriment
(d) notoriety
(e) frugality

_____ 3. **vehemence**
(a) approval
(b) intransigence
(c) calm
(d) emotion
(e) apathy

_____ 4. **remiss**
(a) scrupulously attentive
(b) quietly understanding
(c) reassuringly supportive
(d) noticeably bold
(e) concisely stated

_____ 5. **intransigent**
(a) palpable
(b) profound
(c) tractable
(d) tremulous
(e) lamentable

_____ 6. **germane**
(a) indigenous
(b) ingenuous
(c) sedate
(d) irrelevant
(e) irretrievable

_____ 7. **evanescent**
(a) ethereal
(b) lingering
(c) placid
(d) retreating
(e) pervasive

_____ 8. **stentorian**
(a) buoyant
(b) apprehensive
(c) callous
(d) anomalous
(e) dulcet

_____ 9. **jovial**
(a) parsimonious
(b) squalid
(c) terse
(d) choleric
(e) volatile

_____ 10. **procrustean**
(a) flexible
(b) debatable
(c) devout
(d) complacent
(e) resourceful

Exercise II. Logic.

From the words offered, select the most logical one to fit each phrase.

staccato	apparition	laments	sardonic
infamy	falsetto	hygiene	demise
panacea	consternation	frieze	arias
guile	amazon	sonata	

1. sure hate to meet one in a cemetery _____

2. she'd stand out at a Munchkins' tea _____

3. inappropriate for the "Hallelujah Chorus" _____

4. an ingenuous soul wouldn't resort to this _____

5. may be just the right pitch if you're a guy looking for laughs in a skit _____

6. perfect ornamentation for a Greco-Roman building _____

7. what Beethoven played in the moonlight   _____

8. intimidating tone for rapping out a sharp command   _____

9. the wrong sort of expression at a wedding   _____

10. what showed on your face when you discovered that the cat had her kittens in your bed   _____

11. a reputation to be avoided   _____

12. what Luciano Pavarotti and Beverly Sills probably sing in the shower   _____

13. responsible for sweet breath, sparkling teeth   _____

14. what somebody ought to hurry up and find for the common cold   _____

15. may this never happen to your ambitions   _____

Exercise III. Synonyms and Definitions.
Select the letter of the best synonym or definition for each numbered word.

_____	1. **qualm**	(a) uncouth, rude
_____	2. **nether**	(b) a brief scene
_____	3. **inscrutable**	(c) injurious
_____	4. **torrid**	(d) evildoer
_____	5. **miscreant**	(e) brilliant, scintillating
_____	6. **recondite**	(f) pang
_____	7. **vignette**	(g) difficult to decipher
_____	8. **detrimental**	(h) lower
_____	9. **pious**	(i) talk or write in an ecstatic manner
_____	10. **iridescent**	(j) holier-than-thou
_____	11. **churlish**	(k) steamy
_____	12. **rhapsodize**	(l) abstruse

Exercise IV. Truth or Fiction.

Mark **T** for statements that express truth and **F** for those that are false.

_____ 1. A sadistic person is a likely choice for the main character in a morality play.

_____ 2. If Pandora had exhibited lassitude, she might never have opened her infamous box.

_____ 3. A smart salesperson cultivates an unctuous tone.

_____ 4. Those on diets had better have prodigious appetites.

_____ 5. Flimsy pontoons would be risky underpinnings if you're planning to land in rough waters.

_____ 6. A touch of Attic salt usually improves the stew.

_____ 7. To reach the bottom of Grand Canyon in safety, you'd choose a phaeton rather than a donkey.

_____ 8. Older brothers and sisters often delight in tantalizing a younger sibling.

_____ 9. An impalpable air of mystery or remoteness that often surrounds a film star may add to his or her appeal.

_____ 10. Portrayal of the squalid living conditions in much of Calcutta would detract from the authenticity of a film set in India.

Exercise V. Using the Roots.

Use your knowledge of roots to answer the following questions and complete the statements.

1. What is a *condolence* call? _____

_____

2. A *suspension* bridge is (describe one) _____

_____

3. How are *contiguous* pieces of property situated? _____

_____

4. What is the body's *respiratory* tract? _____

_____

5. What is a *prognosticator?* _____

6. Why would you want to present a *cohesive* argument in a debate? _____

_____

7. The words *exit, circuitous, itinerant, initiate,* and *transit* share the root

_____, meaning _____.

8. What are *noxious* fumes? _____

9. What is the best antonym of *diurnal* (of daytime)? _____

10. The root in *denominator* is _____, meaning _____.

Exercise VI. Decoding with Roots.

a. Circle the root in each numbered word at the left.
b. Enter the meaning of the root on the line shown.
c. Consider any helpful prefixes.
d. Write a brief definition or synonym for each word.

WORD	ROOT MEANING	DEFINITION
1. **dismal**	_____	_____
2. **leguminous**	_____	_____
3. **emit**	_____	_____
4. **remote**	_____	_____
5. **homonym**	_____	_____
6. **misapprehension**	_____	_____
7. **extenuating**	_____	_____
8. **homophone**	_____	_____

Exercise VII. Common Sense Connections.

Join the vocabulary terms with the names, places, or ideas that make the best match. Write the letter of your choice on the line.

_____	1. **fresco**	(a) oil	(b) design	(c) mural
_____	2. **diva**	(a) prima donna	(b) basso	(c) concert
_____	3. **bravura**	(a) Big Bird	(b) Rambo	(c) Barbara Walters
_____	4. **libretto**	(a) composer	(b) W. S. Gilbert	(c) Jackie Joyner-Kersey
_____	5. **chiaroscuro**	(a) darkness	(b) contrast	(c) brightness
_____	6. **concerto**	(a) The Beatles	(b) rap	(c) Tchaikovsky
_____	7. **patina**	(a) metals	(b) rhythm	(c) mercury
_____	8. **sylvan**	(a) tract	(b) nature trail	(c) suburban
_____	9. **Valkyrie**	(a) Hindu	(b) harpy	(c) Valhalla
_____	10. **zephyr**	(a) current	(b) gentle	(c) drafty
_____	11. **frugal**	(a) economy	(b) welfare	(c) education
_____	12. **virtuoso**	(a) professional	(b) instructor	(c) member
_____	13. **centaur**	(a) settler	(b) serf	(c) cowboy
_____	14. **myrmidon**	(a) chief	(b) henchman	(c) duelist
_____	15. **cynic**	(a) deity	(b) devil	(c) angel

UNIT IV

A Book List You
Can Love

A Book List You Can Love
Vocabulary Builders That Are Fun to Read

The following list was compiled from **student recommendations**. No book list is ever complete, but this one can suggest many enjoyable titles for you. Nearly all book lists for college-bound students are pretty similar, but this list is different.

Note that only one or two books are suggested for most authors. If you like one of an author's books, try others!

Books Featuring Teenagers or Young Adults

Anderson	*Speak*
Avi	*Nothing but the Truth; The Barn*
Block	*Weetzie Bat*
Bradford	*Red Sky at Morning*
Cole	*Celine; The Goats*
Conford	*Dear Lovey Hart, I Am Desperate*, et al.
Crew	*Children of the River*
Crutcher	*Staying Fat for Sarah Byrnes; Stotan!; Athletic Shorts: Six Short Stories*
Duran	*Don't Spit on My Corner*
Franklin	*Lone Wolf*
Garden	*Annie on My Mind*
Hentoff	*Does This School Have Capital Punishment?*
Hesse	*Letters from Rifka; Out of the Dust*
Hill	*Take It Easy*
Hudson	*Sweetgrass*
Hurston	*Their Eyes Were Watching God*
Irving	*Cider House Rules; A Prayer for Owen Meany*
Kidd	*The Secret Life of Bees*
LeGuin	*Very Far Away from Anywhere Else*
Lipsyte	*The Contender*
Mazer	*Silver*
McDonald	*Swallowing Stones*
Michener	*The Drifters*
Morrison	*Sula; The Bluest Eye*
Myers	*Scorpions*
Naylor	*Ice; The Fear Place; Outrageously Alice*
Nolan	*Send me Down a Miracle*
Paterson	*Jip, His Story; Lyddie*
Paulsen	*Hatchet; Tasting the Thunder; The Car*
Peck	*Lost in Cyberspace; The Last Safe Place on Earth; Secrets of the Shopping Mall*
Rodowsky	*Lucy Peale*
Salinger	*The Catcher in the Rye*
Sanders	*Clover*
Sebold	*The Lovely Bones*
Tan	*The Joy Luck Club*
Tyler	*Searching for Caleb*
Van de Velde	*User Unfriendly*
Wallace	*Wrestling Sturbridge*
Wersba	*Tunes for a Small Harmonica; Run Softly, Go Fast*

| Westall | *Blitzcat; Time of Fire; Break of Dark* |
| Zindel | *The Pigman* |

Mysteries and Adventure, Suspense, and Science Fiction (SF)

Adams	*The Plague Dogs*
Anthony	*On a Pale Horse* (SF)
Asimov	*Foundation*, plus over 300 more! (SF)
Barlow & Summers	*Barlow's Guide to Extraterrestrials* (SF)
Beach	*Run Silent, Run Deep*
Bradbury	SF and short stories—everything he's written
Card	*Ender's Game* (SF)
Christie	*And Then There Were None*, et al.
Clancy	*The Hunt for Red October*
Cook	*Coma; Brain* (SF)
Crichton	*Jurassic Park; The Andromeda Strain* (SF)
Dean	*Finders*
Dickinson	*Eva* (SF)
Doyle	*The Adventures of Sherlock Holmes*
Duncan	*Don't Look Behind You; Stranger with My Face; The Third Eye*
Dumas	*The Count of Monte Cristo*
Follett	*The Key to Rebecca*
Forsyth	*The Odessa File*, et al.
Herbert	The *Dune* books (SF)
Hillerman	*Skinwalker*, et al.
Hoover	*Away Is a Strange Place to Be* (SF); *Orvis* (SF)
Hughes	*Invitation to the Game* (SF)
Huxley	*Brave New World* (SF)
King	*Salem's Lot; The Stand; The Dead Zone*
London	*The Call of the Wild*
MacLean	*HMS Ulysses; The Guns of Navarone*
Monsarrat	*The Cruel Sea*
Nixon	*Don't Scream*
Peters	*Crocodile on the Sandbank*
Rice	*Interview with the Vampire*
Shusterman	*The Dark Side of Nowhere* (SF)
Singer	*Deal with a Ghost*
Stoker	*Dracula*
Tey	*Brat Farrar*, et al.
Uris	*Battle Cry*
Waddell	*The Kidnapping of Susie Q.*
Zindel	*Loch*

Humor and Satire

Adams	*Hitchhiker's Guide to the Galaxy*
Barry	*The Good Times Are Killing Me*
Dennis	*Auntie Mame*
Durrell	*My Family and Other Animals*
Edgerton	*Walking Across Egypt*
Ephron	*Crazy Salad; Scribble Scribble*
Fleischman	*The Abracadabra Kid*
Gibbons	*Cold Comfort Farm*
Grisham	*Skipping Christmas*

Humor and Satire—(continued)

King	*Southern Ladies and Gentlemen*
Kotzwinkle	*The Bear Went Over the Mountain; E.T.: The Extraterrestrial*
MacDonald	*The Egg and I; The Plague and I*
Marquis	*Archy and Mehitabel*
Pringle	*Preacher's Boy*
Rosten	*The Education of Hyman Kaplan*
Russo	*Straight Man*
Salzman	*The Laughing Sutra*
Shulman	*Guided Tour of Campus Humor*
Sleator	*Interstellar Pig*
Thompson	*Simon Pure*
Townsend	*The Diary of Adrian Mole*
Viorst	*People and Other Aggravations*, et al.
White	*The Second Tree from the Corner*, et al.

Fantasy

Adams	*Watership Down*
Bach	*Jonathan Livingston Seagull*
Bain	*The Dark Tower* series
Bradley	*The Mists of Avalon*, et al.
Jacques	*Redwall* series
Jones	*Howl's Moving Castle*
Klause	*The Silver Kiss; Blood and Chocolate*
LeGuin	*A Wizard of Earthsea*
L'Engle	*An Acceptable Time*
Maguire	*Wicked: The Lives and Times of the Wicked Witch of the West; Confesions of an Ugly Stepsister*
Mahy	*Changeover: A Supernatural Romance*
McCaffrey	*Dragonsinger*
Paolini	*Eragon*
Rowling	*Harry Potter* series
Shetterly	*Elsewhere; Nevernever*
Stewart	*The Crystal Cave*, et al.
Thurber	*The White Deer*
Tolkien	*The Hobbit; Lord of the Rings* trilogy
Wangerin	*The Book of the Dun Cow*
Weis	*Dragons of Autumn Twilight*
White	*The Once and Future King*
Wrede	*Dealing with Dragons*

Fascinating Factual Books and Biographies

Angelou	*I Know Why the Caged Bird Sings*
Armstrong	*It's Not about the Bike*
Baldwin	*If Beale Street Could Talk*
Berne	*Games People Play*
Bryson	*A Walk in the Woods*
Corbett	*Man-Eaters of Kumaon*
Duncan	*Who Killed My Daughter?*
Feynman	*Surely You're Joking, Mr. Feynman*
Gilliam	*Paul Robeson*
Greenfield	*Gypsies*
Grisham	*A Painted Horse*
Hall	*Possible Impossibilities: A Look at Parapsychology*
Hillenbrand	*Seabiscuit*
Kanin	*Tracy and Hepburn*
Kingston	*Warrior Woman*
Markham	*West with the Night*
Mead	*Blackberry Winter*
Meltzer	*Langston Hughes*
Mowat	*Never Cry Wolf; The Dog Who Wouldn't Be*
Myers	*Malcolm X: By Any Means Necessary*
North	*Rascal*
Paulsen	*Winterdance*
Pirie	*Down These Mean Streets*
Slater	*Oddballs*
Steinbeck	*Travels with Charlie*
Stevenson	*A Man Called Intrepid; Intrepid's Last Case*
Tarte	*Enslaved by Ducks*
Tate (Ed.)	*Black Women Writers at Work*
Taylor	*Zoo Vet*
Thomas	*The Lives of a Cell; Medusa and the Snail*
Wright	*Black Boy; American Hunger*
Zindel	*The Pigman and Me*

Great Big Sagas and Historical Novels

Auel	*The Clan of the Cave Bear*
Avi	*Beyond the Western Sea, Vols. I and II*
Clavell	*Tai-Pan; Sho-Gun; King Rat*
Costain	*The Black Rose,* et al.
Diamant	*The Red Tent*
Frasier	*Cold Mountain*
Garland	*Indio*
Hugo	*Les Misérables*
McCullough	*The Thorn Birds*
Michener	*Hawaii*
Mitchell	*Gone with the Wind*
Roberts	*Northwest Passage*
Taylor	*The Bomb*
Undset	*Kristin Lavransdatter*
Uris	*Exodus*
Waltari	*The Egyptian*
Wouk	*The Winds of War; War and Remembrance*

Not-So-Sappy Romances

Alcott	*Little Women*
Austen	*Pride and Prejudice; Emma*
Bronte, C.	*Jane Eyre*
Bronte, E.	*Wuthering Heights*
De la Roche	The *Jalna* series
Du Maurier	*Frenchman's Creek; Rebecca,* et al.
Freedman	*Mrs. Mike*
Hilton	*Lost Horizon*
Holland	*Great Maria*
Kingsolver	*Prodigal Summer*
Marshall	*Christy*
Seton	*Katherine; Green Darkness*

Books Everybody Likes

Adamson	*Born Free*
Braithwaite	*To Sir, with Love*
Burnford	*The Incredible Journey*
Cronin	*The Citadel*
Herriot	*All Creatures Great and Small,* et al.
Holman	*Slakes Limbo*
Kaufman	*Up the Down Staircase*
Kesey	*One Flew over the Cuckoo's Nest*
Kipling	*The Jungle Books*
Lee	*To Kill a Mockingbird*
McCall Smith	*The #1 Ladies' Detective Agency*
Milne	*Winnie the Pooh* (Re-read now that you're older. And try *The Tao of Pooh.*)
Poe	All short stories and mysteries
Rand	*The Fountainhead*
Stevenson	*Treasure Island*
Twain	*The Adventures of Huckleberry Finn; The Prince and the Pauper,* et al.
Walker	*The Color Purple*
Wharton	*Birdy*

Dear Reader,

I may have left your favorite book off the list. If so, please share it with me by writing to the publisher. Let me know *all titles* that should be added, plus the titles of any books so dreadful that we should turn them into confetti. Now—happy reading!

Joan Carris

P.S. If a book hasn't turned you on after 50–75 pages, get another book. You can go back to the one that seemed slow when you're in the mood. It's better to be reading something you enjoy than not reading at all.

UNIT V

Your Best on the Test

Your Best on the Test
Answering the Verbal Questions on Standardized Tests

All standardized tests, especially the SAT and PSAT, ask questions that reveal your language strengths . . . or expose your weaknesses. Some people shine on standardized tests—naturally, or so it seems. Others have trouble.

If you have trouble on tests of major importance like SATs, or if you need "test smarts," this section is for you. Try the suggested approaches to test-taking in general and to each question type on SATs and PSATs. See if these techniques will work as well for you as they have for students in the past. If they don't, try your own methods of attack. *Learn to use what works for you.*

Above all, remember that *the SAT tests your developed ability, not your potential.* Say that you have developed your ability in a particular subject to a 70 percent level. Well, then, you can develop it further, to a higher level. Why not?

HOW TO GET MORE ANSWERS RIGHT THAN WRONG

Just knowing what is on the next few pages could boost your verbal and math scores by a hundred points or more. That's not a joke, and it's not an exaggeration, either. Read on.

VERBAL QUESTIONS ON THE PSAT AND SAT	
PSAT	**SAT**
3 verbal sections	3 verbal sections*
87 questions in three segments (2 25-minute segments; 1 30-minute segment)	78 questions in two 25-minute segments and one 20-minute segment
13 sentence completions	28 sentence completions
35 reading comprehension (critical reading) questions	50 reading comprehension questions
39 English usage and grammar questions	1 essay

*You may get another verbal segment of experimental questions, which do not count toward your score.

Always watch your watch. Time marches on, as they say, but during a test it seems to fly. You must learn to pace yourself by practicing at home with 30-minute timed segments from *Real SATs* (available at your bookstore).

Since questions on reading passages take the most time, be sure to save *at least half* of every verbal test segment for this important job.

Each verbal question on an SAT is worth approximately 7.7 points—10 points on a PSAT—no matter how easy or hard the question or how long it took you to come up with the right answer.

Never dither around on a question you're apt to miss anyway. Mark it in the test booklet and come back to it if you have time. You must pocket all the right answers you can before time runs out.

To guess or not to guess, that is the question—and there's a very definite answer. Whenever you can eliminate one or two answers, always make an educated guess. If you can eliminate two wrong answers, your chances of guessing the correct answer are one in three, more than enough to justify a thoughtful guess. Probability is on the side of the educated guesser.

Example: On a ten-question set on a PSAT, if you get six questions right and *do not guess* on four tough ones, your score will be 60. (Ten points for each correct answer.) If you *do guess* on those same four questions and get just two of them right, your score will be 75.

Wouldn't you rather have the score of 75?

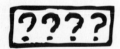

Educated guessing for verbal questions. Ask yourself:

- What is the *real* question here?

- How long will it take to work this out? (If lots of time is needed, I'll circle it and come back later.)

- What help do the answers offer? (For example, what part of speech is needed for the correct answer?)

- Which is the wacko answer? (Nearly always, one choice is hilarious. If I find it, I'm already down to four choices.)

- Do I need negative or positive words here?
  If the word is a mystery, does it have a familiar root or helpful prefix? Have I heard this word used? Where?

- Does this strange word or phrase sound like something I know in a foreign language? Maybe it's related in meaning.

- Have I found all the clues (key words, for instance) in this question?

Omit anything totally unknown. If the entire question comes from outer space and you haven't a clue as to how to proceed, omit the question. The penalty for an omitted question on an SAT is the 7.7 points that a correct answer would have added to your right-answer total. Remember, your goal is to accumulate as big a right-answer total as possible. (For each wrong answer, one quarter of a question's value is subtracted from your right-answer total.)

Never pounce on the first good-looking answer. Smart people eliminate answers one by one, because one of those answer choices is apt to be *awfully tempting*. And wrong. Move too fast and you'll mistakenly choose this answer.

Killer questions do occur. To be honest, any question you cannot answer becomes a killer question on the spot. Most of the really tough ones are near the end of a set of analogies or sentence completions. Really hard critical reading questions can be anywhere in the set because those questions are not arranged in order of difficulty.

Do your best kind of questions first. After all these years in school, you know what sort of questions you do best, next best, et cetera. No matter how the test is arranged, do your best kind first, then the next best, and so on. If you run out of time on your worst kind of question, you won't care so much; you were going to miss some of those anyway.

Record answers in the right places. Check each question number to be sure you're putting its answer where it belongs, every single time. Filling in the wrong ovals makes your heart stop beating, if only briefly.

Idea: Complete a question set, then transfer the answers in a batch from the test booklet to the answer sheet. You'll rarely put an answer in the wrong slot this way.

Vocabulary is the key to all the verbal questions on SATs and PSATs. Both are really giant vocabulary tests. On the most recent tests, over ⅓ of the questions depended on your having an advanced vocabulary, worthy of a college student.

Read to increase your vocabulary.

Make flashcards of words you cannot remember. Flashcards are not babyish. They work.

Simplify long words. Often a big scary word is a friend draped in prefixes and suffixes. Strip away those extra garments before you panic.

predetermined = pre + determined
determined, or decided, beforehand (*pre*) = fated

rejuvenate = re + juven + ate
again/back (*re*) + juven(ile) + *ate* = to make young, like new again

misconception = mis + concep + tion
bad (*mis*) + concept = wrong concept or idea

PREFIX ALERT

You no doubt mastered that ton of prefixes in List 5, "The Incredible Hunk," but here's a quick reminder. Prefixes can be tremendously helpful bits of information on SATs and PSATs when you're faced with a strange word.

Prefixes That Are Usually Negative

a, an	*a*typical	im, ir	*im*pale, *ir*regular
ab, abs	*abs*tain	il, in	*il*legal, *in*ept
anti	*anti*dote	mis	*mis*spell
contra	*contra*dict	non	*non*sense
counter	*counter*act	ob	*ob*tuse
de	*de*mise	of, op	*of*fend, *op*pose
dif, dis	*dif*fer, *dis*agree	un	*un*willing
for	*for*sake		

Prefixes That Are Usually Positive

bene	*bene*fit	com, co	*com*ply, *co*operate
bon	*bon*us	eu	*eu*logy
col, con	*col*laborate, *con*cur	pro	*pro*mote
cor	*cor*roborate		

HOW TO ANSWER SENTENCE COMPLETION QUESTIONS

Sentence completion questions ask you to select the word or words that best complete the meaning of a sentence. Students who read a great deal do well on this question type. The reluctant reader has more trouble, but practice makes a big difference, so let's get to it.

"Test Smarts" You Can Use

Key words point to the answer you want in every sentence. Note the italicized words in the following examples. They are your clues to the needed words and to sentence type.

Example 1. *Although* Janie was *normally* _____, *she became* extremely _____ when it was time to get out of the pool, *insisting* that she needed more practice with the kickboard.

    a. Is Janie behaving normally?

    b. How is she behaving? Is she being insistent?

    c. Is she normally the insistent type?

    d. Is Janie's normal behavior the opposite of how she's acting now? Yes.

    e. **This is a sentence of contrast:** one behavior contrasted with (opposed to) another.

    f. The answer will be opposing words, such as *docile . . . stubborn*. Try reading the sentence with those words inserted, and you'll see that it makes good sense.

Example 2. The critic labeled the film _____, saying that *it was poorly cast and lacked substance.*

    a. Why so many key words in a row?

    b. Do the italicized words after the blank act as a definition of the unknown word? Yes.

    c. **This is a definition sentence:** the key words explain, amplify, or define the missing word.

    d. Try plugging in a word that fits the definition, such as *shallow* or *tasteless*. Now the sentence makes sense.

Example 3. The *aggressive* _____ *and commitment* to opening the American West are *reflected* today in the _____ of modern business entrepreneurs.

    a. Is that little word *and* really significant? You bet it is.

    b. *And* almost always links *similar* words or ideas.

    c. The missing word and *commitment* must be closely linked and well described by *aggressive* to make logical sense.

    d. These two nouns, *blank* and *commitment*, are *reflected* (they show up again) in modern business entrepreneurs—today's pioneers in the business field.

    e. **This is a sentence of comparison or coordination of similar ideas**: the key words told you so.

    f. Try reading the sentence again, with words inserted:

> The aggressive *drive* and commitment to opening the American West are reflected today in the *actions* of modern business entrepreneurs.

or:

> The aggressive *drive* and commitment to opening the American West are reflected today in the *thrust* of modern business entrepreneurs.

Example 4. *Due to* the _____ of qualified instructors, the primary *concern* of modern education *is not the curriculum but* the _____ required to give it life.

    a. *Due to* means *because of*, right?

    b. *Because of* some problem with qualified instructors, the *concern* (worry) in education is *not* curriculum (what is being taught) *but* that problem with teachers.

    c. **This is a cause and effect sentence** or **cause and result**: the key words tell you that one thing/situation is resulting in another.

    d. Go ahead now and plug in your own words. Write your complete sentence here:

_____

    e. Did you come up with something like this? Due to the *lack* of qualified instructors, the primary concern of modern education is not the curriculum but the *personnel* required to give it life.

Key Word Alert!
Certain words should always grab your attention as you read:

Words Indicating Contrast:

but	although	nevertheless	on the other hand
yet	atypically	curiously	uncharacteristically
except	ironically	abnormally	illogically
oddly	however	nonetheless	even though
despite	instead	strangely	on the contrary

. . . and several others. Start watching for them.

Words Indicating Comparison or Coordination:

too	ever	or	repeated
and	also	reflected	moreover
like	always	echoed	similarly
plus	faithfully	commonly	

Words Suggesting Cause and Effect:

so	then	unless	followed
but	since	which resulted in	ensued
after	because	brought about	

. . . just for starters. Watch for others.

You must take the pulse of your sentence by noting these key words—and others like them—right away. Many will be adverbs or conjunctions. Keep an eye out for these critical words until you become "sensitized."

Certain sentence types repeat. Learn these sentence types.
1. Contrast of one thing/situation with another. (Read Example 1.)
2. Definition or explanation. (Read Example 2.)
3. Comparison/coordination of similar ideas. (Read Example 3.)
4. Cause and effect/result. (Read Example 4.)

Knowing what sentence type you are working with will tell you what sort of words must be used to complete the meaning. Although not all sentences on standardized tests fit into these categories, you'll be surprised at how many do.

Negative vs. positive concepts abound. Remember this example? *The critic labeled the film*

_____, *saying that it was poorly cast and lacked substance.* Did the critic like the film? No. The word for this blank must be a *negative* word. Any positive or even neutral word offered as an answer choice will be wrong and can be crossed out immediately.

How about this example? *The aggressive* _____ *and commitment to*

opening the American West are reflected today in the _____ *of modern business entrepreneurs.* Is this a negative sentence as a whole? No, it appears to be fairly positive. Any negative answer choices can be eliminated immediately. *Commitment* is a fairly positive word, and the word linked to it by *and* must also be positive. For the second blank, a positive word or one with no negative connotations is a must. Why? Because the two nouns (*blank* and *commitment*) are *reflected* today. They show up again in modern business pioneers, and they are still positive qualities.

Be alert for negative and positive words. Ask yourself whether you want good words or bad ones? Is the general idea nice or nasty?

The last few sentence completion questions are usually the hardest. In a set of ten questions of this type, the first two are apt to be relatively simple. One-word completions are the easiest and will take you only a few seconds. As you work through the problem set, however, the going may get rougher. As a general rule, the more complex the sentence, the more sophisticated the answer choices, although some very sophisticated sentences depend on simple words for meaning. No rule works all the time on SATs. Eliminate all the answers you *know* to be wrong. Then choose the best of those remaining.

REASONING YOUR WAY THROUGH TO THE ANSWER

Let's work through a question of medium difficulty to demonstrate the reasoning process. This always looks long in print, but your mind is the best computer ever made, and it will do all this work in seconds.

Example: Choose the word or words that best complete the meaning of the entire sentence.

The bygone belief that education was the province of the _____, and not required by the masses, has been supplanted by our conviction that education is absolutely _____ for everyone if our nation is to progress.

(a) monarchy . . . logical
(b) church . . . impossible
(c) populace . . . desirable
(d) elite . . . mandatory
(e) educators . . . required

Step 1. Read the sentence carefully. Read it again.

Step 2. Note key words pointing to the required answer: *not required by the masses* sets up a contrast with the first clause; *supplanted by* (replaced) further emphasizes the contrast with the *bygone belief*. *Conviction* and *absolutely* are strong words, pointing to a strong word for the second blank.

Step 3. Sentence type? An obvious contrast—old with modern. Education long ago compared with now.

Step 4. Whomp up the answer. Let's try: *The bygone belief that education was the province of the wealthy or upper class, and not required by the masses, has been supplanted by our conviction that education is absolutely necessary for everyone if our nation is to progress.* Does the "guess" answer make total sense?

Step 5. Eliminate answers.

(a) **monarchy . . . logical** No. Factually wrong, as the wealthy were also educated. And *logical* makes little sense in the second slot. This sentence poses the problem of *who* must have an education, not whether it is logical or illogical.

(b) **church . . . impossible** True, the church once did most of the education, but *church* is not an opposite of *the masses*, which is required in this sentence. *Impossible* makes no sense in the second blank. No. Cross out.

(c) **populace . . . desirable** *Populace* is a good synonym of *the masses*, not the contrasting word we need. *Desirable* works, but is very weak when you remember the strong words: *conviction, absolutely.* No. Cross out.

(d) **elite . . . mandatory** *Elite* would include the monarchy and the wealthy, who were educated in bygone days, and *mandatory* (essential, vital) completes the idea of contrast between then and now. Circle this one to KEEP.

(e) **educators . . . required** *Educators* is not an opposite of *the masses* and makes little sense, although it's vaguely possible. *Required* works well in the second blank. KEEP, for now.

You are left with *choice (d)* and *choice (e)*. Which one is *more specific*? Which one is closer to your idea of a good answer? Because *elite* fits so much better in the first blank, and because *mandatory* is a stronger word than *required*, you should choose *choice (d)*. *Choice (d)* is correct for this sentence.

Once More, with Feeling

1. *Read and reread the given sentence.* Examine it like a bug under a microscope. Circle key words if it helps you.

2. *Note the key words as clues, especially the "little words"*: so, because, and, yet, since, most, least, although, enough, moreover, typically, normally, curiously, however, uncharacteristically, unless, even though, nevertheless, etc. Note all *adverbs*.

3. *Decide on sentence type—is it one of these?*

   a. *Contrast* of one thing with another?
   b. *Definition*—with the word you're looking for defined or explained in the sentence?
   c. *Comparison* or *coordination* of similar ideas?
   d. *Cause and effect or result?*

4. *Whomp up your own answer for the fill-in word (or words)* **before** *looking at the answer choices.* Do you want a positive or negative word? Positive word in the first blank and negative word in the second blank? What does the sentence *need* to make absolute logical sense?

5. *Eliminate answer choices systematically*, one by one. Cross out the wrong ones in your test booklet, and circle the answers to keep for final decision time.

Note: *Management of your time* is a critical factor on any test. Remember to check the wall clock or your watch frequently during each timed test segment. For these sentence completion questions, allow yourself 15–30 seconds for each, so that a section of ten questions will not gobble more than 3–4 minutes. Easy fill-ins take only a few seconds, and you can ponder longer on the stinkers.

1. Practice Sentence Completions

Directions for all practice exercises: Circle the word or words that best complete the meaning of the entire sentence.

1. Serena, who had a(n)_____ temperament at odds with her name, learned that office work was too dull and predictable for one of her nature.

   (A) placid
   (B) volatile
   (C) remote
   (D) benevolent
   (E) amicable

2. Popular twenty years ago, the young adult problem novel, as it was known in the publishing trade, was basically _____—bent on conveying a moral lesson in modern slang.

   (A) encouraging
   (B) boring
   (C) didactic
   (D) modern
   (E) inspirational

3. Ben's theory that people's lives are predestined, determined by God or perhaps fate, makes his championship of independence and free will especially _____.

   (A) understandable
   (B) incongruous
   (C) suspect
   (D) reprehensible
   (E) interesting

4. Her school performance was consistently _____, causing her parents to debate with her teachers as to whether she was _____ or just plain bored.

   (A) strong . . . inattentive
   (B) insipid . . . gifted
   (C) meteoric . . . brilliant
   (D) lackluster . . . incapable
   (E) erratic . . . deficient

5. The idea behind mediation is _____, wherein people with _____ goals or philosophies reach agreement on common ground, each side conceding a point now and then.

   (A) arbitration . . . identical
   (B) historic . . . classic
   (C) innovative . . . odd
   (D) accord . . . unattainable
   (E) compromise . . . disparate

6. Hal found that his pet monkey had not only a _____ tail, but also a mind to match, as his inventive exploits revealed a _____ intelligence far beyond what Hal had expected in so young an animal.

   (A) simian . . . destructive
   (B) complex . . . primate
   (C) clever . . . naughty
   (D) talented . . . stultifying
   (E) prehensile . . . precocious

7. As anyone who watches TV can _____, the programs are merely sandwiched in between the _____ advertising messages.

   (A) attest . . . ubiquitous
   (B) acknowledge . . . intriguing
   (C) tell you . . . scarce
   (D) deny . . . necessary
   (E) reveal . . . diminishing

8. Possessed of an _____ desire to ride in the red helicopter, Maria stared silently at the glorious machine, willing someone to look her way and _____ the longing she was unable to express.

   (A) insane . . . squash
   (B) inarticulate . . . divine
   (C) inner . . . admit
   (D) incredible . . . refute
   (E) insatiable . . . grant

9. Since Uncle Claymore was normally well groomed and _____, we were caught off guard when we picked him up and discovered him to be not only _____ but also unready.

   (A) shaved . . . undressed
   (B) particular . . . prepared
   (C) punctual . . . disheveled
   (D) imperturbable . . . jaunty
   (E) presentable . . . late

10. Because of our cherished belief in friars as honest _____ with no need of wordly goods, Chaucer's portrayal of an avaricious and _____ cleric comes as a shock.

    (A) priests . . . perspicacious
    (B) clerics . . . charming
    (C) fanatics . . . greedy
    (D) ascetics . . . mendacious
    (E) individuals . . . supercilious

2. Practice Sentence Completions

1. Zora Neale Hurston's *Their Eyes Were Watching God,* noted for its _____ portrayal of African-American life in the thirties, was nonetheless criticized on publication for that very attention to truth.

    (A) riotous
    (B) frenetic
    (C) authentic
    (D) ludicrous
    (E) gritty

2. Unlike last year's bountiful harvest, this year's crop appears somewhat _____.

    (A) slender
    (B) varied
    (C) diseased
    (D) meager
    (E) delayed

3. The theory of _____ states that animal species once alike tend to develop differently over time if their location is changed in a sufficiently dramatic manner.

    (A) fragmentation
    (B) divergence
    (C) confrontation
    (D) expectation
    (E) disassociation

4. Far from being passive puppets, _____ by unseen hands, we should realize that we can _____ the technologies that shape modern life.

    (A) designed . . . alter
    (B) alarmed . . . defeat
    (C) enlivened . . . enhance
    (D) rejuvenated . . . renew
    (E) manipulated . . . govern

5. Old Major's elegant meal of beef sirloin was truly _____, occurring only because he happened to be trotting down the sidewalk just as the meat truck had an accident.

    (A) fortuitous
    (B) outstanding
    (C) unwarranted
    (D) exemplary
    (E) salutary

6. Although weary, the troops were _____ action after a particularly _____ speech from their captain.

   (A) discouraged from . . . terse
   (B) prompted to . . . soporific
   (C) galvanized into . . . cogent
   (D) barred from . . . blistering
   (E) dissuaded from . . . witty

7. As if he'd been trained by a(n)_____, Ralph tried to deceive the customers of the shop with _____ antiques.

   (A) entrepreneur . . . genuine
   (B) connoisseur . . . original
   (C) tyro . . . innovative
   (D) glib salesman . . . classic
   (E) charlatan . . . spurious

8. To the horror of ecologically minded people, objects meant for one-time use or for wholly _____ appeal are surviving almost forever, due to the _____ of some materials.

   (A) ephemeral . . . durability
   (B) fashionable . . . qualities
   (C) modern . . . manufacture
   (D) timeless . . . design
   (E) frivolous . . . affordability

9. Although writers' bodies are, of necessity, _____ during work hours, their minds get a great deal of _____.

   (A) present . . . escape
   (B) subdued . . . excitement
   (C) peaceful . . . turmoil
   (D) sedentary . . . exercise
   (E) immobile . . . thought

10. Rarely are college-bound freshmen without _____; while clearly eager to test their adult wings, they're also _____ about the strength of those wings.

    (A) euphoria . . . unconcerned
    (B) ambivalence . . . anxious
    (C) trepidation . . . dithering
    (D) insecurity . . . confident
    (E) maturity . . . baffled

Again, are you remembering to make careful educated guesses? Note when you guess and keep track of how you're doing. If you're a lousy guesser, a friendly teacher can probably help you to get better.

3. Practice Sentence Completions

1. Although E. B. White enjoyed the success of *Charlotte's Web,* he was _____ to have it made into a movie, fearing that the film would be "cartoony" or inaccurate.

   (A) resigned
   (B) overjoyed
   (C) eager
   (D) reluctant
   (E) careful

2. An optimist by nature, Chris faced a difficult adjustment when his investments turned sour, and he was slow to regain his customary _____.

   (A) sanguinity
   (B) hardiness
   (C) briskness
   (D) wariness
   (E) incisiveness

3. A linguist must discriminate between that which is merely a fad and that which represents actual change in language usage, _____ the former and accurately _____ the latter, regardless of personal preference.

   (A) resenting . . . recording
   (B) disregarding . . . transcribing
   (C) expunging . . . deleting
   (D) enjoying . . . defining
   (E) repeating . . . explaining

4. Juan's young, ingenuous appearance belied his _____ bargaining skill in awkward negotiations, so that opponents were often surprised by his _____.

   (A) honest . . . deviousness
   (B) considerable . . . stalling
   (C) innovative . . . stance
   (D) plausible . . . logic
   (E) canny . . . acumen

5. Society once suffered from a _____ of information about exercise and diet, but recently we've been _____ reams of material on both topics.

   (A) deluge . . . deprived of
   (B) dearth . . . inundated with
   (C) paucity . . . astonished by
   (D) plethora . . . showered with
   (E) narrowing . . . offered

6. Known for her _____, Marlene astounded her community by withdrawing her customary support from a charity and establishing a rival one in her own name, a gesture labeled pure _____ by disgruntled former associates.

   (A) generosity . . . philanthropy
   (B) affluence . . . conceit
   (C) involvement . . . cussedness
   (D) judiciousness . . . wantonness
   (E) altruism . . . narcissism

7. Although her information about space exploration was of incalculable value, the new physicist on our staff was _____ nonetheless; that is, until her advice was sought.

   (A) reticent
   (B) voluble
   (C) confident
   (D) equable
   (E) garrulous

8. When told their ideas are _____, older people often refrain from sharing their patiently garnered knowledge with the young and smug whom they deem too _____ to appreciate it.

   (A) perceptive . . . dimwitted
   (B) ludicrous . . . infantile
   (C) obsolescent . . . myopic
   (D) hidebound . . . compatible
   (E) quixotic . . . self-absorbed

9. The trophies are _____ evidence of Cleo's skill at tennis, yet she's been quite the _____ during her career, having repeatedly taken advantage of her opponents.

   (A) questionable . . . professional
   (B) maturing . . . spoiled brat
   (C) irrefutable . . . opportunist
   (D) insignificant . . . glutton
   (E) immeasurable . . . vixen

10. Tourists in _____ countries, where so many eke out their existence by begging, note that the poor never _____ when the traveler makes a munificent contribution.

    (A) foreign . . . accept
    (B) distant . . . respond
    (C) mendicant . . . acknowledge
    (D) indigent . . . demur
    (E) alien . . . resist

HOW TO ANSWER QUESTIONS ON READING PASSAGES

A written passage followed by questions is designed to test your reading comprehension. The tester wants to know if you understood everything in the passage, not only what was stated but also what was implied.

The majority of reading samples on standardized tests read like textbook material or articles in good magazines. But occasionally you will find some reading passages on standardized tests to be both boring and convoluted.

How can you triumph over these reading passages?

Suggested Strategy

1. **Practice the art of involved reading—with total concentration.** You can read a Gary Larson cartoon book in one way, but you must read textbook material in a totally different way.

   Blank out the world. Immerse yourself in the material to the exclusion of everything else. Only in that way will it make sense and stay in your mind.

   The more you practice being involved with what you are reading, the better you'll get. This technique is invaluable for success with reading passages on standardized tests.

2. **Read the questions first, so that you know what you're looking for as you read the passage.**

3. **Know the kinds of questions that can be asked.** On a sample 30–100 lines long, only certain questions can be asked about the material:

   a. Logical title/main theme?
   b. Facts?
   c. Author's mood or attitude toward the material?
   d. Tone of the piece?
   e. Inferences, e.g., what logically preceded or would follow this material?
   f. Conclusions regarding the information itself—what consequences or implications could it have?

4. **Mark the passage for later reference, as follows:**

   **Asterisks by *meaty sentences.*

   F Put F in the margin or underline for *facts.*

   O Circle words that indicate *tone, mood, author attitude, contrast*—note all words that hint at *change* or *contrast* (e.g., however, but, even though, although, nevertheless, except, on the other hand), plus all adverbs that qualify what has been said (curiously, oddly, and so on).

   C *Cause and effect* relationships must be noted, as they are a great source of questions.

5. **Read the passage once, quickly,** for an overall picture and a good crack at answering any question on central idea or main theme. Read again, slowly, with the questions in mind, marking the passage as you go, if you find that this technique works for you.

6. **Eliminate answer choices one by one.** You will almost always be able to eliminate two of the five answer choices. One answer is usually too broad and all-encompassing, and another answer is typically off the wall—a joke perhaps on the part of the test makers.

    Now you have three answer choices. If you are unsure, make your best guess, record the answer, and go on. Don't dither too long on any question, and *don't worry about it.* (You wouldn't believe how many successful professionals had low test scores at one time or another and it didn't stop them.)

7. **For Paired Reading Passages, specifically:**

    a. This test section will have 11 to 13 questions, which refer to two passages that treat the same topic from different points of view.

    b. Quickly skim over the questions that treat Passage I—about 4 or 5. Read the passage and answer only those questions.

    c. Repeat this process for Passage II, keeping the first passage in mind, maybe circling parts that touch on points you remember from Passage I. Answer the 4 or 5 questions on Passage II.

    d. With both viewpoints in mind, answer the last two or three questions that ask you to compare or contrast opinions in both passages.

WHY ARE READING PASSAGES SUCH A BIG PART OF A VERBAL TEST?

College entrance exams are developed at the request of the colleges themselves and are designed to discover how well you will do with college-level reading materials.

Some authorities have stated that 90 percent of your college studies will directly depend on your reading comprehension. So, you need to practice reading in an involved way not just for a test, but because you'll need to read the same way as a college student.

DO YOU WANT TO SCORE HIGH?

If scoring is your goal, then you must make an effort to answer *every single question.* That means allowing plenty of time for the reading passages.

In 2004, critical reading questions made up 40 of the 78 total verbal questions that count toward your score. (Remember that one test segment, either math or verbal, will be testing for question validity and will not count toward your score. It's tough to tell which segment, though, so do your best on all of them.) Currently, more than half of verbal test questions are on reading comprehension (critical reading skills), so *you must save at least half of every timed segment for these questions.* (I have to save ⅔ of the time as I read slowly.)

Don't skip any questions.

Make your best, most careful guess even on the stinkers. Remember, probability is on your side if you can eliminate even one answer choice.

1. Practice Reading Passage

The following passage is from a history of geology. This portion deals with the first visit to America by the eminent British geologist, Sir Charles Lyell.

Line

1   Lyell's *Principles* had seen six editions in London and a pirated one in Philadelphia. Anyone could see that he had been everywhere, seen everything, and met

5 everybody—on his side of the Atlantic. His talent for synthesizing others' ideas was obvious from his book, and no one in America could approach his stature as a geologist, or so it seemed. The thought of

10 having this "gimlet-eyed Englishman" peering over their shoulders as they struggled to finish their reports caused widespread discomfort among the young surveyors. It was an awkward moment in

15 American geology, but the survey geologists could not help feeling honored by his obvious interest.

      Sir Charles was fascinated by steamships, and in July 1841, he took the

20 fastest he could find, the packet Acadia. It whisked him and Lady Lyell from Liverpool to Boston in just 12½ days, including a day's stop in Halifax. He had been invited to give a dozen lectures at the

25 Lowell Institute in Boston, and that was the main excuse for the trip, but he was intent on seeing all he could see of American geology, and to do justice to that goal he decided to say a whole year. At the

30 same time he was well aware of the potential for book sales in America, and a good part of his baggage must have consisted of the matrices for printing plates of the sixth edition of the *Principles* and

35 the second edition of the *Elements,* which had just appeared in London. It was no accident that the first official American editions of those books "printed from the original plates and wood cuts, under the

40 direction of the author" were published in Boston in 1841.

      Lyell went about his visit with all the single-minded determination he was known

45 for and ultimately succeeded in arranging for himself a field trip through eastern North America, the like of which none had taken before and few since. He and his wife were on the road almost all the time, and they covered the region from Quebec

50 to Savannah in trains, carriages, coastwise steamers, riverboats, and every other conceivable conveyance, usually guided by the best local people.

      Lyell was genial, smooth, and

55 convincing, but he had not known what to expect in America. He was aware that his reputation would serve as his passport with geologists and in the main centers of learning, and it did, but he was pleasantly

60 surprised to find, out in the country, that a polite Englishman traveling for scientific purposes was warmly welcomed wherever he went and could count on all the assistance he could need, even from people

65 who had never heard of geology. Travel in the backwoods of the United States turned out to be easier and much more pleasant than he had expected.

      Any qualms the young survey

70 geologists may have had about being open with him gave way under the impact of his personality. Lyell was not a natural charmer, but he had faced this problem before and knew how to handle it. He

75 praised them all to their faces and behind their backs. In his lectures he made favorable comments and handed out credit right and left. If he had expected American geologists to be half-trained bumpkins, he

80 never expressed the thought, and if their recent accomplishments surprised him, he never showed the surprise. He even found nice things to say about Eaton's stratigraphy of the Niagara district and Percival's

85 map of Connecticut! The few skirmishes that arose were effectively smoothed over with more praise and credit.

1. This passage can most accurately be described as a

    (A) historical account
    (B) gentle lampoon
    (C) journal entry
    (D) character sketch
    (E) professional résumé

2. The phrase "gimlet-eyed" in line 10 most nearly means

    (A) slightly fish-eyed
    (B) extremely perceptive
    (C) somewhat inebriated
    (D) subtly cruel
    (E) haughty or supercilious

3. Overall, the person described in this passage is

    (A) someone exceedingly British and hard to impress
    (B) a pedant, who knows he ranks foremost in his field
    (C) an autocrat, who naturally takes charge
    (D) an autodidact in the field of geology
    (E) an energetic, discerning professional

4. The word "qualms" in line 69 means

    (A) angry thoughts
    (B) resentments
    (C) uneasy fears
    (D) defensiveness
    (E) suspicions

5. Official publication of Lyell's books in Boston was due in part to their excellence, but also to their author's

    (A) opportunism
    (B) egotism
    (C) ability to use the "old boy" network
    (D) vanity
    (E) congeniality

6. The "awkward moment in American geology" (lines 14–15) was actually a time of

    (A) deep scholarly concern
    (B) excitement in geologic circles
    (C) pride mixed with apprehension
    (D) turmoil, due to Lyell's impending visit
    (E) serious self-examination among America's geologists

7. The phrase "his reputation would serve as his passport" (lines 56–57) mostly nearly means that

    (A) everyone in his field would be eager to meet him
    (B) he could offer his books as proof that he belonged in the country
    (C) America, luckily, did not require passports
    (D) he could go anywhere in America he wanted because he held a British passport
    (E) geology was so revered in America that he would be assured of a warm reception anywhere

8. Which of the following descriptions does NOT apply to Sir Charles Lyell as he is depicted in the passage?

    (A) basically pragmatic
    (B) tenacious
    (C) congenial
    (D) obviously charismatic
    (E) magnanimous

9. In the phrase "whisked him and Lady Lyell to Boston in just 12½ days" (lines 21–22), the author's tone is best described as

    (A) mocking
    (B) matter-of-fact
    (C) open to several interpretations
    (D) derisive
    (E) tongue-in-cheek

10. Which sentence best sums up Sir Charles's attitude about America *before* he arrived in America?

    (A) He had numerous doubts, but his desire to see American geology firsthand triumphed.
    (B) He was afraid that travel in rural America would lack many of the amenities.
    (C) He was eager to get out among American academics and exchange ideas.
    (D) He felt that lecturing, selling books, and promoting his reputation in America was a necessity.
    (E) He felt he would only be comfortable in America if he could recreate the amenities he enjoyed aboard the steamship.

11. Of the following attitudes toward American geologists that Sir Charles may have held, which one was he careful to keep under wraps?

    (A) professional respect
    (B) pleasure in mutual interests
    (C) professional skepticism
    (D) professional receptivity
    (E) professional curiosity

12. In line 2, the word "pirated" most nearly means

    (A) imported by American pirates
    (B) conspiratorial
    (C) abridged
    (D) a nonacademic translation
    (E) without legal copyright

2. Practice Reading Passage

Line

1   The central mystery of the Celtic religion, and the ceremonial rituals which embodied its essence, will always be elusive. For many the Celtic mystique, with

5   its romantic emphasis on the fairy and the spirit-world, has obscured the spirituality of these warrior peoples and the fact that they even had a religion. The ancient oral tradition that perpetuated the laws, legends

10   and the tribal teachings, through the trained memories of a group of poets and priests, made the act of writing unnecessary. And, much like the prohibitions laid on the Celtic warrior heroes, which predestined

15   their lives and actions, the taboo on writing continued as long as the old religion lasted.
    The earliest remnants of Celtic culture in Central Europe are usually dated between 800 and 450 BC and assigned to

20   the Hallstatt culture, after the metal artifacts found in a cemetery at Hallstatt in Austria, a centre for salt and copper mining. The later Celtic phase, the La Tène, named after a village in Switzerland,

25   continued in Continental Europe until Roman times. The style of ornament associated with the La Tène culture, with its wild, imaginative but formalized decoration of floral patterns and abstract

30   symbols, was still the dominant characteristic of Celtic metalwork, stonecarving and manuscript illumination in Britain and Ireland a thousand years later.
    The Celts emerged from the Rhine-

35   lands of Central Europe as a distinctive group of clans or tribes between 1000 and 500 BC. Their language, religion, social organization and customs were different from those in the Mediterranean south, or

40   further east by the Danube. In general the Celts seem to have many affinities with Indo-European warrior groups who had overrun the Indus Valley civilizations a millennium or so earlier. A number of

45   archaic linguistic forms, such as *raja,* king (Latin *rex,* Irish *ri* and Gallic *-rix*) or *rigu,* queen, as well as many others connected with sacred customs and social organiza-

tions, are shared by Indo-European

50   languages in Asia and Europe. Cultural affinities between the Celts and India can be also traced in the animal rituals in which the spirit of the new king or queen is rendered incarnate with that of a bull or

55   horse; in the act of fasting to gain recognition for a grievance; in the position of women and the fact they were accorded parity with men (Boadicea in Britain and the legendary Maeve in Ireland) in the

60   warrior class; in metric forms, which in the *Rig Veda,* oldest and most important of the sacred books, are similar to some early Irish and Welsh verse; and in the close relationship between teacher and pupil

65   which is still such a feature of Indian religious life and which was an essential part of the Celtic oral tradition.
    Oral transmission was an entertaining and well-perfected method of imparting all

70   the nuances of important events within the life of the tribe. Woven into the tales, for easy rendition and remembering, were the ritual themes that revolved around the gods: the act of naming, the oracle-stone

75   that screamed during the inauguration of a new king, the divine twins, and the heroic warrior. The constant metamorphoses of these motifs, and the easy intermingling of physical and supernatural realms, made the

80   world of the Celtic imagination tangible through thousands of years of storytelling.
    In the tales, divine beings could shift from supernatural powers to human vulnerability and back without even

85   offending the Christian susceptibilities of the scribes who eventually recorded the legends. No matter how extraordinary the deities were, they were still subject to the rhythms of this life and the demands of a

90   particular locale. Each province or area had its sacred place that was the center of its world; and the name of the place showed the relationship between earth and sky, the tribe and its divinity.

95   Much like the mystery of the inland Maya temples or the Easter Island stone heads, in our time, the effect on the Celtic

sensibility of having to live among so many stone memorials of a bygone race,
100 who appeared to have simply abandoned their temples and disappeared, is unimaginable. The prime function of myth is to explain the inexplicable. This is an undercurrent in the constant repetition and
105 mingling of gods, goddesses, and heroes around a specific ancient site or temple. The use of the sacred centre underlies its traditional appeal as a regular meeting-place and also a mythical arena where
110 momentous events could be shifted into the ever-present timescale of the poem and the story.

Explanations of such phenomena are always in terms of deep psychic need. In
115 common with most nomadic tribes, the Celts on their wanderings through Europe had no pantheon of gods but were at one with the elements and the Great Spirit. Wherever they settled, their poets and seers
120 commingled local deities with others from Greek and Asian legends, suitably altered, to do battle against their own almost human warrior heroes; so all the ancient gods and the residue of rites and folklore
125 connected with them became part of an ancestral dream-world that was essentially Celtic.

Answer questions based on what is stated or implied in the passage.

1. The passage states that the *Rig Veda* is the sacred book of

   (A) continental Europe
   (B) India
   (C) the Celts
   (D) Ireland
   (E) Wales

2. According to the passage, the distinctive and imaginative ornamentation produced by the Celts

   (A) was still their hallmark in the British Isles 1,000 years after the Roman occupation
   (B) was a product of the Celtic culture known as Hallstatt in Austria
   (C) was unique but so wildly imaginative that it never found lasting favor
   (D) dates to the era between 800 and 450 BC in Switzerland
   (E) adorned jewelry and personal belongings, which are the artifacts most commonly unearthed today

3. According to the author, the reason Celtic culture is essentially elusive is that

   (A) there are relatively few artifacts of the Celts
   (B) the Celtic traditions were mingled with those of Wales and Ireland
   (C) other related groups of warrior peoples added their beliefs to those of the Celts
   (D) few archaeologists and historians have been properly trained to sift the available material for facts
   (E) written records are nonexistent

4. The passage states that cultural affinities between the Celts and India include all of the following EXCEPT

   (A) the position of women
   (B) animal rituals involving a bull or horse
   (C) ceremonial feasts as acts of recognition
   (D) forms of language
   (E) metric forms

5. According to the passage, which aspect of the Celts' life has been almost totally overlooked?

   (A) their warring history
   (B) their symbolic art
   (C) their relationship to Indo-European warrior groups
   (D) their spirituality
   (E) their social organizations

6. In contrast to modern peoples, the Celts

   (A) created many abstract artistic symbols
   (B) had clearly defined laws
   (C) greatly enjoyed storytelling
   (D) considered male and female warriors equal
   (E) lived among many stone memorials

7. The purpose of myth, according to the passage, is to

   (A) comfort disheartened or superstitious people
   (B) make understandable that which is not
   (C) enlighten the majority of a population
   (D) eliminate superstitions altogether
   (E) provide a society with memorable literature

8. For the ancient Celts, news about significant current events

   (A) was told in story form interlaced with traditional themes
   (B) had less significance than news holds for us today
   (C) was eerily repetitive of other stories and myths
   (D) assumed a greater significance for a fragmented population on the move
   (E) was told to only a few individuals who were responsible for recording the history of their people

9. The phrase "rendered incarnate" in line 54 most nearly means

   (A) drawn thereafter as this beast
   (B) said to be the same as
   (C) represented by an actual live animal
   (D) memorialized in a holy ritual
   (E) made subservient to the spirit of

10. In contrast to modern cultures, which favor undistorted factual accounts of current events,

   (A) the actual facts of an event touched so few lives directly that few Celts were interested
   (B) the Celts preferred heightened action accounts
   (C) the Celts favored a blending of the supernatural with the real
   (D) ancient peoples in general preferred heroic and familiar accountings to what was currently happening
   (E) the Celtic civilization had a delayed, but more objective accounting entirely

11. The word "commingled" in line 120 most nearly means

    (A) absorbed
    (B) eradicated
    (C) replaced
    (D) compared
    (E) blended

12. Unlike the various gods in religions today, Celtic deities

    (A) were omnipresent and omniscient
    (B) could be as flawed as any human
    (C) played a more significant role in daily life
    (D) intervened on the humans' behalf more often
    (E) were more extraordinary and commanding in all ways

13. According to the passage, which of the following was NOT a primary god-theme for the Celts?

    (A) a screaming oracle-stone
    (B) a set of divine twins
    (C) the naming process
    (D) a heroic warrior
    (E) the dying process

3. Practice Paired Reading Passages

Read the two passages and then answer the questions that follow; questions are based on what is stated or implied in the passages, as well as their relationship to each other.

These passages are excerpts from interviews with prominent contemporary African-American authors: Passage 1 is an interview with Toni Morrison, author of Sula; *Passage 2 is an interview with Toni Cade Bambera, author of* The Salt Eaters.

Passage 1

Line

1   I try to clean the language up and
give words back their original meaning, not
the one that's sabotaged by constant use,
so that "chaste" means what is meant
5   originally. I try to do that by constructing
sentences that throw such words into relief,
but not strange words, not "large" words.
Most large words are imprecise. They are
useful because of their imprecision. If you
10   work very carefully, you can clean up
ordinary words and repolish them, make
parabolic language seem alive again.
      Dialogue done properly can be heard.
Somebody in London told me I seldom use
15   adverbs in my dialogue, that I never have a
character say such-and-such *loudly*. But that
he always knew how something is said.
When I do a first draft, it's usually very bad
because my tendency is to write in the
20   language of everyday speech, which is the
language of business, media, the language
we use to get through the day. If you have
friends you can speak to in your own
language, you keep the vocabulary alive, the
25   nuances, the complexity, the places where
language had its original power; but in order
to get there, I have to rewrite, discard, and
remove the print-quality of language to put
back the oral quality, where intonation,
30   volume, gesture are all there. Futhermore,
the characters have to speak their own
language. Novice writers, even when they
get a good dialogue style, frequently have
everybody talking the same way. If they
35   didn't identify the speaker, the reader
wouldn't know. You've got to be able to
distinguish among your characters. Sula
doesn't use the same language Eva does
because they perceive things differently. If
40   the reader feels he or she can visualize a

character, in spite of the fact no one has
said what the character looks like, that's it!
All I have to do as a writer is *know* it in my
mind. I don't have to write every piece of it.
45   I give a few clues, some gestures . . .
      I try to avoid editorializing emotional
abstractions. I can't bear to read any more
of those books where there is this hopeless,
labored explanation of a simple thing. If
50   you can see the person experiencing the
thing, you don't need the explanation.
      When Eva looks at the back of the
man who abandoned her, she doesn't know
how she's going to feel. It all comes
55   together when he diddy-bops down the
steps, and she hears the laughter of the
woman in the green dress. Her emotional
clarity crystallizes at that moment. When
you think of how it feels to see a man who
60   has abandoned you, to see him after a long
period of time, you can go a number of
ways to convey it. You could use a lot of
rhetoric, but you don't need to do any of
that if you simply see it. You see a person
65   who *is* a simile, a metaphor, a painting. A
painting conveys it better because then the
reader can identify with that feeling,
whether or not he or she has ever experienced it. They can feel it because they see
70   the things that person sees. It's a question of
how to project character, experience from
that viewpoint.
      I don't use much autobiography in my
writing. My life is uneventful. Writing has
75   to do with the imagination. It's being
willing to open a door or think the unthinkable, no matter how silly it may appear.

Passage 2

Line
1   I wasn't raised in the church. I
learned the power of the word from the
speakers on Speaker's Corner—trade
unionists, Temple People, as we called the
5   Muslims then, Father Divinists, Pan-
Africanists, Abyssinians as we called the
Rastas then, Communists, Ida B. Wells
folks. We used to listen to "Wings Over
Jordan" on the radio; and I did go to this
10 or that Sunday school over the years,
moving from borough to country to city,
but the sermons I heard on Speaker's
Corner as a kid hanging on my mama's
arm or as a kid on my own and then as an
15 adult had tremendous impact on me. It was
those marvelously gifted, extravagantly
verbal speakers that prepared me later for
the likes of Charlie Cobb, Sr., Harold
Thurman, Revun Dougherty, and the
20 mighty, mighty voice of Bernice Reagon.
        My daddy used to take me to the
Apollo Theater, which had the best
audience in the world with the possible
exception of folks who gather at Henry
25 Street for Woodie King's New Federal
Theater plays. There, in the Apollo, I
learned that if you are going to call
yourself some kind of communicator, you'd

30 better be good because the standards of our
community are high. I used to hang out a
bit with my brother and my father at the
Peace Barber Shop up in Divine territory*
just north of where we lived, and there I
35 learned what it meant to be a good
storyteller. Of course, the joints I used to
hang around when I was supposed to be
walking a neighbor's dog or going to the
library taught me more about the oral
40 tradition and our high standards governing
the rap, than books.
        The musicians of the forties and
fifties, I suspect, determined my voice and
pace and pitch. I grew up around boys who
45 carried horn cases and girls who couldn't
wait for their legs to grow and reach the
piano pedals. I grew up in New York City,
bebop heaven—and it's still music that
keeps that place afloat. I learned more
        from Bud Powell, Dizzy, Y'Bird, Miss
50 Sassy Vaughn about what can be communi-
cated, can be taught through structure,
tone, metronomic sense, and just sheer holy
boldness than from any teacher of language
arts, or from any book for that matter.

* An area in Harlem around Father Divine's
church.

1. According to the speaker in Passage 1, words

(A) that are deliberately imprecise are the most useful
(B) in constant use tend to lose their original meaning
(C) that are large or Latinate tend to be more precise
(D) are the basis for parabolic language
(E) acquire more fullness of meaning with usage over time

2. The speaker in Passage 1 feels that her first drafts are inadequate because

(A) they came too readily
(B) the characters are speaking too freely
(C) she hasn't yet clarified her vision
(D) they lack adverbs and adjectives
(E) she's using colloquial speech throughout

3. In Passage 1, the speaker's attitude toward her work can best be expressed as

   (A) casual and unassuming
   (B) dedicated, yet occasionally diffident
   (C) perceptive and professional
   (D) authoritative, perhaps even pedantic
   (E) detached and judgmental

4. Which of the following would most likely be abhorrent to the speaker in Passage 1?

   (A) careful exposition of a character's feeling of joy
   (B) writing a first draft in everyday language
   (C) a great number of rewrites
   (D) in-depth analysis of each character prior to and during the writing process
   (E) frequent cutting or discarding of written material

5. According to the speaker in Passage 1, dialogue is right only when

   (A) characters sound like themselves
   (B) readers are comfortable with all the characters
   (C) it is obviously authentic
   (D) readers can both hear and visualize each character
   (E) readers want to read the characters' speeches aloud

6. The speaker in Passage 1 believes that, in comparison to print-quality language, oral quality is better because it

   (A) offers readers both fullness and sound
   (B) possesses a sense of history that print-quality language lacks
   (C) is everyday speech that readers can identify with
   (D) encompasses gesture, volume, and intonation
   (E) includes the language we use to get through the day

7. In Passage 2, the speaker feels that she learned the LEAST about the writing process from

   (A) parents
   (B) books
   (C) her community
   (D) religious orators
   (E) musical greats of her time

8. The tone of the first half of Passage 2 can best be described as

   (A) nostalgic
   (B) drily informative
   (C) derivative
   (D) overly sentimental
   (E) didactic

9. For the speaker in Passage 2, the horn cases and piano pedals in lines 44–46 represent

    (A) her real, enduring interests
    (B) what she learned as a child
    (C) her childhood community's interests
    (D) why she shied away from a career in music
    (E) her youth and New York City

10. In Passage 2, line 52, the speaker uses the phrase "metronomic sense" to mean

    (A) musicality
    (B) regularly repeated verbal elements
    (C) pacing
    (D) the logic of the plot
    (E) plot structure

11. The main similarity between the artistic concerns of the speaker of Passage 1 and those of the speaker of Passage 2 is their

    (A) continued enjoyment of their heritage
    (B) ongoing literary development
    (C) preoccupation with accurately depicting character
    (D) absorption with evocative language
    (E) evolving control over tone, pace, and dialogue

12. With which of the following quotations would both speakers be most likely to agree?

    (A) "Dialogue done properly can be heard." (Passage 1, line 13)
    (B) "All I have to do as a writer is *know* it in my mind." (Passage 1, lines 43–44)
    (C) "My life is uneventful." (Passage 1, line 74)
    (D) "I wasn't raised in the church." (Passage 2, line 1)
    (E) ". . . and it's still music that keeps that place [New York City] afloat." (Passage 2, lines 47–48)

13. Both the speaker of Passage 1 and the speaker of Passage 2 would most likely agree that

    (A) characterization is the ultimate goal of writing
    (B) readers need more explanations than are commonly supplied by writers
    (C) large words are rarely, it ever, useful
    (D) autobiography plays a major role in writers' lives
    (E) language is the most important element of their craft

4. Practice Reading Passage

This material on basic economic principles was published in the late eighties.

Line

1   Traditionally, inflation has hurt creditors and helped debtors. Throughout our history, farmers have been debtors. As a result, during times of deflation or stable

5   prices, the farmers' cries of anguish are heard loud and clear all the way to Washington. But during times of inflation, they may prosper.

    It is easy to see why. Suppose that a

10 farmer borrows $100, which he agrees to pay in one year along with 4 percent interest ($4). In one year he pays back $104. But what if, during that year, prices doubled? The money paid back would be

15 worth much less than the money borrowed.

    Let's say that when the farmer borrowed the money, wheat was selling at $2 a bushel. He would then have been able to buy 50 bushels of wheat ($100/$2). But

20 farmers don't buy wheat—they sell it. So one year later, this farmer harvests his wheat and pays back the loan. If the price level doubles, we can assume that the price of wheat also doubles. How much wheat

25 would the farmer need to sell at $4 a bushel to pay off his loan? He would need to sell only 26 bushels ($104/$4).

    Obviously, this farmer, who is a debtor, benefits from unanticipated inflation

30 because he borrowed money worth approximately 50 bushels of wheat and he later pays back his loan, with interest, in money worth only 26 bushels of wheat. Debtors in general gain from unanticipated

35 inflation because they repay their loans with inflated dollars.

    Just as obviously, those hurt by unanticipated inflation are the people who lend the money—the creditors. We

40 generally think of creditors as banks, but banks are really financial middlemen. The ultimate creditors, or lenders, are the people who put their money in banks, life insurance, or any other financial instrument

45 paying a fixed rate of interest. And the biggest debtor and gainer from unantici-

pated inflation has been the U.S. government. The national debt, which is now approaching $3 trillion*, would be a lot

50 easier to pay off if there were a sharp and lengthy inflation.

    Unanticipated inflation also benefits businesses. Just as businesses suffer losses on their inventory during deflations, they

55 obtain inventory price windfalls during inflations. Between the time inventory is ordered and the time it is actually sold, prices will have creeped upward, swelling profits.

60   Who is hurt by unanticipated inflation? People who live on fixed incomes, particularly retired people who depend on pensions other than Social Security. Those who hold long-term

65 corporate or U.S. government bonds are also hurt. And finally, unanticipated inflation hurts workers whose wages are fixed under long-term contracts and landlords who have granted long-term

70 leases at fixed rent.

    In other words, under unanticipated inflation, some people gain and others lose. In fact, these gains and losses are exactly equal.

75   When inflation is fully anticipated, there are no winners or losers. The interest rate takes into account the expected rate of inflation. Normally, without anticipated inflation, the interest rate would be around

80 5 percent. In 1980 and again in 1981, when the rate of inflation ran at close to 15 percent, the prime rate of interest paid by top credit-rated corporations soared over 20 percent.

85   In order for inflation to be fully anticipated and built into interest rates, however, people need to live with it for several years. Although we have had relatively high inflation for most of the last

90 dozen years, it was only in 1979 that the prime rate finally broke the 12 percent

---

*Over 5.7 trillion in 2004

barrier. Today, though, unanticipated inflation is a thing of the past. Creditors have learned to charge enough interest to
95 take into account, or to anticipate, the rate of inflation over the course of the loan. This would be tacked on to the regular interest rate that the lender would have charged had there been no inflation
100 expected.

Let's work out a few problems. If the real rate of interest—the rate that would be charged without inflation—is 5 percent, and if there is an expected rate of inflation
105 of 3 percent, then obviously the creditors will charge 8 percent.

If the real rate of interest is 4 percent and the expected inflation rate is 6 percent, what will be the nominal rate (the rate
110 actually charged)? Good—I know you said 10 percent. The real rate of interest plus the expected rate of inflation equals the nominal rate of interest.

If the nominal interest rate accurately
115 reflects the inflation rate, then the inflation

has been fully anticipated and no one wins or loses. This is a good thing for our economy because it means that no one is hurt and no one is forced out of business
120 because of inflation.

But if the rate of inflation keeps growing—even if it is correctly antici-pated—our economy will be in big trouble. In a hyperinflation there are ultimately only
125 losers.

Many wage earners are now protected against inflation by cost-of-living adjust-ment clauses (COLA agreements) in their contracts. Some retired workers are also
130 protected, since Social Security benefits are now indexed for inflation—that is, they go up the same percentage as the Consumer Price Index. And so, one way or another, most sectors of our society have learned to
135 protect themselves from at least the short-term ravages of inflation.

Circle the best answer choice based on material stated or implied in the passage.

1. Which one of the following economic conditions is most monetarily beneficial for farmers and business people?

   (A) stable prices
   (B) anticipated inflation
   (C) deflation
   (D) unexpected inflation
   (E) anticipated deflation

2. Inflation that has not been foreseen is most detrimental to which groups of people?

   I.   U.S. government   IV. contract workers
   II. retirees   V. investors in long-term bonds
   III. financial institutions

   (A) II, IV, and V
   (B) IV and V
   (C) I and III
   (D) II, III, and V
   (E) II and IV

2. We can infer that "hyperinflation" mentioned in line 124 would most likely mean

   (A) gradual inflation over a long period of time
   (B) wholly unanticipated inflation
   (C) rapidly escalating inflation, probably in double digits
   (D) astronomically high interest rates over a long period of time
   (E) another nationwide depression like the one in 1929

3. In line 136 "ravages" means

   (A) unexpected downsides
   (B) alarming warnings
   (C) seriously destructive effects
   (D) nasty surprises
   (E) unlooked-for reprisals

5. Overall, the chief beneficiary of any period of unexpected inflation is

   (A) banks and other lending institutions
   (B) businesses operating in most major countries
   (C) pensioners who also collect Social Security
   (D) farmers who are debt-free
   (E) the federal government

6. The nominal rate of interest charged by a lender is

   (A) the fixed rate published by that lender
   (B) the real interest rate plus the anticipated inflation rate
   (C) the expected inflation rate plus the customary fixed rate
   (D) the lowest rate that can be charged if the lender expects to make a profit
   (E) the fully anticipated inflation rate

7. Based on material in this passage, we can infer that one major benefit of modern economic knowledge is

   (A) the loosening of customer credit and reduction of debt
   (B) a steady, dependable rate of inflation
   (C) a predictable interest rate of around 5 percent
   (D) few bouts of totally unanticipated inflation
   (E) businesses being able to rely on nominal interest rates

8. Why might debtors smile at unexpected inflation?

   (A) Because they can repay loans with dollars that are a smaller portion of their current income.
   (B) Because lenders will decrease the amount debtors now owe.
   (C) Because debtors benefit in both unanticipated and anticipated inflationary periods.
   (D) Because they now possess dollars that are worth more.
   (E) Because debtors' payments are suspended in periods of economic flux.

5. Practice Reading Passage

This passage is written by a naturalist living in New York City.

Line

1   Yellow jackets, like all wasps, are members of the insect order Hymenoptera, which includes some of the most social insects ever to evolve. In addition to the

5   wasps, are the ants and the bees. Other groups in the order include the sawflies, ichneumon flies, and the chalcids. When wings are present, hymenopterans have four, which are thin with relatively few

10   veins. The hymenopterans' egg-laying apparatus has been modified into a stinger. Only the females can sting, but most colonies of ants, bees, and wasps consist almost entirely of females, so nearly all

15   members of the colony have this capacity.

It is easy to distinguish any look-alike hymenopterans from other insect orders. The dipterans, or flies, have only two wings; lepidopterans, or butterflies and

20   moths, have four wings that are covered with very small scales, and their mouth-parts include a long, coiled proboscis. The ephemeropterans, or lacewings, and the odonates, or dragonflies and damselflies,

25   have very short antennae and considerably more wing venation.

Among the hymenopterans, in the family Vespidae, the typical wasps, is a subfamily known as the Vespinae, which

30   included the hornets and the yellow jackets. These wasps make their nests out of paper, which is actually composed of fragments of old or decaying wood. Some make their nests in holes in the ground,

35   others attach conspicuous nests to branches or under the eaves of buildings, and some nest in holes in buildings.

Yellow jacket is a common name applied to several species that look quite

40   similar. These small yellow and black wasps are all in the genus *Vespula*. Some of the species referred to as yellow jackets, particularly in the Northeast, are *Vespula arenaria, Vespula flavopilosa, Vespula*

45   *maculifrons, Vespula vidua,* and *Vespula vulgaris.* Though most people fear being stung by these wasps—and the pain can be considerable—the wasps rarely bother anyone unless provoked.

50   Yellow jackets are occasionally seen flying around looking for insects, which they take back to their hives to feed their larvae. However, more often than not, they are usually seen collecting plant nectar and

55   pollen, which is their mainstay. At least that't the way it used to be, until the early 1970s when people started noticing yellow jackets around picnic tables, barbecues, and trash cans, landing on hot dogs, hamburg-

60   ers, soda, and beer. As it turned out, this didn't represent a change in the feeding habits of one of our native species. Rather, this yellow jacket was a new immigrant, *Vespula germanica.* Collectors are now

65   finding them throughout New England, Quebec, Ontario, as far south as Maryland, and west to Indiana. It has been suggested that this yellow jacket be called the picnic wasp because of its habits. Garbage-can

70   wasp would also be an appropriate name.

Picnic wasps are doing incredibly well in urban areas, probably resulting from the abundance of food, nest sites, places to overwinter, and because of the

75   relative lack of predators and competitors. They are also abundant in European cities, but natural checks and balances, such as parasites and predators, keep them in control. In many towns they place their

80   nests in cracks in and underneath the siding of houses. In Ithaca, New York, just one old city block was found to have at least one picnic wasp nest per home. In New York and other very large cities, most of

85   the wooden buildings are in the outer boroughs and suburban areas, but the picnic wasps are also common in midtown, so suitable nest sites must be available.

Among all yellow jackets and paper

90   nest wasps, the queens are produced in the fall. They mate shortly after emergence. The males soon die, and the fertilized queens then hide somewhere. Many go into

95 cracks on the sides of houses or under clapboards, which isn't very different from going under tree bark except that the heat from a home may increase the queen's chances of surviving the winter. The following April or May the wasps resume
100 activity, begin feeding, building a nest, and laying their eggs. Most of the broods develop into female workers and foragers, and by fall the nest may contain thousands of wasps. At this time the queens and the
105 males are produced, and the cycle continues.

Circle the best answer choice based on material stated or implied in the passage.

1. One major assumption underlying this passage is that most of its readers

   (A) are deeply interested in science
   (B) already possess a basic science vocabulary
   (C) live mainly in urban areas
   (D) live primarily in the suburbs
   (E) possess little, if any, real interest or information about insects

2. The author groups yellow jackets with ants, bees, and other wasps because

   (A) they are just like sawflies, chalcids, and ichneumon flies
   (B) their large colonies are nearly all female
   (C) they are distinct from the dipterans (flies), which have only two wings
   (D) as social insects they all make nests or colonies
   (E) females have the ability to sting, have four wings (if they have wings at all), and live in colonies

3. In line 55, "mainstay" is used to mean

   (A) preferred hunting
   (B) traditional habit
   (C) primary fodder
   (D) typical behavior
   (E) customary treat

4. All of the following were cited as reasons why the picnic wasp thrives in cities EXCEPT

   (A) availability of nest sites
   (B) pollution-free environments
   (C) opportunities for surviving harsh weather
   (D) absence of competition
   (E) availability of food

5. The information about *Vespula germanica* primarily supports which one of the following statements?

   (A) As with many species, the female is deadlier than the male.
   (B) Evolution occurs in the insect as well as the human kingdom.
   (C) Humans and insects like the Hymenoptera can usually live in harmonious balance.
   (D) Like humans, insects emigrate in search of hospitable environments.
   (E) Social insects, like social human beings, live according to well-established biological patterns.

6. The observation that "Many go into cracks on the sides of houses or under clapboards" (lines 93–95) serves to emphasize which trait of the yellow jacket?

   (A) creativity
   (B) imagination
   (C) tenacity
   (D) precognition
   (E) opportunism

7. The purpose and tone of this passage are

   (A) basically didactic
   (B) scientific, overall
   (C) explanatory, on a basic level
   (D) somewhat simplistic
   (E) intentionally helpful

TIME TO WRITE RIGHT

"Writing is no trouble: you just jot down ideas as they occur to you.
The jotting is simplicity itself—it is the occurring which is difficult."
—Stephen Leacock, Canadian humorist

Even full-time writers admit that writing is difficult. So is running a marathon, playing in an orchestra, or building a house. That is why all of these things are so profoundly worth doing.

Remember how you felt when your bat connected with a ball the first time? Or when you wrote an entire line in cursive writing? Both of those accomplishments took effort and practice.

Writing is the same. It is a craft you can learn, but basically, we all teach ourselves how to write. It takes practice more than anything else. And you need to know a few things.

When You Write, Remember . . .

1. **Define your audience.** WHO will be reading this masterpiece? WHAT are their expectations? Keep your reader in mind throughout the writing process.

2. **Limit your topic.** Unless you want to write a book, you must narrow your focus so that you can illuminate your material with specific examples, anecdotes, quotes, and other bolstering-type stuff. If you try to cover too much ground, you'll be making sweeping generalizations, and boy, are they boring.

   Remember this rule: *Specifics are fascinating; generalities are dull.*

3. **Outline before writing.** I don't care if it's just a memo, make an outline. Next, rank the items in the outline for logical flow. Readers love a clear and logical piece of writing. They get your message right away, without rereading.

   For example, for a short essay, jot down your main point—the one you want readers to remember above all else. Now list three to five *specific* examples (could include quotes, books, or movies; personal anecdotes; known facts; names of authorities; scientific studies, etc.) that support the point you intend to make. Consider your examples and rank them in order of presentation. Save the best for last . . . or begin with it, but *don't* bury it in the middle. Finally, restate your main point, in different words of course, divinely inspired. Okay, now you have a map. You are ready to write.

4. **Don't try too hard.** Write simply, directly—from the heart. Readers can smell hokum and it stinks. Ernest Hemingway once said, "I have tried simply to write the best I can; sometimes I have good luck and write better than I can."

5. **Avoid the weak verb** *to be*, including *am, is, are, was, were, be, been,* and *being*. Weak verbs accomplish nothing, yet the verb has the major job in every sentence. It is the *sine qua non.*

6. **Show, don't tell**. Writers must paint pictures with words.

Telling	*Showing*
I feel sick.	"Look out, I'm going to heave!"
We are tired of soccer.	We stuffed our soccer ball in the freezer for a few years.
That's a nice cake.	Three layers of dark chocolate cake with nuts and caramel? Bring it on.

7. **Link sentences one to another in a clear manner.** If you have new material or a new term to introduce, begin with what readers know and lead on to the new stuff at the end of the sentence (or paragraph).

8. **Know the stress positions in sentences.** Put what you believe to be the most critical information at the end of the sentence (major stress position) or at the beginning (minor stress position). Readers expect major stuff to be in one of those two places. They don't focus on the middle portions of sentences.

9. **Proofread.** Repair errors neatly and no one will care. Always allot a few minutes at the end of a writing job for proofreading. This applies to writing on a test, of course.
   Given a normal amount of time, writers edit carefully, and enjoy doing it. They're dressing up the new baby to go out in public. I know hundreds of people who write for a living, and not a single one is a writer. They are all *rewriters* and proud of it.

10. **Trust your writing to improve.** You will get better in some way with every writing task. With determination, you can become a competent writer.

When You Write, Please . . .

Avoid all forms of rambling

1. Loose, baggy sentences, one after the other. Aaargh! Good writing offers variety—short, medium, and long sentences. Shorter sentences give prose the life and vigor it needs to keep readers awake.

2. Too many adjectives in a group. Choose the best adjective and let it do the job. In another place, you can add further description.

   > *As to the adjective: when in doubt, strike it out.*
   > —Mark Twain

3. Modifiers that float freely in the sentence. This is a major no-no because it clouds sentence sense. Keep modifiers with the words they modify. Here are two dangling participles as bad examples.

   > *Blowing across the dunes, the dog sniffed the salty air.* (poor dog)

   > *Helen skipped down the street, chewing gum, her hands clutching the wonderful gift.* (Can streets chew gum?)

4. Repeated information. Known as redundancies, few things bore a reader more than seeing the same material multiple times. Speech tends to be chatty and repetitive, but writing needs to be succinct.

Avoid all switching of horses in midstream

1. Switching pronouns from *I* (1st person) to *you* (2nd person), for instance, makes readers wonder who is doing what. Decide on pronouns in the outline stage and be consistent.

2. Shifting from one verb tense to another without regard for time. The verb tense tells the reader when an action took place, which is critical, especially in relation to other action in the paragraph or sentence. If you need to review the English verb tenses, do it now.

3. Lack of parallel structure. Like ideas should be written in the same form.

   > NO: I love marching in the band, learning new songs, and just to be at the game itself. (2 gerund phrases, 1 infinitive phrase)

   > YES: I love marching in the band, learning new songs, and just being at the games. (3 gerund phrases)

4. Sliding from active voice into passive voice. In general, avoid the passive voice unless the person doing the action is wholly irrelevant, or the person hopes to be invisible. E.g., "Mistakes were made."

(active voice)	(passive voice)

   > NO: We needed answers, so in the afternoon a doctor was called.

   > YES: We needed answers, so in the afternoon we called a doctor.

Avoid over-punctuation

Too many commas are worse than too few, yet all prose with lousy punctuation (or none at all) creates instant migraines. If punctuation makes you uneasy, ask your English teacher to review the necessary rules.

> *"All morning I worked on the proof of one of my poems, and I took*
> *out a comma; in the afternoon I put it back."*
>
> —Oscar Wilde

MUST-HAVE LIBRARY FOR WRITERS

Desktop References:

Write Right! by Jan Venolia (ppbk)
The Elements of Style, by W. Strunk and E.B. White, ppbk. (It's all here!)

Supportive, Funny Books on Writing:

On Writing Well, by William Zinsser (My favorite—I re-read it every January)
Bird by Bird, by Anne Lamott (aimed more at fiction writers—great fun)

IF YOU'RE TAKING A STANDARDIZED TEST WITH REQUIRED WRITING . . .

If you're planning (dreading?) to take a test that asks you to write an essay, then why not do it right? And stop fretting. Just practice writing some essays.

Give yourself 25 or 30 minutes to outline, write, and proofread a short essay. One page, maybe two at the most. You don't have to be brilliant! You just have to be well organized and clear. Practice at least two or three times. Going to a test without writing practice essays would be amazingly dumb.

> *"Writing is easy. All you have to do is cross out the wrong words."*
>
> —Mark Twain

And now it's time to practice.

THE
ANSWER
SECTION

Unit I *What You Already Know*

List 1

A. Basic Roots

1. AQUA, AQU = water
2. HYDR = water
3. BIO = life
4. CHROM = color

5. CORP = body
6. EGO = self
7. GE/GEO = earth

8. BIBLI/BIBLIO = book
9. AGR = field
10. MATER/MATRI = mother
    PATER/PATRI = father

B. No Surprises

1. AUD/AUDIT = hear
2. COGN = know
3. DICT/DIC = speak, say
4. DORM = sleep

5. ERR = wander
6. FLECT/FLEX = bend
7. LABOR = work
8. SCI = know

9. SCRIB/SCRIPT = write
10. VID/VIS = see
11. SENS/SENT = feel

C. More Roots You Know

1. CHRON = time
2. COSM = universe, world (sometimes, harmony)
3. CIV = citizen
4. PED and POD = foot

5. PSYCH = mind
6. PED = child
7. VIA = way
8. URB = city

9. TEMP (tempor) = time
10. ZO = animal
11. EQU = horse

D. Roots One More Time

1. CYCL = circle   a. (2)   b. (3)   c. (1)
2. FALS/FALL = deceive   a. (2)   b. (1)   c. (3)
3. GRAV = weigh, heavy   a. (2)   b. (3)   c. (1)
4. AM (AMI) = love, like   a. (2)   b. (3)   c. (1)
5. NEG = deny   a. (2)   b. (3)   c. (1)
6. NOV/NEO = new   a. (4)   b. (2)   c. (1)   d. (3)
7. VAC = empty   a. (1)   b. (3)   c. (2)
8. EQU = equal   a. (3)   b. (1)   c. (2)
9. FRAG/FRACT = break   a. (2)   b. (4)   c. (3)   d. (1)
10. MIN/MINIM = little, least, or smallest   a. (2)   b. (3)   c. (1)   d. (4)

I. Fill-Ins

1. corpulent
2. amorous
3. dissension
4. biopsy
5. matron

6. trivial
7. fraction
8. hydroponics
9. dormant
10. audience

11. podium
12. novice
13. collaborated
14. temporal
15. pedant

II. Antonyms

1. (c) unsophisticated
2. (d) attentive care
3. (b) impolite
4. (i) bright, intelligent

5. (f) huge or vast
6. (e) correct
7. (g) ignorant

8. (j) narrow in scope
9. (a) patriarchal
10. (h) regular, dependable

III. Fill-Ins

1. anachronism
2. geological
3. equestrian
4. dictatorial
5. patrimony
6. envision

7. grave
8. polychrome
9. agrarian
10. psychology
11. precognition
12. equivocal

13. cyclic
14. inscription
15. protozoans
16. deflect
17. egotistical

List 2

E. Demi to Dec

1. DEMI/SEMI/HEMI/MED/MEDI = half
2. UNI/MONO/SOL = one
3. SESQUI = one and a half
4. DI/BI/DU/DUO/DIPLO = two
5. TRI/TER = three
6. QUADR/TETR = four
7. PENTA/QUINT/QUINQUE = five
8. SEX/HEX = six
9. SEPT/HEPT = seven
10. OCT/OCTA/OCTO = eight
11. NON/NOVEM/ENNEA = nine
12. DEC = ten

F. Duodec to Omni/Pan/Panto

1. DUO and DO have been added to *dec*, which means *ten. Duodec/dodec* = twelve; twelve faces.
2. Ten and is written -teen.
3. Times ten is written -ty.
4. CENT/HECTO/HECATO = 100
5. MILLI/KILO = 1,000
6. MYRIA = 10,000 or great, vast
7. MEG/MEGA = million or great, large
8. ARCH/PRIM/PRIN/PROTO = first
9. AMBI/AMPHI = both, around
10. OLIGO/PAUCI = few
11. MULTI/MYRIA/POLY = many
12. OMNI/PAN/PANTO = all

I. Matching

1. (g) in all places all the time
2. (e) times ten
3. (k) two letters pronounced as one sound, e.g., *chorus, bread*
4. (h) great slaughter
5. (i) model or prototype
6. (j) four plus ten
7. (c) 500th anniversary
8. (1) paralysis of one side of the body
9. (a) speaker using lengthy words
10. (b) one great stone, or a single impressive structure
11. (d) first five books of the Bible
12. (f) scant quantity

II. Fill-Ins

1. megalomaniac
2. multitudinous (or myriad)
3. triad
4. sextet
5. millipedes
6. octet
7. pandemonium
8. ambivalent
9. solitude
10. omnivorous
11. ennead
12. myriad (or multitudinous)
13. principal
14. dodecahedron
15. decennial
16. one

III. Logic

1. An octogenarian is eighty or in his eighties.
2. Because a few people share the rule in an oligarchy, it is difficult to keep the balance of power equal. A group of 4 or 5 people who can consistently agree on policy is extremely rare. Humankind's basic nature is egocentric; one person wants to have final say. Even the old Roman triumvirate (3 joint rulers) had a short life.
3. A pentavalent element has a valence of 5.
4. The thigh's quadriceps is divided into four parts.
5. An ambiguous answer lacks focus, may present too many points of view, or may "beat around the bush." It is anything but definite.
6. The ancients thought that the Mediterranean Sea was in the middle of the Earth. On a map you can see that it is almost entirely surrounded by land, literally *in the middle of land*.
7. *Two-faced* people are guilty of duplicity—literally *double fold*.
8. There are 6 metrical feet to most lines in *The Aeneid*.
9. A millennium is a period of 1,000 years.
10. A triptych has *three* folding panels. A *tripod* supports a movie camera, and many still cameras also.

List 3

G. Prefixes

1. a. to view or go over again
   b. to put back
   c. It fires in the reverse direction to the motion of the aircraft.
   d. *retro*spectively
   e. to put it off, to set a later date for it
   f. postbellum = after the Civil War

2. a. not sociable or congenial; not fond of people
    b. literally *against aircraft,* usually referring to a defense system set up to detect aircraft
    c. literally *against the thesis;* the exact opposite
    d. bad luck, ill fortune
    e. lacking sense; illogical
    f. mentally uncomfortable; upset or apprehensive
    g. to act against or contrary to
    h. to function improperly or badly
    i. not irritating to allergies, as *nonallergenic makeup*
    j. to speak against or in opposition, to disagree
3. a. large or great in size or importance
    b. enlarges objects so that we may see them
    c. extremely tiny or invisible to the naked eye
    d. minuscule (tiny) organisms or germs
4. a. forward
    b. in favor of it
    c. in favor of liberal causes
5. a. autodidact
    b. auto; automobile = self-propelled
    c. autonomous

H. Yes, More Prefixes
1. a. circumference = the distance around a circle
    b. circumnavigate = to sail or travel around the globe
    c. circumvent = to get around someone or something, as *he circumvented his friend's plans by making a good plan of his own*
2. a. introspective
    b. intramural
    c. intramolecular
    d. introvert
3. a. warned ahead of time
    b. in the front of a picture, closest to the viewer
    c. going before, preceding
    d. *fore*tell it *pro*gnosticate it, or *pro*phesy it
    e. An idea that takes precedence over another comes before it in rank or importance.
4. a. beyond the ordinary; therefore, special
    b. external
    c. extrovert
    d. ESP refers to perceptions, knowledge, or feelings (vibes) attained in some inexplicable way outside the scope of the five senses.
5. a. between (rex, regis = ruler)
    b. between
    c. between
6. a. overcooked
    b. overlord
    c. hyperactive
    d. hyperbole
    e. superimpose
    f. supranational
    g. surmount
7. a. something beyond rage—causing profound anger, even disgust or contempt
    b. supposed to be as pure as possible
    c. way beyond the norm, far out, exotic

I. Antonyms
1. (i) antitoxic
2. (h) regress
3. (g) agree with
4. (a) prospect
5. (c) preliminary study
6. (e) antagonist
7. (d) outré
8. (b) normal
9. (f) dependent on others
10. (j) conservatism

II. Chart Fill-In

1. [example]
2. misbegotten
3. contra; to go against, contradict, or deny
4. non; nonreader
5. galact (Gr. *milk*, as in Milky Way); intragalactic
6. micro; cosm; a tiny portion typical of the whole
7. magniloquent; speaking in a very grand manner
8. mal; maladroit
9. circum; scrib; to encircle, mark off, or limit
10. ballein (Gr. *to throw*); hyperbole

III. Fill-Ins

1. recurrent
2. postmortem
3. counteract
4. malevolent
5. profusely
6. superhuman
7. extrajudicial
8. misnomer
9. foregone
10. unassuming

Unit II *Vocabulary In and Out of Context*

List 1

I. Antonyms

1. (b) refined, sensitive, polite
2. (a) major, important
3. (f) timidity, lack of nerve
4. (i) lacking zest or flavor
5. (h) youthful
6. (j) absent
7. (e) full of body, springy
8. (c) straight (not winding)
9. (d) restrained
10. (g) noticeably bright or interesting

II. Logic

1. A *petty* act is mean-spirited or spiteful and atypical of someone normally well-behaved and considerate.
2. *Lank* hair often appears stringy, dirty, and unkempt. Its lifelessness is unappealing, as it indicates lack of care.
3. A brain *teeming* with ideas is stuffed full of ideas.
4. Other words ending in *-ling,* where the suffix indicates young or little, include *yearling, gosling, duckling, foundling, fledgling, fingerling* (young fish), *nestling,* and *sapling.*
5. Ask any mother of five under the age of 5!

III. Fill-Ins

1. lucrative
2. paltry
3. haggling
4. rift
5. teeming
6. puling
7. dank
8. pestilence
9. reverie
10. petty
11. ubiquitous
12. stripling
13. crass
14. sinuous
15. vapidly

List 2

I. Fill-Ins

1. razed
2. scrutiny
3. capitulation
4. pert
5. tyro
6. smirk
7. rapture
8. filching
9. bizarre
10. vacillating

II. Thinking About the Words

1. A *salutatory* address is given by the second-ranked senior at graduation. *Salutary* means promoting good health and derives from salut, salus = *health,* which also happens to mean *greeting.* When we salute someone, we are really saying, "to your health," if we remember our roots.
2. A typical ranking of these adjectives would begin with *contentment* first, then *happiness, delight, exultation,* and finally *rapture,* as the utmost in joy. (Any group that wishes may debate this ranking!)
3. In the phrase "only a semblance of her former self," *semblance* means a faint reminder—an appearance we recognize, yes, but just barely. She *resembles* herself, but she is not herself.
4. The *sloth* is a lazy creature, often taking hours to move an inch or two. Indolence, sloth, laziness, and idleness are often given as synonyms, yet each word has slightly different connotations. Sloth is the most negative one, as it suggests ideas like a dirty house, an unkempt appearance, etc.
5. Synonyms for *ruse,* each with slightly different connotations, include trick, stratagem, artifice, subterfuge, ploy, hoax, deception, dodge, flimflam, humbug, pretext, feint, gimmick, snare, trap, and game.
6. *Marauding* means plundering or thieving.

UNIT III: THE VOCABULARY LISTS

III. Antonyms

1. normal, commonplace, everyday, customary, accepted
2. sophisticate, an urbane man, a learned or erudite person, a cosmopolitan individual, a savvy person
3. to refuse to budge, be adamant or stubborn, refuse to yield, "dig in," plant your heels
4. energy, dynamism, get-up-and-go, activity, drive, ambition
5. detrimental to health, harmful, injurious
6. to remain static, to be unwavering or steady
7. to build, construct, restore, institute
8. to tell the truth, be honest and trustworthy
9. one who is truthful, honest, straightforward; an ingenuous person who is without guile
10. cheerful, jovial, optimistic, jolly, sunny, merry, sociable, convivial
11. a purifying substance
12. droopy, lifeless, drab, lank (referring to a hairstyle); if referring to behavior or remarks, antonyms could include polite, respectful, deferential, well-mannered
13. disagreement, noncompliance, refusal to accede to the wishes of another, lack of consent, demurral
14. despair, despondence, misery, grief, woe
15. to give only a cursory look, glance over

Unit III   *The Vocabulary Lists*

List 1

I. Definitions

1. stigmatize
2. perpetrate
3. relinquish
4. truckle
5. nurture
6. evince
7. intimate
8. defile
9. feign
10. entice

II. Switcheroo

1. (g) force
2. (e) lure
3. (f) urgent appeal
4. (j) hint, suggestion
5. (a) reparation or satisfaction
6. (i) one who commits a foul deed
7. (b) downgrading
8. (h) compensation or correction
9. (d) brand of infamy
10. (c) one who profanes or desecrates

III. Analogies

1. wax : wane :: burgeon : wither (Antonyms)
2. nurture : growth :: exhort : action (Cause and effect)
3. philosopher : wisdom :: Anglophile : England (Person related to thing he or she is most attracted to)
4. disparate : praise :: truckle : command (Antonyms)
5. evince : interest :: redress : wrong (Implied relationship)

IV. Fill-Ins

1. redress (*to atone* is also possible)
2. medieval
3. truckle
4. stigmatized
5. relinquishing
6. philologist
7. enticed
8. *Invincible*
9. coerced
10. perpetrated

V. Antonyms

1. (b) citation
2. (c) philanthropist
3. (a) futuristic
4. (d) conceal
5. (d) cajole
6. (a) stunt
7. (c) be truthful
8. (c) respect
9. (b) brevity
10. (a) proclaim

VI. Word Analysis

1. Possibilities are nearly endless. Some of the more well-known include Kipling's *Just So Stories, Alice in Wonderland, Charlotte's Web, Stuart Little, Trumpet of the Swan,* most Disney cartoons, *The Wizard of Oz,* Aesop's *Fables,* the *Nutcracker* ballet, *The Wind in the Willows, Rabbit Hill, Uncle Remus* tales, *Knight Rider* (TV), *Christine,* and so forth.

2. a. 1. hard-fought (it was a tough election)
      2. barely or not at all
   b. 1. make me feel awful
      2. push down
   c. 1. sloped upward
      2. apt or likely
   d. 1. stick together
      2. break asunder, divide, split
   e. 1. absolutely, totally
      2. examine in careful detail
   f. 1. hint or suggest indirectly
      2. close, well-known

3. *At one in harmony* suggests the accord (as well as the feeling of self-satisfaction) that comes from atoning for a wrong. You have "paid the price," whatever it was, and now feel harmonious within, not divided by anxiety or guilt.

4. *Yield, surrender, abandon, resign,* and *waive* all share the idea of giving up completely. *Yield* suggests that you have given way after being forced to do so, as a team is forced to *yield yards to the opposition,* or a driver is compelled by law to *yield right of way.*

   Surrender implies that somebody on an opposing side resisted for a while, as *he surrendered to the impassioned pleas of his constituents.*

   Abandon is a term of finality and suggests a complete giving up, as *she abandoned her child, knowing she could not care for him.*

   Resign is used in more formal contexts, such as *resigning a position* or *he was resigned to defeat,* meaning that he had given himself up to defeat and had come to terms with it.

   Waive implies less force and more willingness to concede, as *they waived their right to the beach property.* Signing a *waiver* means that you sign a legal document giving over a right or claim.

5. A person who "insinuates" himself into a group was not *invited* to join. He wormed his way in through devious means, clever enough that no one is absolutely sure how he did it.

   Teacher Note: This lesson contains a number of meaty quotes that spark good classroom discussions. You might wish to consider the quotes used in "Word Study" for sentences 1, 6 (interesting word order, too), 13, and 14.

List 2

I. Fill-Ins

1. Gothic	5. genre	8. thespian
2. free verse	6. denouement	9. rococo
3. classic	7. protagonist	10. lampoon
4. travesty		

II. Matching

1. (h) elaborate seventeenth-century artistic style
2. (c) a medieval architectural style
3. (j) a tale using figurative characters and language
4. (a) the opposite of tragedy
5. (i) mockery through caricature
6. (b) illogical, often unrealistic slapstick comedy [answer (i) is possible]
7. (d) wit used as a weapon to evoke scorn or contempt
8. (e) low or distorted imitation of the real thing
9. (f) ridiculing verbal portrait of a person (i is possible)
10. (g) high burlesque ridiculing a literary work or well-known literary style

III. Analogies

1. thespian : comedian :: doctor : pediatrician (One of a kind)
2. Notre Dame Cathedral : Gothic :: Parthenon : classical (Implied relationship—building to predominant architectural style)
3. classical : Attic :: genre : category (Synonyms)
4. prologue : denouement :: beginning : culmination (Antonyms)
5. comedy : amusement :: satire : contempt (Cause and effect/result)

IV. Identification

1. satire (also classical)
2. thespian
3. allegory (also classical)
4. Gothic
5. farce (also comedy)
6. (fantasy) genre
7. allegory (also fantasy genre)
8. protagonists
9. classical
10. free verse
11. classical
12. (fantasy) genre; classical; allegorical in part
13. free verse
14. classical
15. thespian
16. Gothic (novel); classical
17. protagonist
18. classical
19. satire (also classical)
20. Gothic

V. Word Analysis

1. Literally, *belles lettres* means *fine letters*. This term refers to literature written as "pure" literature, not as informative or instructive material. It is typically light, sophisticated writing meant for the reader's aesthetic pleasure. Popular, current fiction, concerned primarily with plot or satisfying readers of a particular genre (e.g., mysteries or Gothic novels) is *not* considered *belles lettres*. Essays by E. B. White, however, fit this description, as do the short stories of Flannery O'Connor and other accomplished modern authors.

2. a. photogenic
   b. genus
   c. gentleman
   d. genius
   e. genesis
   f. gene
   g. genetic
   h. engender
   i. indigenous
   j. ingenue

3. *Arts Antonyms*
   1. protagonist—(d) antagonist
   2. tragedy—(g) comedy
   3. assonance—(e) dissonance
   4. realism—(a) romanticism
   5. hyperbole—(j) understatement
   6. travesty—(b) honest representation
   7. overture—(c) finale
   8. ancient—(i) modern
   9. ingenue—(f) sophisticate
   10. rococo—(h) classical

4. *Divers* means *various* or *several* and refers to number. *Diverse* means *unlike* or *different*, also having various shapes or characteristics. If you are studying this course on your own, please show your sentences to a teacher or helpful friend. In class, judgment of students' sentences may be at teacher's discretion.

5. *Fill-Ins*
   a. bona fide
   b. benefactor
   c. bons mots
   d. bon voyage
   e. benediction
   f. bonhomie
   g. beneficiary
   h. benefit

6. A *protagonist* is depicted as someone struggling to achieve something, often a victory, in personal terms, over his own character. Usually, he must struggle to surmount some difficulty, solve some problem. Opposing him in the struggle is an *antagonist,* usually a person, sometimes an entire political body or government, that seeks to defeat the protagonist.

VI. Current examples are best judged by the individual teacher, as new books, movies, and television productions will be different from year to year. If you are studying on your own, show your list to any knowledgeable person.

List 3

I. Fill-Ins

1. dupe
2. sect
3. coup
4. abuts
5. flayed
6. warily
7. crux
8. gibes
9. rank
10. whit

II. Synonyms

1. (b) attest, (c) avow
2. (a) jargon, (c) argot
3. (c) distribute, (d) parcel (out)
4. (a) bog, (d) entangle (Note that one synonym is a noun for the noun meaning of mire; the other synonym is a verb for the verb meaning.)
5. (a) gross, (b) excessive
6. (a) feign, (d) hypocrisy (Again, a verb for the verb meaning, a noun for the noun meaning.)
7. (b) guile, (c) entice (Same explanation as with 4 and 6.)
8. (a) decree, (b) edict
9. (c) fraction, (d) party
10. (b) complete, (d) flagrant

III. Analogies

1. truth : sham :: honesty : guile (Antonyms)
2. gull : dupe :: touch : abut (Synonyms)
3. sect : political :: verdict : guilty (One of a kind)
4. coup : downfall :: credentials : employment (Cause and effect/result. One may lead to the other.)
5. noticeable : rank :: wily : ingenious (Degree)

IV. Famous Fill-Ins

1. mire
2. wiles
3. shamming
4. cant
5. rank
6. flayed
7. verisimilitude
8. gibes
9. coup

V. Antonyms

1. (f) commend or (b) praise
2. (h) nervousness
3. (j) foolhardy
4. (e) disclaim
5. (i) extraneous detail
6. (a) circumspect
7. (b) praise or (f) commend
8. (d) reality
9. (c) large amount
10. (g) unbelievable

VI. Word Analysis

1. Because prefixes *in-* and *dis-* most often mean *not,* the attachment of them makes a word opposite of its original meaning. *Incredible* means not believable or exceedingly difficult to credit as truth. *Discredit* means lack of credit or esteem. A discredited story is no longer believed.
2. a. (4) sacred choral music, usually with accompaniment
   b. (3) musical direction: in a singing manner
   c. (5) a religious song from the Bible
   d. (1) one segment of a long poem
   e. (2) a singer or chanter in a synagogue
3. The root **crux** means *torture,* and *excruciating* refers to something intensely painful, with a synonym of torturous. One favorite old method of execution was death on the *cross,* the other meaning of **crux.**
4. Modern uses of *crusade* can refer to anything from a determination to sell play tickets (I'm on a crusade to fill the house opening night) to a weight-loss crusade. As soon as Crusade is capitalized, however, it refers to Christian religious/military expeditions in the eleventh, twelfth, and thirteenth centuries to fight the Muslims in the Holy Land.
5. a. (5) sudden, violent overthrow of government
   b. (4) a fatal blow or finishing event
   c. (1) two-door automobile
   d. (6) theatrical success
   e. (3) detachable ticket, certificate
   f. (2) to deal with successfully
6. *Nonsectarian* suggests a much broader outlook on issues (or an issue in particular) than that held by the narrow-minded *sectarian.* A *nonsectarian* group is not affiliated with any specific religion, for instance, but can be composed of people of many religious faiths.

List 4

I. Fill-Ins

1. titan
2. somnolent
3. mnemonic (seventeenth-century Dutch painters: Hals, Rembrandt, Rubens, Terborch, Vermeer)
4. nemesis
5. mentor
6. ethereal
7. hierarchy
8. narcissistic
9. bacchanal (or saturnalia)
10. cynosure
11. terpsichorean
12. stygian
13. Promethean
14. mercurial
15. theology
16. cupidity, saturnine
17. solons
18. draconian

II. Analogies

1. titan : weakling :: giant : midget (Size)
2. saturnine : dour :: mercurial : inconstant (Synonyms)
3. deity : Zeus :: nymph : Echo (One of a kind)
4. miser : cupidity :: mentor : leadership (Type related to main characteristic)
5. alert : somnolent :: selfless : narcissistic (Antonyms)
6. Cynosure : sky :: Styx : underworld (Location)
7. physician : medicine :: solon : law (Person related to field)
8. religion : Deism :: Muse : Terpsichore (One of a kind)
9. daringly inventive : Promethean :: brutally harsh : draconian (Synonymous relationship)
10. *The Mikado* : opera :: "The Raven" : poem [One of a kind; answer (a) is incorrect since *The Iliad* is a narrative poem, and a *saga* is a form of prose.]

III. Antonyms

1. (c) soft, lax, weak
2. (h) steady, constant
3. (f) responsible government
4. (i) extend, lengthen
5. (a) funeral
6. (b) cheerful, pleasant, bright
7. (d) deadening (Promethean does mean life-giving)
8. (b) cheerful, pleasant, bright
9. (e) hellish
10. (g) generosity

IV. Word Analysis

1.
  a. (5) capable of walking
  b. (4) stroll idly
  c. (1) vehicle for moving those who cannot walk
  d. (6) walk on an inspection
  e. (3) introductory remarks
  f. (2) baby carriage

2.
  a. protean
  b. junoesque
  c. Uranus
  d. aeolian
  e. erotic
  f. martial
  g. Olympian

3.
  a. complete, unobstructed view of an entire region
  b. referring to all North and South American republics
  c. wild tumult, uproar, uncontrolled behavior
  d. relating to all Greece or Greeks
  e. relating to all humanity
  f. a mime show, with no talking
  g. a cure-all, perfect remedy

4.
  a. short poem, epigram, or any abbreviated piece of writing
  b. alert, "bright-eyed and bushy-tailed," peppy
  c. cheerful, optimistic, bright, pleasant
  d. selflessness, concern for (and interest in) others
  e. steady, constant, dependable, changeless
  f. weak, lax, loose, mild
  g. generosity

5. *Planets:* Mercury, Venus, Mars, Jupiter, Saturn, Uranus, Neptune, Pluto.
   Constellations (zodiacal): Aries, Taurus, Gemini, Cancer, Leo, Virgo, Libra, Scorpio, Sagittarius, Aquarius, Capricorn, and Pisces.
   Constellations (partial list): Ursa Major, Ursa Minor (Cynosura), Cassiopeia, Andromeda, Cepheus, Pegasus, Perseus, Orion, Cygnus, Pleiades (Seven Sisters, the daughters of Atlas), Draco, Boötes, Aquila.
   Ceres, goddess of agriculture, leaves her name in the asteroid Ceres, a minor planet revolving around the sun.

Review

Lists 1–4

I. Fill-Ins

1. coup	6. whit	11. cynosure
2. mnemonic	7. titan	12. wiles
3. relinquished	8. satire	13. dole
4. sect	9. atoned	14. thespian
5. feign	10. classic	15. defile

II. Analogies

1. genre : Gothic :: disposition : mercurial (One of a kind)
2. nemesis : jinx :: coercion : force (Synonyms)
3. dim : stygian :: smelly : rank (Degree)
4. books : bibliophile :: French : Francophile (Person related to outstanding trait; *stampophile* is a made-up word)
5. classic : rococo :: complimentary : disparaging (Antonyms)
6. dupe : credulous :: Prometheus : inventive (Character related to outstanding trait)
7. episode : saga :: Norman Conquest : Dark Ages (Part of a whole)
8. somnolence : yawn :: burlesque : laughter (Cause and effect)
9. satirist : words :: philosopher : wisdom (Person related to significant tool of the trade)
10. mire : entanglement :: lampoon : ridicule (Synonyms; also, cause and effect/result)

III. Find the Oddball

1. (c) omnipresent	Others are synonyms.
2. (d) duplicity	Others share *arch-* prefix.
3. (e) heavenly	Others share a root meaning *god*.
4. (b) laud	Others are synonyms.
5. (a) disclaim	Others are synonyms.
6. (a) allegory	Others are types of comedy.
7. (d) baroque	Others are literary/theatrical terms.
8. (e) germane	Others share the root *gen*.
9. (c) nursery	Others are synonyms.
10. (b) solon	Others are gods/goddesses in Roman mythology.
11. (a) nemesis	Others are synonyms.
12. (d) bond	Others share the root *bon, bene*. (*Bond* is English and Norse.)
13. (c) whim	Others are synonyms.
14. (c) assist	Others are synonyms.
15. (b) vestments	Others share the root *vers, vert*.

IV. Antonyms

1. nurture	6. cupidity	11. brevity
2. evince	7. verify	12. coerce
3. abutted	8. animated	13. somnolence
4. gibe	9. denouement	14. narcissism
5. wary	10. invincible	15. free verse

V. Fill-Ins

1. baroque	5. flayed	9. crux
2. fiat	6. perpetrated	10. exhorted, redress
3. truckles	7. anthropomorphic	11. ethereal
4. cant	8. mentor	

List 5, Part 1

I. Antonyms

1. postpone	5. anticipate	8. miniature
2. preliminary	6. microcosm	9. illiterate
3. postpartum	7. paucity	10. offense
4. predate, antedate		

II. Fill-Ins

1. misanthrope or misanthropist
2. ob-, to disagree, voice a contrary opinion
3. unfeigned
4. im-, stolid, revealing no emotion
5. foresee
6. pan-, the gods of a people or a temple of the gods
7. ambi-, ambidextrous
8. for-, to give up, renounce
9. nonentity
10. omni-, literally, all-knowing

III. Definitions

1. bonny = attractive or appealing; good (Scots)
2. discredit = to cause loss of belief or trust; doubt, loss of reputation
3. invalidate = to render not valid, to discredit
4. irrational = not rational or logical, not sensible
5. atheism = lack of belief in God; denial of God's existence
6. eurythmic = harmonious
7. proclivity = tendency toward, leaning, natural inclination
8. anthithesis = an opposite; direct contrast
9. apolitical = not connected with politics
10. counteract = to go (or work) against, to offset

IV. Find the Oddball

1. (d) quinine
2. (a) semantic
3. (b) decant
4. (c) monetary
5. (e) oculist
6. (b) trip
7. (a) equestrian
8. (d) prim
9. (c) hector
10. (e) novel
11. (e) mulct
12. (c) hepatoma
13. (b) squadron
14. (a) sexton
15. (d) ominous

V. Missing Prefixes

line 1. excited, anticipatory
line 2. forward
line 3. Presently, into, forehead
line 4. irritated, again, intoned, opposed
line 5. unless, experienced, beside
line 6. Uncomprehending, confusion, retorted, dismay
line 7. object, accused
line 8. destroyed, replied
line 9. Distraught, automobile
line 10. Understanding, replaced, confusion, recognized
line 11. postponing, enjoyment, exactly
line 12. belongs, mistake

List 5, Part 2

I. Fill-Ins

1. de-, defame
2. se-, segregate
3. em-, path; the sharing of another's feeling; knowing exactly how he or she feels
4. e-, emit
5. gen (type, kind), homogeneous
6. apo-, apogee
7. ad-, her/hes (cling, stick to); to cling to, stick with
8. fer (carry, bear), transfer
9. para-, paradigm
10. ana-, chron (time); something out of place in time

II. Antonyms

1. (f) orthodox
2. (j) endoderm
3. (d) emerge
4. (h) epilogue
5. (g) include
6. (k) refutable
7. (a) extramundane
8. (c) reject
9. (e) extramural
10. (b) asymmetry
11. (1) anthithesis
12. (i) synthesis

III. Analogies

1. disaster : catastrophe :: permeation : seepage (Synonyms)
2. submarine : periscope :: tank : turret (Implied relationship)
3. interjection : between :: epilogue : end (Implied relationship of location)
4. apocryphal : doubtful :: eccentric : odd (Synonyms)
5. orthopedist : skeleton :: orthodontist : teeth (Person with major concern/focus)

IV. Add-a-Prefix

1. ob + ject = object
2. tra + jectory = trajectory
3. re + ject = reject
4. e + ject = eject
5. con + jecture = conjecture
6. e + jaculation = ejaculation
7. pro + ject = project
8. ad + jective = adjective
9. de + jected = dejected
10. ab + ject = abject

V. Fill-Ins

1. contingent
2. alleged
3. suffused, writhed
4. metamorphosis, wrought
5. effected
6. effaced
7. correlation
8. annealing
9. aberration, diaphanous

List 6

I. Fill-Ins

1. stolid
2. requisite
3. nebulous
4. plausible
5. lithe
6. incumbent
7. eldritch
8. diffident
9. brusque or brazen
10. astringent

II. Synonyms

1. pastoral = bucolic, rural
2. pristine = fresh, uncorrupted
3. expedient = advisable, politic
4. incorrigible = uncontrollable, delinquent
5. catholic = comprehensive, wide-ranging
6. diffident = shy, unassertive
7. eldritch = weird, eerie
8. astringent = dry, puckery
9. brusque = bluff, curt
10. brazen = forward, insolent

III. Analogies

1. rabbi : synagogue :: pedagogue : school (Implied relationship, of leaders and their locations)
2. dog : fidelity :: cheetah : speed (Noted characteristic of each)
3. diffident : gregarious :: timorous : brazen (Antonyms)
4. catholic : parochial :: open : restricted (Antonyms)
5. repeated offender : incorrigible :: impassive judge : stolid (Implied relationship, appropriate adjective for each person)

IV. Fill-Ins

1. incorrigible
2. pristine
3. astringent
4. incumbent
5. nebulous
6. egregious
7. demagogue
8. brazen
9. infidel
10. expedient

V. Antonyms

1. Plausible is the opposite of implausible, unbelievable.
2. Incorrigible is the opposite of compliant, docile, amenable.
3. Catholic is the opposite of parochial, narrow, provincial.
4. Diffident is the opposite of confident, sure, aggressive, brazen, bold, assertive.
5. Lithe is the opposite of inflexible, rigid, stiff.
6. Pastoral is the opposite of urban, metropolitan.
7. Pristine is the opposite of impure, sullied, tainted, stale.
8. Requisite is the opposite of unneeded, unnecessary, extra.
9. Stolid is the opposite of sensitive.
10. Stringent is the opposite of lax, weak, lenient, relaxed.

VI. Word Analysis

1. Roman Catholic schools are often called parochial schools, and thus the words catholic and parochial have joined hands in our minds. Instead, we should remember that *parochial* means limited or restricted, provincial. Parochial schools are normally supported by private, not public, funds and managed privately as well.
2. Works that show country or rural life as peaceful, innocent, and idyllic are the ones that qualify as pastoral or bucolic. Students working alone should share their lists with any knowledgeable adult.
3. Simpler, usually Anglo-Saxon, words as substitutes for the Latinate/Greek words include *dry*, for astringent; *shy,* for diffident; *needed,* for requisite; *harsh,* for stringent; *teacher,* for pedagogue; *gather,* for congregate; *broad,* for catholic; *sure*, for confident; and *church,* for synagogue. As noted, however, these are rarely exact synonyms, which explains why the English dictionary keeps growing.

   The point, of course, is that writing composed of entirely Latinate words becomes ponderously slow going at times. The briefer, punchier words give life to prose. (Remember List 3, "Four-Letter Words"?)
4. The most appropriate tone is humorous. In this context, the journalist didn't "keep faith" with the old saw "never split an infinitive," and therefore he was an unbeliever, an infidel. In fact, splitting infinitives has never been *grammatically* wrong; it used to be considered *stylistically* incorrect. This old view is changing as modern grammarians urge common sense. When the phrase *sounds* better with the adverb inserted mid-infinitive, leave it there.

List 7

I. Synonyms

1. sangfroid
2. concierge
3. insouciance
4. dossier
5. rapport
6. entrepreneur
7. précis
8. debacle
9. avante-garde
10. détente
11. echelon
12. ménage
13. outré
14. soupçon
15. ennui
16. pique

II. Antonyms

1. (d) agitation
2. (c) large amount
3. (e) follower
4. (c) success
5. (a) heightened tension
6. (c) common
7. (d) discord

III. Fill-Ins, Parisian Dream

1. concierge
2. ménage
3. ennui
4. Dossier
5. insouciance
6. piqued
7. soupçon
8. précis
9. (an) entrepreneur

IV. French in Print

1. (d) select group, set
2. (g) unpleasantly familiar, known or seen before
3. (e) proper, what is required by society's rules of behavior
4. (k) a social false step, a boo-boo
5. (i) an accomplished fact, usually unchangeable
6. (b) the responsible obligations of those with rank, nobility, position
7. (l) outstanding item, the showpiece
8. (j) special, favored pupil
9. (c) savvy, know-how, social competence
10. (h) private conversation between two
11. (a) feat of strength, skill, ingenuity
12. (f) related to, compared with

V. Roots of Derived Words

1. **tent,** prefix *re-*
2. **port,** prefix *sup-*
3. **tent,** prefix *dé-*
4. **dos** (from dors)
5. **port,** prefix *rap-*
6. **tens**
7. **port,** prefix *com-*
8. **tend,** prefix *ex-*
9. **dors,** prefix *en-*
10. **port,** prefix *de-*
11. **dors**
12. **port,** prefix *ex-*
13. **tent,** prefix *at-*
14. **port,** prefix *im-*
15. **dors** (root as prefix)

VI. Word Analysis

1. Sans Souci means *without care,* which is how people wish to feel on vacation at the seaside.
2. As they say in England, there's a "bloody great" difference between *sanguine,* meaning optimistic and confident, and *sanguinary,* meaning bloody, bloodthirsty, or murderous. As for *exsanguinate,* it means to bleed to death. Note that helpful prefix *ex-* as a key to the meaning of this word.
3. a. 4, middle-class, common
   b. 5, expert, specialist, or professional
   c. 1, meeting, usually secret
   d. 3, young woman formally entering society
   e. 2, trite remark
4. A Francophile is a lover of *(phil)* France and things French, while the Francophobe strongly dislikes things French; he or she has a *phobia* (fear or hatred) of everything French.
5. Webster tells us that our modern meaning of *canard,* a false or unjustified story, or trumped-up report, derives from the Middle French language period when the phrase *vendre des canards à moitié* meant to cheat, literally *to half-sell ducks.*
6. Words come into the language through need. For example, the phrase *a little bit* is not as precise as *soupçon,* which is a hint or suggestion of something, actually *less* than a little bit. We needed *soupçon* (or a word like it) to describe more accurately what we wanted to say. Likewise, we needed the word *astronaut,* with its solid Latin and Greek base, once we began to have such a person as an astronaut. Before that, there was no need. Moreover, words that are better than the English equivalents come into the language so that writers and speakers can express themselves with greater clarity and precision. We have no exact equivalent for *ennui,* a brief word that suggests boredom, dissatisfaction, and a yearning for something exciting—all in five letters!

   Last, words enter the language through popular usage. The word *swivet,* derivation unknown, did not appear in *Webster's Collegiate Dictionary* as published in the early fifties, yet it is lined up with fellow respectable words in the 1983 edition of this same dictionary. *Her announcement struck him forcibly, leaving him in a perfect swivet. What should he do now?* Obviously, we can use the word *swivet,* and we did—enough to bring it formally into the language.

List 8

I. Synonyms

1. (b) stale and (d) hackneyed
2. (a) redundancy and (d) repetition
3. (b) cite and (e) set forth as possible
4. (c) understandable and (e) intelligible
5. (a) loquacious and (c) voluble
6. (b) terse and (c) concise
7. (d) retort and (e) rejoinder
8. (a) chatter and (e) babble
9. (b) repartee and (d) banter
10. (c) sarcasm and (d) wit

II. Analogies

1. anecdote : book :: epigram : monologue (Part of a whole)
2. laconic : garrulous :: novel : trite (Antonyms)
3. Oscar Wilde : raconteur :: Mark Twain : satirist (Example of general type)
4. repetition : speech :: tautology : writing (Implied relationship)
5. malapropism : words :: gibbering : speech (Implied relationship)

III. Fill-Ins

1. cliché
2. repartee
3. double entendre
4. raconteur
5. riposte
6. malapropism
7. banal
8. persiflage
9. badinage
10. bon mot (pl. bons mots)

IV. Terms in Use

1. anecdote
2. malapropism (He meant *varicose* veins, not warlike ones.)
3. double entendre
4. irony, and an epigram as well
5. etymology (example of entry)
6. irony
7. riposte, and a double entendre
8. tautology (This sentence needs to be cleared of clutter. "The foal gamboled in the meadow fragrant with spring grass," does the job better.)

V. Roots

1. (k) disparaging
2. (m) inherited trait, possession, privilege
3. (f) extremely vivid and clear
4. (h) to move or bend
5. (i) unyielding
6. (n) record player
7. (a) special right or privilege
8. (j) thought or image
9. (b) story of a life
10. (c) to turn aside or away
11. (d) to question
12. (g) easily bent, yielding
13. (e) study of handwriting
14. (o) to enact laws

VI. Word Analysis

1. a. actual, real, verifiable
   b. inarticulate, mute, silent
   c. laconic, terse, concise
   d. fresh, novel, original
   e. garrulous, talkative, loquacious, verbose, voluble
2. Badinage, repartee, banter, persiflage, *possibly* raillery, epigrams; irony also possible; a riposte is often witty enough to be termed a bon mot.
3. *Apropos* means *fitting, suitable,* or *opportune,* depending on the context. Additionally, as illustrated by example *b,* it means *relevant.*
4. Voices change in both pitch and loudness to reflect feelings such as fear, sorrow, joy, and anger. The need for secrecy usually brings on a whisper or lowered volume. Psychologists have confirmed that much of our opinion of people is based on their voice characteristics—their inflection, in other words. A newscaster with a whiny, high-pitched voice might never land a job.

VII. Just for Fun

a. fly guy
b. jet set
c. glad dad or happy pappy
d. fryer buyer
e. pink sink
f. mouse house, mole hole
g. shivery delivery
h. jerky turkey
i. dramatic fanatic
j. sunk monk

Incidentally, what would be the definition given for the name of the game itself, Stinky Pinkies? Smelly hands? Warning: This game can degenerate!

Review

Lists 5–8

I. Antonyms

1. (g) macrocosm
2. (d) shy
3. (i) parochial
4. (a) extra, superfluous
5. (k) agitation, nervousness
6. (b) ordinary
7. (n) success
8. (m) concise thought
9. (c) gibber
10. (e) original
11. (o) urban
12. (h) definite
13. (f) amenable
14. (j) bold
15. (l) laconic

II. Know Those Roots and Prefixes

1. Root = *bon;* an extra, unlooked-for reward
2. Prefix = *inter;* root = *rog;* to question, often with persistence
3. Prefix = *rap* (from *re*); root = *port;* accord, mutual understanding
4. Prefix = *mal;* root = *a + propos;* humorous misuse of words
5. Prefix = *in;* root = *flect;* change in pitch or loudness of voice
6. Prefix = *epi;* root = *gram;* short, witty saying

7. Prefix = *al;* root = *leg;* to presume or assume without proof; to offer as a reason or excuse
8. Prefix = *de;* root = *tent;* suspension of tension or relaxation of mutual distrust or animosity
9. Prefix = *in;* root = *souci;* cheerful nonchalance, lack of care
10. Prefix = *ex;* root = *ped;* advisable, practical; what will "get the job done"—even if not moral or honorable

III. Chart Fill-In

1. Prefix = *re;* root = *strict;* bound by law or convention or kept within boundaries; confined
2. demagogue
3. Prefix = *in;* root = *fid;* an unbeliever
4. Prefix = *en;* endorse
5. Prefix = *de;* root = *port;* to send away/out of the country legally
6. metamorphosis
7. Prefix = *de;* derogatory
8. Root = *gram;* epigram
9. Prefix = *a;* root = *string, strict;* dry, as *an astringent comment* (also, wry); drying, as a styptic pencil
10. Prefix = *se;* segregate

IV. Sentence Completion

1. incumbent
2. irony
3. dossier
4. avant-garde
5. pristine
6. anecdotes
7. brusquely
8. raconteur
9. plausible
10. précis
11. eldritch
12. badinage

V. Analogies

1. dancer : lithe :: entrepreneur : resourceful (One desirable characteristic for each)
2. stolid : impassive :: ironic : sarcastic (Synonyms)
3. enthusiasm : ennui :: plausibility : illogic (Antonyms)
4. repartee : riposte :: détente : compromise (Implied comparison—one logically leads to the other, and one is implicit in the other)
5. words : etymology :: mind : psychology (Implied comparison)

VI. Word Analysis

1. See Answers for List 7, Part VI, question 6, page 412.
2. The root of *echelon* means rung(s) of a ladder, which corresponds directly to our current meaning of level or rank.
3. *Good, Well, Favoring:* bene-, bon-, eu-, and pro-

   Bad, Negative, Not: a-, anti-, ant-, dif-, dis-, in-, il-, im-, ir-, non-, un-, mal-, mis-, de-, cata-

   Above, Over: over-, super-, ultra-, hyper-, exter-, extra-, extro-

   Out/Away: for-, ab-, abs-, apo-, ap-, e-, ex-, ec-, ef-, de-, cata-

   Below, Under: sub-, suc-, suf-, sug-, sum-, sup-, sus-, hyp-, hypo-

   With, Together: com-, co-, col-, con-, cor-, syn-, syl-, sym-, sys-, sy-

   Indicating Time/Place: amphi-, circum-, peri- (around); epi-, ecto- (outer); ab-, abs-, apo-, ap- (from, away, down) se- (away, apart); inter- (within); tele- (far, distant); anti-, ante- (before); ex- (former); fore- (before); pre- (before); post- (after).

   Size/Amount: micro-, min-, pan-, panto-, omni-.

   In, Into, Within: in-, im-, ir-, il-, endo-, en-, em-, intro-, intra-.
4. Each person's description of his or her household will be different.
5. In sentence (a), *pique* means annoyed or peeved. In sentence (b), it means aroused or awakened.
6. At teacher's or student's discretion.
7. A *soupçon* of chili powder would result in bland Mexican food, and those who love it tend to love it hot.

List 9

I. Definitions

1. hirsute
2. prehensile
3. asinine
4. leonine
5. ruminate
6. denizen
7. simian
8. fodder
9. spoor
10. porcine
11. bovine
12. vivisection
13. whelp
14. fledgling
15. vixen
16. reptilian

II. Adjectives

1. piscatory
2. elephantine
3. canine
4. taurine
5. ursine
6. feline
7. lupine
8. simian
9. asinine
10. reptilian
11. leonine
12. porcine
13. equine
14. bovine
15. ovine

III. Antonyms

1. (h) celestial
2. (e) intelligent
3. (j) alien
4. (b) whelp
5. (i) hirsute
6. (a) ace
7. (c) variable
8. (f) nebulous
9. (g) stable
10. (d) to dig up

IV. Fill-Ins

1. vixen
2. vivisection
3. whelp
4. viviparous mammals
5. disinter
6. carnage
7. meat *and* vegetation (everything)
8. vixen
9. ruminants
10. simians

V. Word Analysis

1. Fishing is the piscatorial art. (*Pisces* = fish)
2. Astrologers say that Leos are the "kingly" ones, like their namesake, the lion. Pride and a love of being the center of attention are common traits. Many Leos are stage actors, film stars, and professional speakers. (Those who become teachers enjoy having all those captive audiences, day after day.) Leos like bright, true colors, sunshine, and parties. They tend to have flashing tempers, especially if their pride is wounded, but they are staunch friends, as they value friendship highly.
3. *Matching*
   a. (3) swan
   b. (5) fox
   c. (6) dog (canine)
   d. (2) horse (equine)
   e. (1) cow (bovine)
   f. (4) kangaroo
4. An aviary is a "bird zoo" or enclosure to preserve/protect/display birds. A *rara avis,* literally rare bird, is a rare (unusual) person, a character. *Rara avis* can also refer to any rare thing.
5. A pussycat should come to the French girl's call. This Anglicized usage is modern French slang and won't appear in many dictionaries, but it typifies the words that the French have adopted from English: *pullover* (sweater) and *l'uppercut* (uppercut) are other examples.
6. *Matching*
   a. (4) words
   b. (1) birds
   c. (5) insects
   d. (2) mind and behavior
   e. (3) mammals
7. Educational fodder is the food that school offers: math, science, languages, etc., plus any information that adds to our store of knowledge.
8. At teacher's and student's discretion. It might be fun to compile a group list and discover how many animals have found their way into common sayings/old saws.

List 10

I. Synonyms

1. (a) whims, (d) caprices
2. (b) enmity, (c) animosity
3. (d) tenacity, (e) perseverance
4. (c) double-dealing, (e) hypocrisy
5. (a) behavior, (b) appearance
6. (c) trifle, (d) trinket
7. (a) keen, (c) shrewd
8. (b) precise, (d) clear
9. (b) persistent, (e) determined
10. (a) atmosphere, (d) environment

II. Antonyms

1. honesty, straightforwardness, openness, frankness
2. caution, circumspection, timidity, timorousness
3. accord, friendship, harmony
4. modesty, restraint, humility, reserve, unpretentiousness
5. normal, regular, customary, expected, typical

III. Fill-Ins

1. ambience
2. pertinacity
3. demeanor
4. respite
5. bigot
6. attrition
7. exigency
8. quisling
9. vagaries
10. anomaly

IV. Analogies

1. amenities : desirable :: vagaries : unpredictable (Implied relationship)
2. attrition : reduction :: bearing : demeanor (Synonyms)
3. bigoted : tolerant :: ostentatious : modest (Antonyms)
4. temerity : effrontery :: pertinacity : obstinacy (Synonyms)
5. annoyance : rancor :: display : ostentation (Degree)

V. In Your Own Words

At teacher's discretion. If working on your own, consult with a knowledgeable adult about your sentences. Also, reread the sentences using these words in your lesson.

VI. Word Analysis

1. logistics
2. a. buddy, pal, companion, crony, confidante, soul mate, alter ego, comrade, sidekick, classmate, roommate
   b. Make of car specifically named; auto, machine, motor, tin can (to suggest cheap construction), jalopy, buggy, convertible, station wagon, sedan, vehicle
   c. odor, stench, stink, reek, foulness, fetidness, must, mustiness, moldiness, mildew, etc. (bad smells)—fragrance, perfume, scent, aroma, redolence, bouquet, spiciness, muskiness, sweetness (good smells)
   d. sandals, loafers, brogues, wingtips, tennies, sneakers, trainers (e.g., running shoes), pumps, slingbacks, huaraches (Mexican woven-leather sandals), flats, duckboots, oxfords, boots (specific boot varieties perhaps)
   e. tension, anxiety, apprehension, strain, stress, misgiving, "the willies," distress, unease, jumpiness, agitation, disquiet, malaise, "the jitters," plus any current, appropriate slang expressions
3. Some nouns always appearing in plural form are news, trousers (or pants), scissors, molasses, mathematics, measles, mumps, economics (the study), politics, alms, hysterics, headquarters, and vermin.
4. *Vagariously* is an adverb meaning capriciously, or in a whimsical way, therefore unpredictable. *Vicariously* refers to something experienced secondhand, as through reading or watching a movie. A vicarious experience is *felt,* not actually lived.
5. Annoyance or harassment requires constant rubbing interaction by persons determined to wear each other down through persistence—just as the stones are worn down tumbling against one another in the rock polisher. The current, popular usage of attrition to mean reduction in workforce seems (to me) to be more related to the action of stones, pebbles, or shells near the seashore. Gradually, many are moved up onto the shore or beach by the action of the other stones and waves. Those that are beached are, in a sense, cast off or discarded. Those members of a workforce who retire, resign, or die have also moved out of their system in a gradual, natural manner.

6. A few examples from *plex, plic, -ply* are complex, Plexiglas, duplex, perplex, complicate, explicit, replica, replicate, duplicate, imply, implicate, reply, multiply, supplicate, complexion, and duplicity.

From *spec, spic, spect:* spectator, speculate, inspect, respect, disrespect, inspector, perspicacity, specimen, spectacles, species, aspect, special, specter, circumspect, expect, introspection, prospect, suspect, auspice(s), conspicuous, despicable, etc.

From *ten, tin, tain, tent:* tenacious, tenacity, tenable, tenant, tenement, tenet, tennis, tenor, tenure, abstinence, abstain, attain, contain, detain, maintain, obtain, pertain, retain, sustain, abstention, attention, etc.

List 11

I. Synonyms

1. connive
2. discern
3. improvise
4. adulterate
5. extrapolate, infer
6. peruse
7. promulgate
8. succumb
9. succor
10. ascertain
11. inundate
12. portend

II. Antonyms

1. spurn
2. adulterate
3. exacerbate
4. connive
5. conciliate
6. improvise
7. extrapolate
8. vilify
9. succor
10. succumb

III. Switcheroo—Verbs into Nouns

1. (g) omen
2. (k) corruption
3. (n) spontaneous creation
4. (h) deduction
5. (a) appeasement
6. (c) discrimination
7. (b) declaration
8. (l) relief, help
9. (e) consent to wrongdoing
10. (m) abuse, defamation
11. (d) aggravation
12. (o) examination
13. (i) flood
14. (f) discovering beyond doubt
15. (j) prediction based on past knowledge or experience

IV. Analogies

1. criticism : vilification :: shower : inundation (Degree)
2. spurn : hanker for :: exacerbate : relieve (Antonyms)
3. improviser : ingenuity :: conciliator : diplomacy (Person related to most desirable characteristic)
4. ascertainment : conclusion :: perusal : knowledge (Cause and effect or result)
5. discern : differences :: infer : conclusions (Implied relationship, as one leads to the other)

V. Fill-Ins

1. incubate
2. recumbent
3. confer
4. acrimonious
5. cursory
6. acumen
7. defer
8. deference
9. acrid
10. recourse

VI. Word Analysis

1. To *infer* is to draw conclusions based on evidence. To *imply* is to hint or suggest, often in a negative or critical manner; something implied is hinted or suggested, never stated directly. To *intimate* is to hint or suggest indirectly, and it often substitutes for the word *imply*. All of these words can mean suggest or hint, but *anything inferred involves conclusions drawn from somewhere.* To *impute* means (1) to blame unfairly and (2) to attribute, as *many qualities that now seem extremely fanciful were once imputed to the Greek gods. Ascribe* or *assign* are good synonyms for impute.

    Sentences at the instructor's discretion. If you are working alone, share your sentences with a knowledgeable adult.

2. A *cursory inspection* is not really an inspection, as it is hasty and not thorough, whereas *perusal* means careful study.

3. Words derived from *fer* include transfer, transference, conference, refer, reference, inferential, prefer, preference, suffer, indifferent, indifference, referendum, circumference, vociferous, odoriferous, coniferous.

4. a. ascertain, discern (at times)
    b. improvise, extemporize
    c. peruse
    d. connive
    e. inundate
    f. spurn
    g. succumb
    h. confer
    i. defer
    j. adulterate

5. *Aggravate* is most commonly used to mean annoy or irritate, as *Her violin practicing aggravated her tired father.* This usage is considered *wrong,* no matter how common. However, the sentence *Don't aggravate the situation any further* is correct usage.

6. *To course* is *to run* and is a direct translation of the Latin root, *currere.* Coursing with hounds, therefore, is running with them and is popular in several parts of the world. Hounds of small size, known as beagles, course after hares in England, and the accompanying runners charge along after them. A beagle pack flourishes in Pennsylvania, and the sport is popularly called "beagling." Foxhounds course after a fox, while their human companions ride horses. Fox hunting continues in parts of America, notably the East and the South, as well as in England.

7. Working with prefix and root meanings usually gives a student a close idea of word meaning, especially if the word in question is in context. In context, *refer,* literally *to carry back* or *to bear again (over),* will be quite clear in meaning, as will *confer,* literally *to bear or carry with (someone else).* But *defer* would elude quick definition, as it has more than one meaning and would be even more dependent upon context for definition. Its meaning of *put off, postpone,* literally *carry down, off, away,* is usually clear in context. To *defer* to another's wisdom or superior position seems further away in meaning from the original root and prefix. No wonder we have to study the meanings of words.

List 12

I. Substitution

1. vascular
2. resuscitating
3. phobia
4. lesion
5. carcinogen
6. euthanasia
7. Gastric
8. paranoia
9. salutary
10. cardiac

II. Matching

1. obstetrician
2. cardiologist (also internist)
3. toxicologist/internist
4. psychiatrist
5. oculist or ophthalmologist
6. dermatologist
7. pathologist (possibly, an internist skilled in diagnosis)
8. vascular specialist
9. podiatrist or chiropodist
10. psychiatrist
11. internist
12. pediatrician
13. physical therapist
14. podiatrist or chiropodist
15. orthodontist
16. neurologist

III. Chart Fill-In

1. in-; cide/cis; a surgical cut
2. em-; empathy
3. derm; hypodermic
4. anti-; antidote
5. fratri-; cide/cis; the killer of a brother
6. virulent
7. mania; megalomania
8. eu-; thanatos; mercy killing or allowing the death of someone terminally ill
9. suscitare; resuscitate
10. anti-; antitoxin

IV. Antonyms

1. (a) incisive, (e) clear-cut
2. (b) toxic, (d) harmful
3. (b) soothe, (e) alleviate
4. (c) vivacious, (d) sparkling
5. (a) sane, (c) composed

V. Definitions

Refer to the definitions given earlier in List 12, page 422.

VI. Word Analysis

1. A *carcinoma* is a cancerous tumor.
2. Patients who abandon orthodox medical treatment usually do so for religious reasons or because traditional forms of treatment have been unsuccessful. Those patients with intractable or incurable illnesses are most prone to seek an alternative.
3. a. (5), b. (4), c. (7), d. (6), e. (2), f. (1), g. (3)
4. A *salutation* is a greeting, and its root is **salut**, **salus**, which means health, safety, and also *greeting*. In Italian, *saluto* is a salutation or salute; *saluer* means to salute, greet, or bow in French; and *to your health* in Spanish is *¡a su salud!* A friendly greeting is also a wish for good health, the ancient root meanings well intact in modern usage.
5. a. tonsils (removal of)
   b. lobe of the brain, usually an operation that severs nerve fibers for relief of mental illness or tension (Have you read Kesey's *One Flew over the Cuckoo's Nest*, in which a lobotomy was performed on any mental patient "out of control" according to the authorities? Thought-provoking book.)
   c. appendix (removal of)
   d. uterus (removal of)
   e. stomach (removal of diseased portion)
   f. breast (removal of)
6. To *exsanguinate* is to die as result of excessive blood loss.
7. Death is the subject; root, **thanatos**.
8. a. (5) surgical cut
   b. (9) outer skin layer
   c. (7) compulsion to steal
   d. (6) lack of feeling or interest
   e. (2) cause of infectious disease
   f. (8) irritation or disease of skin
   g. (10) study of viruses
   h. (1) optimistic, cheerful
   i. (4) science of nervous system
   j. (3) division into two parts

Review

Lists 9–12

I. Antonyms

1. (g) judicious
2. (c) honesty
3. (j) to purify
4. (e) to mollify, appease

5. (a) to welcome
6. (h) parent
7. (d) hairless

8. (f) alien
9. (b) variable
10. (i) to antagonize

II. Analogies

1. rumination : idea :: mutation : anomaly (Cause and effect or result)
2. whims : vagaries :: trinket : bagatelle (Synonyms)
3. bovine : herbivorous :: leonine : carnivorous (General kind plus typical characteristic)
4. dismay : phobia :: glance : perusal (Degree)
5. spoor : pawprint :: temerity : backtalk (General category plus specific example [or one of a kind])
6. grain : fodder :: anemia : illness (Specific example of general category. Answers *a* and *c* show exact synonyms.)
7. duplicity : truth :: confusion : logic (Implied relationship—the one impedes or prevents the other)

III. Definitions

1. prehensile
2. vivisection
3. vascular
4. torso
5. therapeutic

6. paranoia
7. lymph
8. cardiac
9. ambience
10. logistics

11. ascertain
12. extrapolate
13. improvise
14. gastric
15. euthanasia

IV. Fill-Ins

1. portends
2. connived
3. succor
4. antidote
5. infer

6. salutary
7. Succumbing
8. vilifies
9. resuscitate
10. attrition

11. Promulgation
12. carcinogens
13. lesion, discern
14. fester

V. Remembering Roots

1. spec, spic, spect meaning to look
2. plex, plic, ply meaning to fold
3. cid, cis meaning to cut, to kill
4. cur, curr, curs, course meaning to run
5. ten, tin, tain, tent meaning to hold

6. ac, acr meaning bitter, sharp, sour
7. fer meaning to carry, bear
8. ter, terr meaning earth, land
9. vita, viv meaning life
10. path meaning feeling, suffering, disease

VI. Find the Oddball

These are the words crossed out, the oddballs.

1. needle
2. idea
3. thought
4. health

5. mask
6. taste
7. indigence

8. timorousness
9. alteration
10. accord

List 13

I. Antonyms

1. (b) sober
2. (e) flawed
3. (a) morose
4. (b) revulsion
5. (d) boorish
6. (c) humorless: Answers (a) and (b) may be momentarily tempting, but they lack reference to humor, which is necessary for an antonym of jocular.
7. (a) apathetic
8. (e) ill-fitting
9. (d) credulous
10. (d) ill-omened: Answers (a), (b), and (e) are all wide of the mark.

II. Analogies

1. friend : congenial :: Daffy Duck : zany (Individual related to logical or expected trait)
2. temperament : sanguine :: writing : belles lettres (One of a kind or general type)
3. happiness : exhilaration :: naughtiness : rebellion (Degree)
4. homage : respectful deference :: calmness : placidity (Synonyms)
5. fortress : indomitable :: warrior : bellicose (Thing/person related to most desirable characteristic)

III. The Right Word

1. belle
2. docile
3. postbellum
4. homo sapiens
5. levity, jocularity, or jocosity
6. levitate
7. sanguine
8. impeccable
9. congeniality (Jocularity, jocosity, jocundity, or levity are also possible, but not as precise. A *close* friend is usually a kindred soul, one like you.)
10. adulation
11. astute (perhaps impeccable)
12. exhilaration
13. felicitous
14. homage
15. fervent

IV. Switcheroo

1. (c) boding ill
2. (e) state of delight
3. (g) enliven, excite, refresh
4. (h) unconquerably
5. (b) merry, jolly
6. (j) serenely
7. (i) in a polished manner
8. (f) relief
9. (a) teach with a definite opinion/point of view
10. (d) adorned, decorated

V. Truth or Fiction

1. F
2. T
3. T
4. F
5. F (Bloodthirsty is a synonym for *sanguniary*.)
6. T
7. F
8. F
9. F
10. T

VI. Word Analysis

1. Usually the context will tell the reader whether the subject refers to war (*bellum*) or to something beautiful (*bell*). However, hunters refer to their weapons as beautiful pieces, so the chance for confusion certainly exists. Alas, there is no substitute for a large working vocabulary.
2. (a) At teacher's discretion. Most students will think of moth*er*, fath*er*, broth*er*, and sist*er* at least. Maybe even teach*er*. If you are working alone, show your list to any knowledgeable adult.
   (b) When you are faced with a strange word on a standardized test, it may be very helpful to use the suffixes *-or* and *-er* to denote a person, perhaps even an animal (otter). That basic knowledge might help to begin the logical deduction process leading toward a word's meaning.
3. (a) Pug, pugn- means *to fight*. A *pugilist* is a boxer or prizefighter, who is probably *pugnacious*, at least when in the ring. If not, his career is apt to be short. The words *pugnacious, truculent*, and *belligerent* are nearly interchangeable.
   (b) The *pug dog* got his name from a seventeenth-century word, *pug*, meaning imp or monkey, according to the O.E.D. By the eighteenth century, pug referred to the small breed of dog we know now—the short, stubby fellow with a curled tail and funnily wrinkled face who originated in Asia.
4. At teacher's discretion. If you are working alone, discuss these girls' names with your friends or any adult.
5. (a) To *placate* someone is to mollify, soothe, or appease that person, typically by promising to be good eternally: to carry out the trash, to write faithfully once a week, or to remember all of those things that you have no hope of remembering. (A person in need of placating someone else will promise the most outlandish things.)
6. Words from the root stup include *stupefy, stupor, stuporous, stupid, stupidity, stupendous*, and the colloquial *stupe*, meaning a dope.

List 14

I. Definitions

1. morbid
2. pompous
3. scurrilous
4. specious
5. heinous
6. inimical
7. furtive
8. choleric
9. captious
10. atrocious, execrable
11. ludicrous
12. plaintive

II. Fill-Ins

1. (d) lurid
2. (c) nefarious
3. (a) sordid
4. (b) macabre
5. (b) intercept
6. (c) mortal
7. (d) duress
8. (c) captivate
9. (a) obdurate
10. (b) specious

III. Antonyms

1. (a) placid
2. (b) admirable
3. (c) buoyant
4. (d) not fatal
5. (e) genuine
6. (c) self-effacing
7. (b) cheerful
8. (d) aboveboard
9. (a) congenial
10. (a) accepting

IV. Analogies

1. pollute : waterway :: desecrate : temple (Implied relationship)
2. slander : scurrilous :: enemy : inimical (Concept or person related to logical characteristic)
3. sacrilege : heinous :: squalor : sordid (Concept related to logical characteristic)
4. deed : nefarious :: motion : furtive (Implied relationship)
5. moribund : sick :: atrocity : misdeed (Degree)

V. Matching

1. (g)
2. (i)
3. (a)
4. (j)
5. (b)
6. (d)
7. (c)
8. (e)
9. (f)
10. (h)

VI. Word Analysis

1. A *heinous crime* is one that appalls or shocks. Unfortunately, the theft of a pencil is rather common and not particularly shocking —unless it's your best pencil.
2. *Derisive laughter* (at something ludicrous) is scornful laughter. You feel superior to or in some way better than that which is merely ludicrous. Therefore, both *superiority* and *scorn* figure in derisive laughter, whereas we laugh with simple pleasure at beloved comedians. (They'd be upset if we didn't!)
3. *Matching*
   a. (3) lacking necessary possessions or resources
   b. (5) morally loose, unrestrained
   c. (6) unable to be consoled, downcast
   d. (8) notorious
   e. (1) utter shame or disgrace
   f. (4) worn out, useless, dead
   g. (7) foul, rotten, malodorous
   h. (2) base, low, contemptible
4. A crime may be of various degrees, some not terribly serious, but an *atrocity* is an *outrage*, an affront to our sense of morality and humanity. The torture of prisoners of war, murder, and genocide qualify as genuine atrocities.
5. *Furtive* means *stealthy* or *sly*, and sometimes *stolen*. Anything you do furtively is done with the hope that no one will see you. *Wary* implies both *caution* and *careful watchfulness*, not deliberate secretivenss.

List 15

I. Synonyms

All definitions and synonyms found in "Word Study."

II. Substitution

1. spores
2. antipodes
3. refraction
4. Axis (The three powers, Germany, Italy, and Japan, in World War II get a capital letter to distinguish them from any other axis.)
5. laser
6. centrifugal
7. shards
8. inertia
9. dross
10. fusion; also, axis is possible but not preferred.

III. Analogies

1. washing machine : centrifuge :: plant stem : axis (One example of a general type)
2. biology : life systems :: anthropology : humankind's development (The study related to what it studies.) **Note:** Don't be tempted by answer (a), which is off the mark. Science is a collection of facts, as well as unproven hypotheses and theories, but not a study of facts per se. Answer (d) is too narrow.
3. wine : dregs :: metal : dross (Implied relationship—the impurities of each general type)
4. Dark Ages : unenlightened :: tyrannosaurus : antediluvian (Implied relationship—the most typical adjective applied to each) **Note:** Anyone tempted by answer (e) should remember that not all fossils are by definition prehistoric.
5. concave : convex :: invigorated : inert (Antonyms)
6. axis : periphery :: tree heart : twig (Location)
7. shower : deluge :: pause : doldrums (Degree)
8. medicine : antibiotic :: rock : igneous (One of a kind/general type)

IV. Matching

1. (c) violation
2. (d) opposite
3. (i) splitting into parts
4. (f) bending of light
5. (a) resistant single cell
6. (j) the study of rocks
7. (k) kindling
8. (e) unruly
9. (l) to wash
10. (h) rapidity
11. (b) hollow, depression
12. (g) separatist

V. Completion

1. biomedicine
2. alluvial
3. paleontologist
4. pyre
5. igneous
6. fusion
7. axis
8. doldrums
9. antipodes
10. laser

VI. Word Analysis

1. *Velocipede* is an old term for a wheeled vehicle propelled by a rider, such as a bicycle or even a tricycle. The term is still in use to refer to a railroad handcar with three wheels.
    A *velodrome* is a racing track for cyclists and may be enclosed or out of doors.
2. At teacher's discretion. If working alone, you decide which quotation you prefer and why. *Both* are worth thinking about.
3. EC- or ECO- is Greek for *habitat* or *environment*; thus, ecology studies the habitats or environments of organisms and their interrelationship.
4. *Matching*
    a. (5) the study of Earth's history, makeup, etc.
    b. (6) the study of crime and criminal behavior
    c. (4) the study of civilizations' artifacts or remains
    d. (10) the study of bacteria
    e. (3) the study of the nature and cause of diseases
    f. (9) the study of viruses
    g. (2) the study of mammals
    h. (8) the study of insects
    i. (1) the study of birds
    j. (7) the study of the origin and history of words

List 16

I. Fill-Ins

1. cabana	5. quixotic	9. sierra
2. siesta	6. vendetta	10. mañana
3. presto	7. bonanza	11. salvo
4. portfolio	8. imbroglio	12. sotto voce

II. Synonyms and Definitions

1. (b) outdoors and (c) in the open air
2. (a) coalition with a definite purpose and (c) plotters [As to (e), remember that a faction is within the political party and not representative of the whole.]
3. (c) dabbler and (d) one lacking commitment
4. (b) fan and (d) devotee [Are you familiar with the word swain, answer (c)?]
5. (c) chaperone and (d) companion
6. (a) experts and (d) connoisseurs
7. (b) outstanding and (c) of major importance
8. (b) easily molded and (e) malleable
9. (a) sham and (c) artificial
10. (c) embroilment and (e) hostile, confusing argument

III. Logic

1. duenna
2. vendetta
3. dilettante
4. aficionado
5. quixotic or quixotism

IV. Contrasting Ideas

1. (i) indoors	6. (c) mansion	11. (j) introduce
2. (f) tyros	7. (m) entire political party	12. (n) honor, praise
3. (h) fortissimo	8. (b) yesterday	13. (k) fact
4. (l) andante	9. (e) desert	14. (d) reduce
5. (a) meager amount	10. (o) unaware	15. (g) single shot

V. Logic

1. Almost anyone would enjoy receiving a leather portfolio as a gift, but especially an artist or anyone in business or recordkeeping who must tote papers around.
2. Siestas and warm climates seem to go together, as people naturally seek to escape the fierce heat of midday. Over time, the life style of an entire country logically revolves around the siesta, and business is conducted during cooler hours. Evening meals are typically late, when it is cooler and people feel more like eating. England's weather stands in direct contrast, as does weather in any of the more northern countries. There, business is often transacted over long lunches, leaving no time for the luxury of a siesta.
3. *Sierra,* by derivation, refers to jagged or saw-toothed mountains, whereas *mountain* can refer to any of the rather worn-down humps we fondly think of as mountains, such as the Sourland Mountains in central New Jersey. Geologically, sierras are younger mountains, less eroded by weather and time than older ones like the Appalachians or Sourlands.
4. The practical, sober nondreamer is the opposite of the quixotic person.
5. Women's liberation, which has come in moderate form even to Spain and Portugal, means that young women have freedoms formerly denied them, thus eliminating the cultural need for a constant chaperone prior to marriage.
6. Even in America, where teenagers have unusual freedom, we have kept the idea of chaperonage at dances and parties for young people. In college dorms and fraternities and sororities, we have a housemother, hoping that she will maintain a respectable level of decorum and act as an older adviser.
7. A *vendetta* or blood feud always demands retribution. As soon as one person is killed, another on the opposite side will be killed, and then it starts all over, never ending, as a circle never ends.
8. An *imbroglio* is always complex, usually quite hostile or bitter. Chances for one side misunderstanding the other are great, because of the complexity of the difference between them. An *argument,* on the other hand, can be quite straightforward and simple.

9. The *dilettante* dabbles, typically in one of the arts, and lacks serious commitment, therefore accomplishing nothing of worth. Many flit from one art to another. But America, established by the rigid Puritans, admires stick-to-it-iveness and commitment—major ingredients of the Protestant work ethic, still firmly in place. A dilettante may be a fine, upstanding person without a mean bone in his or her body, but someone *is* going to inquire, "And what do you plan to *do with yourself,* dear?"

10. A *general factotum* around the office is one who fetches and totes, who often does the jobs no one else will or can do. The factotum usually can turn a hand to anything and everything. No wonder the office is a gloomy place when that person goes on vacation.

VI. Word Analysis

1. A *junta* is a council or deliberative body for the purpose of government and is explained in Word Study. Junto is a group joined for a common purpose.
2. *Peccadillo* means a small sign, a slight fault.
3. Rephrasing Irving is a bit presumptuous, but to aid understanding, here is one suggestion: *There is no chaperone as rigidly cautious and unfailingly proper as an old flirt.*
4. At teacher's discretion. The dictionary definitions are helpful, but examples worked out within the class will be even more so. If you are working alone, consult with any knowledgeable adult about the material contained in your dictionary.

Review

Lists 13-16

I. Analogies

1. connoisseur : dilettante :: neighbors : antipodes (Antonyms)
2. sanguine : exhilarated :: satisfied : pompous (Degree)
3. sluggish : inert :: bad : heinous (Degree)
4. presto : music :: rushing : current (Implied comparison—the rapidity of moving water) [Answer (d) will not work, because friendship is by definition between congenial people.]
5. saleswoman : portfolio :: aficionado : scrapbook (Person related to logical possession)
6. plaintive : sentence :: morbid : outlook (One of a kind)
7. shard : pottery :: ethic : doctrine (Part of a whole)
8. sophistication : suavity :: chaperone : duenna (Synonyms)
9. stance : ludicrous :: attitude : inimical (One example or description of a general type, or one of a kind)
10. cognoscente : respect :: murder : execration (Person related to logical/expected attitude from the public)

II. Chart Fill-In

1. em-, embellish
2. re-, bell, characteristic of a rebel, resisting control or discipline, unruly, refractory
3. indoctrinate
4. al-, alleviate
5. anti-, anticipate
6. ob-, dur, stubborn, unwilling to yield or give way
7. mort, immortal
8. desecrate
9. anti-, antibiotic
10. refractory
11. re-, ign, to light or fire again
12. petrology, the study of rocks
13. de-, deluge
14. re-, capit, to review the main points or summarize
15. duc, traduce

III. Affect and Effect

1. affects	4. affected	7. effect
2. effected	5. effect	8. effected
3. effects	6. Affecting	

IV. Antonyms

1. (d) discourage
2. (b) practical
3. (e) accord
4. (e) current
5. (a) open
6. (c) cheerful and jocular
7. (b) noble
8. (c) sordid
9. (a) above suspicion
10. (b) fervent
11. (d) toward a center
12. (d) placid

V. Story Fill-In

1. auspicious
2. felicitous
3. nefarious
4. impeccable
5. sanguine
6. pompously
7. inimical
8. placid
9. choleric
10. fusion
11. velocity
12. shards

VI. Substitution

1. plaintive
2. cabana
3. mañana
4. ludicrous
5. execrable
6. homage
7. dilettante
8. captious
9. zany
10. siesta
11. indomitable, exhilarating
12. fission, fusion
13. spores
14. salvo

List 17

I. Identification

1. solecism
2. pun
3. hyperbole
4. aphorism (also an epigram, if anyone is fortunate enough to remember an earlier lesson)
5. innuendo

II. Definitions

1. bombast
2. rhetoric
3. vociferous
4. spiel
5. construe
6. terse
7. prate (or prattle)
8. soliloquy
9. dissent
10. reticent
11. glib

III. Aphorisms

1. Birds of a feather flock together.
2. Beauty is only skin deep.
3. The pen is mightier than the sword.
4. Beginner's luck.
5. People in glass houses shouldn't throw stones.
6. Sticks and stones may break my bones, but names can never harm me.
7. You can't teach an old dog new tricks.
8. Dead men don't talk.
9. Too many cooks spoil the broth.
10. A rolling stone gathers no moss.
   Note: At this point you might think about *conciseness* in speech and writing, exemplified here by the old, simple adages. Our finest language critics and writers, such as E. B. White, William Safire, and Edwin Newman, have repeatedly implored us to use direct, uncluttered English if we wish to make our meanings absolutely clear.

IV. Antonyms

1. (g) dissent
2. (j) lacking fluency
3. (i) hyperbole
4. (a) accusation
5. (c) reticent
6. (h) wordy, verbose
7. (b) vociferous
8. (e) unintelligible
9. (f) dull, insensitive
10. (d) establish

V. Analogies

1. construe : gesture :: interpret : language (Implied comparison)
2. prate : speak haltingly :: run : stumble (Implied comparison)
3. play on words : pun :: grammatical error : solecism (One the definition of the other)
4. demagogue : rhetoric :: door-to-door salesperson : spiel (Person related to typical form of speech delivery, i.e., stock in trade)

5. bombast : lucubration :: innuendo : insinuation (Synonyms)
6. compassion : Lucifer :: mortality : deity (Person related to what he or she does not have)
7. presentiment : future :: review : past (Implied comparison)
8. thespian : soliloquy :: minister : invocation (Person related to one probable form of speech)

VI. Word Analysis

1. Your *avocation* is what you do for a hobby. Some, like Charles Schulz, creator of Peanuts and Snoopy, are fortunate to have combined both vocation and avocation.
2. Sentimentality is thought of as too much sentiment, an excess of gooey emotion, which would mar any book for current readers.
3. Anyone described as "not lucid" is incapable of intelligent speech or understanding. A person in shock or recovering from anesthesia or a blow on the head is often not lucid for a short time afterward.
4. Just for starters: dispose, depose, impose, imposition, juxtaposition, position, expose, exposition, repose, appose, apposite, apposition, appositive, suppose, supposition, presuppose, exponent, and exponential.
5. A *rhetorical question* is usually one asked for effect, with no reply expected or possible. People often ask a rhetorical question because they feel it is something that should be raised, an important matter to consider, perhaps with the hope of eventually securing an answer.
6. *Aphorisms.* Students will undoubtedly be more creative than these suggestions, but here they are.

   a. *Reticence is auriferous.* Note the root fer in this last word. It also occurs in *coniferous* (cone- bearing, which refers to some evergreens), *odoriferous,* and *vociferous.* Remember that fer means *to carry, bear.*
   b. *Prating involves negligible pecuniary expenditure.*
      Prattle requires negligible pecuniary expenditure.
   c. It is inadvisable to postpone until mañana that which could conceivably be expedited precipitately.

7. *Paronomasia* is from the Greek word *paronomazein,* to call with a slight change of name. It is now simply a pun, a play on words.

List 18

I. Definitions

1. subpoena
2. ad hoc
3. in extremis
4. magnum opus
5. sine qua non
6. alter ego
7. non sequitur
8. quid pro quo
9. caveat emptor
10. ex post facto
11. extempore
12. bona fide

II. Fill-Ins

1. quid pro quo
2. ex post facto
3. ad hoc
4. status quo
5. magnum opus
6. in extremis
7. caveat emptor
8. sine qua non
9. alter ego
10. habeas corpus
11. extempore
12. subpoenaed
13. corpus delicti
14. bona fide
15. non sequitur
16. persona non grata

III. Logic

1. You could be served a writ of habeas corpus if you were required to appear in court.
2. If you felt that illegal, unjust imprisonment faced you, then you might secure a writ of habeas corpus as protection against imprisonment until you'd had a chance to testify in court, or produce exonerating documents and/or witnesses.
3. Welcome, acceptable persons would include all regular governmental employees and elected or appointed officials. Also, those officials in good standing from other countries would be persona grata. Any in disgrace or under suspicion would, of course, be persona non grata.
4. Corporeal beings are material ones that have earthly substance, as opposed to spiritual beings, who exist only in our minds or imaginations.
5. Progress inevitably brings change, and change disturbs the status quo, which requires that everything stay the same.

IV. Matching

1. (i) to go before
2. (g) to interpose
3. (k) an act of repentance
4. (l) unformed, vague, shapeless
5. (h) to play for time
6. (j) current
7. (a) change of form, type
8. (c) earthly
9. (b) withdrawal
10. (d) language unit
11. (f) contrite
12. (e) movement

V. Useful Latin Bits

1. *Abbreviations:*
   a. ibid.
   b. i.e
   c. e.g.
   d. N.B.
   e. et al.
2. *Story.* In order: per annum, per se, per capita, and per diem.
3. *Matching opposites:*
   a. (5) bogus
   b. (2) ex post facto
   c. (1) rehearsed, planned
   d. (3) welcome
   e. (4) sine qua non
4. Graduating magna cum laude, with great distinction, or summa cum laude, with highest distinction, certainly would be worth considering.

VI. Word Analysis

1. Pro tem is the abbreviated form of pro tempore.
2. *Latin phrases.*
   a. in loco parentis = in place of the parents, or as foster parents
   b. in toto = in total, in all
   c. mirabile dictu = marvelous (or miraculous) to tell (or relate)
   d. pax vobiscum = peace be with you
   e. sub rosa = in secrecy is the idea; literally, under the rosebush
   f. tempus fugit = time flies (or flees)
   g. terra firma = solid earth, or firm ground
3. Penance, or the idea of atoning for a wrong, is the same as an act of contrition. One can do penance mentally as well as through some overt act.
4. Penitent and contrite are fine synonyms as both indicate sincere sorrow or regret for something one has done.
5. Latinate words often have longer root stems to begin with than many of the short Anglo-Saxon words. We tend to add prefixes and lengthy suffixes to these roots, expanding the whole business. *Destine,* for example, is not long, but by the time we add *pre-* and *-ation* to form *predestination,* we have an extremely healthy word. *Fer* is brief, but we make *transference* and *interference* out of it, and so on. Anyone familiar with the German language will be aware that it adds suffixes and prefixes with even greater abandon than English.

List 19

I. Definitions
Refer to "Word Study."

II. You're the Lawyer

1. commuted
2. law of torts
3. perjury (I had sworn to tell the *whole* truth.)
4. verdict
5. an annulment
6. injunction
7. larceny (petit larceny)
8. vagrant
9. lawyer, advocate
10. sanctions
11. misdemeanors, felony
12. extortion
13. forensic
14. malfeasance
15. litigation
16. adjudicates
17. extradite
18. indicated
19. acquitted
20. jurisdiction

III. Antonyms

1. (c) to sanction
2. (f) to abrogate
3. (h) disapprove of, also (i)
4. (a) to indulge in
5. (b) to absolve, acquit
6. (i) to discourage, go against; (h) disapprove of also okay
7. (d) stable, fixed
8. (e) dictatorship
9. (j) to beg, plead with to discourage, go against
10. (g) separation

IV. Analogies

1. felony : indictment :: libel : litigation (Cause and logical effect or result)
2. death : legacy :: trial : verdict (Cause and effect or logical outcome)
3. noble : plebeian :: fixed : vagrant (Antonyms)
4. curse : malediction :: interdict : prohibition (Synonyms)
5. oath : perjury :: public office : malfeasance (Implied comparison. Perjury is a serious offense while under oath just as malfeasance is a serious offense while in office.)

V. The Root of It All

1. Other words from tor- include torture, torturous, tortuous, retort, distort, distortion, contort, contortion, contortionist, torment, tormentor, torque, torsion, etc.
2. Words from dict- include dictate, dictation, dictatorial, predict, prediction, edict, dictaphone, diction, abdicate, dedicate, indicate, predicate, vindicate, addict, addiction, benediction, dictionary, etc.
3. A *plebe* is the lowest of the low at West Point, and since it is rooted in the word meaning common people, with modern connotations of low, coarse, vulgar, the label of plebe for the freshman suits the upperclassmen just fine.
4. The *conjunction* is a function word in the English language, serving as a go-between to link portions of a sentence or phrase. A conjunction is a joiner, which is its root meaning. Literal meaning = *join with.*
5. *Pandemic* refers to anything occurring throughout a large area and affecting a high proportion of the population. In contrast, an *epidemic* is an outbreak (typically of disease) within a more localized area, which is short-lived and affects a smaller percentage of people.

VI. Word Analysis

1. A civil lawsuit takes place between one citizen and another to determine each person's rights under the law. A criminal lawsuit involves a citizen and the state or federal government in such crimes as treason, hijacking a vehicle, corporate misbehavior (e.g., monopolistic practices), the abducting of a minor across state lines, homicide, etc.
2. At teacher's discretion. If working on your own, discuss Descarte's quote with any knowledgeable adult.
3. Quincy, or any doctor whose specialty is forensic medicine, must be able to present his facts in a court of law. In a case of murder or grave bodily damage, the doctor's factual findings will become part of the evidence collected on the case and may be used during a trial.
4. *Vagabond, rover,* and *wanderer* can be used in a positive way, or at least a neutral manner. *Vagrant* and *tramp* have fairly strong negative connotations. For most people the word *vagabond* (or perhaps *rover*) suggests someone who is independent and carefree, bouncing from place to place by choice.
5. A larcenous thought comes to all of us at times, if we admit the truth. Most young children have gazed a bit avidly at the collection plate in church, wondering what it would be like to have all that money to do with as they please. Most people don't give in to thoughts of theft, however minor, but now and then weak human natures are subject to fleeting temptations.

List 20

I. Substitution

1. suffused
2. vindicated
3. expurgate
4. suffice
5. imputed
6. remonstrate
7. tempered
8. instigate
9. extricate
10. imbibe

II. Fill-Ins

1. Admonished, abstained
2. sated, premonition
3. divulged, condescend
4. annihilating
5. influx, supplanted

III. Switcheroo

1. (h) self-indulgent
2. (d) unaffected, natural, not superior in manner
3. (g) concealed
4. (j) lacking
5. (a) exuded
6. (c) fulfilled or satisfied
7. (b) drained
8. (i) weakened
9. (e) agreeable
10. (f) unavenged

IV. Rhyme Completion

1. satiety
2. temper
3. abstention
4. expurgation
5. instigation
6. extrication
7. compulsion
8. condescension
9. annihilations
10. imputation

V. Find the Oddball
(These are the words to be crossed out in each question.)

1. imbed
2. defy
3. maintain
4. discuss
5. expel
6. suffice
7. annoy
8. remonstrance
9. revile
10. precipitate
11. trickle
12. dispute (All others are synonyms of the verb *temper.*)

VI. Word Analysis

1. *Nihilism* rejects the idea that there is an objective ground for truth, especially moral truth. Nihilists say the world is such a total mess that we should give up and wipe ourselves off the face of the earth. To them, annihilation seems like a desirable thing, and if war would accomplish that goal, they'd be in favor. An alarming number of terrorists are nihilists; others are blind idealists who will stop at nothing to achieve their goals.
2. A *confluence* is a junction where two or more streams or bodies of water join each other. *Junction, conjunction,* and *confluence* can often be used interchangeably.
3. A *vindicatory* remark might be said in justification of something done, an opinion held, an action taken, etc. Also, it might be a "gotcha" comment in retribution or as verbal punishment.
   A *vindictive* remark is a vengeful one, made by someone seeking revenge. Vindictive statements are spiteful, meant to wound the listener. (The second sense of vindicatory is close to this meaning, though not exact.)
4. *Precognition* refers to knowledge gained ahead of time, before the knowledge should logically be known. It does not necessarily refer to anything ill-omened.
   A *premonition* is a foreboding that something bad is going to happen, but it is not knowledge. Often, a premonition is unfounded and does not come to pass.
5. At teacher's discretion. If you are working alone, compare your answer to the definition of *intricate* found in a dictionary.
6. Because there are several hundred words in current use that are exactly the same as the Latin words, we can't print them all, but here are some of the most common: abdomen, actor, administrator, agenda, alter, antenna, apostrophe, apparatus, aquarium, area, aroma, basis, biceps, character, cinnamon, color, coma, conductor, confine, crisis, deficit, diploma, doctor, echo, ego, exit, exterior, favor, geranium, gymnasium, horizon, hyphen, index, instructor, junior, lens, major, minor, maximum, monitor, motor, murmur, narrator, neuter, odor, opera, pathos, pelvis, plasma, plus, pollen, professor, propaganda, quota, rabies, ratio, recipe, rhododendron, rumor, saliva, sector, senior, simile, siren, species, spectator, spectrum, sponsor, stadium, status, tenor, terror, thesis, thorax, translator, trio, tuba, tumor, ulterior, vapor, veto, vice versa, video, vigor, virus, and vortex.

Review
Lists 17-20

I. Antonyms
1. (c) loquacious
2. (a) establish
3. (b) disapprove
4. (b) spurious
5. (d) open statement
6. (c) reticence
7. (e) judicious statement
8. (c) status quo
9. (d) indulge
10. (a) concur

II. Truth or Fiction
1. F
2. T
3. T
4. F
5. F
6. F
7. T
8. T
9. T
10. F (Remember that the verb is determined by the subject nearer to the verb in either-or constructions.)

III. Chart Fill-In
1. vociferous
2. ex-, tempor; unrehearsed, on the spur of the moment
3. feasance, malfeasance
4. ex-, expurgate
5. moni, premonition
6. a-, morph; lacking definite form or shape, unformed
7. ex-, extricate
8. loqu, soliloquy
9. insatiable
10. en-, dem; native to a people or country, or restricted to or particular to one people or their region

IV. Analogies
1. rootless : vagrant :: glib : spiel [Main characteristic of the type/kind. Answer (a) is grossly understated.]
2. felon : persona non grata :: adjudicator : impartial (Logical characteristic of the type)
3. fondness : sentimentality :: talk : prating (Degree)
4. legal code : law of torts :: trees : maple (One of a kind)

5. condescend : stoop :: ascribe : impute (Synonyms)
6. progress : regress :: instigate : discourage (Antonyms)
7. suffice : sate :: suggest : dictate (Degree)
8. sine qua non : essential :: extortion : intimidating (Main characteristic of kind/type)

V. Fill-Ins

1. alter ego
2. hyperbole
3. reticent
4. divulging
5. litigation
6. Caveat emptor
7. in extremis
8. pun
9. forensic
10. construed
11. annihilate
12. aphorism
13. ad hoc
14. remonstrated
15. larceny
16. vindicated

VI. Matching

1. (l) retroactively, after the fact
2. (i) exonerate, free
3. (k) surrender to another
4. (j) absorb, take in
5. (n) flush, fill, infuse
6. (a) take the place of
7. (o) moderate
8. (d) withdraw, go back
9. (e) continued flow, movement
10. (m) marital
11. (g) clear, sane authority
12. (f) postulate
13. (b) repentant, contrite
14. (c) low or common
15. (h) urge forward

List 21

I. Definitions

1. staccato
2. patina
3. frieze
4. fresco
5. diva
6. chiaroscuro
7. bravura
8. vignette
9. virtuoso/a
10. aria
11. sonata
12. libretto
13. rhapsody
14. dynamics
15. falsetto
16. concerto

II. Fill-Ins

1. dynamics
2. vignette
3. bravura
4. rhapsodize
5. virtuosa
6. aria
7. frieze
8. patina
9. chiaroscuro
10. Diva
11. staccato

III. Logic

1. A *nocturne* might help a baby drift off to sleep because it is dreamy, peaceful music. (Of course, anyone who knows babies realizes that they will go to sleep to any sort of music—or *not* go to sleep until they're darn good and ready.)
2. *Innocuous* means *harmless,* and a rabid dog can be very harmful.
3. *Dynamo* usually has positive connotations when applied to people, as it suggests energy and a desire to accomplish.
4. *Aspirations* are hopes, dreams, plans for the future.
5. *Illegible*—incapable of being read.
6. *Libretto* and *library* share the root LIBR, meaning book.
7. The name Fresca, so close to fresco, suggests a closeness to nature—a freshness and lack of artificiality that appeals to today's diet-conscious consumers.
8. People acting "in concert" are acting together, cooperating as a group. A "concerted effort" is the effort made by people working together in harmony, usually with determination.
9. From the softest to loudest: pianissimo, piano, forte, fortissimo. (Think for a moment about our word fort. How is it related to *forte, fortissimo,* and *fortitude*?)
10. *Falsetto* and *false* share the root fals, meaning to deceive. Obviously, the Italian *falso* meaning false is derived from this same root.

IV. Analogies

1. wall : fresco :: canvas : oil painting [Implied relationship. Answer (d) is too narrow.]
2. Beethoven : sonatas :: Gilbert and Sullivan : operas (Name related to stock-in-trade or typical product)
3. mountain climbing : bravura :: Windsor family : dynasty (Specific example of a general type, or one of a kind)
4. physics : thermodynamics :: play : vignette (Part of a whole)
5. overture : finale :: onset : expiration (Antonyms)

V. Antonyms

1. (d) bravura	5. (b) sloth	8. (f) diurnal (in the daytime)
2. (h) full color spectrum	6. (c) harmless	9. (e) flowing, connected
3. (j) bass	7. (i) unsuitable	10. (g) lacking emotion
4. (a) dampen, discourage		

VI. Word Analysis

1. The suffix *-ette* or *-etta* limits the meaning of the root word in some way, often by giving the idea of little, or perhaps short. A novelette is not as long as a novel, nor a cigarette as large as a cigar, etc. An operetta is less serious, and usually shorter, than an a opera.
2. In order, beginning with the lowest (deepest) singing voice: basso, baritone, tenor, alto (contralto), mezzo soprano, soprano.
3. *Staccato* is the opposite of *legato*.
4. De + crescendo = *decrescendo,* gradually decreasing in force or loudness.
5. To different people the phrase "exhibiting the patina of age" may have varied connotations, but in general it would suggest gray or white hair, wrinkles, a less erect carriage, slower movement, and perhaps a general softening or mellowing of appearance.
6. A funeral *dirge* would be somber, and slower and altogether heavier in tone than a rapturous *rhapsody.* It would tend to repeat musical themes, whereas a rhapsody is typically improvisational and may change form at will. (Musically speaking, the two are contrasting terms.)

List 22

I. Multiple Choice

1. (b)	7. (b)	13. (a)
2. (c)	8. (a)	14. (c)
3. (b)	9. (c)	15. (c)
4. (a)	10. (b)	16. (a)
5. (a)	11. (a)	17. (b)
6. (c)	12. (b)	

II. Who Said That?

1. a Valkyrie	7. Sylvanus	12. Iris
2. Pandora (or Epimetheus)	8. Stentor	13. Pontus
3. a myrmidon	9. Panacea	14. Zephyrus
4. Tantalus	10. Procrustes	15. Hygeia
5. Phaeton	11. Jove (Jupiter)	16. an amazon
6. centaur		

III. Analogies

1. Attic salt : wit :: compensation : emolument (Synonyms)
2. suspense : denouement :: research : panacea (Implied comparison in time/direction; also cause and result.)
3. pleasant : jovial :: bright : iridescent (Degree)
4. amazon : gnome :: stentor : whisperer (Antonyms)
5. manage : conduct :: tantalize : bedevil (Synonyms)

IV. Fill-Ins

1. manacled	5. myrmidon	9. pontoons
2. Pandora's box	6. Attic	10. zephyr
3. pending	7. sylvan	11. agnostic
4. hygienic	8. intangible	12. centaur

V. Word Analysis

1. The obvious parallel is that one, at most two, persons were burdened with the guilt of letting evil loose in the world. Most Christians blame Eve for tasting the forbidden fruit, just as the Greeks thought that Pandora was their troublemaker. In Christian belief, Eve was the first mortal woman, just as Pandora was the first for the Greeks. Both were fashioned by a male god. Both were warned not to do something that they promptly went ahead and did anyway.
2. Either *brilliant* or *glittering* might be substitutes for iridescent in the Ingalls quote, but neither word is a precise equivalent of iridescent, which suggests the shimmering ethereal quality possessed by the rainbow.

3. The major reason for the continued existence of the words in List 22 is that we have no exact equivalent in English for any of them. Because each carries myriad associations with its myth, each is unique. Most of these words lack synonyms in English, and when some are suggested, they are weak.

4. A Valkyrie was an awesome maiden because she chose which warriors were to die in battle, and the image of a life-threatening female still clings to this word. An amazon is supposed to be tougher, taller, and stronger, but the threat of death is not implicit in her.

5. The American Indian warriors went to the Happy Hunting grounds. I can find no mention of where their women went after death but would love to hear from anyone who knows. The Christian equivalent of the Elysian Fields is heaven, a concept much more vague than that of other religions, but where women are welcome to show up if they wish.

6. Aurora was the goddess of dawn, and Boreas, god of the north. Thus, the words literally mean "northern dawn."

List 23

I. Synonyms and Definitions

All synonyms and definitions shown in Word Study are acceptable as answers, plus those agreeable to each teacher.

II. Antonyms

1. (b) dutiful
2. (a) eternal
3. (b) wasteful
4. (c) immaterial
5. (e) imperceptible
6. (e) insignificant
7. (d) readily comprehensible
8. (e) lukewarm
9. (a) gelid [Answer (d), tepid, is close but not an exact opposite.]
10. (b) easily swayed
11. (c) open and easily understood
12. (d) upper

III. Famous Descriptions

1. evanescent
2. frugal
3. prodigious
4. intransigent
5. nether
6. sardonic
7. inscrutable
8. piety

IV. Know Those Roots

1. (g) sticky
2. (f) a course or route
3. (j) babbling, illogical
4. (k) to send back
5. (a) false, assumed name
6. (i) going from place to place, roving, wandering
7. (c) drive, enterprise
8. (e) follower, believer
9. (l) to name, suggest, propose
10. (h) name derived from a paternal ancestor or father
11. (d) projectile
12. (b) inborn, innate

V. Analogies

1. warm : torrid :: difficult : recondite (Degree)
2. unctuous : sincerity :: sardonic : sympathy (Implied relationship)
3. palpable : touch :: audible : hear (Implied relationship)
4. irreverent : pious :: remiss : attentive (Antonyms)
5. annoyed : vehement :: frugal : miserly (Degree)

VI. Word Analysis

1. *To scrutinize* is to examine carefully. It shares the root scrutari (to search) with *inscrutable*.
2. In Arnold's poem, *dumb* merely means without speech, as a cat certainly would be.
3. Over time the meaning of *pious* has come in some contexts to suggest false or hypocritical devotion to religion, whereas originally it meant devout in an honest sense. Today we are more apt to think of a pious person as one who displays religion or thrusts it upon us, one who is religious above all else. Any word whose meaning changes toward the negative is said to have *degenerated*.
4. A *misnomer* is literally a false name. Usually, misnomers are names that are grossly inappropriate.
5. A *palpable spleen* is one that can be felt, or palpated, by the physician. Normally, the spleen is an organ that is tucked up under the ribs for protection, but in some people it is situated far enough below the rib cage to be felt.
6. At teacher's discretion. This may sound silly, but it is an enjoyable class discussion and may encourage some to participate who typically are silent. Also, students may wish to judge which extenuating circumstances are logical or acceptable and which ones simply ridiculous.

List 24

I. Knowing the Words

1. *Antonyms*

   a. life, or continuation
   b. honesty, openness, candidness
   c. energy, liveliness, verve, vivacity, etc.
   d. generosity, extravagance, or perhaps philanthropy
   e. cleanliness

2. *Synonyms*

   a. ghost, specter, or phantom
   b. boor or lout
   c. wail, moan, or cry
   d. villain, criminal, or wrongdoer
   e. harm, damage, or injury

3. *Explanations*

   a. one who enjoys hurting others and witnessing their pain
   b. a twinge of conscience or pang of unease, worry
   c. utter disgrace, usually as a result of a profound wrong or evil
   d. one who believes that mankind is motivated by self-interest
   e. worry or concern about what the future will bring
   f. amazement often mixed with dismay

II. Switcheroo

1. (g) fearful of something ahead
2. (j) notorious
3. (i) stingy, niggardly
4. (a) to understand or to seize
5. (f) boorish
6. (b) wantonly cruel
7. (d) sadly regrettable
8. (l) distrustful of human nature
9. (e) innocent, free of artifice
10. (k) harmful
11. (h) to please by charming
12. (c) to bemoan, regret exceedingly

III. Chart Fill-In

1. example
2. prehens, prehend; tending to take from others for your gain at their expense
3. motive; motion, emote, emotion, mobile, mobility, move, immobile, etc.
4. abysmal; maleficent, maladroit, malfunction, dismal, malady, maladjusted, etc.
5. dol; to sympathize in time of sorrow or grief
6. infamy; famous, infamous, defame, fame, etc.
7. cynic; one who distrusts mankind
8. demise; missile, remit, submit, emit, missive, intermittent, commit, etc.
9. squalidus; utter filth/degradation
10. reprehensible; apprehend, apprehensive, apprehension, comprehend, comprehension, prehensile, etc.

IV. Substitution

1. qualms
2. miscreant
3. detrimental
4. consternation
5. apparitions
6. lassitude
7. demise
8. parsimoniously
9. sadist
10. squalor

V. Find the Oddball

1. (c) appreciate   Others share the same root.
2. (d) fool   Others refer to churl.
3. (a) impious   Others relate to miscreant.
4. (b) wound   Others relate to qualm.
5. (b) unease   Others relate to lassitude.
6. (a) terror   Others relate to consternation. [Answer (e) belongs in the group because it lacks the intensity of (a), the oddball.]
7. (e) motley   Others share the same root.

8. (c) satiated   Others are negative in meaning.
9. (d) dismal   Only one with a negative connotation. (The name Dolores does not have a negative connotation, in spite of its etymology.)
10. (c) medical   Others define malady.

VI. Word Analysis

1. Anyone wearing a "determinedly guileless smile" could be suspected of duplicity. Innocence should be natural to be believed.
2. The suspect is apt to be at the police station, possibly in jail.
3. At teacher's discretion. Some well-known homophones are to, two, and too; right and write; boil (v.) and boil (n.); horde and hoard; bored and board.
4. A maladroit individual is typically clumsy—may drop things, bump into furniture, miss hitting the ball, etc. He or she is physically inept, in other words.
5. This definition is often termed an *epigram,* and Wilde was known for his epigrams. (See List 8.) The class might be interested in briefly discussing the truth, or lack of it, that they see in Wilde's definition of a cynic. What does he mean by someone who knows the price of everything and the value of nothing?

Review

Lists 21–24

I. Antonyms

1. (c) lethargic
2. (b) philanthropy
3. (e) apathy
4. (a) scrupulously attentive
5. (c) tractable
6. (d) irrelevant
7. (b) lingering
8. (e) dulcet
9. (d) choleric
10. (a) flexible

II. Logic

1. apparition
2. amazon
3. laments
4. guile
5. falsetto
6. frieze
7. sonata
8. staccato
9. sardonic
10. consternation
11. infamy
12. arias
13. hygiene
14. panacea
15. demise

III. Synonyms and Definitions

1. (f) pang
2. (h) lower
3. (g) difficult to decipher
4. (k) steamy
5. (d) evildoer
6. (l) abstruse
7. (b) a brief scene
8. (c) injurious
9. (j) holier-than-thou
10. (e) brilliant, scintillating
11. (a) uncouth, rude
12. (i) talk or write in an ecstatic manner

IV. Truth or Fiction

1. F   5. T   8. T
2. T   6. F   9. T
3. F   7. F   10. F
4. F

V. Using the Roots

1. We make *condolence* calls to express our sympathy and friendship to people who are grieving, usually after a death.
2. A *suspension* bridge is suspended in air from cables swung over towers between two banks. It has no pilings for support along its length, which makes it look more precarious than it really is.
3. *Contiguous* pieces of property are situated next to each other, touching along a common border.
4. The *respiratory* tract conducts air (breath) in and out of the body. It includes the nose, mouth, windpipe (trachea), and lungs.
5. A *prognosticator* is one who foretells the future, who claims to know ahead of time what will happen.
6. A *cohesive* argument hangs together, somewhat in the way an *adhesive* bandage sticks to skin. In a debate, only a well-organized, *coherent,* and cohesive argument can stand up to examination by the opponents.
7. *Exit, circuitous, itinerant, initiate,* and *transit* share the root IT meaning *to go.*
8. *Noxious* fumes may be merely harmful, or actually deadly, like the carbon monoxide exhaust from a car.
9. The best antonym of diurnal is *nocturnal.*
10. The root in *denominator* is *nomin,* meaning name.

VI. Decoding with Roots

1. Circle MAL; note prefix dis-; bad or badly; gloomy, depressing, or poor, as *dismal prospects.*
2. Circle LEG; note legum-, meaning pea or bean; to choose, select, read; referring to peas or beans.
3. Circle MIT; note prefix e-; to send; to give off or out, as a noise or odor is emitted.
4. Circle MOT; note prefix re-; to move; moved or set away or apart, as *a remote village.*
5. Circle ONYM; note prefix homo-; root = name, prefix = same; homonyms are words spelled exactly the same but with different meanings, as *quail* (n.) and *quail* (v.); *bear* (v.) and *bear* (n.).
6. Circle PREHNS; note prefix mis-; to seize or grasp; a misunderstanding or misconception.
7. Circle TEN; note prefix ex-; to stretch, extend; referring to a reason or excuse that mitigates or lessens the severity of an occurrence, as *extenuating circumstances may convince me to accept a late assignment.*
8. Circle PHON; note prefix homo-; sound; words that sound the same but are spelled differently, as *bear* and *bare*, *horse* and *hoarse*.

VII. Common Sense Connections

1. (c) mural
2. (a) prima donna
3. (b) Rambo
4. (b) W. S. Gilbert
5. (b) contrast
6. (c) Tchaikovsky
7. (a) metals
8. (b) nature trail
9. (c) Valhalla
10. (b) gentle
11. (a) economy
12. (a) professional
13. (c) cowboy
14. (b) henchman
15. (b) devil

Unit V *Your Best on the Test*

1. Practice Sentence Completions

1. (B) volatile (Answer must contrast with the name Serena.)
2. (C) didactic (Answer is defined in "bent on conveying a moral lesson," the last 1/3 of the sentence.)
3. (B) incongruous (Word chosen must make clear the unusual contrast in Ben's beliefs.)
4. (D) lackluster . . . incapable (Sentence of coordination; logic permits only this answer. Note *consistently*.)
5. (E) compromise . . . disparate (Definition plus logic)
6. (E) prehensile . . . precocious (Coordinated ideas)
7. (A) attest . . . ubiquitous (Logic, common sense)
8. (B) inarticulate . . . divine (Definition: "longing she was unable to express" = *inarticulate*, which is why someone has to divine what she wants.)
9. (C) punctual . . . disheveled (Sentence of contrasts: *punctual* vs. *unready* and *disheveled* vs. *well-groomed*)
10. (D) ascetics . . . mendacious (Sentence of definition—an *ascetic* "with no need of worldly goods"—and contrast: *honest* vs. *mendacious*)

2. Practice Sentence Completions

1. (C) authentic (Definition required; the answer must mean "attention to truth.")
2. (D) meager (Contrast; answer is the opposite of *bountiful*.)
3. (B) divergence (Logic; answer sums up the meaning of the entire sentence.)
4. (E) manipulated . . . govern (Definition—puppets are always *manipulated by unseen hands*—and contrast; we can *govern* technologies rather than be manipulated by them.)
5. (A) fortuitous (Definition)
6. (C) galvanized into . . . cogent (Contrast and logic)
7. (E) charlatan . . . spurious (Logic and common sense require two negative words to coordinate with "deceive.")
8. (A) ephemeral . . . durability (Logic, coordinated ideas)
9. (D) sedentary . . . exercise (Contrast; note "*although*.")
10. (B) ambivalence . . . anxious (Contrast; note "*while*" and "*they're also . . .*")

3. Practice Sentence Completions

1. (D) reluctant (The answer must logically complete the meaning of "fearing that the film would be 'cartoony' or inaccurate.")
2. (A) sanguinity (Vocabulary is key here; answer must coordinate with "optimist by nature" and the idea of Chris's "customary" good nature.)
3. (B) disregarding . . . transcribing (The first blank must pertain to "that which is merely a fad," and the second blank explains and defines what a linguist does with an "actual change" in language usage. This sentence requires understanding of the word linguist.)
4. (E) canny . . . acumen (Coordinated ideas require Juan to be a canny, or very shrewd, bargainer, or else opponents wouldn't be "surprised by his acumen.")

5. (B) dearth . . . inundated with (Sentence of contrast; the first word must contrast sharply with the idea in the second half of the sentence.)

6. (E) altruism . . . narcissism (Logic leading to contrast. Marlene was know for something good, her altruism, until she withdrew her "customary support" or charity she set-up in her own name. Only *narcissism* is strong enough to fit all the meanings in this sentence.)

7. (A) reticent (Sentence of contrast. Note "*although.*")

8. (C) obsolescent . . . myopic (Vocabulary and logic are the keys. "*Smug*" points to *myopic* for the second blank.)

9. (C) irrefutable . . . opportunist (Definition; only *opportunist* defines the phrase "repeatedly taken advantage of her opponents.")

10. (D) indigent . . . demur (First blank must be filled by a word describing a country "where so many eke out their existence by begging," and the second blank must mean *object* or *resist,* and so *demur* is perfect.)

1. Practice Reading Passage

1. (D) (Although the passage is certainly historical, most of it is devoted to an explanation of Lyell's personality, hence, a character sketch.)
2. (B) extremely perceptive (See Webster.)
3. (E)
4. (C)
5. (A) (Lyell took advantage of his trip to America to make sure that his books would be published there.)
6. (C) (This is the point of the first paragraph.)
7. (A)
8. (D) (Lines 72–73 and following make the point that Lyell was not a natural charmer, but that he worked at being congenial.)
9. (E) (Tongue-in-cheek describes gentle irony.)
10. (A) (Check lines 28–29.)
11. (C) (Check lines 78–82.)
12. (E) (A pirated edition of a book is illegal because it lacks legal permission or copyright.)

2. Practice Reading Passage

1. (B) (Note last half of the third paragraph.)
2. (A) (See the second paragraph.)
3. (E) (See the first paragraph.)
4. (C) (Note the last half of the third paragraph.)
5. (D) (See the first paragraph.)
6. (D) (Read lines 58–59.)
7. (B) (Read lines 102–103.)
8. (A) (See lines 68–77.)
9. (C) (Animal rituals involved live beasts; see the third paragraph.)
10. (C) (This idea is throughout the passage.)
11. (E)
12. (B) (Read the fifth paragraph.)
13. (E)

3. Practice Reading: Paired Passages

1. (B) (Read the first two lines.)
2. (E) (Everyday speech is colloquial for the speakers and the places involved.)
3. (C)
4. (A) (Read lines 46–51.)
5. (D) (Read lines 30–42.)
6. (D) (See lines 28–30.)
7. (B) (See lines 35–40 and 48–54 in passage 2.)
8. (A) (Nostalgia is viewing the past with affection.)
9. (E) [Next-best choice is (C), although it's hard to make a case for the entire community based on the limited sample.]
10. (C) (Pacing is timing in a book.)
11. (D)
12. (B)
13. (E)

4. Practice Reading Passage

1. (D) Read lines 9–59 for this answer.
2. (A) Read lines 60–70, where this list is the focus of the paragraph.

3. (C) Read lines 75–84, and then lines 114–125.
4. (C) The word *ravages* always means serious destruction/damage.
5. (E) Read lines 46–47, where this is stated specifically.
6. (B) Read lines 111–113, where this is stated specifically.
7. (D) This is the only answer choice that is correct and is supported in the passage.
8. (A) This answer can be deduced from the example of the farmer selling his wheat in times of inflation, when he needs to sell only 26 bushels (not 50) to repay his loan amount.

5. **Practice Reading Passage**

1. (B) Note that the author never explains scientific words or phrases, such as "social" insects, *proboscis* (line 22), *antennae* (line 25), and "wing venation" (line 25)—just for starters.
2. (E) Read lines 1–26, where this is explained.
3. (C) Check the dictionary. Whenever *mainstay* is used, it will refer to the primary (main) thing. Here, the topic is food (fodder).
4. (B) Read lines 67–88. Pollution-free environments are never discussed.
5. (D) Read lines 55–88, which discuss how successful the new wasp immigrant is in North America and Canada. While the other statements are true, the distinctive thing about *Vespula germanica* is that it emigrated (left somewhere else), and is now a thriving immigrant species.
6. (E) Read lines 93–98. An opportunist takes advantage of any situation, regardless of consequences. (Wasps, of course, have no conscience.)
7. (A) Didactic means "for the purpose of instruction or information." This is a passage written in a factual, unemotional manner, lacking figures of speech and humor, its sole purpose being to inform the reader.

INDEX

This index lists words that are taught, referred to frequently, or used as synonyms or antonyms. Pages shown in bold type give a definition of the words.

a- 102
a-, ad-, af-, ag-, al-, an-, ap-, as-, at- ab-, abs- 109
abandon 55
abbreviate **90**
abduct **236**
aberration **108**
abhorrence 200
abhorrent 201
adjure **275**
abominable 212, 213
abrogate 270, **272**
abscond **108**
absolve 274, 287
absorb 285
abstain 282, 284
abstinence **167**
abstruse 326
absurd 154, 204
abut 73, **75**
abysmal **337**
ac/acr 177
accord 166, 250
accordance 250
accretion 164
accuse 272, 274
ace 155
acquiesce **43**
acquit 270, **272**, 287
acquittance **272**
acrid **177**
acrimonious **177**
acrophobia 186
ACT exam 2
actor 66
actress 66
acumen **177**
acute **177**
adage 250
addition 164
adhere **109**, **327**
ad hoc 259, **261**
adjudicate 270, **272**
adjure **275**
admirable 212, 213
admonish 54, **288**
adulation 199, **200**

adulterate 43, 172, **174**
adverse 213
advisable 118
advocate (n., v.) 270, **272**
Aeneid **332**
Aeolus **95**
affect **236**, **244**
affirm 75
aficionado/a 232, **234**
aggravate 175
agnostic **316**
agog **120**
agon **67**
agony 67
agoraphobia **186**
agr 12
agree 250
agreement 250
agriculture **12**
agronomy **12**
aid 176
alarm 54
alert 89
alfresco 231, **233**
alien 155, 324
allay 175
allege 109, 136, **138**
alleged **138**
allegory 62, **64**
alleviate 175, 186, **204**
alliance 222
allure 54
alluvial **225**
alma mater **261**
alter- **110**
alter ego **12**, 259, **261**
alternative 110
altruism 88
alumna, alumnae **261**
alumnus, alumni **261**
am/ami (examples of) 16
amateur 233
Amazon **312**
amazon 310, 312
ambi/amphi 22
ambidextrous **22**
ambience 162, **164**

amenable 118
amenities 162, **164**
amoral **102**
amorphous **263**
amphi- 108
amphitheater 22, **108**
ana- 109
analogy questions, How To **363**, 365
anaphase **110**
anarchy **90**
anastrophe **109**
andante 234
anecdote 136, **138**
anemia 183, **185**
Anglophile **56**
anima 78, 183, **185**
animal **78**
animated **78**
animosity 166
animus **78**
anneal **109**
annihilate 282, **284**
announce 54, 176
annul 272
anomaly 162, **164**
anonymous **327**
antagonism 166
antagonist **67**
antagonize 174
ant-, anti- (against) **25**, **102**
antarctic **102**
ante-, anti- (before) **104**
antedate **104**
antediluvian 220, **222**
anteroom **104**
anthrop **56**
anthropology **56**, 226
anthropomorphism **56**
antibiotic **225**
anticipate **215**
anticipation 104
antidote 102, 183, **185**
antipathy **102**
antipodes 220, **222**
antiquated 222
anthithesis **102**

apo- **108**
apathetic 202
apathy 102, 185, **188**
aphorism 248, **250**
apocryphal **108**
apogee **108**
Apollo 314
appalling 212
apparition 333, **334**
appealing 77
appease 174
applaud 54
appreciative 212
apprehend **338**
apprehension 333, **335**
appropriate 202
approve 274
apt 202
aqua/aqu 11
Aqua-lung **11**
aquarium **11**
aqueduct **11**
arch- (pre.) **90**
arch **90**
archaeology **90**
arctic **102**
ardent 326
Ares **312**
argot 75
aria 299, **301**
articulate (v., adj.) 136, **138**, 139
artificial **236**
ascertain 172, **174**
Asclepius **312**
ascribe 285
asinine 153, **154**
aspire **304**
assent 250
assert 75, 138
asslike 154
assume 77
astigmatism **55**
astringent 116, **117**
astute 199, **201**
atheist **90**
Atlas 90
atmosphere 164

atone 51, **53**
atrocious 210, **212**
attention **130**
attentive 326
attest 75
Attic **64**, 310, **312**
Attic faith **312**
Attic salt **312**
attribute 285
attrited **164**
attrition 162, **164**
atypical 102
audacity 167
aud/audit 13
audible **13**
augur 201
auspex 201
auspices **201**
auspicious 199, **201**
authentic 261
authorization 274
authorize 274
auto- **26**
autumnal equinox **304**
avant-garde (n., adj.)
   126, **128**
avarice 86
avenge 55, 287
aver 73, **75**
avi **161**
avis **201**
avow 75
awesome 326
axis 220, **222**

Babbitt **165**
babble 139, 251
bacchanal 84, **86**
Bacchus **86**
badinage 136, **138**
bagatelle 162, **164**
banal 141
bane 88
banter 138
barbaric 212
baroque 62, **64**
battology **144**
bearing 165
befoul 53
beginner 155, 303
behave 272
behavior 165
believable 119
belittle 54
bell (war) **204**
bell (beauty) **204**

belle **204**
belles lettres 71, **204**
bellicose **204**
belligerence **204**
bellowing 315
bene **67**
bene- **102**
benediction **102**
beneficent **67**
benevolent **67**, 214
besmirch 53
bi 20
bibli 12
bibliograph 12
bibliophile 12
bigot 162, **165**, 364
bio 11, **225**
biography 11, **141**
biology 11, **225**
biomedicine **225**
biophysics **225**
biopsy **11**
biplane **20**
bit 77
bizarre **41**, 129
bland 118, 203
blasphemous 215
bliss **201**
blithe 199, **201**
blood-feud 234
bloom 53
blossom 53
blues 223
bluff 118, 203
bode 176
bog 76
bogus 261
boil **128**
bold 77, 118
bombast 248, **250**, 252
bon **67**
bon- **102**
bona fide 259, **261**
bona fides **261**
bonanza 232, **234**
bonbon **102**
bonhomie **67**
bonny **67**
bons mots **145**
bonus **67**
book list **349–355**
booming 315
boor 335
boorish 203
border 75
boreal **316**
boredom 129

Boreus **316**
both **104**
bovine (adj. n.) 153, **155**
bowdlerize **290**
brand 55
brash 77
bravura 299, **301**
brazen (v., adj.) 116,
   117, 118, 213
brev **90**
breviary **90**
brevity **90**
brilliant 313
broad 118
brusque 116, **118**
bucolic 119
buoyant 214
burgeon 51, **53**
burlesque (n., adj.) 62,
   64

cabana 232, **235**
cabin 235
cagey 201
Calliope **88**
calm 203
canard **135**
canine 161
canny 201
cant (n., v.) 73, **75**
cap/capt/cept/ceive/cip
   215
capit **236**
capital **236**
capitulate **44**
caprice 167
captious 210, **212**
captivate **215**
carcinogen 183, **185**
carcinoid **185**
carcinoma **185**
carcinomatosis **185**
cardiac 183, **185**
cardialgia **185**
cardiopulmonary **185**
-cardium **185**
careful 326
careless 326
caricature 64, 66
carn **157**
carnage **157**
carnivorous **157**
cata- 108
catacomb 108
catholic, Catholic 116,
   118

caution 54, 167
cautious 77
caveat **261**
caveat emptor 259, **261**
cave canem **261**
cede, ceed, cess **263**
celestial 87
cent 22
centaur 310, **312**
Centaurus **312**
centenarian **22**
centennial **22**
centrifugal 220, **222**
centrifuge 222
chagrin **42**
charge 285
charitable 214
Charon **89**
chatter 139, 251
chauvinist 165
cheer 54
cheerful 201, 214
cheerfulness 223
chiaroscuro 299, **301**
choleric 203, 210, **212**,
   313
chrom 12
chromatin **12**
chromides 12
chronological **14**
chronometer **14**
churl 333, **335**
chutzpah 35, 167
cide/cis **188**
circum- **26**, 108
circumnavigate 108
circumspect 77
circumspection 167
cite 55
civic **14**
civil **14**
civilization **14**
claim 138
clamorous 253
classic 66, 129
classical 62, **64**
claustrophobia **186**
clear 119
Clio **88**
close-mouthed 252
cloudy 119
coach 87
coalition 223
co-, col-, com-, con-,
   cor- **108**
coerce 51, **53**
cogn 13, 236

cognition **236**
cognizant **13**, **236**
cognoscenti 231, **233**
coherent 108, **327**
collaborate 108
collude 174
comedy 62, **65**
comical 213
commend 76
commit 55
common 141
commute (v., n.) **157**, 270, **273**
compel **288**
compensate 55
compensation **316**
complaisant 118
complete 77
complex (adj.) 108, **167**
compliant 118
compliment 76
composure 130
comprehend **338**
comprehensive 118
compress (v.) 108
compunction 336
concave 220, **223**
conceal 54, 285
concerto 299, **301**
concierge 126, **128**
conciliate 172, **174**
concise 140, 253
conclude 175
condescend 282, **284**
condole **337**
conduct (n.) 165
confer **177**
confident 118, 203
confidential **120**
confirm 387
congenial 199, **201**, 213
congregate **120**
conjugal **276**
connive 172, **174**
connoisseur 233, **236**
connotation **61**
consecrate **216**
consecutive **78**
consider 176
considered 251
consonant 201
conspicuous **167**
conspire 174
constant 87
consternation 333, **335**
constrict **120**
construe (v., n.) 248, **250**

contaminate 53
contemporary **15**, 64, **264**
contention **167**
context **33**
contiguous **316**
contingent 108, **316**
contra- **25**, **102**
contradict 102, 138
contrary 102
contravene 138
conventional 129
convex 223
convince **56**
convivial 313
coolness 130
coordinate 108
corp 12
corporation **12**
corporeal 261
corps 12
corpulent 12
corpus delicti 259, **261**
correct 55
corrupt 53, 174
cosmic **14**
cosmopolitan **14**
coterie 133
counselor 87
counter- **25**, **102**
counterattack 102
counterfeit 261
coup 73, **75**
crass **36**
crave 176
crazy 204
create 284
cred **78**
credence **78**
credential **78**
credible **78**
credit **78**
credo **78**
credulous 201
crescendo **309**
criminology **226**
critical 212
critical reading questions, How To 381
cruel 87
crux 73, **75**
cumb/cub **177**
cum laude **268**
Cupid **86**, **95**
cupidity 84, **86**
cur/curr/curs/course **177**
cure-all 313

current **177**
cursory **177**
curt 118
cycl (examples of) 15
cynic 333, **335**
Cynics **335**
Cynosura **86**
Cynosure **86**
cynosure 84, **86**

dabbler 233
dank **34**
danse macabre **214**
dash 130
dauntless 203
de- **108**
deadness 202
death 335
debacle 126, **128**
debase 53, 174
dec 21
decapitate 108, **236**
decathlon 21
deceive **215**
December 21
deciduous **108**
declare 75, 176
decline 176
decorate 55
decree 76
decry 54, 272
deduce 175
defame 108, 177
defer **177**
deference **177**
defile 51, **53**
deflect 141
deflower 53
dehydration 11
dei **90**
deism **90**
deity **90**
delightful 202
delinquent 118
deluge 175, **225**
dem **275**
demagogue **120**, **275**
demean **165**
demeanor 162, **165**
demi- 20
demise (n., v.) 333, **335**
demitasse **20**
democracy **275**
denigrate 54
denizen 153, **155**
denouement 62, **65**

denounce 55
deny 138
deport **130**
depraved 118
depreciate 54
derisive 326
derm **188**
dermatitis **188**
dermatologist **188**
derogatory **141**
desecrate **216**
destroy 284
détente 126, **128**
deter 286
detestable 212
detriment 333, **335**
devotee 234
devout 325
di- 20
dialect 75
diaphanous **110**
dic/dict 13, **275**
dictate 13
dictator **275**
di-, dia- **110**
dif-, dis- **103**
differ 103, 250
difference 250
diffident 116, 117, **118**
dilettante 231, **233**
Dionysus **86**
diplo- 20
diploma 20
diplomatic 203
disagree 250
disagreement 250
disapproval 274
disapprove 274
disavow 75
discern 172, **174**
discerning 201
disclaim 75
discord 130
discover 174
discriminate 174
diseased 214
disencumber 285
disentangle 285
dishonor 53
disinter **157**
dislocate **263**
dismal 337
dismay 103
disparage 51, **54**
display 54
dissemble **44**
dissent 248, **250**

dissolution 223
distinct 119
distraught 103
distribute 76
div **90**
diva 299, **301**
diverse **67**
divert **67**
divine 90
divulge 282, **285**
doc/doct **204**
docile 118, **204**
doctor **204**
doctrine **204**
document (v., n.) **204**
dol **337**
doldrums 220, **223**
dole 73, **76**
doleful **337**
Dolores **337**
dolt **41**
Don Quixote **235**
dorm 13
dormant 13
dors **130**
dorsal **130**
dossier 126, **128**
double-dealing 165
double entendre 136,
  139
dour **41**
downcast 201
downgrade 54
Draco **87**
draconian 84, **87**
dramatis personae **261**
dregs **223**
dross 220, **223**
drowsy 89
dry 117
duc/duct **236**
ductile **236**
du, duo- 20
duenna 232, **235**
duet **20**
dull 89
dullness 185, 202
duo **20**
duodec-, dodec- 21
dupe 73, **76**
duplicity **20**, 162, **165**
dur **215**
duration **215**
duress **215**
dutiful 326
dwindle 53
dynamics 299, **302**

dynamism 336
dynamite **304**
dynamo **304**
dynasty **304**
dyn/dynam **304**
dyne **302**

eccentric **108**
echelon 126, **129**
Echo **88**
ecto- **108**
ectomorph **108**
edict 76
educe 273
e-, ec-, ef-, ex- **108**
eerie 118
efface **108**
effect **108**, **244**
effluent **287**
effrontery 167
effusive **36**
e.g. (*exemplia gratia*)
  267
ego **12**
egocentric **12**
egocentrism **88**
egoism **88**
egregious **120**
egress **287**
eight **104**
eldritch 116, **118**
Elements of Style, The
  75, 284, 324
elevator **204**
elicit 273
eligible **304**
elucidate **253**
Elysian fields **321**
emaciated **212**
embellish **204**
embrace 176
embroilment 233
em-, en-, endo- **109**
emit 108
emote **337**
emotionless 202
empathize **109**
empathy **188**
encumber 285
endemic **275**
endocrine 109
endorse **130**, 274
endurance **215**
enduring 324
engender **67**

English language,
  history of **11**
enigmatic 325
enmesh 285
enmity 166
ennea 21
ennead **21**
ennui 126, **129**
entangle 76, 285
entice 51, **54**, 77
entrepreneur 126, **129**
environment 164
ephemeral 324
epi- **108**
epidemic **275**
epidermis **108**, **188**
epigram 136, **139**
epilogue 108
equ (examples of) 15
equal **104**
equanimity **78**, 130
equerry **15**
equestrian **15**
equine **15**
equinox **304**
Erato **88**
Eros **86**, **95**
err 13
err **13**
errant 275
errare humanum est 261
escalation 128
essential 120
establish 272
et al. (*et alia*) 267
eternal 324
Ether **87**
ether 87
ethereal 84, **87**
etymology 136, **139**
eu- **102**
eulogize 177
eulogy 102
euphony **102**
euphoria **200**, 223
Euterpe **88**
euthanasia 183, **186**
ev (aev) **56**
evanescent 322, **324**
evil 212, 214
evince 51, **54**
ex- **104**
exacerbate 172, **175**
exalt 53
examine 176
excessive 77
ex-convict 104

excoriate 76
exculpate 272, 274, 287
execrable 210, **212**
execute **78**
exhale 108, **304**
exhilaration 199, **202**
exhort 51, **54**
ex-husband 104
exigencies 162, **165**
exit 327
exonerate 272, 287
expansion 164
expedient 116, **118**
expert 155, 233
expiate 53
expire **304**
explicit **167**
export **130**
ex post facto 259, **262**
expostulate 286
expurgate 282, **285**
extemporaneously 262
extempore 259, **262**
extemporize **175**
extenuating 322, **324**
exter-, extra-, extro- **27**,
  110
external 110
extort 270, **273**
extortion **273**
extract **273**
extradite 270, **273**
extramundane **110**
extrapolate 172, **175**
extricate 282, **285**
extrovert **110**
exude 285

fac, fect, fic, fict, -fy **236**
faction 77
factitious **236**
factotum **236**
faire **133**
fait **133**
fall, fals (examples of)
  16
falsetto 299, **302**
farce 62, **65**
fat 156
faultfinding 212
faultless 202
faulty 202
faux **133**
favorable 213
fawn 56
feed 55

feign 51, **54**, 77
felicitous 199, **202**
felon **273**
felonry **273**
felony 270, **273**
fer **177**
fertile **177**
fervent 199, **202**, 327
fervid 327
fester (v., n.) 183, **186**
few **104**
fiasco 128
fiat 73, **76**
fiat money 76
fiction **236**
fid **120**
fidelity **120**
fiery 224
filch **41**
first **104**
fission 220, **223**
fit 202
five **104**
flagrant 77
flawed 202
flawless 202
flay 73, **76**
flect/flex 13, **141**
fledgling 153, **155**
fleece 76
flex 13, **141**
float 314
flourish 53
fluctuate **287**
flu, fluct, flux **287**
fodder 153, **155**
fool 76
foolhardy 77
for- **103**
forbade 103
force 53
fore- **27**, **104**
forebode 176
foreign 324
forensic 270, **273**
foreshadow 176
forewarn 104, 176
forgo **103**
forsake 103
forte **234**
forthright 213
fortissimo **234**
foster 55
foul 77, 212
four **104**
frag, fract (examples of)
   17, **225**

fragile **225**
fragmentation **225**
Francophile **56**
fraudulent 261
free verse 62, **65**
fresco 299, **302**
fresh 141
friendly 213
friendship 166
frieze 299, **302**
frighten 54
frigid 326
frugal 322, **324**
furtive 210, **213**
fusion 221, **223**
fustian 250

gabble 139
gall 167
garrulous 136, **139**, 140,
   252
gastric 183, **186**
gastronome **186**
gastronomy **186**
gather 175
ge/geo 12
gelid 326
gen **67**
genesis **67**
genial 201
genre 63, **65**
genuine 261
geology 12
geometry 12
geophysics 12
germane 322, **324**
ghost 334
gibber 136, **139**
gibberish 139
gibe (n., v.) 74, **76**
Gilbert, Wm. S. 165,
   300
glib 248, **251**
glittering 313
gloomy 89, 313
glum 201
glut 286
gnome **316**
gnos, gnom **316**
goad 286
goldmine 234
gorge 286
Gothic 63, **65**
grad, gress **287**
gradual **287**
graduate **287**

gramophone **141**
grandiloquence 250, 252
graph/gram **141**
graphic **141**
grav (examples of) 16
greed 86
greg **120**
gregarious **120**
grisly 214
gross 77
grovel 56
gruesome 214
guessing on the
   SAT/PSAT **360**
guile 77, 333, **336**
gull 76
gullible 201

habeas corpus 259, **262**
hackneyed 141
Hades **89**, 330
haggle **35**
hairless 155
hairy 155
hal **304**
half **104**
Halley's comet 110
hanker (for) 176
harsh 87
healthful 187
heavenly 87
hecatomb **22**
hect-, hecto-, hecato- 22
hectometer **22**
heinous 210, **213**
Helios 314
help 176
hemi- 20
hemisphere **20**
Hephaestos 314
hept 21
heptameter **21**
Hera 313
her, hes **327**
Hermes 87
hetero- **110**
heterodox **110**
hex 21, 88
hex 21
hexagon **21**
hidden 77
hide 54
hierarchy 90
hint 54, 175
Hippocrates 312

Hippocratic oath 284,
   285, 312
hirsute 153, **155**
hirsutism **155**
hirsutulous **155**
hoary **35**
hoax 76, 77
hom **204**
homage 199, **202**
homager **202**
hombre **204**
homburg **204**
homicide **188**, **204**
homo- **110**
homogeneous **110**
homonym **110**
homophone **337**
Homo sapiens **204**
honor 53, 55, 202
honorable 215
horrifying 212
hostile 213
hostility 166
household 129
humility 166
humor 65
humorless 203
hundred **104**
hydr **11**
hydrant **11**
hydrate **11**
Hygeia **312**
hygiene 310, **312**
hyper- **27**, **110**
hyperactive **110**
hyperbole 248, **251**
hyp-, hypo- **110**
Hypnos **89**
hypochondria **110**
hypocrisy 77, 165
hypodermic **110**

ibid. (*ibidem*) **267**
icy 326
idolatry 200
idyllic 119
i.e. (*id est*) **267**
ign **225**
igneous 221, **224**
ignis fatuus **225**
ignition **225**
Iliad 117, 303
il-, im-, in-, ir- (not) **103**
il-, im-, in-, ir- (in, into,
   or within) **109**
illiterate **103**

ill-mannered 203
illogical **167**
ill-omened 201
illuminate 109
imbibe 282, **285**
imbroglio 231, **233**
immaterial 324
immovable **337**
immutable **157**
impalpable 325
impassioned 202, 327
impassive 87, 103, 120
impeccable 200, **202**
imperceptible 325
imperfect 119, 202
imperturbable 212
impious 325
implausible 119
imply 54
import **130**
imposture 77
impromptu 262
improvise 172, **175**
impudent 117
impulse **288**
impure 119
impurity 223
imputation **285**
impute 282, **285**
inane 154
inappropriate 202
inarticulate 138
inauspicious 201
incarnate **157**
incise **188**
incision 109, **188**
incisive **188**
incite 286
incognito **236**
inconstant 87
incorrigible 116, **118**
incredible 119
incubate **177**
incubator **177**
inculpate 272, 274
incumbent (adj., n.) 116, **119**, **177**
indict 271, **274**
indigenous **363**
indistinct 119
indolence **44**
indomitable 200, **203**
indoors 233
inductive **236**
indulge **284**
inertia 221, **224**
inexpedient 118

in extremis 260, **262**
infamy 333, **336**
infelicitous 202
infer 173, **175**, 250
infidel **103**, **120**
infinitesimal 326
inflame 186
inflection 13, 137, **139**
inflexible 119, **141**
influx **287**
infraction **225**
infuse 286
ingenue **67**
ingenuity **67**
ingenuous **67**
inhabitant 155
inhalator **304**
inhale **304**
inherent **327**
inhibit 286
inimical 210, **213**
initiative **327**
injunction **276**
innocent **304**
innocuous **304**
innuendo 248, **251**
inscrutable 322, **325**
insignificant 326
insinuate 54
insinuation 251
insipid 141
insolent 117
insomnia **90**
insouciance 126, **129**
inspector **167**
instigate 283, **286**
intangible 316
intensify 175
inter- **27**, **109**
inter **157**
intercede **263**
intercept **215**
interdict **275**
interject 109
interpose **253**
interpret 250
interrogate **141**
interrupt 109
intimate (v., adj., n.) 52, **54**
intra-, *intro-* **26**, **109**
intramural **109**
intransigent 322, **325**
intravenous **109**
intrigue 174
introductory **109**
inundate 173, **175**

invigoration 202
invincible **56**
invoke **253**
irascible 212
iridescent 310, **313**
Iris **313**
irony 137, **140**
irradiate 109
irregularity 164
irreligious 103
irrevocable **253**
irritable 313
irritate 175
Isles of the Blessed 321
it **327**
itinerary **327**

jabber 139
jargon 75
jinx 88
jittery **203**
jocular 200, **203**
joint **276**
jointed 138
jolly 313
Jove **313**
jovial 310, **313**
joyful 201
judge 175
judicial **275**
judicious 154
jud, jur, jus **275**
junction **276**
junct, jug, join **276**
junctures 165
Juno **95**
junta 232, **235**
junto **235**
Jupiter **313**
jurisdiction **275**
jurisprudence **275**
justice **275**
justify **287**

keening **34**
keep 55
key word alert 372
key word concept **34**
kilo **22**
kind 214
kindred 201
kindred soul 261

labor **13**
Laconia **140**
laconic 137, **140**

lament 333, **336**
lampoon 63, **66**
languor 336
lank **34**
larceny 271, **274**
laser 221, **224**
lassitude 334, **336**
lasting 324
laud 54, 55
laughable 213
lavatory **225**
lave **225**
lav, lu **225**
lawsuit 274
lawyer 272
lax 87
leg **141**
legacy **141**
legality **141**
legato 309
legible **304**
legislature **141**
leg, lig, lect **304**
legume **304**
lento 234
Leo **155**
Leonid **155**
leonine 153, **155**
lesion 183, **186**
lethargic 89
lev **204**
level 129
levitate **204**
levity **204**
librettist 302
libretto 300, **302**
life 335
limited 118
lionize 155
lithe 116, **119**
litigant (n., adj.) **274**
litigation 271, **274**
liveliness 185
livery 364
loathing 200
loc **263**
location **263**
locomotion **263**
logic **167**
logical 204
logistics 163, **165**
logos **167**
-logy **226**
longevity **56**
long (for) 176
long-lived 324
long-winded 139

loose 87
loquacious 140, 252
lout 335
lucid **253**
Lucifer **253**
luc, lux **253**
lucrative **35**
lucubration 250, **253**
ludicrous 210, **213**
lugubrious 214
lull 166
lup 159
lupine 159
lure 54, 77
lurid 210, **213**
luscious 77
lust 86
lymph 183, **186**
lymphoma **186**

macabre 211, **214**
macro- **103**
macrocosm **103**
macroeconomics **103**
magna- **26**
Magna Carta 262
magna cum laude 268
magnanimous 200
magnify **236**
magnum opus 260, **262**
maintain 55
mal (root) **337**
mal- **25**, 103
malady **337**
malapropism 137, **140**
Malaprop, Mrs. **140**
malcontent **103**
malediction **275**
malfeasance 271, **274**
malfunction **337**
malign 177
malodorous 77
manacle **316**
manage **316**
mañana 232, **235**
mania **188**
maniac **188**
manic-depressive **188**
manu **316**
manuscript **316**
many 104
mark 55
Marquis de Sade **337**
Mars **95, 312**
marsh 76
master 155

material 324
mater, matri 12
maternal 12
matriarch 12, **90**
mean **215**
med 20
medieval **56**
mediate 156
medium 20
megacycle **22**
megalomania **188**
meg, mega **22**
melancholic 203
melancholy **214**
mellifluous **287**
melodramatic 64
Melpomene **88**
ménage 127, **129**
Mentor **87**
mentor 84, **87**
mercurial 84, **87**
Mercury **87**
merry 201, 214, 313
meta- **110**
metamorphosis 110, **263**
metaphase **110**
metropolitan 119
micro- 26, **103**
microcosm **14, 103**
milli **22**
million **104**
min- **103**
miniature 103
minimal 77
min, minim (examples
    of) 17
mire (n., v.) 74, **76**
mirthful 313
mis- **25**, 103
misanthrope 56, **103**
misbehavior 103
miscreant 334, **336**
missionary **327**
missive **327**
miss, mit **327**
mnemonic 84, **88**
Mnemosyne **88**
mobile **337**
mob, mot, mov **337**
mockery 65
moderate (v.) **287**
modern 64, 222
modest 214
modesty 166
mollify 174
monarch 90
moni **288**

monitor **288**
mono 20
monotone **20**
morbid 211, **214**
moribund **216**
mor, mort **216**
morose 201
morph **263**
morpheme **263**
Morpheus **89**
morphology **263**
mortal **216**
mortician **216**
mortify **216**
motive **337**
Mount Olympus 88, **95**
multi **22**
multiply **167**
muse (n., v.) **88**
Muses **88**
mutation **157**
mute 138
mut, mutat **157**
myria **22**
myriad **22**
Myrmidon **313**
myrmidon 310, **313**
mysterious 325

naive 201
narcissism 85, **88**
Narcissus **88**
narrow 118
N.B. (*nota bene*) 267
nebulous 117, **119**
necessary 120
needs (n.) 165
nefarious 211, **214**
neg (examples of) 16
negative/positive
    concepts 370, 372
negligent 326
Nemesis **88**
nemesis 85, **88**
neo/nov (examples of)
    16
neophyte 155, 303
nerve 167
nether 322, **325**
netherworld **325**
neur **189**
nihil **292**
nine **104**
noble 212, **215**
noc/nox (harm) **304**
noc/nox (night) **304**

nocturnal **304**
nocturne **304**
nocuous **304**
nomenclature **327**
nomen, nomin, -onym,
    onoma **327**
nominal **327**
nonagon **21**
nonchalance 129
nonentity **103**
nonessential 120
non- (no, not) **25, 103**
non, novem (nine) 21
nonsensical 204
non sequitur 260, **262**
nonviolent 103
Norman Conquest 275
nourish 55
novel 141
November 21
novena 21
novice 155, 303
Nox **87, 88**
noxious 303, **304**
nullify 272, 284
nurture 52, **55**

obdurate **215**
obese 156
object (v.) 286
objection 103
obligatory 119
ob-, oc-, of-, op- **103,**
    109
obscene 215
obstacle 109
obstinance 166
Oceanus 90
octave **21**
October **21**
oct, octa, octo **21**
octopus **21**
Odin **89, 315**
odious 213
Odysseus **87**
Odyssey 303
offensive 103, 109
oligarchy **22**
oligo **22**
-ology **226**
omni- 22, **103**
omnivorous 22, 103
one **104**
one and a half **104**
onomatopoeia **64, 327**
ooze 285

opthalm **189**
oppose 103, 109, 174
optimistic 203
ordinary 141
orgy 86
original 141
orth- **111**
orthodontist **111**
orthopedics **111**
ostentation 163, **166**
outcast 262
outdoors 233
outr **27**
outrageous 212, 213
outré 127, **129**
over- 27, **110**
overabundance 110
overthrow 75
overwhelm 175
ovine **159**
ovus **159**

pachyderm **188**
pacify 174
paleontology **226**
palpable 322, **325**
paltry **35**
pan- 22, **95**, **103**
Panacea **312**
panacea **103**, 310, **313**
pandemic 22, **275**
Pandora **314**
Pandora's box 310, **314**
pantheon **90**, **103**
panto- 22, **103**
pantomime 22, **103**
paradigm **111**
paradise **111**
paradox 164
paralegal **111**, 276
paramedical **111**
paranoia 184, **186**
parcel (out) 76
pariah 262
parochial 118
parody 63, **66**
paronomasia 258
par-, para- **111**
parsimony 334, **336**
particle 77
partnership 222
party 77
pastoral 117, **119**
paternal 12
pater, patri 12
path **188**

pathology **188**
patina 300, **302**
patine 302
patriarch 12
patriotism 12
pauci **22**
paucity **22**
pause 166
peccadillo **202**
ped (child) 15
pedagogue **15**, **120**
pedal **14**
pedant 15, **316**
pediatrician 15
pedometer **14**
ped, (foot) *pod* (examples of) 14
pel, puls **288**
penalize **264**
penance **264**
pendant 15, **316**
pend, pens **316**
penitent **264**
penitentiary **264**
pen (poena) **264**
penta- **20**
pentathlete **20**
per- **110**
per annum **267**
perambulate 174
per capita **267**
perceptible 325
per diem **267**
performer 66
peri- **108**
periscope 108
perjury 271, **274**
permeate 110
perpetrate 52, **55**
per se 261, **267**
persecute **78**
perseverance 166
persiflage 138
persona grata **262**
persona non grata 260, **262**
perspicacious **167**
pert **42**
pertinacity 163, **166**
peruse 173, **176**
pessimistic 203
pestilence **37**
petrology **226**
petty **37**
Phaeton (Phaethon) **314**
phaeton 311, **314**
phantom 334

phil **56**
philanthropist **56**
philatelist **56**
philologist **56**
philosopher **56**
philosophy **56**
phlegmatic 87, 120
phobia 184, **186**
phon **337**
phonetics **337**
phonograph **337**
pianissimo 234
pigeon 76
pious 214, 322, **325**
piquant **36**
pique 127, **129**
pisces **159**
piscine 159
pitch 252
pithy 140, 253
placate 174
placid 200, **203**, 212
plaint 214
plaintive 211, **214**
plausible 117, **119**, 215
pleasant 202
pleb **275**
plebeian **275**
plebiscite **275**
plex, plic, -ply **167**
podiatrist **14**
poisonous 187
politic 118, 203
poly- **22**
Polyhymnia 88
polymath **22**
pomposity 250
pompous 211, **214**
ponder 156
pon, pos **253**
pontiff **314**
pontonier **314**
pontoon 311, **314**
Pontus **314**
porcine 153, **156**
port **130**
portable **130**
portend 173, **176**
portfolio 231, **233**
posit **253**
post- 25, **104**
postbellum **204**
posthumously **104**
postpartum **104**
postpone 104, **253**
postscript 25
potsherd 224

practical 204
praise 76, 177
praiseworthy 77, 212, 213
prate 248, **251**
prattle **251**
pre- 25, 27, **104**
precede **263**
précis 127, **130**
predatory **338**
predestine 104
predetermine 104
prefix 25, **102**
prefix alert **362**
prefixes, negative 362
prefixes, positive 362
prehend, prehens, pris **338**
prehensile 153, **156**
prehension **156**
preliminary 104
premonition **288**
prerogative **141**
presentiment 14, **253**
press 54
prestissimo **234**
presto (adj., n.) 231, **234**
pretend 77
pretense 77
pretentious 214
pretentiousness 166
prevaricate **44**
prim, prin (examples of) 22
primeval **56**
prison **338**
pristine 117, **119**
pro- **26**, **102**
proclaim 54, 176
proclivity 102
procrustean 311, **314**
procrustean bed **314**
Procrustes **314**
prodigious 323, **326**
professional 233
prognosis **316**
progress 102
pro-liberal 102
prolix 139, 140, 253
Promethean 85, **88**
Prometheus 88, **314**
promising 201
promulgate 173, **176**
prophase **110**
propitate 174
propitious 201
propose **253**

protagonist 63, **66**
Proteus 95
proto (examples of) 22
Protozoa **15**
provincial 118
provoke 129, 286
PSAT facts 359
PSAT/SAT exams **1**, **2**
psyche **14**
psychiatry **14**
psychosomatic **14**
puckery 117
puling **34**
pulsate **288**
pun 248, **251**
puny 326
purge 285
purify 174
putrid 77
pyr **225**
pyre **225**
pyretic **225**
pyrite **225**
pyromaniac **188**

quad 20
quadruped 20
qualm 334, **336**
quick(ly) 234
quid pro quo 260, **263**
quiet 203
quinque 20
quinquennium **20**
quint 20
quintuplet **20**
quisling 163, **166**
Quisling, Vidkun **166**
quixotic 232, **235**

raconteur 137, **140**
raillery 138
rancid 77
rancor 163, **166**
random 275
rank (adj., v., n.) 74, **77**, 129
rankle 186
rapid(ly) 234
rapidity 225
rapport 127, **130**
rapture **44**
rash 77
rashness 167
ration 76
raze **41**
re- 25, **109**

reading comprehension questions 381
rebellious **204**
recapitulate **236**
recklessness 167
recognize **236**
recondite 323, **326**
recourse **177**
rectify 55
recumbent **177**
recur **177**
redress 52, **55**
redundancy 141
reflect 156
reflection **141**
refraction 221, **224**
refractory **225**
refrain 284
regress 109, **287**
reincarnation 151
reiterate **327**
reject 176
rejoinder 140
relevant 324
relieve 175, 176
relinquish 52, **55**
remiss 323, **326**
remission **326**
remonstrate 283, **286**
repartee 138
repel **288**
repentant **264**
replace 287
report **130**
reprehensible **338**
reptilian 154, **156**
repugnance 200, **209**
requisite 117, **120**
resentment 129
reserve 166
reserved 118, 139, 252
resign 55
resist 177
respect 53
respiration **304**
respite 163, **166**
rest 166
restrained 252
restraint 166
resuscitate 184, **187**
retain 55, **167**
reticent 139, 249, **252**
retort 140
retro- 25, **109**
retrogress 109
reveal 54, 285
reverie **37**

reversal 109
reverse **67**
revitalize 187
revive 187
revoke **253**
revolting 212
revulsion 200
rhapsody 300, **303**
rhetoric 249, **252**
ridicule 66
ridiculous 154, 213
rift **35**
rigid 119
rigorous 87
rigueur **133**
riposte (n., v.) 137, **140**
rire sardonique **326**
rococo 63, **66**
rog **141**
rout 128, 284
rover 275
roving 275
ruffled 203
rumen **156**
ruminant (n., adj.) **156**
ruminate 154, **156**
rural 119
ruse **42**

sacrilege **216**
sacr/sacer **216**
sadist 334, **337**
Saga **89**
saga 85, **89**
salutary **43**, 184, **187**
salve! **234**
salvo 231, **234**
sanction 271, **274**
sangfroid 127, **130**, 203
sang/sangui **134**
sanguinary **203**
sanguine 200, **203**
sanguinity 223
sarcasm 140
sarcastic 326
sardonic 323, **326**
sate 283, **286**
SAT facts 359
satiate 286
satire 63, **66**
Saturn **89**
saturnalia 89
saturnine 85, 87, **89**
savoir **133**
saying 250
scare 54

sci 13
science **13**
scoff 76
scold 157
Scopes trial 156
scorching 326
scorn 176
scrib/script 13
scruple **336**
scrutinize **42**
scurrilous 211, **215**
se- **109**
secession **263**
secluded 109
secret 213
sect 74, **77**
sectarian **77**
segregate 109
select **304**
self-effacing 214
self-important 214
selflessness 88
semi- 20
semicolon **20**
sensation **253**
sensational 213
sense **14**
sensible 154, 204
sensitive 120
sens, sent 14, **253**
sentence completion questions, How To **370**
sentence types **370–372**
sentient **253**
sentiment **253**
separatist 222
sept 21
September **21**
sequel **78**
sequence **78**
sequ, secut **78**
serene 203
sesqui 20
sesquicentennial **20**
sesquipedalian **20**
seven **104**
severe 87
sex 21
sextet 21
sham (n., v.) 74, **77**
shard 221, **224**
shining 313
show 54
showiness 166
shrew 157
shrewd 201

shrink 53
shy 117, 118
sierra 232, **235**
siesta 232, **235**
silent 139, 252
Silvanus **315**
simian (n., adj.) 154, **156**
simple 66
sine qua non 260, **263**
sinful 214
sinuous **36**
six **104**
slack 87
slander 177
sleepy 89
slick 251
slight 77
slow(ly) 234
slump 223
smirk **43**
smooth 203
sneer 76
sober 204
sociable 201
sol 20
solecism 249, **252**
solicitor 272
soliloquy 249, **252**
Soloi **252**
Solon **89**
solon 85, **89**
somn **90**
somnambulism **90**
somnambulist **90**, 95
somnolent 85, **89**
Somnus (Hypnos) **89**
sonata 300, **303**
sonatina **303**
soothe 186
sordid 211, **215**
sotto voce 231, **234**
souci 134
soupçon 127, **130**
sparing 324
sparkle 185
Sparta/Spartans **140**
specialist 155
specimen **167**
specious 211, **215**
spec/spic/spect **167**
spectator **167**
specter 334
speed 225
spiel 249, **252**
spir **304**
spiritual 87

splenetic 212
spoor (n., v.) 154, **156**
spore 221, **225**
sprout 54
spur 54
spurn 173, **176**
squalor 334, **337**
staccato 300, **303**
staccato mark **303**
stale 141
starve 55, 286
state 75
status **263**
status quo 260, **263**
stealthy 213
Stentor 117, **315**
stentorian 311, **315**
stentorophonic **315**
stigmata 55
stigmatize 52, **55**
Stinky Pinkies **146**
stolen 213
stolid 117, **120**
stoop 284
storyteller 140
straightforward 213
strategy for critical
  reading questions 383
strict/string **120**
stricture **120**
strident 253
stringent **120**
stripling **36**
stroll 174
Strunk, William 284
stubborn 154
stubbornness 166
study 176
stupefaction 202
stupefy **209**
stygian 85, **89**
Styx **89**
suave 200, **203**
submerge 110
submissive 118
subpoena 260, **263**
substantiate 287
sub-, suc-, suf-, sug-,
  sum-, sup-, sus- 110
suburbs 15
succeed **263**
success 128
succinct 253
succor 173, **176**
succumb 173, **177**
suffice 283, **286**
suffuse 110, 283, **286**

suggest 54, 175
sulky 201
sullen 201
sully 53
summa cum laude 268
summon 110
superficial 251
supersede 110
super-/supra- 27, **110**
supplant 283, **287**
support 272, 274
sur- 27
surfeit 286
surly 89
surrender 55
surreptitious 213
suspense **316**
sylvan 311, **315**
symmetrical 108
sympathy **188**
synagogue **120**
synchronize **14**
synthesis **108**
sy-, syl-, sym-, syn-, sys-
  108

taciturn 139, 252
tactile **316**
tainted 119
talkative 139, 140, 252
tangible **316**
tang, ting, tact, tig **316**
tantalize 311, **315**
Tantalus **315**
tantalus **315**
taunt 76
taurine **159**
taurus **159**
tautology 137, **141**
techniques for sentence
  completion questions
  376
teeming **35**
-teen 21, **104**
tele- **109**
telecourse **109**
telegram **141**
telepathy **109**
temerity 163, **167**
temper (v.) 283, **287**
tempo **15**
tempor **264**
temporal **264**
temporary **15**, 264
temporize **264**
tempt 54

ten **104**
tenacious **167**
tenacity 166
tendency **130**
tend/tens/tent **130**
tensile **130**
ten thousand **104**
ten/tin/tain/tent **167**
termagant **157**
Terpsichore **88**
terrace **157**
terra firma **157**
terrestrial **157**
terrier **157**
terr/ter **24**, **157**
terse 118, 140, 249, **253**
tertiary **20**
test techniques **359–399**
testy 313
tête **133**
tetr 20
tetrarch/tetrarchy **20**
Thalia **88**
the **90**
theft 274
theology **90**
therapeutic 184, **187**
thermodynamics **304**
thespian 63, **66**
thoughtful 251
thousand **104**
three **104**
thunderous 315
timid 117
timing for the SAT/
  PSAT **360**, 374, 382
timorous 117
tiny 326
titan 85, **90**
titanic **90**
titanism **90**
Titans **90**
tit for tat **263**
toady 56
-tomy **192**
tonic 117
torrid 323, **326**
torso 184, **187**
tort 271, **275**
tor/tort 280
total 77
touch 75
toughen 287
toxic 184, **187**
trace 130
track 156
traditional 129

traduce **236**
tragedy **65**
trail 156
traitor 166
trajectory 110
tramp 275
transfer 110
transient 324
translucent **253**
transmit **327**
transmute **157**
tra/trans **110**
traverse 138, 174
travesty 63, **67**
tricae **285**
trick 76, 77
trifle 164
trimester 20
trinket 164
trite 137, **141**
tri/ter **20**
trivial **15**
Trojan War 87, 117, 312, 313, 315
truckle 52, **56**
truckle bed **56**
trunk 187
truth 77
tutor 87
Twain, Mark 109, 110, 128, 136, 138, 154, 161, 201, 231, 262
twelve **104**
two **104**
-ty **21**, **104**
tyro 42, 155, 233, 303

ubiquitous **37**
ultraconservative 110
ultr-/ultra- **27**, **110**
Ulysses **87**
un- **25**, **103**
unadorned 66
unassertive 118
unbelievable 119
unbend 284
uncommunicative 252

uncompromising 325
uncongenial 201
unconquerable 203
uncontrollable 118
unctuous 118, 323, **327**
understand 250
understatement 251
unearthly 118
unemotional 120
unfeigned **103**
uni- **20**
unicycle **20**
unintelligible 138
unnecessary 120
unnoticeable 77
unpretentious 214
unrefined 203
unruffled 203
untangle 285
unworldly 87
upset 75
up-to-date 64, 222
Urania 88
Uranus **314**
urban **15**, 119
urbane **15**, 203
urge 54
ursa **159**
Ursa Minor **86**
ursine **159**

vac (examples of) 16
vacillate **43**
vagabond 275
vagaries 163, **167**
vagrant (n., adj.) 271, **275**
vague 119
Valhalla **315**
Valkyrie 311, **315**
vanquish 284
vapid **37**
variable 87
vascular 184, **187**
vehement 323, **327**
velocity 221, **225**
vendetta 231, **234**

veneration 200
ver **78**
veracious **78**
veracity 77, **78**
verbose 139, 140, 253
verbs 53, **174**, **284**
verdict **78**, 275
verify **78**
verisimilitude **78**
vernal equinox 304
vers, vert **67**
versatile **67**
verse **67**
verve 185
via **15**
viaduct **15**
vicious 214
victorious **56**
victory 128
vid/vis **14**
vignette (n., v.) 300, **303**
vigor 336
vile **177**
vilify 173, **177**
villain 336
villainous 213
vinc, vict **56**
vindicate 283, **287**
violate 53
virago 157
viricide **188**
virology **188**
virtuoso/a 300, **303**
virulent **188**
virus **188**
vis **133**
vital 120
vitality **158**, 185
vitamin **158**
vita/viv **158**
vivid **158**
viviparous 158
vivisection 154, **157**
vixen 154, **157**
vocal **253**
vocation **253**, 257
vociferate **253**
vociferous 249, **253**

voc, voke **253**
voluble 118, 139, 140
vu 133
Vulcan 314

waive 55
wakeful 89
wanderer 275
wandering 275
wary 74, **77**, 89
wasteful 324
weak 87
weird 118
whelp (n., v.) 154, **157**
whim 167
whit 74, **77**
White, E. B. 139, **284**, 381
wholesome 214
wicked 214
wide-ranging 118
wile 74, **77**
wise 154
wit 140
wither 53
witty 203
woeful 214
wooded **315**
wordy 139, 140, 253
worship 200
wrath **111**
wretched 212
wri-/wro- **111**
wry **111**

yearn (for) 176
yield 55

zany (n., adj.) 200, **204**
zephyr 311, **316**
Zephyrus **315**
Zeus 86, 88, 313, 314, 315
zoo **15**
zoology **15**